HISTORY OF KANAUJ

HISTORY OF KANAUJ

To the Moslem Conquest

RAMA SHANKAR TRIPATHI

With a foreword by

L.D. BARNETT

MOTILAL BANARSIDASS

Delhi Varanasi Patna

Bangalore Madras

First Edition: *1964*
Reprint: *Delhi*, *1989*

MOTILAL BANARSIDASS
Bungalow Road, Jawahar Nagar, Delhi 110 007

Branches

Chowk, Varanasi 221 001
Ashok Rajpath, Patna 800 004
24 Race Course Road, Bangalore 560 001
120 Royapettah High Road. Mylapore, Madras 600 004

ISBN: 81-208-0404-x (Cloth)
ISBN: 81-208-0478-3 (Paper)

PRINTED IN INDIA

BY JAINENDRA PRAKASH JAIN AT SHRI JAINENDRA PRESS, A-45 NARAINA INDUSTRIAL AREA, PHASE I, NEW DELHI 110 028 AND PUBLISHED BY NARENDRA PRAKASH JAIN FOR MOTILAL BANARSIDASS, DELHI 110 007.

TO THE AFFECTIONATE MEMORY

OF

MY REVERED FATHER

PANDIT JANAKI SHARANJI TRIPATHI

FOREWORD

It gives me exceeding pleasure to see at last in print Dr. Tripathi's admirable history of his native land.

Magna parens frugum, magna virum, the realm of Kānyakubja is a land of old and high renown, and from the spacious days of the great Harshavardhana onwards for many centuries it held a dominant position in Northern India. Nature favoured it, and indeed made its success almost inevitable as soon as strong and wise rulers ascended its throne. Lying in the centre of the Gangetic Valley, it held vital control over the trade-routes on all sides, and especially those reaching eastward into Bengal and westward into the Panjab; and to this fact, no less than to the personal feuds and ambitions of their kings, may be ascribed the fierce antagonism which prevailed between Kanauj and Bengal from the time of Śaśāṅka until almost to the end of Hindu rule in Northern India. Thus in its splendours and tragedies alike the history of Kanauj is intensely Indian and profoundly fascinating; and the tale is well told in the pages which follow.

L. D. Barnett

PREFACE

Kanauj is of high antiquity and renown. Founded long before the dawn of the Christian Era, it first rose to importance in the sixth century A. D., when it became the capital of the Maukharis. Under Īśānavarman and Sarvavarman this dynasty rapidly grew in authority and influence, which brought them into conflict with the Later Guptas. The struggle between the two powers had far-reaching effects, for it ended in transferring the centre of political gravity from Magadha to Kanauj.

In the beginning of the seventh century, however, the fortunes of the Maukharis took such a sudden and catastrophic turn that Harṣa of Thanesvar had to assume control of affairs in Kanauj. It is usually asserted that he extended his suzerainty throughout Northern India, but in my opinion his dominions comprised only parts of Eastern Panjab, almost the whole of modern United Provinces, Magadha, Orissa and Bengal. I have devoted a disproportionately large space to this subject mainly because it bristles with knotty points, and is a frequent source of controversy. An attempt has also been made here to give a critical account of Harṣa's administration and achievements of peace. His death plunged Kanauj into anarchy and darkness that lasted for about half-a-century. When the curtain rises again, a striking figure flits across the political stage. Yaśovarman gained some successes at the start of his career, but was ultimately reduced to subservience by Lalitāditya of Kashmir.

The next rulers of note were the Pratīhāras, whose power reached its zenith during the time of Bhoja I and Mahendrapāla I. As a result of their protracted campaigns the empire of Kanauj grew to enormous dimensions comprising territories as widely apart as Saurāṣṭra and North Bengal, Magadha and Rajputana, Gorakhpur district and Ujjain, Karnal and Bundelkhand. The most interesting feature of this epoch is the tripartite struggle that continued intermittently between the Pratīhāras, the Pālas, and the Rāṣṭrakūṭas. Later on, the prosperity of Kanauj received a rude shock from the ever-victorious arms of Mahmūd, but it partially revived its glories under the Gāhaḍavālas, who after Govindacandra's conquest of Magadha once more regained control of the lower course of the Ganges, which was so vital to its trade and political ascendancy. Eventually Sihābuddin Ghori involved the contemporary Hindu states in one common ruin, and thus Kanauj fell from its high position. Such in short is the fascinating story of this ancient realm, full of political vicissitudes and ephemeral grandeur. Today Kanauj is an insignificant town, but from the downfall of the Guptas until the avalanche of the Moslem invasions it was the centre of culture and crafts, religion and riches, power and politics, and was the *ultima thule* of each aspirant to supreme dignity in Northern India.

The Volume substantially represents my Thesis, which was approved by the University of London in 1929 for the Degree of Ph. D. It could not be sent to the press so long on account of pressure of University duties and other unavoidable circumstances. The delay has, however, in a way been to my advantage, for it has enabled me to bring the work up-to-date, and to improve and revise it carefully in the light of the guidance given by the distinguished Board of Examiners. I take this opportunity of offering my respectful thanks to Dr. L. D. Barnett, M.A., D.LITT., Mr. J. Allan, M.A., and Professor H. H. Dodwell, M.A., for their valuable suggestions. To Dr. L. D. Barnett, I am particularly indebted for writing a Foreword to this book. Further, I owe special acknowledgments to such scholars as have illumined my path by their contributions on any topic dealt with here. My thanks are also due to my wife, Hemavatī Devī, for occasional help in preparing the Index.

The system of transliteration adopted in the text will be apparent from the following examples: Candra, Viṣṇu, Īśvara, Kṛita, Rāṣṭrakūṭa. But I have followed the ordinary spelling of proper names, and diacritical marks have been omitted in case of well-known place-names. I have also retained the usual forms of Chinese words and names, as given in the translations of Watters and Beal.

In conclusion, may I crave the indulgence of the reader for any lapses and blemishes, typographical or other, that may still be found in the book, in spite of my best efforts to weed them out. A monograph on the history of Kanauj has been a desideratum, and if the present work usefully supplies this long-felt want, I shall consider my labours amply rewarded.

January 1, 1937 RAMA SHANKAR TRIPATHI

CONTENTS

LIST OF ABBREVIATIONS

Ind. Ant.—Indian Antiquary.

Ep. Ind.—Epigraphia Indica.

J. R. A. S.—Journal of the Royal Asiatic Society.

J. B. B. R. A. S.—Journal of the Bombay Branch of the Royal Asiatic Society.

J. B. O. R. S.—Journal of the Bihar and Orissa Research Society.

Jour. Am. Or. Soc.—Journal of the American Oriental Society.

J. A. S. B.—Journal of the Asiatic Society of Bengal

Proc. A. S. B.—Proceedings of the Asiatic Society of Bengal.

Mem. As. Soc. Beng.—Memoirs of the Asiatic Society of Bengal.

Jour. Dept. Lett.—Journal of the Department of Letters.

Jour. U. P. Hist. Soc.—Journal of the United Provinces Historical Society.

Jour. And. Hist. Res. Soc.—Journal of the Andhra Historical Research Society.

Jour. Ind. Hist.—Journal of Indian History.

Ind. Hist. Quart.—Indian Historical Quarterly.

Ind. Cult.—Indian Culture.

Proc. & Trans. Ori. Conf.—Proceedings and Transactions of the Oriental Conference.

Ann. Bhand. Inst.—Annals of the Bhandarkar Institute.

Cal. Rev.—Calcutta Review.

Arch. Surv. Ind. Rep.—Archæological Survey of India Report.

Ann. Rep. Arch. Surv. Ind.—Annual Report of the Archæological Survey of India.

Prog. Rep. Arch. Surv., W. Circle—Progress Report of the Archæological Survey, Western Circle.

Arch. Surv. Rep., E. Circle—Archæological Survey Report, Eastern Circle.

Ann. Prog. Rep. Arch. Surv., C. Circle—Annual Progress Report of the Archæological Survey, Central Circle.

Ann. Rep., Luck Mus.—Annual Report, Lucknow Museum.

My. Arch. Surv. Rep.—Mysore Archæological Survey Report.

Raj. Mus. Rep.—Rajputana Museum Report.

C. I. I.—Corpus Inscriptionum Indicarum, volume III.

Imp. Gaz.—Imperial Gazetteer.

Bom. Gaz.—Bombay Gazetteer.

Rāmāy.—Vālmīki Rāmāyaṇa.

Mbh.—Mahābhārata.

Pad.—Padma Purāṇa.

Viṣ.—Viṣṇu Purāṇa.

Bmd.—Brahmāṇḍa Purāṇa.

Br.—Brahma Purāṇa.

Bhāg.—Bhāgavata Purāṇa.

Ag.—Agni Purāṇa.

Vā.—Vāyu Purāṇa.

Hv.—Harivaṁśa.

Anc. Ind. Hist. Trad.—Ancient Indian Historical Tradition (Pargiter).

Hc.—Harṣacarita (Bāṇa).

Hc. C. T.—Harṣacarita (English Translation by Cowell and Thomas).

Rājat.—Rājataraṅgiṇī (Kalhaṇa).

Stein.—English Translation of the Rājataraṅgiṇī.

Anc. Geo. Ind. *or* A. G. I.—Ancient Geography of India (Cunningham).

Sangam Age.—The Kāverī, the Maukharis and the Sangaṁ Age (Aravamuthan).

Early Hist. Ind. *or* E. H. I.—Early History of India (Smith).

H. M. H. I.—History of Mediæval Hindu India. (C. V. Vaidya).

Pol. Hist. Ind.—Political History of India (Raychaudhuri).

Anc. Hist. Dec.—Ancient History of the Deccan (Jouveau Dubreuil).

Cam. Hist. Ind.—Cambridge History of India, Vols. I and III.

Life.—Life of Yuan Chwang (Samuel Beal).

Watters.—On Yuan Chwang's Travels.

Beal.—Buddhist Records of the Western World.

Cat. Coi. Ind. Mus.—Catalogue of Coins in the Indian Museum (Calcutta).

Coi. Med. Ind.—Coins of Mediæval India (Cunningham).

Elliot.—History of India as told by its own Historians.

Briggs.—History of the Rise of the Mahomedan Power (Tárīkh-i-Firishta).

Sachau.—Alberuni's India.

PART I

CHAPTER I

INTRODUCTORY

Position and importance of Kanauj

The petty town of Kanauj, lying in latitude 27°5′ North and longitude 79°55′ East in the Farrukhabad district of the United Provinces, is one of the few cities that have played a noteworthy part in the political life of Ancient India.[1] It has been the witness of the rise and fall of mighty empires, the appearance and disappearance of successive dynasties; and although this fascinating panorama of events chiefly unfolds itself during the centuries that intervene between the decline of the Guptas and the Moslem conquest, we may trace faint beginnings of its chequered career back even to the misty past of the Brahmanic age.

[1] The importance of Kanauj in ancient times was probably due to its strategic advantages. The city stood on a cliff on the right bank of the Ganges, which was then the highway of commerce and communication, and it must have, therefore, been a convenient centre for river traffic in the upper Doab [see Samuel Beal, *The Travels of Fa-hian* (*Fo-kuo-ki*), ch. XVIII, p. xliii; Thomas Watters, *On Yuan Chwang* (*Si-yu-ki*), Vol. I (1904), p. 341; *Bāla-Rāmāyaṇa* of Rājaśekhara, Act X, p. 306, ed. Govindadeva Śāstrī (Benares, 1869). The river, however, now flows at a distance of some miles to the east (see *Gazetteer of Farrukhabad*, p. 217; *Imperial Gazetteer of India*, XIV, p. 370]. Besides, as observed by Cunningham, "the situation is a commanding one, and before the use of the cannon the height alone must have made Kanauj a strong and important position" (Cunningham's *Ancient Geography of India*, ed. S. N. Majumdar, (Calcutta, 1924), p. 436).

Origin and derivation of the name

The *Rāmāyaṇa* of Vālmīki and other works contain an amusing story, describing its foundation and how it got the name Kānyakubja, from which Kanauj is said to be a modern derivation.[1] We are told that in early times there was a king named Kuśa, who married the daughter of the king of Vidarbha or Berar. He was blessed with four sons : (*a*) Kuśanābha, (*b*) Kuśāṁbha, (*c*) Asūrtaraja and (*d*) Vasu. Each of them, on being requested by the reigning monarch to protect the kingdom, founded a town after his own name. Of these, Kuśanābha founded a town called Mahodaya, meaning "of high prosperity."[2] King Kuśanābha begot a hundred beautiful daughters by the celestial damsel Ghṛitāci,[3] and one day, when they were sporting together in the royal gardens, Vāyu

[1] Compare also : "Kannojaṁ kila Kānyakubja-nagaraṁ sā rājadhānī purā" (*Kānyakubja-Mahākāvya*, p. 194). Moslem writers usually write Qannauj قنوج (see e.g., *Tabaqāt-i-Akbarī*, Vol. I, p. 39, ed. B. De). Raverty, however, gives the form Kinnauj in his translation of the *Tabaqāt-i-Nāsirī* (I, p. 470, etc.). From the *Śarh-i-Ta'rīkh-i-Yamīnī* also the proper way of pronouncing Kanauj appears to be "Kinnauj" with the last letter but slightly enunciated (see Extracts in Elliot, II, p. 52). Fa-hian transliterates it as Ka-nao-yi or Kanoyi, and Thomas Watters is of opinion that it represents "the name which was probably in use among the natives" (Watters, I, p. 341). Accordingly Vincent Smith asserts that the name Kanauj is "ancient" and was "current fifteen hundred years ago" (*J. R. A. S.*, 1908, p. 767). Whatever be the truth, this much is certain that the Prakrit transliteration used by Rājaśekhara in the beginning of the ninth century A. D. is Kaṇnaujja (Konow and Lanman, *Karpūra-mañjarī*, III. 5. p. 74, Harvard Oriental Series, 1901).

[2] "Kuśanābhas tu dharmātmā puraṁ cakre Mahodayaṁ" (*Vālmīki Rāmāyaṇa*, Bālakāṇḍa, canto 32, Verse 6, Calcutta, 1881).

[3] "Kuśanābhas tu rājarṣiḥ kanyāśatamanuttamaṁ
Janayāmās dharmātmā Ghṛitācyāṁ Raghunandana"
(*Ibid.*, verse 11).

(the wind god)[1] became enamoured of their surpassing charms. He made a proposal to marry all the hundred sisters, but was met with a scornful refusal. Their rebukes further enraged the wind god to such an extent that he instantly changed them all into hunchbacks by his curses. From this circumstance (kanyānāṁ kubjatvaṁ) the city got its name Kānyakubja or Kanyākubja, meaning "the city of hunchbacked maidens."[2] Historically the story is no doubt worthless except that it proves the high antiquity of both the town and its name.

Variety of names

Owing to a fondness for synonyms, the ancient Hindu often used different names for the same place, and this laxity of nomenclature is perhaps nowhere so noticeable as in the case of Kanauj. Its most commonly recognised name was, of course, Kānyakubja or Kanyākubja or Kanyakubja,[3] which continues to occur in literature and inscriptions from the earliest to the

[1] Also called a Riṣi or "Great Tree Riṣi" (Watters, I, p. 341; Samuel Beal, *Buddhist Records of the Western World*, Vol. I, pp. 207-08).

[2] "Yad Vāyunā ca tāḥ kanyāḥ tatra kubjīkṛitā purā,
Kānyakubjamiti khyātaṁ tataḥ prabhriti tat puraṁ."
(*Vālmīki Rāmāyaṇa*, (North-Western Recension, ed. Bhagvad Datta, 1931), Bālakāṇḍa, canto 33, verses 34-35). Yuan Chwang narrates a similar story with minor variations (cf. Watters, I, p. 341; Beal, I, pp. 207-09). See also *Śiva Purāṇa*, Dharmasaṁhitā, ch. 11, verses 39-52 (Calcutta, 1890); Kalhaṇa's *Rājataraṅgiṇī*, ed. Durgāprasāda (Bombay, 1892), Vol. I, Bk. IV, verse 133, (Stein's Translation, p. 132); Dowson's *Hindu Classical Dictionary* (1914), pp. 149, 344, etc.

[3] Compare : "........ Athokanya-kanyā-kānyebhyaḥ kubjamityapi ......" (Keśava's *Kalpadrukoṣa*, verse 16, p. 10, Gaekwāḍ's Oriental Series, No. XLII, 1928), or, cf. "Daratstriyām ca Daradā Kanyakubjaḥ Kuśasthalaṁ Kanyākubjaḥ Kānyakubjaḥ Kośalaḥ Kosalopi ca" (*Ibid.*, verse 22, p. 6).

latest period of its history.[1] Next, we find mention of the name Mahodaya or Mahodayā, meaning "full of high prosperity." Although there are references to this name in earlier literature,[2] it did not hold the preference until the time of the Pratīhāras, when Kanauj was renovated to a life of opulence and power.[3] That Kānyakubja and Mahodaya were names of one and the same city is also testified by Hemacandra's *Abhidhānacintāmaṇi*,[4] Halāyudha's *Abhidhānaratnamālā*,[5] and other lexicons.[6]

Gādhipura or Gādhinagara was another name of Kanauj in early times.[7] Gādhi, as we shall see below,

[1] See also for the forms :

(*a*) Kanyakubja—*Ind. Ant.*, XVIII, pp. 13, 133; Kalhaṇa's *Rājataraṅgiṇī*, ed. Durgā Pd. (Bombay, 1892), Vol. I, Bk. I verse 117, (Stein's Trans. p. 22); Bk. IV, verse 145, (Stein, p. 134, etc.).

(*b*) Kānyakubja—*Ibid.*, Bk. VIII, verse 2453, (Stein, p. 191); *Rāmāyaṇa*, ante; *Mahābhārata*, III, ch. 116, verse 19; *Padma Purāṇa*, V (Sriṣṭi-khaṇḍa), ch. 35, verse 1; *Harṣacarita*, ed. Jīvānanda Vidyāsāgara, (Calcutta, 1892), p. 425; *Ep. Ind.*, I, pp. 197, 203, verse 3, etc.

(*c*) Kanyākubja—*Ind. Ant.*, XVIII, pp. 16, 18; *Śiva Purāṇa*, Dharmasaṁhitā, ch. 11, verse 52; *Ep. Ind.*, I, pp. 219, 222, verse 22, etc.

[2] See e.g., *Vālmīki Rāmāyaṇa*, Bālakāṇḍa, canto 32, verse 6; *Padma Purāṇa*, V, ch. 35, verse 193.

[3] *Ep. Ind.*, V, p. 208; IV, p. 131; *Ind. Ant.*, XV, p. 305; *Bālarāmāyaṇa*, X, p. 306; *Kāvyamīmāṅsā*, ed. C. D. Dalal (1916), p. 8, etc.

[4] Cf. "Kanyakubjaṁ Mahodayaṁ" (verse 39, p. 166).

[5] Cf. "Kanyakubjā Mahodayā" (II, verse 132, p. 32).

[6] See also the *Śabdārtharatnasamanvaya-koṣa*, line 6, p. 79 (Gaekwāḍ's Oriental Series, 1932); and the *Vaijayantī* of Yādavaprakāśa, ed. Gustav Oppert (1893), Bk. I, Sec. 4, verse 7, p. 159, etc.

[7] Compare e.g., "........ Mahodayaṁ Gādhipuraṁ......" (Keśava's *Kalpadrukoṣa*, verse 16, p. 10); *Śabdakalpadruma* (Calcutta, 1889), Vol. II, p. 85; Kalhaṇa's *Rājataraṅgiṇī*, Vol. I, Bk. IV, verse 133, (Stein, p. 132). The name Gādhinagara occurs in the

was one of its celebrated legendary rulers, and it appears that the city came to be called after him owing to his great deeds.

It was also known as Kuśasthala,[1] which in its etymological sense means "a spot of *kuśa* grass." Probably it derived this name from the fact that the *kuśa* grass, considered sacred for sacrificial purposes, grew there in abundance.[2] Or, alternatively it may be suggested that the place was called after king Kuśa, father of Kuśanābha, and thus signified "the residence or possession of Kuśa." Of a piece with this name is the synonym Kauśa, which is almost certainly a derivation of Kuśa.[3]

The records of the Gāhaḍavāla dynasty represent its kings as protecting the four sacred places (*tīrthas*)—Kāśī, Kuśika, Uttara Kośala (Ayodhyā) and Indrasthāna; and Kielhorn was of opinion that in this list the name Kuśika stands for Kanauj.[4]

Lastly we learn from Yuan Chwang that Kusumapura (*Keu-su-mo-pu-lo*) or "the city of flowers" was the original name, and it came to be invested with the name of Kanyākubja ("city of hunchbacked maidens")

Gwalior Sāsbahū inscription, see *Ind. Ant.*, XV, pp. 36, 41, verse 6.

[1] Cf. "Kuśasthalaṁ Kānyakubjaṁ" (*Abhidhāna-saṁgraha*, II (puravarga), verse 193, p. 9); *Śabdakalpadruma*, Vol. II, p. 85; *Harṣacarita* (Calcutta, 1892), p. 603; Cambay plates of Govinda IV: *Ep. Ind.*, VII, p. 43; *Mahābhārata* (P. C. Roy's Sanskrit text) V (Uddyogaparva), section 30, verse 19, etc.

[2] We may compare this name with Kuśāgarapura, the designation of the old city of Rājagriha. According to Yuan Chwang the city derived its name from the excellent fragrant reed grass which abounded there (Watters, II, p. 148; Beal, *Life of Yuan Chwang*, p. 113).

[3] "Kanyākubjaṁ Gādhipuraṁ Kauśaṁ Kuśasthalaṁ ca tat" (Hemacandra's *Abhidhānacintāmaṇi*, verse 40, p. 166). See also Keśava's *Kalpadrukoṣa*, verse 16, p. 10, etc.

[4] *Ind. Ant.*, XV, p. 8, note 46; *Ibid.*, XVIII, p. 13, note 33.

only after the curses of the "great Tree Riṣi".[1] Hindu authority in support of this synonym is wanting, but such a name seems to have been fairly current in ancient times. Indeed, the pilgrim notes that Pāṭaliputra—the earlier Imperial city—bore the same name.[2]

Wider application of the name

There are indications that the title of Kānyakubja was not restricted to the city only, but also extended to the neighbouring territory, or even to the kingdom of which it was the centre. Yuan Chwang gives the name *Ka-no-kü-she*, i.e., Kanyākubja both to the capital and the country, which he describes as being 4,000 *li* in circuit.[3] Similarly, the Barah copper plate shows that at that period (836 A. D.) both the names Mahodaya and Kānyakubja were current, the former being used for the capital city, and the latter for a *bhukti* or province of the kingdom,[4] of which Kālañjara-*maṇḍala* formed a part. Again, we learn from Rashid-ud-din's *Jami-ut-Tawārīkh* that according to the Persians the designation Kanauj stood for Mahades (Madhyadeśa) or middle-land, one of the traditional nine divisions of Hind.[5] In support of this, it may be added here that the Somnāthpattan *praśasti* of Bhāva Bṛihaspati, dated 1169 A. D., mentions

[1] Watters, I, p. 341; Beal, I, p. 207.

[2] *Ibid.*, II, p. 87; *Ibid.*, II, pp. 83, 85.

On the authority of certain Jain chronicles of Gujarat Dr. Vincent Smith affirms that Kalyāṇa was another name of Kanauj (*J. R. A. S.*, 1908, p. 768). The fact that '*Mahodaya*' and '*Kalyāṇa*' are almost synonymous words in Sanskrit, no doubt, lends some support to this view. See also Bühler, *Ind. Ant.*, VI, pp. 181, 183; D. R. Bhandarkar, *J. B. B. R. A. S.*, XXI, pp. 427-28.

[3] Watters, I, pp. 340-41.

[4] *Ep. Ind.*, XIX (January, 1927), pp. 17, 19.

[5] Elliot's *History of India*, Vol. I, p. 54; see also *Alberuni's India*, (Sachau's Trans.), Vol. I, 9. 199.

the Kānyakubja-*viṣaya* as including Bānārasī i.e., Benares.[1] In the Gāhaḍavāla plates the city itself is called the Kuśika *tīrtha* and the name Kānyakubja is given to the kingdom. Thus Candradeva, the founder of the line, is invariably extolled as "one who had acquired the kingdom of Kānyakubja by the prowess of his arm."[2]

Legendary rulers of Kanauj

One of the weakest spots in Sanskrit literature is the almost entire absence of any history. Thoroughly permeated with the idea of the unreality of material things, the ancient Brahmans have seldom cared to mark the footprints which kings and dynasties leave upon the sands of time. Their earliest attempts—the *Rāmāyaṇa*, the *Mahābhārata*, and the *Purāṇas*—are veritable mines of information for the then religious and social life, but as chronicles of political events they seem lamentably full of tale-telling and chronological absurdities. It is my object in the following pages to glean the kernel of historical fact from these authorities by winnowing as far as possible the outer husks of legends.

According to all forms of tradition the progenitor of the ancient royal lineages was the mythical Manu Vaivasvata. He had a daughter named Ilā, who consorted with Budha and bore a son, Purūravas, also known as Aila.[3] Purūravas is represented as a powerful ruler, holding sway over distant regions. He begat by the celestial damsel Urvasī six sons named Āyu, Dhīmān,

[1] *Vienna Oriental Journal*, III, pp. 7, 13, verses 5-6.

[2] See *Infra*.

[3] *Harivaṁśa*, ch. 10, verses 7f.; *Śiva Purāṇa*, VII (Dharma Saṁhitā), ch. 60, verses 2-19. See *Mbh.* (P. C. Roy's edition), I (Ādiparva) section 75, verses 12-20; Sec. 95, verse 7, (P. C. Roy's English Translation, I, Sec. 75, p. 229; Sec. 95, p. 282) for another fantastic version giving the birth of Purūravas from the hermaphrodite Ilā.

Amāvasu, Driḍhāyu, Vanāyu and Satāyu.[1] Of these sons, as asserted by Pargiter, Āyu succeeded Purūravas at Pratiṣṭhāna, identified with the modern Jhusi on the confluence of the Ganges and the Jumna in Allahabad; and Amāvasu[2] founded "another kingdom, the capital of which was then or afterwards Kānyakubja (Kanauj)".[3] Amāvasu's descendants continued to rule over this kingdom, and the *Purāṇas*[4] give their names in the following order: (*a*) Bhīma, (*b*) Kāñcanaprabha[5], (*c*) Suhotra,[6] (*d*) Jahnu, (*e*) Sumanta,[7] (*f*) Ajaka,[8] (*g*) Balākāśva, (*h*) Kuśa. Before we proceed further with the genealogy, let us pause to consider another account, which traces the origin of the dynasty to Ajamīḍha. It is given in the *Mahābhārata*[9] and the *Agni Purāṇa*,[10]

[1] *Ibid.*, I, Sec. 75, verse 24 (Eng. Trans., p. 230). The names slightly vary in certain *Purāṇas* (Cf. e.g., *Vāyu P.*, ch. 91, verse 51, Apte's edition, 1905).

[2] Called Vijaya in *Bhāgavata P.*, IX, ch. 15, verse 3.

[3] Pargiter, *Ancient Indian Historical Tradition*, p. 258, to which I owe some valuable suggestions and references utilised here.

[4] *Viṣṇu P.*, IV, ch. 7, verses 2-17; *Brahmāṇḍa P.*, III, ch. 66, verses 22 f.; *Vāyu P.*, ch. 91, verses 91 f.; see also *Mbh.*, I, Sec. 75.

[5] Called merely Kāñcana in *Viṣ.* and *Bhāg. P.*

[6] Called Hotraka in *Bhāg.*

[7] Called Puru in *Bhāg.* and Sunaha in *Bmd.*

[8] The *Bhāg. P.* inverts the order of Ajaka and Balākāśva, whom it calls simply Balāka.

[9] *Mbh.*, XIII (Anuśāsanaparva), Sec. 4, verses 2-7, (Eng. Trans. *Ibid.*, pp. 15-16). In the Śāntiparva (cf. *Mbh.*, XII, Sec. 49, verses 3-7) Sindhudvīpa is called Rajas, and the name of Vallabha is omitted.

[10] Cf. "Ajamīḍhasya Keśinyāṁ jajñe Jahnuḥ pratāpavān,
Jahnor abhūd Ajakāśvo Balākāśvas tadātmajaḥ,
Balākāśvasya Kuśikaḥ Kuśikād Gādhirindrakaḥ,
Gādheḥ Satyavatī kanyā Viśvāmitraḥ sutottamaḥ"

(*Agni P.*, ch. 277, verses 16-17; Calcutta, 1882). It should be noticed here that Ajakāśva is substituted for Sindhudvīpa, and Vallabha is again omitted.

and is further corroborated by the *Brahma*[1] and *Harivaṁśa Purāṇas*,[2] which, unmindful of any inconsistency, give the first version as well.[3] According to this tradition, the divergent part of the genealogy would stand thus :

(*a*) Ajamīḍha.
|
(*b*) Jahnu (son of no. *a* by Keśinī).
|
(*c*) Sindhudvīpa (son of *b*).
|
(*d*) Balākāśva (son of *c*).
|
(*e*) Vallabha (son of *d*).
|
(*f*) Kuśika (son of *e*).
|
(*g*) Gādhi (son of *f*).
|
Satyavatī (daughter) ... Viśvāmitra.[4]

This derivation, however, does not seem to be correct. First, it goes against most of the *Purāṇas*, and those that give it do not in any way merit superior credence. The *Agni* is a late production, and the other two mar their value by their inconsistent accounts. Secondly, on this point the *Mahābhārata* also appears to make confusion worse confounded. At one place it refers to Ajamīḍha as belonging to the race of Bharata,[5]

[1] *Brahma P.*, ch. 13, verses 82-92 (Apte's edition, 1895).

[2] *Harivaṁśa*, ch. 32, verses 43-53.

[3] *Br.*, ch. 10, verses 13-60; *Hv.*, ch. 27, verses 1f.

[4] In the second version also the names as given in the *Mahābhārata* and the *Purāṇas* slightly vary, but from Gādhi onwards all the lists agree.

[5] Cf. "Bharatasyānvaye caivājamīḍho nāma pārthivaḥ,

and thus makes Viśvāmitra—if the above genealogy be correct—a remote descendant of Bharata. Elsewhere again it represents Bharata as the grandson of Viśvāmitra begotten on his forsaken daughter, Śakuntalā, by Duṣmanta or Duṣyanta.[1] These conflicting statements would lead us to believe that Viśvāmitra was both an ancestor and a descendant of Bharata—a supposition which is impossible in the natural course of things. One of them must, therefore, be untrue, and as the story of Duṣyanta is "one of the best alleged tales in ancient tradition"[2] it follows that Viśvāmitra was anterior to Bharata and consequently to Ajamīḍha, a descendant of Bharata.

To turn to the accounts of these kings, we have unfortunately very little information of value. One of them, Suhotra, is described as having "performed many *Rājasūya* and *Aśvamedha* (horse) sacrifices. He brought under his sway the whole earth surrounded by her belt of seas, and full of elephants, kine and horses, and all her wealth in gems and gold."[3] He freed the earth from Mlecchas and forest thieves (vasumatīṁ mlecchāṭavika varjitāṁ), which expression perhaps signifies that he succeeded in clearing out the aboriginal inhabitants from his kingdom. Another, Jahnu, who was probably two generations below Yauvanāśva Māndhātri, being married to his grand-daughter Kāverī,[4] must have also

Babhūva Bharataśreṣṭha yajvā Dharma-bhṛitāṁvaraḥ" *Mbh.*, XIII (Anuśāsanaparva), Sec. 4, verse 2, (Eng. Trans. *Ibid.*, p. 15).

[1] Cf. "Duṣyantaḥ khalu Viśvāmitra-duhitaraṁ
Śakuntalāṁ nāmopayeme tasyāmasya jajñe Bharataḥ"—*Ibid.*, I (Ādiparva), Sec. 95, verse 28, (Eng. Trans., *Ibid.*, p. 284).

[2] Pargiter, *Anc. Ind. Hist. Trad.*, p. 100. For further discussion see the same.

[3] *Mbh.*, I (Ādiparva), Sec. 94, verses 26-29, (Eng. Trans. *Ibid.*, p. 279.

[4] "Upaninyur mahābhāgā duhitritvena Jāhnavīṁ,
Yauvanāśvasya pautrīṁ tu Kāverīṁ Jahnurāvahat"

been a king of great renown, since the river Ganges is said to have been named after him as Jāhnavī.[1] These kings must have ruled over the surrounding regions from some capital situated on the very site of, or near Kanauj, since according to the Rāmāyaṇic legend, given above, the city was founded by Kuśanābha, son of Kuśa. It is noteworthy that even in the *Mahābhārata* the first definite mention of Kānyakubja as the capital is made during the time of Gādhi.[2]

Continuing the genealogy further, we are told that Kuśa was succeeded by his son Kuśanābha or Kuśāṁbha. He practised severe austerities in order to have a son equal to Indra, who, beholding the intensity of his devotions, took birth as his son[3] and was known to the

(*Bmd.*, III, ch. 66, verse 28; *Vāyu*, ch. 91, verse 58; *Br.*, ch. 13, verses 86-87, etc.).

[1] A fable, however, is told to explain this name. Jahnu is represented as having drunk the waters of the river Ganges, and released them atter the intercession of sages and celestials, whence the river came to be known as Jāhnavī, i.e., issuing from Jahnu (*Viṣ.*, IV, ch. 7, verses 2-3; *Vāyu*, ch. 91, verses 54-58; see also *Mbh.*, XIII, Sec. 4, verse 202; *Vālmīki Rāmāyaṇa*, Bālakāṇḍa, canto 43, verses 35-38).

[2] See e.g., *Mbh.*, V (Uddyogaparva), Sec. 118, verse 4, (Eng. Trans., *Ibid.*, p. 345).

[3] Cf. "Kuśastambas tapastepe puttrārthī rājasattamaḥ,
Pūrṇe varṣa sahasre vai śatakratuṁ apasyata,
Sudurgaṁ tāpasaṁ driṣṭvā sahasrākṣaḥ purandaraḥ,
Samarthaḥ putrajanane svayaṁ evāsya śāśvataḥ,
Putratvaṁ kalpayāmās svyaṁ eva purandaraḥ,
Gādhir nāmābhavat puttraḥ Kauśikaḥ pākaśāsanaḥ"

(*Vāyu P.*, ch. 91, verses 63-65; *Bmd.*, III, ch. 66, verses 33-35; see also *Viṣ.*, IV, Sec. 7, verse 4; *Mbh.*, XII, Sec. 49, verses 4-6). According to another account of the *Mahābhārata* (I, Sec. 177, verse 3) Gādhi was the son of Kuśika: Cf.

"Kānyakubje mahān āsīt pārthivo Bharatarṣabha,
Gādhīti viśruto loke Kuśikasyātmasaṁbhavaḥ."

The *Brahma P.* (ch. 13, verses 90-91) and the *Harivaṁśa* (ch. 32, verses 51-52) also make Gādhi the son of Kuśika, whereas

world as Gādhi or Gāthi.[1] The legend of the god of thunder incarnating himself as Gādhi perhaps suggests that the latter had Indra, or one of its numerous synonyms, as his name. Or, it may be that he started some special form of Indra-worship, and thus became popularly associated with that god. He appears to have been a powerful prince and a contemporary of Arjuna, the Haihaya ruler, since we are told in the *Mahābhārata* that "at the time when Arjuna the king of the Haihayas was harassing the world, there lived on the earth a mighty monarch in the land of Kānyakubja, a sovereign whose military force was exceedingly great. And his name of Gādhi was famous in the world."[2] Being childless and desirous of a son, Gādhi repaired to the forest, where he was blessed with a daughter named Satyavatī. Ricīka, the son of Bhrigu Aurva, asked for her hand, but the king did not like to bestow his daughter on the Riṣi with matted locks, and at the same time he hesitated to provoke his wrath by direct refusal. The king, therefore, made an impossible demand of a thousand fleet horses, each horse to be brown in colour, and each to have a sable ear. Ricīka Aurva, however, with the help of the god Varuṇa complied with the king's request,[3] and thereupon in the very city of Kānyakubja Satyavatī was married to the Riṣi. Ricīka then consecrated two special mixtures (*caru*), one for

according to the *Rāmāyaṇa* (Bālakāṇḍa, canto 51, verse 19) he was the son of Kuśanābha.

[1] The *Purāṇas* and the *Epics* call him Gādhi, whereas in the *Aitareya Brāhmaṇa* (VII, 18) and the *Sarvānukramaṇī* (see *Vedic Index of Names and Subjects*, Vol. I, p. 225) he is known as Gāthi.

[2] *Mbh.*, III (Vanaparva), Sec. 115, verses 20-21, (Eng. Trans., *Ibid.*, p. 356).

[3] The steeds are said to have issued from "Aśvatīrtha" (*Viṣ. P.*, IV, ch. 7, verse 7), which, according to Wilson, is in the district of Kanauj at the confluence of the Kālīnadī and the Ganges (Wilson's Trans., *Viṣ. P.*, p. 399, note 2).

his wife and the other for her mother, infusing in them qualities suited to a Brahman and a Kṣatriya respectively.[1] These preparations, however, were interchanged with the result that Satyavatī's mother, i.e., the wife of Gādhi, gave birth to Viśvāmitra or Viśvaratha[2] naturally inclined towards peace and piety; while Satyavatī herself was blessed with Jamadagni, whose son was the fiery Paraśurāma, who had a warrior's propensities. This fable, otherwise historically worthless, is important for two reasons. It helps us to determine the historical position of Viśvāmitra, who is one of the most intriguing riddles in ancient Brahmanic tradition. He seems to figure at all times in defiance of chronology from the *Ṛigveda* down to the Epic period.[3] But here we learn definitely that Viśvāmitra of Kānyakubja was contemporary with the Bhārgava Jamadagni, who was afterwards killed by Arjuna Kārtavīrya of the Haihaya clan.[4] Secondly, the story records the simple fact of king Viśvāmitra's translation from the Kṣatriya class to Brahmanhood. This change of class was quite natural in early Brahmanic history, but the narrators of the

[1] *Viṣ.*, IV, ch. 7, verses 8-16; *Mbh.*, XII (Śāntiparva), Section 50, verses 8f; XIII (Anuśāsanaparva), Sec. 4, verses 1f. (Eng. Trans., Śāntiparva, XII, Sec. 50, pp. 148-150; XIII, Sec. 4, pp. 17-18, etc.).

[2] Viśvaratha seems to have been the Kṣatriya name. Cf.
"Viśvāmitrastu dharmātmā nāmnā Viśvarathaḥ smṛitaḥ,
Jajñe Bhriguprasādena Kauśikād vaṁśavardhanaḥ"
(*Vāyu P.*, ch. 91, verse 93; *Bmd.* P., III, ch. 66, verse 65, etc.).

[3] Probably there were more than one Viśvāmitras bearing the name as a patronymic or a personal designation, and in course of time owing to a lack of historical sense the Brahmans confused them all.

[4] Another synchronism may be established from the fact that after becoming a Brahman Viśvāmitra meddled in the affairs of the Ayodhyā kingdom, and successfully espoused the cause of Satyavrata Triśaṅku in opposition to Vasiṣṭha (see *J. R. A. S.*, 1913, pp. 885-904; *Ibid.*, 1917, p. 37f.).

Epics and the *Purāṇas* were obliged to invent this monstrous fiction of the interchange of *caru* to explain it during a priest-ridden age, when such a "promotion" could hardly happen. But how this was actually brought about is again the subject of a fanciful legend.[1] Having ascended the throne of Kānyakubja, king Viśvāmitra is said to have gone out ahunting one day in the vicinity of the hermitage of Vasiṣṭha. There he seized the Cow of Plenty named Nandinī,[2] but the sage having created an army of uncivilised tribes, such as Pahlavas, Draviḍas, Savaras, Kirātas, etc., routed the forces of Viśvāmitra and got back the cow. Mortified at this defeat by "Brahman prowess" (brahma teja), Viśvāmitra abandoned his kingship,[3] and after practising severe penances successively earned the titles of Rājarṣi, Maharṣi and Brahmarṣi.[4]

After Viśvāmitra's relinquishment of the rulership of Kānyakubja in favour of a life spiritual, the lordship of the Gāthins passed over to Aṣṭaka born of Mādhavī.[5]

[1] *Mbh.*, I (Ādiparva), Sec. 177, verses 1f. (Eng. Trans., *Ibid.*, pp. 501-04); *Vālmīki Rāmāyaṇa*, Bālakāṇḍa, cantos 51-56.

[2] The cow is called Kāmadhenu or Śabalā in the *Rāmāyaṇa* (*Ibid.*, ch. 53, verse 1, etc.). There are references in later works and inscriptions also to Viśvāmitra's carrying away the prized cow (see e.g., Padmagupta's *Nava-sāhasāṅkacarita*, XI, verses 64f. pp. 182-84; Nagpur stone inscription, *Ep. Ind.*, II, p. 180; Arthuna inscription of Cāmuṇḍarāja, Ibid., XIV, p. 295).

[3] Macdonell and Keith, however, are doubtful about Viśvāmitra's kingship. They say, "it may probably be dismissed as a mere legend with no more foundation at most than that Viśvāmitra was of a family which once had been royal. But even this is doubtful" (*Vedic Index of Names and Subjects*, Vol. II, p. 312). Against this we may also add the testimony of the *Pañcaviṁśa Brāhmaṇa* (XXI, 12, 2), which calls Viśvāmitra king.

[4] *Vālmīki Rāmāyaṇa*, Bālakāṇḍa, ch. 56f.

[5] *Mbh.*, V (Uddyogaparva), Sec. 118, verse 18, (Eng. Trans., *Ibid.*, p. 347); see also *Matsya P.*, ch. 37, verse 6; *Brahma P.*, ch. 13, verse 91.

He seems to have been a virtuous ruler as among others Bhīṣma recommends his name to be recited both at sunset and sunrise.[1] We further learn from the *Mahābhārata* that he performed the horse-sacrifice.[2] Aṣṭaka was succeeded by the shadowy Lauhi,[3] with whom the ruling dynasty of Kānyakubja abruptly comes to an end.[4]

Later notices of Kanauj

Darkness then descends upon the fortunes of Kanauj, and the city sinks into oblivion for a long period except for the glimpse that we catch of it about the time of the Mahābhārata war. In his peace overtures Yudhiṣṭhira is represented to have said to Duryodhana: "We are desirous of peace; give us even a single province of the empire. Give us even Kuśasthala, Vrikasthala, Mākandī, Vāraṇāvata, and for the fifth any other that thou likest. Even this will end the quarrel."[5] Kuśasthala evidently stands for Kanauj, and we may, therefore, assume from Yudhiṣṭhira's readiness to compromise his claims for these five towns that they were of some importance at that time.

We are next told that it was at Kānyakubja that the Buddha "descended to earth again after his glorious ascent to the Trayastriṁśa heaven." The spot was

[1] *Mbh.*, XIII (Anuśāsana parva), Sec. 165, verses 55, 59, (Eng. Trans., *Ibid.*, p. 772).

[2] *Ibid.*, III (Vanaparva), Sec. 197, verse 1, (Eng. Trans., *Ibid.*, p. 599).

[3] *Vāyu P.*, ch. 91, verse 103; *Bmd.*, III, ch. 66, verse 75, *Brahma P.*, ch. 13, verse 92.

[4] Pargiter conjectures that the sudden disappearance of this family was due to the northward depredations of the Haihayas that began about this time (see *Anc. Ind. Hist. Trad.*, pp. 267-70).

[5] *Mbh.* V, Sec. 30, verse 19, (P. C. Roy's Eng. Trans. V, Sec. 31, p. 77). In T. R. Kriṣṇāchārya's edition of the *Śrīmanmahābhāratam*, based on South Indian texts, we have the name 'Avisthalaṁ' instead of 'Kuśasthalaṁ' (V, Sec. 31, verse 19).

marked by the erection of a Tope, which was the fifth of the eight great Topes connected with the Master's career[1]. He also preached there a sermon on sorrow and impermanency, representing the body as being like a bubble or foam[2]. Strangely enough, the story of Kanauj itself presents a striking illustration of the truth of this discourse!

During the rule of the Mauryas Kanauj, like other towns in the north, must have formed part of their wide dominions, but it was otherwise an obscure place that played no part in their history. After the death of Aśoka, the Maurya empire crumbled to pieces, and seems to have been parcelled out amongst his sons. One of the latter, named Jalauka, pushed his conquests as far as Kānyakubja in the east.[3] The statement, however, is very confused, and should not be implicitly relied upon as authoritative evidence of the alleged fact.

The next mention of Kanauj is to be found in the *Mahābhāṣya* of the celebrated grammarian Patañjali usually assigned to *circa* 150 B. C.[4] He gives the form Āhicchatrī and Kānyakubjī in the sense of a woman born at these two towns respectively.[5] The use of the adjective derived from the name of the town thus clearly shows that Kānyakubja was a well-known place in the second century B. C. and it must have been founded considerably earlier.

It is again assumed that Kanauj is mentioned twice, firstly under the name of Kanagora; and secondly, under

[1] Watters, I, p. 337.

[2] Beal, *The Travels of Fa-hian* (*Fo-Kuo-ki*), ch. xviii, p. xliii. The insignificance of Kanauj at the time of the Buddha is, however, demonstrated by its omission in the *Jātakas*.

[3] *Rājat.* Vol. I, Bk. I, verse 117, (Stein, Trans., p. 22).

[4] Smith, *Early History of India* (4th ed.), p. 228; Keith, *A History of Sanskrit Literature* (1928), p. 428.

[5] Kielhorn, *Mahābhāṣya*, II, p. 233 (see under "Gotrāvayavāt," *Adhyāya* 4, *Pāda* 1, *Sūtra* 79 of *Pāṇini*).

that of Kanogiza, in the *Geography* of Klaudios Ptolemy, who wrote his great work sometime about 140 A. D.[1] Kanagora is placed in longitude 135°, latitude 30°40′, and is enumerated as one of the seven towns belonging to the Prasiake (Prācya), or the East. Among other cities mentioned are Sambhalaka, Adisdara, and Sāgala, which perhaps represent respectively Sambhal in Rohilkhand, Ahicchatra (Ādikoṭa) identified with Ramnagar in the Bareilly district,[2] and Sākala, the modern Sialkot in the Punjab according to Smith.[3] Saint Martin, however, believes that it stands for Sakula or Saghela, mentioned in the Ceylonese chronicles among the royal cities of Northern India, and which in the opinion of Turnour is the same as Kuśinagara, so well-known in Buddhist traditions.[4] As observed by Dr. Vincent Smith, "it would be natural to find Kanauj in this company, and it is possible that Kanagora may be intended for that city".[5] But from the form of the name it would seem more reasonable to identify it with Karṇapura or Kanakapura, i.e., modern Cawnpore, a trading centre not far from Kanauj.

The second name, Kanogiza, which bears a great resemblance to Kānyakubja, is placed in longitude 143° and latitude 32°. It occurs in a list of inland towns of transgangetic India.[6] Ptolemy, while giving here the name more correctly, has put the city hopelessly out of position with reference to the Ganges, from which he has removed it several degrees although it was

[1] *Ancient India as described by Ptolemy.*, ed. S. N. Majumdar Śāstrī (Calcutta, 1927), pp. 134, 227-28; *Ind., Ant.* XIII, pp. 352-353, 380-81.

[2] Compare also *Kāśikā* on Pāṇini, I, 75, where both Ahicchatra and Kānyakubja are included in the Prācya.

[3] *J. R. A. S.*, 1908, p. 766.

[4] Ptolemy's *Ancient India*, p. 135.

[5] *J. R. A. S.*, 1908, p. 766.

[6] Ptolemy's *Ancient India*, pp. 224-25.

actually situated upon its bank. To add to our difficulty, none of the towns Selampura, Kassida, Eldana, and Asanbara, mentioned in the list containing Kanogiza, can be identified with any degree of certainty. Thus, though it is tempting to identify the one on the ground of affinity in sound to Kānyakubja, and the other because it is more correctly placed, we have no positive evidence to show that these names represent Kanauj.[1]

The first notice of Kanauj with some scanty details is in the work of Fa-hian, who visited the town about the beginning of the fifth century A. D. So far, the references to Kanauj were purely legendary and incidental, but the record of Fa-hian is of historical importance, as it contains the impressions of an eye-witness. His meagre account is as follows: "Fa-hian resided in the Dragon *Vihāra* during the summer retreat. After this was over, going south-east seven *yojanas*, he arrived at the city of Ki-jou-i (Kanauj). This city borders on the Ganges. There are two *Sanghārāmas* here, both belonging to the system of Little Vehicle. Going from the city six or seven *li* in a westerly direction, on the north bank of the river Ganges, is the place where Buddha preached for the good of his disciples. Tradition says that he preached on impermanency and sorrow, and also on the body being like a bubble or foam. On this spot they have raised a tower, which still remains."[2] It is evident from the above description that during the pilgrim's itinerary, when the power of the Guptas was at its meridian, Kanauj was quite an unimportant and negligible

[1] On the other hand Kennedy says, "We have certain reasons for thinking that both Ptolemy's Kanagora and Kanogiza refer to Kanauj, and we know no reason to the contrary" (*J. R. A. S.*, 1908, p. 880). See also Cunningham, *Arch. Surv. Ind. Rep.* Vol. I (1862-63), p. 280; Smith, *J. R. A. S.*, 1908, p. 766.

[2] Beal, *The Travels of Fa-hian (Fo-Kuo-ki)*, ch. xviii, p. xliii.

place[1]. The sun of the glory of Pāṭaliputra was still in the ascendant, but it soon began to decline, and the next century saw the rise of another political centre that was destined to hold pre-eminence till the avalanche of the Moslem conquest.

[1] Notwithstanding this testimony, it was at one time asserted that the Guptas had their capital at Kanauj (See Prinsep, *Indian Antiquities*, I, p. 284; Burgess, *Arch. Surv. W. India*, II, p. 80; Frazer, *Literary History of India*, p. 251). In the light of later researches, however, the error has become too obvious even to need any refutation or discussion (see Smith, *J. R. A. S.*, 1908, pp. 769-70; *J. A. S. B.*, 1884, p. 184 f; Fleet, *C. I. I.* Vol. III; Allan, *Gupta Coins*; Raychaudhuri, *Political History of India*, etc.).

PART I

CHAPTER II

THE MAUKHARIS OF KANAUJ

Section A

Decline of the Guptas and its effect

The latter half of the fifth century A. D. was a period of great ferment in Northern India, as it saw the beginning of that process which ultimately undermined the stability of the Imperial Gupta dynasty. The empire became involved in a disastrous war with the Puṣyamitras or Puṣpamitras who "had developed great power and wealth",[1] and although the danger of immediate subversion was averted by the energy and military strategy of Skandagupta, the shock of the struggle, during the course of which he was reduced to such straits that he had to spend "a whole night on the bare ground," was none the less serious. It was closely followed by a greater menace to the safety of the empire; this was the "irruption of the savage Hūṇas," who at this time began to pour down the North-Western passes like an irresistible torrent. At first Skandagupta, "by whose two arms the earth was shaken, when he .... joined in

[1] *Corpus Inscriptionum Indicarum*, vol. III, pp. 54, 55: Bhitari stone pillar inscription. Fleet locates the Puṣyamitras in Central India "somewhere in the country along the banks of the Narmada" (*Ind. Ant.*, 1889, p. 228), but Smith places them in the North (*Early Hist. of India*, 4th ed., p. 326, Note 2). Mr. H. R. Divekar, on the other hand, suggests a different reading (*Ann. Bhand. Res. Inst.*, 1919-20, p. 99 f).

close conflict with the Hūṇas,"[1] succeeded in stemming the tide of their advance into the interior; but the repeated attacks of these nomadic hordes eventually broke the stubborn resistance, and the Gupta dynasty began to totter to its fall.[2] History undoubtedly records the continuance of the rule of the Guptas till long afterwards,[3] but the Hūṇa onrush appears to have brought to the surface the latent disruptive forces, which readily operate in India at the least manifestation of a slackening of the grip of the central power upon the outlying provinces.

The earliest defections from the empire were evidently Saurāṣṭra and Western Malwa. There is a curious break in the silver currency after Skandagupta, and we have no inscriptions to prove that his successors, had any direct connection with these regions.[4] Besides, it is almost certain that towards the last quarter of the fifth century the Maitrakas rose to power in Valabhī under the leadership of Senāpati Bhaṭṭāraka. This is obvious from the fact that the first known record of this family belongs to Mahārāja Dhruvasena I, the third son of Bhaṭṭāraka, and bears the Gupta-Valabhī date 206 =525 A. D. Between them there intervened the other two sons of Bhaṭṭāraka-Senāpati Dharasena I and Mahārāja Droṇasiṁha. If we, therefore, roughly assign 40 to 45 years for the first three reigns, the kingdom must have been founded in *circa* 480-85 A. D. We know from the inscriptions that the first few Maitraka rulers were not absolutely independent,[5] but it is not clear

[1] *C. I. I.*, III, pp. 54, 55. Cf. "Hūṇair-yyasya samāgatasya samare dorbhyāṁ dharā kampitā bhīmāvarttakarasya........."

[2] *Early Hist. of India*, 4th ed., p. 328.

[3] Raychaudhuri, *Pol. Hist. of India*, 3rd ed., p. 391f.

[4] *Ibid.*, p. 390; see also Allan's *Gupta Coins*, Introd., p. xlix.

[5] We learn, for instance, from the Maliya copperplate that

whose suzerainty they acknowledged. Possibly they owed allegiance to the Hūṇas, who gradually overwhelmed the western and central parts of India. Or perhaps, for sometime they nominally kept alive the tradition of Gupta paramountcy.

Presumably about the same time the Maukharis also, who, as we shall see below, originally governed as feudatories certain parts of Magadha, taking advantage of the weakness of the central government established themselves at Kanauj, and initiated a line which was destined to play a very important rôle in the politics of Northern India.

We learn from the Madhuban plate[1] that in Thāneśvar Naravardhana became the founder of a dynasty immortalised by the deeds of Harṣa. The latter is definitely known to have ascended the throne in A. D. 606, and as he represented the fifth generation in descent, we may well feel certain that Naravardhana must have carved out the kingdom about the close of the fifth or the beginning of the sixth century.

But the greatest disturbing factors were doubtless the Hūṇas, who by the year 510 A. D. advanced into the heart of India under the leadership of Toramāṇa,[2] and established their settlements in Central India, where they

Mahārāja Droṇasiṁha was installed as king "by the paramount master in person." (*C. I. I.*, *III*, pp. 165, 168).

[1] *Ep. Ind.*, *I*, pp. 72, 73. According to Bāṇa the founder of the house was the shadowy Puṣyabhūti or Puṣpabhūti.

[2] This date rests on the evidence of three inscriptions:

(*a*) Fleet, *C. I. I.*, III, No. 19, pp. 88-90; Eran stone pillar inscription of Budhagupta, dated Gupta year 165.

(*b*) *Ibid.*, No. 20, pp. 91-93; Eran posthumous inscription of Goparāja, dated Gupta year 191.

(*c*) *Ibid.*, No. 36, pp. 158-61; Eran inscription dated in the first year of Toramāṇa. See also *Gupta Coins*, p. lxii, where Mr. Allan rightly remarks that "it was in resisting the invader (Toramāṇa) that Goparāja fell."

ruled practising the most horrible cruelties till a new chief arose to deliver the land from an intolerable foreign thraldom. This was the "*Janendra*" Yaśodharman, who won a powerful position for himself by inflicting a crushing defeat on the tyrannical Hūṇa chief, Mihiragula, "the Attila of India." His Mandasor inscription[1] further claims that he brought under his sway lands which even the Guptas and the Hūṇas could not subdue, and made himself master of India from the Brahmaputra to the western ocean, and from the Himalayas to the Mahendragiri, i.e., Kaliṅga (cf. the Allahabad Pillar Inscription. According to Smith, however, it denotes the southernmost peak of the Travancore Ghats; *E. H. I.*, 4th ed. p. 339). Making due allowance for hyperbole in this contemporary epigraph, it appears that Yaśodharman exercised some sort of loose hegemony over the north during the heyday of his power, but his success was short-lived and the Guptas soon emerged from their temporary eclipse. For, the Khoh inscription of Saṁkṣoba, dated in the Gupta year 209=528 A. D. "in the enjoyment of sovereignty by the Gupta kings",[2] and according to Mr. R. G. Basak, another record of Ucchakalpa Mahārāja Sarvanātha of the Gupta year 214=533 A. D.,[3] show that at that time Gupta authority was recognised, even though nominally, in Central India. Besides, Dr. Raychaudhuri has well pointed out that "in A. D. 543-44, ten years after the Mandasor inscription, which mentions the *Janendra* Yaśodharman as victorious, the son (?) and Viceroy of a Gupta Paramabhaṭṭāraka Mahārājādhirāja Prithivīpati, and not any official of the Central Indian *Janendra*, was governing the Puṇḍravardhana *Bhukti*—a province which lay

[1] *C. I. I.*, vol. III, No. 33, pp. 146, 148.

[2] *Ibid.*, pp. 114, 115.

[3] *Ibid.*, No. 31, pp. 135-39; *Ep. Ind.*, XV, p. 125.

between the Indian interior and the Lauhitya."[1]

Thus, amid these political convulsions the Later Guptas tried to revive their lost glories, but what they achieved was only the ghost of their former existence, as the process of disintegration had gone too far, and fresh complications had arisen owing to the growth of new powers. The Maukharis, who had grown rich and prosperous by their possession of the fertile Doab, were also at this time bidding for supremacy in the north, and they had now to be reckoned with before the Guptas could reclaim the allegiance of the greater part of Northern India. This contest for overlordship between the Maukharis and the Later Guptas forms the most arresting feature of the major portion of the sixth century A. D. It was a struggle between the waning glories of Magadha and the rising power of Kanauj. It ended in transferring the political centre of gravity to the latter; and the credit for effecting this mighty change is due to the Maukharis, who reaped a rich harvest out of the prevailing confusion, and suddenly leaped from obscurity to great importance.

Sources

Unfortunately, our data for the history of Kanauj under the Maukharis[2] are very meagre, and so we have to depend mainly on guesswork supported by a few coins, epigraphic documents, and casual literary references.

(*a*) The first record of some value is the seal of

[1] *Pol. Hist. of India*, 3rd ed., p. 403. Compare the Damodarpur Copper-plate inscription of 543-44 A. D., (*Ep. Ind.*, XV, p. 113f.).

[2] The records of the dynasty use the term Mukhara and Maukhari in a loose way. The Jaunpur (*C. I. I.*, III, pp. 229, 230) and the Haraha inscriptions (*Ep. Ind.*, XIV. pp. 115, 119) call its kings "Mukhara," whereas Bāṇa uses both terms indiscriminately (see *Hc. C.T.*, pp. 122, 194; *Kādambarī*, ed. Peterson (Bombay, 1900), p. 1, verse 4.

Sarvavarman found in Asirgaḍh, which is a hill-fort (formerly belonging to the Scindia) in the Burhanpur *tahsil* of the Nimad district of Central Provinces.[1]

(*b*) Next, we have what are known as the Nālandā seals.[2] They are several in number, and were discovered in the ruins of Nālandā in the Patna district of the Bihar Province. These records are preserved in a fragmentary state, and the lacunæ are evidently too many to yield us any substantial information. A seal of Sarvavarman, which Dr. Hīrānanda Śāstrī calls "a replica of the Asirgaḍh seal," is, however, almost entire.

(*c*) The third inscription was found in the Juma Masjid of Jaunpur in the United Provinces.[3] It is supposed to detail the victories achieved by Īśvaravarman, but its value is somewhat vitiated by the dubious character of its testimony.[4]

(*d*) The most important epigraph, however, is the one found at Haraha in the Bara Banki district of the United Provinces.[5] Its object is to record the reconstruction of a dilapidated temple of Śiva by Sūryavarman, son of Īśānavarman, the reigning king of the Maukhari dynasty. It not only enumerates the achievements of Iśānavarman, but also contains a date which we shall discuss further at length, as it offers certain difficulties in interpretation.

(*e*) The history of the Maukhari dynasty is also supplemented by inscriptions of a line known to historians as that of the Later Guptas. One of them was found at Aphsad in the Nawada subdivision of the Gaya

[1] *C. I. I.*, III, No. 47, pp. 219-21.

[2] *Arch. Surv. Ind. Rep.*, Eastern circle, 1917-18, p. 44; *Ep. Ind.*, XXI (April, 1931), pp. 73-74.

[3] *C. I. I.*, III, No. 51, pp. 228-30.

[4] See *Infra.*

[5] *Ep. Ind.*, XIV, pp. 110-20, edited by Hīrānanda Śāstrī; *Ind. Ant.* XLVI, pp. 125-27, commented upon by Mr. N. G. Majumdar.

district.[1] It throws a flood of light on Gupta-Maukhari relations, and without its help we should have been left to grope in the dark about these points.

(*f*) Another inscription, belonging to the time of Jīvitagupta II, was found in Deo Baranārk in the Shahabad district.[2] It is the only epigraphic record in which the name of Avantivarman occurs.

(*g*) We may also mention here the hoard of Maukhari coins discovered in Bhitaura in the Fyzabad district of the United Provinces.[3] It is considered that they furnish certain dates, and we shall try to determine later on how far we can fix the chronological position of these Maukhari kings by their help.

(*h*) Further, we may take into account the evidence of Bāṇa. The *Harṣacarita* narrates the last stages of the Gupta-Maukhari feud, and tells how eventually the young Maukhari ruler was engulfed in the political whirlpool of the times.

(*i*) Lastly, the *Mañjusrī-Mūlakalpa* alludes to the Maukharis and their contemporary powers. This late Buddhist work, however, demands cautious and critical use.

Antiquity of the Maukharis

It appears from these records that the Maukharis came into prominence during the sixth century A. D., but there are certain indications which enable us to trace their existence to much earlier times. First, Kaiyaṭa's commentary on the *Mahābhāṣya* "which may belong to the 12th century A. D., but which tradition places earlier,"[4] gives us only three illustrations:

[1] *C. I. I.*, III, No. 42, pp. 200-08.

[2] *Ibid.*, No 46, pp. 213-18. Also see *Arch. Surv. Ind. Rep.*, XVI, pp. 73-75.

[3] *J. R. A. S.*, 1906, pp. 843-50.

[4] Keith's *History of Sanskrit Literature* (1928), p. 429.

Paunikyā, Bhauṇikyā, and Maukharyā, under the aphorism (Pāṇini, IV. I. 79) explaining the formation of the words with the *syan* suffix. The *Kāśikāvṛitti* of Jayāditya and Vāmana, "written before I-tsing visited India,"[1] again cites the term, under the same rule of Pāṇini, as an instance of *Gotrāvayava*, i.e. non-famous *gotras* or names, *kulas* or families. From these references it has been conjectured that the term Maukhari was "possibly known to Pāṇini and also Patañjali"[2] who have been assigned to about the sixth century B. C. and *circa* 150 B. C. respectively.

Fleet further pointed out the antiquity of the Maukharis by the Pāli legend "*Mokhalīṇaṁ*," written in Mauryan Brāhmī characters on a clay-seal, which was secured by Cunningham at Gaya.[3] This is evidently an equivalent of the Sanskrit word "*Maukharīṇām*," which is a derivative of Mukhara and signifies "of the Maukharis." The use of the Mauryan characters unmistakably shows that they were well-known in the 3rd and 4th centuries B. C., and Sir Alexander Cunningham even tried to prove some connection between the Maukharis and the Mauryas.[4] In his opinion the term Maukhari is only a variant form of Maurya, and that "in fact Maurīya would be a legitimate contraction of

[1] *Ibid.* The itinerary of I-tsing falls between the years 671-695 A. D.

[2] *Ep. Ind.*, XIV, p. 112. The term Mukhara actually occurs in Patañjali's *Mahābhāṣya*, *Adh.* V. II., *Sūtra* 107, Kielhorn's ed., p. 397.

[3] *C. I. I.*, III, *Introd.*, p. 14. Recently Dr. A. S. Altekar of the Benares Hindu University has discovered three short inscriptions of a Maukhari family with the title Mahāsenāpati in the Kotah State. They yield us the date 294 of the *Krita* era, and if it stands for the Mālava *Saṁvat*, we have got definite epigraphic reference to the political importance of the Maukharis in the middle of the third century A.D.

[4] *Arch. Surv. Ind.*, *Rep.*, XV, p. 166.

Maukharīya." But there does not seem to be any substantial ground for this view except the mere similarity in sound.

Who were the Maukharis?

Both Vāmana and Kaiyaṭa—the famous expositors of the Pāṇinian system of grammar—take the term Mukharyā as "a patronymic, signifying the descendants of Mukhara, who must have been the *Ādipuruṣa* or the first to bring his family into prominence and thereby caused it to be known after his name."[1] It is not possible to determine whether Mukhara was a proper or an attributive name. Dr. Hīrānanda Śāstrī, however, definitely assumes that it was a surname, and that the man was "so called for his being a 'leader,' or for his fighting in the forefront of the armies, which he led into action, as it is such characteristics only which would go to make a man the founder of a line."[2]

It is interesting to note that Bāṇa also considers Mukhara to be the progenitor of Grahavarman's line, as Puṣyabhūti was of the Thānesvar dynasty.[3]

But the Haraha inscription appears to trace their origin to another remarkable personage, since it informs us that "the Mukhara princes, who have vanquished their foes and checked the course of evil, are the descendants of the hundred sons, whom king Aśvapati got from Vaivasvata (*Manu*), and who were conspicuous on account of their excellences."[4] Ancient Indian

[1] *Ep. Ind.*, XIV, p. 111.
[2] *Ibid.*
[3] *Hc. C. T.*, p. 128.
[4] *Ep. Ind.*, XIV, p. 119, verse 3. Cf.
"Sutaśatam lebhe nṛipaḥ Aśvapatiḥ
Vaivasvatādyadguṇoditaṁ,
Tat prasūtā durita-vrittirudho Mukharāḥ Kṣitīśāḥ
Kṣatārayaḥ" (*Ibid*, p. 115).

literature doubtless knows of many individuals with the name Aśvapati,[1] but it is difficult to ascertain whom the author of the *praśasti* had in view. The learned editor of the Haraha inscription further connects this dynasty with the Solar race. He thinks that Vaivasvata, from whom Aśvapati obtained the hundred sons, is the seventh Manu, "supposed to be born of the Sun and to preside over the present age."[2]

On the other hand, Mr. N. Ray tries to prove in the *Calcutta Review* that the Maukharis belonged to the *Somavaṁśa* or Lunar race.[3] He draws this conclusion from the following passage in the *Harṣacarita* : ...... "Rājyaśrī has at length united the two brilliant lines of Puṣpabhūti and Mukhara, whose worth, like that of the Sun and Moon houses, is sung by all the world to the gratification of wise men's ears."[4] The learned writer argues that the Puṣpabhūtis were of the Solar race, as they were mostly Sun-worshippers (paramā-dityabhakta), and they had such names as Ādityavardhana and Prabhākaravardhana. Granting this—it is contended—Bāṇa's manner of description would necessarily imply that the Maukharis belonged to the Somavaṁśa. But the hypothesis is gratuitous, since there are grounds to hold that the Vardhanas were not of the Solar line. Besides the suffix *bhūti*, indicating that Puṣpabhūti, the founder, was a Vaiśya, we have the explicit testimony of Yuan Chwang that Harṣa was a Vaiśya (*Fei-she* caste). Curiously, this obtains confirmation from the *Mañjuśrī-*

[1] See Monier-Williams' *Sans-Eng. Dictionary*, p. 101.

[2] *Ep. Ind.*, XIV, p. 111. Dr. H. C. Raychaudhuri is of opinion that Vaivasvata is Yama, and not Manu (*Pol. Hist. of India*, 3rd ed., p. 406).

[3] February, 1928, vol. XXVI, No. 2, p. 203. See also C. V. Vaidya's *H.M.H.I.*, vol. I, p. 335.

[4] *Hc. C. T.*, p. 128. Compare the Sanskrit passage: Somasūrya Vaṁśāviva Puṣpabhūti-Mukharavaṁśau.

Mūlakalpa, which describes the Thanesvar ruling family as Vaiśya.[1] It appears, therefore, that in the above passage Bāṇa was not actually connecting the two dynasties with the Sun and Moon respectively, but he was merely comparing them with the two well-known Kṣatriya houses, that are famous in history and legend alike. Thus though we cannot be certain as to who was the progenitor of the Maukharis, at least this much seems probable from the evidence of the Haraha inscription, as also from the termination *varman*, that they were Kṣatriyas. But in after times they appear to have gone down in the social scale, for in an interesting letter, quoted by Mr. Aravamuthan, Mr. K. P. Jayaswal observes, "I think that the modern *Mauhari* caste, almost solely located in the Gaya district, are their representatives. They are Baniyas, i.e. Vaiśyas now."[2] Was this degradation due to loss of sovereignty and subsequent change of occupation?

Their original status and territories

The Maukhari seal, written in Mauryan Brāhmī characters, to which we have referred above, contains the earliest epigraphic notice of the Maukharis. Regarding its importance Mr. Jayaswal says, "The Maukhari seal probably denotes that they were a political (republican) community in origin; they must have been bereft of power in B. C. (3rd century) as there is no room for a secondary, real political power near Gaya and Rājagṛiha in those days when the Mauryas were ruling. The seal may refer to a social (*Jātisaṅgha*) organisation only at the time. I feel that their seat has always been the district of Gaya."[3] Besides this seal there are three

[1] Gaṇapati Śāstrī's ed. (Trivandrum, 1925), pp. 626, 634.
[2] *The Kaveri, the Maukharis and the Sangam Age*, p. 80, Note 1.
[3] *Ibid.*

other inscriptions which give us a clue to the original territory and dignity of the Maukharis. They are inscribed in characters of the same type, which Indraji and Bühler think are "a little later than those of the Guptas, and hence probably belonging to the fifth century A. D."[1] Kielhorn was also of opinion that on palæographic grounds they cannot be placed later than the first half of the sixth century.[2] Mr. C. V. Vaidya, on the other hand, suggests for these inscriptions "a date later than that of Harṣa."[3] But there does not seem to be any warrant for this assumption. As is well pointed out by Mr. N. G. Majumdar, the script used in these inscriptions is far more archaic than that of the Haraha inscription of 554 A. D. clearly indicating that "they are of a considerably earlier date."[4] They were discovered in the Barabar and Nagarjuni hills, two of the easternmost parts of the Vindhyas, abutting on the Gaya district.[5] These inscriptions mention a set of three rulers, viz. Yajñavarman, Śārdūlavarman, and Anantavarman, who belonged to the Maukhari lineage, since one of them describes Anantavarman having "adorned by his own (high) birth the family of the Maukhari kings."[6] These Maukharis are given the unassuming general title of "*nṛipa*" or ruler;[7] and in one of the records Śārdūla is specifically called a "*Sāmanta-cūḍāmaṇi*," the best among "chieftains." Considering, therefore, the date and find-spots of these documents, it does not seem unreasonable to hold that

[1] *Ind. Ant.*, XIII, p. 428, Note 55.
[2] *Ep. Ind.*, VI, p. 3.
[3] *H. M. H. I.*, vol. I, p. 34.
[4] *Ind. Ant.*, XLVI, p. 127.
[5] *C. I. I.*, III, Nos. 48-50, pp. 221-28.
[6] *Ibid.*, No. 48, pp. 222, 223.
[7] See on Nripa, *Amarakoṣa*, VIII, 2—(Nṛipo nyo Maṇḍaleś-varaḥ).

about the close of the fifth century A. D. the Maukharis were still settled in Magadha round the Gaya region, and that they were feudatories to some power—very possibly the Later Guptas—as even at this time they were powerful enough to curb the rise of an independent state in the very heart of their home-territories.[1] But owing to the Hūṇa invasions and perhaps family feuds the hold of the Guptas was gradually being sapped in the outlying provinces, and this must have afforded a splendid opportunity for bold spirits to seek fresh fields and pastures new. Probably Harivarman, the first king in the Kanauj line, was one such daring adventurer, who in the prevailing confusion migrated westwards and succeeded in carving out a kingdom in the fertile Doab with his seat of government at Kanauj.[2]

Was Kanauj the capital of the Maukharis?

It is unfortunate that the records of the Maukharis do not mention the kingdom over which they ruled, and at such a distance of time this omission, coupled with the scantiness of known details about them, causes us a good deal of doubt and difficulty. Śaṅkar Pāndurang Pandit was the first to express his scepticism as

[1] Mr. N. Ray, however, thinks that these three Maukhari chiefs "ruled in the Bihar region as governors of the Kanauj Maukharis. They were perhaps charged with the viceroyalty of the Magadhan region after its loss by Dāmodaragupta" (*Cal. Rev.*, Feb., 1928, p. 210). But in view of the archaic character of the script of their inscriptions this conclusion seems unjustified.

[2] The fact that the Gaya line of feudatory chiefs ends with Anantavarman, and Harivarman founded his power about the close of the fifth century (see *Infra*), may lend additional support to this theory of westward migration during the decline of the Gupta power.

regards accepting Kanauj as the Maukhari capital;[1] and sharing this diffidence Dr. Vincent Smith remarked that the "assumption is a natural and legitimate inference from Bāṇa's narrative, but not a necessary one."[2] He further adds that the Pandit may be right in the view which he "definitely adopted that up to the time that Rājyaśrī's husband was murdered, Kanauj was the capital of the Mālava kings."[3] Elsewhere Smith summarises his views on the Maukhari territories in these words: "These 'Later Guptas of Magadha', as they are called by archæologists, shared the rule of that province with another dynasty of *Rājās*, who had names ending in *varman*, and belonged to a clan called Maukhari. The territorial division between the two dynasties cannot be defined precisely, but the Maukhari dominion in the middle of the sixth century included Oudh. Their relations with one another were sometimes friendly and sometimes hostile, but the few details known are of little importance."[4]

On the contrary, there are other scholars who definitely affirm that Kanauj was the Maukhari capital. Dr. Hoernle calls Īśānavarman the Maukhari chief of Kanauj,[5] and in another place refers to the attack of the Mālava king in 606 A. D. on Kanauj, which he captured after killing the king Grahavarman.[6] We are again told in the *Imperial Gazetteer* that "when the Gupta Empire fell to pieces it (Kanauj) became the capital of the Maukharis, one of the petty dynasties, which arose

[1] *Gauḍavaho*, Introd., pp. cxxix, note, cxxxiii. (*Bom. Skt. Series*, 1887).

[2] *J. R. A. S.*, 1908, p. 771.

[3] *Ibid.*, p. 772.

[4] *Early Hist. of India*, 4th ed., pp. 330-31.

[5] *J. R. A. S.*, 1903, p. 554.

[6] *Ibid.*, pp. 557-58.

in its place.[1]

Opinion being so divided, let us examine how far our original authorities justify us in concluding that Kanauj was the Maukhari seat of government. In the first place, the testimony of Bāṇa seems to be very valuable in this connection. He makes Saṁvādaka, the servant of princess Rājyaśrī, deliver the following sad tidings to Harṣa and Rājyavardhana: "On the very day on which the king's death was rumoured, His Majesty Grahavarman was by the wicked lord of Malwa cut off from the living along with his noble deeds. Rājyaśrī also, the princess, has been confined like a brigand's wife with a pair of iron fetters kissing her feet, and cast into prison at Kānyakubja."[2] If Kanauj was the capital of Grahavarman's adversary, as S. P. Pandit and Smith would have us believe, does it not appear incomprehensible why Bāṇa should call him "the wicked lord of Mālava?" Besides, the statement in the *Harṣacarita* that Kānyakubja was "*seized* by the man named Gupta"[3] clearly proves, it was in the possession of some other power, which could be no other but the Maukharis at this time. Thus, in my humble opinion, the evidence of Bāṇa naturally leads to the conclusion that Rājyaśrī was residing in Kanauj when it was attacked by the "wicked lord of Malwa," and it was there that she was imprisoned after her husband's murder. This tragedy was followed by the relief of Kanauj by Rājyavardhana,

[1] Vol. XIV, p. 370 (new edition). See also *Hc. C.T.*, Preface pp. xi-xii; C. V. Vaidya, *H. M. H. I.*, p. 39f; Peterson, *Kādambarī*, Introd., p. 53; F. E. Hall, *Vāsavadattā*, p. 52; Bühler, *Ep. Ind.*, I, p. 69, for this view.

[2] *Hc. C. T.*, p. 173.

[3] *Ibid.*, p. 224. "Devabhūyaṁ gate deve Rājyavardhane Guptanāmnā ca grihīte Kuśasthale" (Calcutta ed., p. 603). Does the man named Gupta here refer to Śaśāṅka? Bühler at any rate noted that in one *Ms.* of the *Harṣacarita* he is called Narendragupta (*Ep. Ind.*, I, p. 70). See also Allan's *Gupta Coins*, Introd., p. lxiv on this point.

but its effects were soon counteracted by the recapture of the Maukhari capital by Śaśāṅka, the king of Gauḍa, who had come all the way from Bengal to assist the Mālava king in his aggressive designs against the allied houses of Thānesvar and Kanauj.[1]

Moreover, our authorities indicate that Rājyaśrī returned to Kanauj after her wanderings in the Vindhyas, and the vacant throne was offered by the statesmen to Harṣa.[2] If Kanauj had not been the Maukhari capital there is no reason why she should have settled there, and administered the government in conjunction with her brother according to the *Fang-chih*.[3] Our conclusion probably gains additional support from the provenance of the Maukhari inscriptions and coins. Considering the portability of the latter this evidence is of course flimsy, but here it gains some weight when taken in conjunction with that of Bāṇa. As stated above, a large number of coins was found associated with those of Śīlāditya Pratāpaśīla in Bhitaura in the district of Fyzabad. Some were found by Rivett Carnac at Ayodhyā and others were obtained in Ramnagar, in Rohilkhand, the ancient Ahicchatra.[4] The two chief inscriptions of Harivarman's line were discovered in the city of Jaunpur and Haraha in the Bara-Banki district, near Lucknow. All these findspots lie in the United Provinces, and are not situated far from Kanauj too. Besides, we know that except the Nalanda seals all the Maukhari inscriptions discovered in Magadha belong

[1] That Kānyakubja was first annexed by the king of Malwa after Grahavarman's death seems also implied in the statement, "There is moreover a report that the villain purposes to invade and *seize this country* (Thānesvar) *as well* (*Hc. C.T.*, p. 173).

[2] Beal, *Buddhist Records of the Western World*, vol. I, p. 211; Watters, I, p. 343. See for a detailed discussion, *Infra*, Chapter III.

[3] *Ibid.*, p. 345; Smith, *Early Hist. of India*, 4th ed., p. 351.

[4] *Arch., Surv. Ind., Rep.*, IX, p. 27.

to the line of Yajñavarman. The records of the Later Guptas, in which we have incidental notices of some Maukhari kings, further show that the Maukharis could not possibly flourish in Magadha side by side with them. We may, therefore, say in conclusion that the available evidence and the consensus of opinion of scholars point to Kanauj as the capital of Harivarman's line, and there is nothing to prove the contrary.

Section B

Harivarman

Harivarman appears to have been the founder of the Maukhari house of Kanauj, as he is the first to be named in the known records of this dynasty. Probably he or one of his immediate ancestors moved westwards to Kanauj during the decline of the Guptas, but with the materials at hand it is impossible to guess what relation this successful adventurer bore to the line of the Maukharis mentioned in the Barabar and Nagarjuni hill cave inscriptions. The Haraha inscription gives him the proud epithet of *Jvālāmukha*, or flame-faced; and the Asirgaḍh seal further testifies that "his fame stretched out beyond the four oceans; who had other kings brought into subjection by (his) prowess, and by affection (for him)".[1] He bears, however, only the subordinate title of Mahārāja, which perhaps shows that the use of laudatory expressions in the inscriptions is due not to any considerable power wielded by him, but to the simple fact that he was the first Maukhari to attain distinction.

Ādityavarman

Harivarman was succeeded by his son, Āditya-

[1] *C. I. I.*, III, pp. 220, 221; also see *Ep. Ind.*, XIV, pp. 115, 119, verses 4-5.

varman, "begotten of the Bhaṭṭārikā and Devī Jayasvāminī." He seems to have been a staunch follower of the Brahmanical cult, and the Haraha inscription describes his "sacrificial performances" in very eloquent terms.[1] The anonymous predecessor of Īśvaravarman, who is represented in the Jaunpur inscription as acquiring "religious merit arising from sacrifices",[2] may therefore be identified with Ādityavarman. He is also called merely Mahārāja, and is recorded to have married Devī Harṣaguptā. She was probably the sister of the Later Gupta king, Harṣagupta, as it was a common practice in those days for brothers and sisters to bear such identical names, of course with variation of gender in the ending to indicate the sex[3].

Īśvaravarman

The fragmentary condition of the Jaunpur inscription unfortunately causes some difficulty in the correct attribution of the exploits recorded therein. The lacunæ being extensive, Fleet remarked that "it is impossible to say whether the historical information given in them refers to Īśvaravarman, or to one of his descendants."[4] Let us, therefore, closely follow the evidence of the extant portion. Īśvaravarman is described in it as having "allayed the trouble (caused) by the approach of cruel people, and which affected the happiness of mankind," and as being "a very lion to (hostile) kings."[5] Immediately after this description occurs an account of some of his victorious engagements. We

[1] *Ibid.*, pp. 116, 119, *verse* 7.
[2] *C. I. I.*, III, pp. 229, 230.
[3] *Ibid.*, *Introd.*, p. 14.
[4] *Ibid.*, No. 51, p. 229. See also Hīrānanda Śāstrī, *Ep. Ind.*, XIV, p. 112, note 6; Aravamuthan, *The Kaveri, Maukharis and the Sangam Age*, p. 90.
[5] *C. I. I.*, III, p. 230.

are told that "a spark of fire that had come by the road from (the city of) Dhārā ... the lord of the Andhras, wholly given over to fear, took up (his) abode in the crevices of the Vindhya mountains .... went to the Raivataka mountain ...... among the warriors of the Andhra army who were spread out among the troops of elephants (and) whose arms were studded with the lustre of (their) swords drawn out."[1] The specific mention of these achievements in the very next passage after a tribute in general terms to Īśvaravarman for his heroic qualities probably shows that the author intended to ascribe them to the same king. But the damaged condition of the inscription does not make it clear whether the claims of instilling fear in the minds of the "lord of the Andhras" and the adversary who "went to the Raivataka mountains" are mere rhodomontade, or actually refer to some victories achieved by Īśvaravarman against these southern monarchs. One thing, however, appears certain from the description that "a spark of fire," i.e., the king of Dhārā, undertook an aggressive campaign against Īśvaravarman, and the latter probably emerged triumphant in this trial of arms[2]. His successful resistance against these odds must have considerably enhanced Īśvaravarman's power and prestige, and we may therefore consider him as the first Maukhari king who really brought the family into prominence. He did not, however, attain to imperial dignity, as the Asirgaḍh seal gives him the unostentatious title of Mahārāja only. This seems an additional reason to hold that the Jaunpur inscription simply registers Īśvaravarman's successful defence of the kingdom, and has no bearing on any of his "imperial

[1] *Ibid.*

[2] Was there any confederacy formed by these southern powers against the rising state of Kanauj ?

ambitions," or the extension of his "conquests towards the west up to Dhārā, to the Vindhya and Raivataka (Girnar) mountains in pursuit of the Andhras," as Dr. R. K. Mookerji would have us believe.[1] Like his predecessors, Īśvaravarman was also a Brahmanist, and he is said to have "invoked Indra in many a sacrifice" performed "in accordance with the canons."

Īśānavarman

Īśvaravarman was succeeded by his son, Īśānavarman, whose mother was the Bhaṭṭārikā and Devī Upaguptā. Presumably the second element of her name indicates that Upaguptā was also a Gupta princess. Thus, the marriages of two successive Maukhari kings—Ādityavarman and Īśvaravarman—with Gupta princesses clearly show that the two houses were at first on very cordial terms. Indeed, the subordinate title Mahārāja given to the first three Maukhari rulers may even lend some colour to the view that they recognised the suzerainty of the Later Guptas, who were yet powerful in the north.

It appears that Īśvaravarman did not long survive the disturbances that had occurred during his reign, and so his successor was called upon to avert the falling fortunes of his dynasty like a second Skandagupta. This fact seems to be metaphorically alluded to in the following statement of the Haraha inscription: "By whom the earth was forcibly upheld, like a broken boat, after fastening it on all sides by hundredfold virtues (or, strings), when it was sinking below the invisible ocean of the nether regions, being shaken by the storm of Kali."[2] Fortunately, the record also makes specific mention of the foes against whom Īśānavarman had to

[1] *Harṣa* (Rulers of India Series), p. 54.
[2] *Ep. Ind.*, XIV, pp. 117, 120, verse 15.

contend before he could feel his position secure, or exercise any power effectively. We are told that Īśānavarman occupied the throne after :—

(*a*) "conquering the lord of the Andhras, who had thousands of threefold rutting elephants;

(*b*) vanquishing in battle the Śūlikas who had an army of countless galloping horses;

(*c*) causing the Gauḍas, living on the seashore, in future to remain within their proper realm."[1]

Unhappily the data for the history of the period are very scanty, and this makes it difficult for us to identify the kings over whom Īśānavarman is recorded to have achieved victories. It is not clear who is signified here by the tile of "lord of the Andhras." The old Andhra empire had crumbled to pieces long ago, and the country had been partitioned among three or more dynasties (see Prof. K. R. Subramanian's *History of Andhra between* 225 *to* 610 *A. D.*). The Viṣṇukuṇḍins were the dominant power in the sixth century A. D., and so Īśānavarman's Andhra opponent must have belonged to this family. It appears probable that he was either Indravarman or Vikramendravarman, but until their chronological position is more definitely established the identification cannot be regarded as beyond doubt. Dr. H. C. Raychaudhuri, however, thinks that the Andhra king probably was Mādhavavarman II of the Viṣṇukuṇḍin family,[2] who "shortly before the invasion of Pulakeśi II ...crossed the river Godāvarī with the desire to conquer the eastern region."[3] Whoever he

[1] *Ibid.*, verse 13. Cf. "Jitvā Āndhrapatiṁ sahasragaṇita-tredhākṣaradvāraṇaṁ, Vyāvalgan-niyutātisaṁkhyaturagān bhaṁkhāraṇe Śūlikāṁ (n), Kritvā cāyatimocita-sthalabhuvaḥ Gauḍān samudrāśrayān, Adhyāsiṣṭha natakṣitīśacaraṇaḥ siṁhāsanaṁ yaḥ jitī."

[2] *Political Hist. of India*, 3rd ed., p. 405; *J. A. S. B.*, 1920, p. 391 note 5.

[3] Jouveau Dubreuil, *Anc. Hist. of the Deccan*, p. 92.

might be, it appears certain that he was particularly active about this time, since the Jaunpur inscription also records warlike relations between the Maukharis and the Andhras during the reign of Īśvaravarman, and it is possible that both the father and the son had to fight against the same Andhra king. Nor are we in a better position to identify the Śūlikas and locate them correctly. Possibly they are identical with the Śaulikas of the *Bṛihatsaṁhitā* (xiv, 8) and the *Mārkaṇḍeya Purāṇa*, and are to be located in the south-east, near Kalinga, Vidarbha, and Cedi.[1] But Mr. B. C. Mazumdar makes the suggestion that the Śūlikas lived on the sea-coast near the modern district of Midnapore (Bengal).[2] According to Dr. H. C. Raychaudhuri, on the other hand, they are to be identified with the Cālukyas. He argues that "Śūlika may be another dialectic variant,"[3] since in the Mahākūṭa pillar inscription[4] the name appears as "Calikya," and in the Gujarat records we find the forms Solaki and Solanki.[5] The Mahākūṭa

[1] *Ind. Ant.*, XXII, p. 189. Fleet, however, connected them with the Mūlikas mentioned in the *Bṛihatsaṁhitā* (XIV, 48, 23) as a people living in the north-west division (*Ind. Ant.*, XXII, p. 186). See also Rapson's *Catalogue of Coins of the Andhra Dynasty*, p. xxxi; and *Ind. Ant.*, 1917, p. 127.

[2] *Orissa in the Making*, p. 105.

[3] *Pol. Hist. of India*, 3rd. ed., pp. 405-06; *J. A. S. B.*, 1920, p. 319, n. 6.

[4] *Ind. Ant.*, XIX, pp. 16-20; *Bom. Gaz.*, vol. I, pt., II. p.336.

[5] *Ibid.*, vol. I, pt. I, p. 156. Father Heras identifies the Śūlikas with the Coḷas (*Jour. And. Hist. Res. Soc.*, I, pp. 130-31). In support of this view attention may be drawn to a Tamil work, *Kalingattupparani*, by Jayagoṇḍāṇ, which according to Mr. Aravamuthan (*The Kaveri, the Maukharis, and the Sangam Age* p. 14f.) narrates the circumstance of the Coḷa king's conflict with Mukari. But I venture to say that the identification of the latter with a Maukhari ruler does not at all appear to be convincing. Presumably it was the name of a place in the South, and as Mr. Aravamuthan himself points out elsewhere (*Ibid.*, p. 72; see also pp. 24-26), a

pillar inscription further informs us that about this time the Cālukyas were extending their power on all sides, and one of their kings Kīrtivarman I, claims to have made conquests in Aṅga, Vaṅga, Magadha, Madraka, and Kaliṅga, etc.[1] Probably in their northward progress they came into conflict with Īśānavarman, and suffered a defeat at his hands.

Regarding the Gauḍas as a political power, we get the earliest definite epigraphic reference in the Haraha inscription. It appears from the term *Samudrāśrayān* applied to them that they occupied the seaboard of western Bengal, but we do not know with certainty what local dynasty was ruling there at that time.[2] They had now distinctly entered upon a career of aggrandisement, since not only does this record represent them as "issuing forth from their proper realm", but the Aphsad inscription also mentions Jīvitagupta I's struggles against these "haughty foes" who "stood on seaside shores."[3] Considering this, and the fact that between the kingdoms of Gauḍa and Kanauj intervened the Gupta dominion of Magadha, it may not be unreasonable to suggest that both Īśānavarman and his Gupta contemporary may have co-operated to check the advance

Tamil inscription of Ceylon mentions a certain Mukari-Nāḍāḻvan, and the *Kaṇakkadhikāram* refers to a chief of Mukari on the banks of the river Poṇṇi (Kāveri).

[1] *Bom. Gaz.*, Vol. I, pt. II, p. 345; *Ind. Ant.* XIX, pp. 17, 19.

[2] See the Faridpur copper plates for a set of three kings of Gauḍa. Perhaps they were slightly later in date than the one referred to in the Haraha inscription (*Ind. Ant.*, XXXIX, p. 193f; *J. A. S. B., N. S.* X, p. 425f; *Ibid., N. S.* VII, p. 289f). Dr. R. G. Basak conjectures—(see *The History of North-Eastern India*, p. 113) that the Gauḍa opponent of Īśānavarman was possibly Jayanāga, referred to in the Vappaghoṣāvaṭa grant (*Ep. Ind.*, XVIII, 1925, pp. 60f) and the Buddhist work *Mañjuśrīmūlakalpa*, (see p. 636, ed. Gaṇapati Śāstrī).

[3] *C. I. I.*, III, no. 42, pp. 202, 205.

of the Gauḍas towards the north. These successes spurred on the ambitions of Īśānavarman, and he began to claim imperial dignity by assuming the title of Mahārājādhirāja. But the Guptas could not long tolerate Īśānavarman's pretensions to supremacy or any growth in his strength, and so an appeal to arms became inevitable. This open rupture between the two houses is one of the most important events of Īśānavarman's reign, and is thus recorded in the Aphsad inscription: "By whom playing the part of the mountain Mandara, there was quickly churned that formidable milk-ocean, the cause of the attainment of fortune, which was the army of the glorious Īśānavarman, a very moon among kings."[1] This passage occurring in a record of a different dynasty is indeed remarkable, as besides testifying to the defeat of Īśānavarman it also implies his great power.[2] It must have been a severe blow—although only temporary—to the rise of the Maukharis, and probably after this victory Kumāragupta even pushed his territories as far west as Prayāga, for there are indications that his funeral rites took place there.[3]

Lastly, we may mention that, like his predecessors, he was also a Brahmanist, and during his reign it is claimed that "the three Vedas were born afresh."

[1] *Ibid.*, pp. 203, 206.

[2] Dr. R. K. Mookerji, on the other hand, seems to think that Kumāragupta was the vanquished party in this duel. He says: "Īśānavarman, who achieved three important victories in three different regions and according to inscription No. 1 (his number)—a fourth victory over the Malwa king Kumāragupta ......" (*Harṣa*, pp. 54-55; see also N. Ray, *Cal. Rev.*, Feb., 1928, p. 207, for the same view).—But if one reads between the lines of the verse, this conclusion seems utterly unwarranted. It may be remarked that the view adopted in the text is also endorsed by Fleet.

[3] *C. I. I.*, III, p. 206. note 3.

Sarvavarman

Īśānavarman was succeeded by his son, Sarvavarman, whose mother was the Bhaṭṭārikā and Mahādevī Lakṣmīvatī. The Haraha inscription discloses to us that Īśanavarman had another son named Sūryavarman, who during the lifetime of his father caused a dilapidated temple of Andhakāri, Śiva, to be "raised at his wish and made an ornament of the earth." He is not mentioned in any other record, which probably shows that either he predeceased his father, or there was a struggle for succession, and Sūryavarman being worsted in the fight was ousted or put to death. Dr. H. C. Raychaudhuri, on the other hand, tries to identify the Maukhari Sūryavarman with the ruler of the same name mentioned in the Sirpur stone inscription of Mahāśivagupta.[1] He is there described as "born in the unblemished family of the Varmans, great on account of their supremacy (ādhipatya)." But there seems little reason to uphold this identification, since according to the learned editor of this undated inscription its characters "belong to the 8th or 9th century A. D.," which indicates that Sūryavarman "must have flourished about the 8th century A. D."[2]

Sarvavarman turned out to be a chip of the old block; and he thoroughly avenged his father's defeat by his successful engagements with the Guptas. We are told in the Aphsad inscription that Dāmodaragupta "breaking up the proudly-stepping array of mighty elephants, belonging to the Maukhari became unconscious (and expired in the fight)."[3] Although the poet appears to make the conventional claim for his hero's

[1] *Pol. Hist. of India*, 3rd ed., p. 407, note 3. See for the inscription, *Ep. Ind.* XI, p. 185f.

[2] *Ep. Ind.*, XI, p. 185.

[3] *C. I. I.*, III, pp. 203, 206.

victory, the result of the struggle was in effect certainly adverse to Dāmodaragupta, as he is reported to have been killed on the battlefield itself. Now, who was this rival of the Guptas with the unassuming epithet of "Maukhari"? There seems little doubt that it refers to Sarvavarman, for in the Asirgaḍh seal he alone is specifically mentioned as "Sarvavarman, the Maukhari." The significance of this term, occurring in an inscription of the dynasty, would be lost unless we do suppose that owing to some reason it had become specially associated with Sarvavarman's name. Besides, we have already seen that the rivalry between the Guptas and the Maukharis in the preceding generation had ended against Īśānavarman, and this must have made his successor smart keenly under the blow. Sarvavarman, therefore, tried to retrieve the disaster, and his efforts against his Gupta contemporary met with conspicuous success.[1]

Perhaps after the defeat and death of Dāmodaragupta, Magadha or at least its western portion was annexed by Sarvavarman. This conclusion seems evident from the Deo-Baranark inscription in which one Sarvavarman, identified with the Maukhari king of the same name, confirms a grant that was previously made by Bālāditya, the famous conqueror of the Hūṇas[2]. We can explain this grant in the modern Shahabad district of Bihar Province only on the assumption that the supremacy over Magadha had passed to the

[1] Cunningham thinks that this rivalry is indicated in the coins as well. He says: "As a curious proof of the antagonism between the Guptas and the Maukharis, I may cite the fact that on the coins the Maukhari king has his face turned to the left, in the opposite direction to that of the Gupta kings. This opposition is also seen on the coins of Toramāṇa, the successor and probable supplanter of Budhagupta" (*Arch. Surv. Ind., Rep.* XVI, p. 81; also see *J. R. A. S.*, 1906, pp. 849-50).

[2] *C. I. I.*, III, pp. 216, 218.

Maukharis after this victory. What happened to the Later Guptas cannot be ascertained definitely, but the *Harṣacarita* probably gives a faint trace of their movements. Bāṇa calls Kumāragupta and Mādhavagupta, *Mālavarājaputra* (sons of the king of Malwa); and as the latter has been accepted on almost all hands as identical with Mādhavagupta of the Aphsad inscription, it may not be unreasonable to suggest that Mahāsenagupta, the son of Dāmodaragupta, retired to some part of Malwa, which continued to acknowledge the Gupta supremacy even after the downfall of the Imperial family.[1] This was probably Eastern Malwa, corresponding to the Bhilsa district on the Vetravatī, for we are told in the commentary of the *Kāmasūtra* of Vātsyāyana (Adhikaraṇa, III) that Ujjayinī or Ujjain denoted Western Malwa, and where only Malwa is mentioned it should be taken to mean Eastern Malwa.[2] It appears that Mahāsenagupta established himself in this region after being ousted from Magadha in order to pursue his schemes to regain the lost possession with greater vigour and unhampered by the enemy's proximity.[3]

The same passage, which records Sarvavarman's successful encounter with his Gupta rival also informs us that the "proudly stepping array of mighty elephants belonging to the Maukhari ... had thrown aloft in battle the troops of the Hūṇas (in order to trample

[1] Raychaudhuri, *Pol. Hist. of India*, 3rd ed., pp. 391-92; see the Betul plates of Parivrājaka Mahārāja Saṁkṣoba dated G. E. 199 =A. D. 518 (*Ep. Ind.*, VIII, pp. 284-87); Khoh inscription of the year 209 G. E. = 528 A. D. (*C. I. I.*, III, pp. 113-16) etc. Also consult *Ep. Ind.*, XV, p. 124f.

[2] *Ujjayinīdeśabhavyāstā evāparamālavyaḥ Mālavya iti pūrvamālavabhavāḥ* (*Ind. Ant.*, 1878, p. 259, footnote 4; see also *Cal. Rev.* Feb., 1928, p. 210).

[3] It is only by this assumption that we can reconcile the testimonies of the *Harṣacarita* and the Deo-Baranārk and Aphsad inscriptions.

them to death)."[1] Now, who were the Hūṇa opponents of Sarvavarman? There are indications in the *Harṣacarita* that the Hūṇas had retained their hold in the north-west, in spite of their expulsion from Central India. Prabhākaravardhana had fought against them and towards the close of his reign he had to send the crown-prince again to defend the frontiers of the kingdom against their attack. Probably these Hūṇas began their movements during the time of Sarvavarman, and being a great power in Northern India the Maukharis were then called upon to hold these nomads in check. The Vardhanas were not strong in this generation, and, as Thānesvar lay between Kanauj and the Hūṇa territories in the south-east of the Punjab, it may not be unreasonable to suppose that Sarvavarman's undertakings against the Hūṇas were a sort of help given to the Vardhanas to repel their depredations and save northern India from another Hūṇa upheaval.

Avantivarman

Unfortunately we do not stand on firm ground in regard to Sarvavarman's successor owing to a curious break in the records. Scholars are at variance, but the general opinion appears to be that Susthitavarman wore the Maukhari crown after Sarvavarman.[2] This is usually assumed on the strength of the following passage in the Aphsad inscription : "The illustrious Mahāsena-

[1] It appears from the manner of description that Sarvavarman inflicted a defeat on the Hūṇas before he came into conflict with Dāmodaragupta.

[2] Fleet, *C. I. I.*, III, *Introd.*, p. 15; C. V. Vaidya, *H. M. H. I.*, vol. I, p. 34; Dr. R. K. Mookerji, *Harṣa*, p. 55; Cowell and Thomas, *Harṣacarita*, Trans. Preface, p. xi. note 3. For the opposite view see Dr. Raychaudhuri, *Pol. Hist. of India*, 3rd. ed., p. 408; R. D. Banerji, *J. B. O. R. S.*, June, 1928, p. 254f; Aravamuthan, *Sangam Age*, pp. 93-94.

gupta ...... whose mighty fame, marked with the honour of victory in war, over the illustrious Susthitavarman, (and) (white) as a full-blown jasmine flower or water-lily, or as a pure necklace of pearls pounded into little bits (?) is still constantly sung on the banks of (the river) Lohitya the surfaces of which are (so) cool, by the siddhas in pairs, when they wake up after sleeping in the shade of the betel-plants, that are in full bloom."[1]

It is contended that as two generations of the Later Guptas, viz., Kumāragupta and Dāmodaragupta, were on terms of enmity with two successive Maukhari rulers —Īśānavarman and Sarvavarman—the opponent of the third Gupta king Mahāsena must necessarily have been a Maukhari. The conclusion, however, seems to be rather oversanguine, and even unwarranted for several reasons. In the first place, none of the epigraphs mentions Susthitavarman as a Maukhari, and the Aphsad inscription also does not say a word indicating that he belonged to the Maukhari lineage. Secondly, the description of Mahāsena's victory as "still constantly sung on the banks of (the river) Lohitya" or Brahmaputra shows beyond doubt that the reference here is to his rivalry with some king of Assam, and not to a Maukhari ruler, as the Maukharis were never masters of the Brahmaputra valley. But it is not clear from the passage whether the Brahmaputra is mentioned as the farthest limit of Mahāsenagupta's conquest or simply refers to the place where the actual battle was fought. In my humble opinion the latter interpretation seems more convincing.

Curiously enough, the Nidhanpur plates mention a Susthitavarman[2] as the father of Bhāskaravarman contemporary with Harṣa. He is perhaps identical with

[1] *C. I. I.*, III, pp. 203, 206.
[2] *Ep. Ind.*, XII, pp. 74, 77.

the king called in the *Harṣacarita* Susthiravarman.[1] That Susthiravarman and Susthitavarman were one and the same person is also proved by the identity of the names of his son and of his three immediate ancestors, as furnished by the *Harṣacarita*, the Nidhanpur plates, and the Nalanda seals.[2]

Thirdly, the Deo-Baranark inscription omits the name of Susthitavarman, and makes Avantivarman confirm a grant previously made by Sarvavarman.[3] This probably shows that Avantivarman was considered to be the successor of Sarvavarman.

Fourthly, no coins of Susthitavarman have been found associated with those of the other Maukhari rulers. On the other hand, coins of Avantivarman have been discovered in Bhitaura along with those of Īśānavarman and Sarvavarman. Thus, the trend of evidence favours the elimination of Susthitavarman from the Maukhari genealogy, and proves that it was Avantivarman who succeeded Sarvavarman.

Very little is known about Avantivarman. We do not even know what relationship he bore to Sarvavarman, but considering the fact that he came to the throne after the latter, and there is no case in the Maukhari dynasty of a brother succeeding a brother, it may be tentatively assumed that Avantivarman was a son of Sarvavarman. Bāṇa calls him the pride of the Mukhara race, which stood "at the head of all royal houses," and was "worshipped, like Śiva's footprint, by all the world."[4] There are also indications that he was a patron of Viśākhadatta, the celebrated author of

[1] *Hc. C. T.*, p. 217.
[2] *J. B. O. R. S.*, V, pp. 302-04.
[3] *C. I. I.*, III, pp. 216, 218.
[4] *Hc. C. T.*, p. 122. Cf. "Dharaṇīdharāṇāṁ ca mūrdhni sthito Māheśvaraḥ pādanyāsa iva sakala-bhuvana-namaskrito Maukharo vaṁśaḥ" (Hc., Cal. ed., p. 298).

the *Mudrārākṣasa*. This hypothesis is based on the reading Rantivarma or Avantivarman, instead of "Candraguptaḥ," in the *Bharatavākya*, which occurs in some manuscripts, as is noticed by Mr. Telang in his edition of the play[1]. That the Maukhari rulers were patrons of literature is evident from the introductory stanza of the *Kādambarī* in which Bāṇa represents his *guru* Bhatsu or Bharva as being "honoured by crowned Maukharis."[2]

Grahavarman

According to the *Harṣacarita*, Avantivarman was succeeded by his eldest son (sūnuragrajaḥ) named Grahavarman. He "a prince like the lord of planets, descended upon earth,"[3] is further recorded to have won the hand of princess Rājyaśrī of Thāneśvar. Bāṇa gives a very vivid description of this marriage; how the royal palace was thronged with feudatories ready to do service, and how the nuptial ceremony was performed at the auspicious time with oriental splendour.[4] It is not clear whether Avantivarman was alive at the time of this union. Bāṇa, at any rate, represents Grahavarman as opening the matrimonial negotiations, which probably shows that his father was then dead. On the other hand, we should be cautious in drawing any conclusion from Avantivarman's absence during the ceremonies, for he may have stayed behind deeming it imprudent to leave the capital unprotected. From

[1] *Ind. Ant.*, XLIII, p. 67; *J. R. A. S.*, 1900, p. 535; Aravamuthan's *Sangam Age*, p. 95. Mr. K. P. Jayaswal, however, believes that the true reading in the *Bharatavākya* is "Candraguptaḥ," whom he identifies with Candragupta II (*Ind. Ant.*, XLII., p. 265; *J. R. A. S.*, 1923, pp. 586-87).

[2] *Kādambarī*, Trans. by Ridding, p. 1. Cf. "Saśekharaiḥ Maukharibhiḥ kṛitārcanaṁ."

[3] *Hc. C. T.*, pp. 122-23. [4] *Ibid.*, pp. 123-28.

the political point of view it was a very important alliance. It linked up the two powerful houses of the Maukharis of Kanauj and the Vardhanas of Thāneśvar, and was largely instrumental in shaping the course of history during that momentous period. The Later Guptas, who owing to their inveterate rivalry with the Maukharis, were courting the Vardhana alliance—as is evident from the marriage of Mahāsenaguptā—finally broke off all old relations and formed an *entente* with the Gauḍas. This policy at first seemed to augur well for the Guptas. Devagupta of Malwa[1] advanced against Kanauj with the support and co-operation of Śaśāṅka, king of Gauḍa[2], just at the opportune moment when Prabhākaravardhana had died. Thus says Bāṇa: "On the very day on which the king's death was rumoured, his majesty Grahavarman was by the wicked lord of Malwa cut off from the living along with his noble deeds."[3] Kanauj was seized and occupied; and Rājyaśrī was thrown into a dungeon "like a brigand's wife with a pair of iron fetters kissing her feet." Such brutal treatment meted out to a young lady—the wife of the dead monarch—incidentally throws light not only on the inhuman character of the Gupta king, but also on the immoral laws of war during that age. So far the Gupta-Gauḍa scheme was eminently successful, and Kanauj lay prostrate before their combined forces. We shall deal in the next chapter with its relief and subsequent fate.

[1] See *Infra*, chapter III.
[2] *Ibid.*
[3] *Hc. C. T.*, p. 173.
Cf. "Yato yasmin ahani avanipatiḥ uparata ityabhūdvārtā tasminneva Devo Grahavarmā durātmanā Mālavarājena jīvalokaṁ ātmanaḥ sukritena saha tyājitaḥ. Bhartridārikāpi Rājyaśrīḥ kālāyasnigaḍa yugalacuṁbitacaraṇā caurāṅganā iva saṁyatā Kānyakubje kārāyāṁ nikṣiptā." (Hc., Cal. ed., pp. 424-25).

Section C

Extent of the Kingdom under the Maukharis

Although it is difficult to fix the limits of the Maukhari jurisdiction during the zenith of their power with any considerable degree of certainty, a consideration of the provenance of coins and inscriptions of the dynasty, along with their internal evidence, will help us to some extent to lift the obscurity that hangs over this problem.

To begin with the coins, some of them were found in Ahicchatra, a few miles to the north-west of Kanauj,[1] and others were procured at Ayodhyā. Sir Richard Burn has further discussed a large hoard of Maukhari coins that was discovered in Bhitaura in the Fyzabad district of the United Provinces.[2]

Two seals were discovered in Nalanda;[3] but as the "lower right quadrant with about half the writing is lost," we cannot say definitely to which reign they belong. Recently some more Maukhari seals came to light from the same site, and fortunately one of them, issued by Sarvavarman, is almost entire.[4]

The Jaunpur (U. P.) inscription[5] records some achievements of Īśvaravarman, and we have made the surmise that they do not refer to any of his actual conquests; but merely to his bold stand against the enemies' aggressions.

Next, the Haraha inscription, found in the Bara-Banki district (near Lucknow) of the United Provinces,[6]

[1] *Arch. Surv. Ind. Rep.*, IX, p. 27; *J. R. A. S.*, 1889, p. 136.
[2] *J. R. A. S.*, 1906, pp. 843-50.
[3] *Arch. Surv. Ind. Rep.*, Eastern circle, 1917-18, p. 44.
[4] *Ep. Ind.*, XXI (April, 1931), pp. 73-74.
[5] *C. I. I.*, Vol. III, No. 51, pp. 228-30.
[6] *Ep. Ind.*, XIV, pp. 110-20. These findspots have already been indicated elsewhere. I have been compelled to repeat them

mentions Īśānavarman's victories over the Andhras, the Śulikas, and the Gauḍas, who, according to Mr. N. G. Majumdar "were all compelled to accept his sovereignty."[1] But a close perusal of the inscription hardly justifies our drawing this conclusion. It describes the Gauḍas as being forced "in future to remain within their proper realm," which shows that they were only checked in the course of their aggrandizement. Besides, Īśānavarman could not extend his suzerainty as far as Gauḍadeśa, when he had to bow to the steel of a king of an intermediate territory, viz. Kumāragupta, the later Gupta monarch of Magadha. Probably the Andhras and the Śūlikas were likewise the aggressors, and Īśānavarman's engagements with them were more or less of the nature of a successful trial of arms, no annexation of their territories or imposition of Īśānavarman's authority being implied.

Here we must also consider a seal that was found in Asirgaḍh in the Nimad District of the Central Provinces[2]. Its discovery at a place situated so far south should not, however, be taken as proof that Asirgaḍh was a sort of a "Maukhari outpost" in the Deccan, as observed by Mr. Aravamuthan[3]. Fleet rightly points out that the mere finding of the inscription at Asirgaḍh of course does not suffice in any way to connect the members of this family of Maukharis with that locality. Their territory probably lay some hundreds of miles more to the east.[4] Coins and seals, being small and portable, can easily be carried far away from the actual place of their origin. As an instance, we

here for the sake of convenience, and to make my point more explicit.

[1] *Ind. Ant.*, 1917, p. 127.

[2] *C. I. I.*, III, No. 47, pp. 219-221.

[3] *The Kaveri, the Maukhari, and the Sangam Age*, p. 97.

[4] *C. I. I.*, III, No. 47, p. 220.

may observe that a seal of Bhāskaravarman of Kāmarūpa or Assam was found in Nalanda, although it is known beyond doubt that this region was never included within his realm.

The Aphsad inscription further informs us that Dāmodaragupta suffered a fatal defeat at the hands of a "Maukhari",[1] whom we have identified with Sarvavarman. We have also suggested that probably the death of this Later Gupta king was followed by the annexation of Magadha—or at least its western parts—to the Maukhari dominions. The Deo-Baranark inscription[2] appears to lend welcome support to this theory, since it records the confirmation of a grant by two Maukhari rulers—Sarvavarman and Avantivarman—in the region of Arrah (Shahabad District).

Lastly, we may notice the testimony of the Nirmand inscription, found at a place almost on the bank of the Sutlej in the Kangra District of the Punjab[3]. It mentions the grant of a Mahārāja Sarvavarman; and "as we know of no other Sarvavarman of about this period," says Mr. Aravamuthan, "we may tentatively assume that the Maukhari Sarvavarman had been able to extend his dominions so far west in the course of his wars with the Hūṇas."[4] The assumption, however, does not seem cogent. The Maukhari Sarvavarman is uniformly given the paramount titles of Mahārājādhirāja and Parameśvara in the dynastic records, whereas the Sarvavarman of the Nirmand inscription is a mere Mahārāja. Moreover, it would involve the supposition that the Maukharis exercised suzerainty over the intervening Vardhana dominions, and Prabhākara, who certainly was an independent king, had to fight against the Maukharis

[1] *Ibid*, pp. 203, 206.
[2] *Ibid.*, pp. 216, 218.
[3] *Ibid.*, No. 80, pp. 286-91.
[4] *The Kaveri, the Maukhari, and the Sangam Age*, p. 93.

to wrest independence. Of this there is not a shred of evidence, but on the contrary the manner of description in the *Harṣacarita* shows that both the powers were on very amicable and cordial terms.

Excluding Asirgaḍh and Nirmand, we may therefore summarily say that during its fullest expansion the Maukhari kingdom of Kanauj extended up to Ahicchatra and the frontier of the Thanesvar kingdom on the West; to Nalanda on the East; on the North it may have touched the Tarai districts; and on the South it probably did not go beyond the southern boundaries of the present United Provinces[1]. These territories were undoubtedly of sufficient dimensions to justify the assumption of imperial titles by the later Maukhari rulers after Īśāṇavarman.

Some Maukhari Dates

One of the chief items of information furnished by the Haraha inscription is a date for Īśānavarman, which we may profitably utilise here to determine the chronological setting of these Maukhari rulers. It is expressed in the following verse: "When six hundred had increased by eleven, while the illustrious Īśānavarman, who had crushed his enemies, was the lord of the earth."[2] The record thus yields us the year 611; but, as according to the dictionary one of the alternative senses of the word "*atirikta*" is "superfluous or redundant",[3] it has been suggested that "the other possible meaning will be 589[4]." We may, however, throw doubt on this interpretation on the ground that there is no instance

[1] *See* for a different view, *Ibid.*, pp. 96-101; C. V. Vaidya's *H. M. H. I.*, Vol. I, pp. 1, 39.

[2] Ekādaśātirikteṣu ṣadu* sātītavidviṣi Śateṣu śaradāṁ patyau bhuvaḥ Śrīśānavarmaṇi (*Ep. Ind.*, XIV, pp. 118, 120, verse 21).

[3] Monier-Williams' *Sans-Eng. Dictionary*, p. 15.

[4] *Ann. Rep., Lucknow Museum*, 1915, p. 3, footnote. (**Read** ṣaṭsu)

known where the term is used in this sense. Unfortunately, the inscription does not specify the era, but from the use of the word *śaradām* it has rightly been pointed out that it indicates the Mālava or Vikrama era, which in the opinion of Dr. Kielhorn began in *śarad* or autumn.[1] This reference to the Vikrama era is, as affirmed by Mr. Mazumdar, "also not opposed to palæographical considerations."[2] Converting, therefore, the Vikrama year 611 into the corresponding date of the Christian era, we find that Īśānavarman was ruling in the year 554 A. D

Sir Richard Burn, on the other hand, has shown that some coins of Sarvavarman, the son and successor of Īśāna, bear the date 553 A. D.[3] If we accept this, we must reject the date mentioned in the Haraha inscription, for unless we do so the dates of the father and son overlap each other, which is obviously contrary to the natural course of events.

Another way of reconciling this chronological impossibility is to accept the other "possible" date for the Haraha inscription, viz., 589 Vikrama year or 532 A. D., but before we adopt any such view let us first carefully consider the dates on the coins. Mr. N. G. Mazumdar, who had the opportunity of examining these coins deposited in the Indian Museum, Calcutta, says: "I am sorry to say that the date marks on the coins of Sarvavarman (as well as of other Maukhari kings) have totally disappeared and as such it is impossible to say at which particular date these coins were issued. So it is better not to infer anything from them, and hazard a doubtful reading that may or may not be correct. I may also add that Mr. R. D. Banerji is also of the same opinion, and I am sure that will be

[1] *Ind. Ant.*, XX, p. 407. [2] *Ibid.*, XLVI, p. 126.
[3] *J. R. A. S.*, 1906, p. 849.

the opinion of all who examine the coins with any care."[1] Our difficulty in relying on these coins is further augmented by the widely divergent readings proposed by scholars, which we now proceed to analyse in the following table :

NAME OF KING	RAPSON : (1)	CUNNINGHAM : (2)	SMITH: (3)	FLEET: (4)	BURN: (5)	BROWN: (6)	DIKSHIT (7)
(a) Īśānavarman	54,55	55or155 or 257	54	40,60 70,or5	4×	××5	245 257 54 55 57
(b) Sarvavarman			58		234 23-	234 23-	258 259 25× 58
(c) Avantivarman					250 57 71	250 57 70(?)	260 26× 57 17

(1) "There is some doubt as to the reading of these dates; and the era to which they should be referred is altogether doubtful" (*Indian Coins*, p. 27).

(2) "Imperfect date in front of face. Legend in old Gupta characters : "*Devajanita Vijitāvaniravanipati Srī Sānti Varma*"......The date appears to be the same on all the three specimens in the plates. I read it as 55, and would complete it to 155, if I could be certain that this Sāntivarma is the same king who is mentioned in the Aphsad inscription (*Ann. Surv. Ind. Rep.*, ix, p. 27). In a subsequent report, while admitting that the name is "clearly and unmistakably Īśānavarma," Cunningham remarked: "I possess two of these coins, one of which has a date in front of the face, which may be read as 257" (*Ibid.*, xvi, p. 81).

[1] *Ind. Ant.*, XLVI, p. 126.

(3) "Date, apparently in the same era as Toramāṇa's, 54. This coin is probably one of Īśānavarman. A specimen of his coinage with the same date as Dr. Hoey's coin is figured in *Coins of Med. India*, pl. II, 12. ... Although the date is quite plain Cunningham notes it as "not read" (*J. A. S. B.*, 1894, p. 193). Again, Dr. Hoey's coins now published add the dates 54 and 58. The legend on the coin dated 58 is damaged, and every letter of the king's name cannot be read with certainty. But the name begins with *Sa*, and I have no doubt that the reading above given is correct" (*Ibid.*, p. 194).

(4) The marginal legend commencing above the peacock's head is: "*Vijit-āvan(i)r-avan(i)-pati-śṛ-ī-śānavarma deva jayati.*" "On the obverse of the coin figured by Cunningham as no. 22, ... in front of the king's face there are two marks, which may perhaps be the numerical symbols for 40, 60, or 70 and 5. But they are very imperfect and doubtful" (*Ind. Ant.*, xiv, p. 68).

(5) (a)...*Coins of Īśānavarman*: "As usual the name is written Śrīśānavarma, the initial ī being merged in the title Śrī. One coin bears a date which I read as 4x, but even the tens figure is doubtful" (*J. R. A. S.*, 1906, p. 844).

(*b*) *Sarvavarman:* "Name written Śrīśarvavarma. Two coins bear dates which I read as 234 and 23—. The face is to right, and the reading of 200 is thus not quite certain, as the mark denoting the number of hundreds which stands at the right of the symbol is not on the coin" (*Ibid.*).

(*c*) *Avantivarman:* "Name written Śrīvantivarma. Three distinct dates are found, viz., 250 (one coin); 57 (five coins); 71 (one coin). There are also six coins on which the dates are very doubtful, and four from which they have disappeared (*Ibid.*, p. 845). Later on, Sir Richard Burn adds: "It will be noticed that Sarvavarman's and Avantivarman's dates overlap, and it is possible that what I have read as 57, for the latter should be 67" (*Ibid.*, p. 849).

(6) Mr. Brown evidently concurs with Sir Richard Burn in most of his readings, (See *Catal. of Coins of the Guptas, Maukharis etc. in the Luck. Mus.*, 1920, p. 29).

(7) I owe the readings, as given by Mr. Dikshit in his unpublished paper to Mr. Aravamuthan's *Sangam Age*. I have read Mr. Aravamuthan's scholarly discussion (pp. 102-07) with profit.[1]

It is thus evident how very uncertain and various the readings on these coins are. The only dates on which there is some degree of agreement are 54 and 257 for Īśānavarman; 58 and 234 for Sarvavarman; and 57, 71 and 250 for Avantivarman. These must evidently refer to two distinct eras, as some of the numbers are expressed in two digits only, and others in three. Sir Richard Burn is of opinion that the numbers in three digits are in the Gupta era, and those in two point to years in the Maukhari era beginning from about 500 or 499 A. D., when Ārya Bhaṭa composed his great astronomical work and exactly 3,600 years of the Kaliyuga had elapsed.[2] But the Haraha inscription shows that the Maukharis used a third era, whether we take its date to be the year 589 or 611 *Vikrama*. It therefore baffles explanation why, if the Maukharis had started an era of their own, an inscription of the dynasty does not use it. Besides, the years 257 for Īśāna, and 234 or 250 for the later kings; 58 for Sarvavarman and 57 for his successor, are gross absurdities; and there is no known case of the prevalence of several eras in such a circums-

[1] Further references to Maukhari coins occur in the *Supplementary Catalogue of the Coins in the Indian Museum*, Calcutta (Non-Muhammadan Series), Vol. I, pp. 36-37; C. J. Brown, *Coins of India*, p. 49; *Ep. Ind.*, XIV, pp. 113-14; *Ind. Ant.*, XLVI, pp. 125-26; Dr. R. K. Mookerji, *Harṣa*, pp. 57-58.

[2] *J. R. A. S.*, 1906, p. 848.

cribed territory as that of the Maukharis. Thus, any reliance on the dates supplied by the coins only makes confusion worse confounded; and we must, therefore, choose the alternative of accepting the date given in the Haraha inscription, which, as discussed above, is the Vikrama year 611=554 A. D. This is one of the starting points in the Maukhari chronology, and the other is 606 A. D., when Grahavarman was killed. Hence assigning an average of twenty years to each of the six rulers, the seventh reign being extremely short, we feel justified in assuming that the Maukharis began their rule over Kanauj sometime about the close of the fifth century A. D.

PART II

CHAPTER III

HARṢA

Beginning of the 7th century A. D.

When we enter upon the seventh century A. D., we are no longer embarrassed by the paucity of materials, and the history of our kingdom also claims to make a special appeal to the interest of the historian of Ancient India. The period begins with the appearance of a remarkable figure on the political stage, and although Harṣa[1] had neither the lofty idealism and missionary zeal of Aśoka nor the commanding personality and constructive statesmanship of Akbar, yet he has succeeded in arresting the attention of the historian like both those great rulers.

Ample sources

Without under-rating or exaggerating Harṣa's importance we may at the outset say that this has partly been due to the abundance of information, which we

[1] The form Harṣa occurs, for instance, in the Aihole inscription (*Ep. Ind.*, VI, p. 6, verse 23), the Madhuban (*Ibid.*, I, p. 72, line 8) and the Banskhera copper plates (*Ibid.*, IV, p. 211, line 7; see also the autograph in line 18). He is called Harṣadeva in the Aphsad inscription (*C. I. I.*, III, No. 42, p. 204, line 15) and in the *Harṣacarita* (see p. 112, Calcutta edition). The Sonpat copper seal, however, gives the full name Harṣavardhana (*C. I. I.*, III, No. 52, p. 232).

get for his life and reign.[1] "When all the sources are utilised," as observed by Dr. Vincent Smith, "our knowledge of the events of the reign of Harṣa far surpasses in precision that which we possess respecting any other early king, except Candragupta Maurya and Aśoka."[2]

Besides the usual epigraphic documents,[3] we have the "*Si-yu-ki*," the well-known narrative of the celebrated Chinese pilgrim, Yuan Chwang, who travelled in India from A. D. 629 to 644. He has left a copious wealth of details in his *Records*, and the fact that they preserve the impressions of an eye witness adds considerably to the value and merits of their testimony. The "*Life of Yuan Chwang*," written by his friend Hwui-li, also throws welcome light as a supplement to the pilgrim's account. Lastly, Harṣa's early life and career are the subject-matter of the historical romance entitled "*Harṣacarita*", composed by Bāṇa, who wielded his forceful pen to immortalise the deeds of his patron and hero.

Difficulties unsolved

But in spite of the existence of these contemporary works, which supplement and corroborate each other

[1] We use the expression considering how vague and deficient our sources for Ancient Indian History are.

[2] *Early Hist. of India.*, 4th ed., p. 348.

[3] We are fortunate in possessing several records of Harṣa:
(*a*) Banskhera copper plate of the year 22 or 628 A. D. (*Ep. Ind.*, IV, pp. 208-11).
(*b*) Madhuban copper plate of the year 25 or 631 A. D. (*Ibid.*, I, pp. 67-75).
(*c*) Sonpat copper seal (*C. I. I.*, III, No. 52, pp. 231-32).
(*d*) The Nalanda seals (*Ep. Ind.*, XXI, April 1931, pp. 74-76). Some interesting information is also furnished by the southern inscriptions, especially of his rival Pulakeśi II Cālukya.

on many topics of general interest, the results of up-to-date researches on Harṣa are far from decisive. The first problem that confronts us is: What was the real political position of Harṣa at the start of his career, and how did he (if Yuan Chwang is to be believed) come to occupy the throne of Kanauj, although we know from Bāṇa's *Harṣacarita* that he was a prince of Thanesvar only? Now, in order to arrive at a satisfactory solution of the puzzle let us take full note of the course of events in both Thanesvar and Kanauj, as at this period owing to matrimonial connections and the danger of common enemies the affairs of the two kingdoms had become inextricably intertwined.

Circumstances leading Harṣa to the throne of Kanauj and his position before and after the event

After the death of Prabhākaravardhana, the king of Thanesvar, the task of governance fell upon the eldest son, Rājyavardhana, who, after having defeated the Hūṇas of the North-West, had returned to the capital with "limbs emaciated" and "long white bandages, bound about arrow-wounds received in battle."[1] The young prince, however, was so much overwhelmed with grief at the loss of his father that instead of accepting sovereignty and regal glory, he determined to retire from worldly concerns, and seek solace in the sylvan retreats of a hermitage; and he asked his younger brother, Harṣa, to assume the reins of Government.

Just at this juncture, when strange feelings of renunciation and aversion from worldly power were passing through the minds of both the brothers, and the tears of their bereavement had hardly had time to

[1] *Harṣacarita* (English Translation by Cowell and Thomas, 1897), p. 165.

dry, they were struck by another bolt from the blue. For suddenly a courier named Saṁvādaka arrived with the tragic news that the king of Malwa had killed their brother-in-law, Grahavarman, and their sister, Rājyaśrī, had been thrown into a dungeon in Kānyakubja.[1] He added: "There is moreover a report that the villain, deeming the army leaderless, purposes to invade and seize this country as well. Such are my tidings : the matter is now in the king's hands."[2] Hearing of this calamity that had overtaken the house of Kanauj, and the Malwa king's reported designs against Thanesvar, a "deadly frown broke forth" on the "broad brow" of Rājyavardhana, who addressed his younger brother thus: "This task is my royal house, this my kin, my court, my land...this day I go to lay the royal house of Malwa low in ruin. The repression of this beyond-measure unmannerly foe—this, and no other is my assumption of the bark-dress, my austerities, my stratagem for dispelling sorrow."[3]

He gave instructions to Harṣa to remain behind with all the "kings and elephants," probably with a view to guarding the rear against any fresh Hūṇa upheaval, and asked only Bhaṇḍi[4] to follow him "with

[1] *Ibid.*, p. 173.

[2] *Ibid.*

[3] *Ibid.*, pp. 174-75.

[4] Bhaṇḍi was the son of Queen Yaśovatī's brother, who is identified by Dr. Hoernle—without much justification (see C. V. Vaidya, *H. M. H. I.*, Vol. I, p. 38)—with the Emperor Śīlāditya of Malwa (*J.* R. *A. S.*, 1903, pp. 559-60; see also *Harṣa*, p. 12, note 1). He was sent to the Thanesvar court at the age of eight to serve the princes (*Hc. C. T.*, p. 116). Dr. R. K. Mookerji remarks that "the name Bhaṇḍi itself is a Hūṇic rather than a Sanskrit name" (*Harṣa*, p. 61). It is difficult to follow on what grounds the learned Professor makes this assertion. Dr. Hoernle made a similar suggestion (*J. R. A. S.*, 1903, p. 560) arguing that Bhaṇḍi meaning "buffoon was a strange name for a prince." But

some ten thousand horse."[1] But Destiny had decreed trouble for the ill-starred brothers at every step, and now it was young Harṣa's turn to take a plunge into the stirred waters of the political storm. After sometime Harṣa learned from one of the favourite cavalry officers that Rājyavardhana, "though he had routed the Malwa army with ridiculous ease, had been allured to confidence by false civilities on the part of the king of Gauḍa, and then, weaponless, confiding and alone, despatched in his own quarters."[2] Who the miscreant allies of Gauḍa and Malwa were, we have no means of ascertaining from the *Harṣacarita*, but we can identify them with the help of other authorities. The Madhuban and Banskhera inscriptions affirm that "the kings Devagupta and others, who resembled wicked horses, were all subdued with averted faces"[3] by Rājyavardhana. If we remember that young Rājyavardhana could get opportunities to fight against two enemies only, viz., the Hūṇas of the North-West (against whom he was despatched by his father), and the king of Malwa[4] who had taken Grahavarman of Kanauj by

such cynical names were not uncommon in ancient India. To give some instances we have: king Gardabhilla (*J. B. B. R. A. S.*, IX, p. 148); or Śūdraka, authenticated from inscriptions (*Ind. Ant.*, XVI, p. 64; *Proc. A. S. B.*, 1879, pp. 220, 221).

[1] *Hc. C. T.*, p. 175.

[2] *Hc. C. T.*, p. 178. Cf. "Tasmāt ca helānirjita Mālavānīkaṁ-api Gauḍādhipena mithyopacāropacitaviśvāsaṁ mukta-śastram ekākinaṁ viśrabdhaṁ svabhavana eva bhrātaraṁ vyāpāditaṁ aśrauṣīt" (*Hc.*, Cal. ed., p. 436).

[3] *Ep. Ind.*, I, pp. 72, 74; *Ibid.*, IV, p. 210. Cf.
"Rājāno Yudhi duṣṭavājina iva Śrī-Devaguptādayaḥ,
Kritvā yena Kaśāprahāra-vimukhāḥ sarve samaṁ saṁyatāḥ."

[4] Bühler thought that this Malwa was "in the Panjab much nearer to Thanesvar" (*Ep. Ind.*, I, p. 70). But Dr. Hoernle rightly pointed out that this was "obviously an error" (see *J. R. A. S.*, 1903, p. 561, note). We have adopted the view in the

surprise with the tragic consequences described above, we feel no hesitation in identifying the latter with the Devagupta of the Madhuban and Banskhera inscriptions.[1] Fanciful as the guess may be, it would seem that Bāṇa did not like to mention this suggestive and auspicious name of Rājya's adversary—Devagupta literally means "protected by the gods"—owing to his foul deed. For the same reason probably he places the following statement in the mouth of Harṣa with regard to the king of Gauḍa: "My tongue seems soiled with a smirch of sin as I take the miscreant's very name upon my lips."[2] According to the testimony of Yuan Chwang, the king of Gauḍa was Śaśāṅka (She-shang-kia)[3] the wicked king of Karṇasuvarṇa in East India[4] who per-

previous chapter that this Malwa denoted Eastern Malwa as distinguished from Western Malwa, which was Malwa proper.

[1] See also Bühler, *Ep. Ind.*, I, p. 70; C. V. Vaidya, *H. M. H. I.*, Vol. I, p. 35. Devagupta appears to have been a scion of the later Gupta family, but we do not know with certitude what relationship he bore to Mahāsenagupta (see *supra*). According to Dr. Hoernle it was the Emperor Śīlāditya of Western Malwa, son of Yaśodharman, who was defeated by Rājya (*J. R. A. S.*, 1903, p. 559), and Dr. R. K. Mookerji subscribes to the same view (*Harṣa*, pp. 16, 62). It seems, however, inexplicable how, if Śīlāditya was the principal opponent, his name is omitted in the Madhuban and Banskhera inscriptions and left to be implied by the vague term "others."

[2] *Hc. C. T.*, p. 179.

[3] Watters, I, p. 343; Beal, I, p. 210. See also the Commentator on the *Harṣacarita* (Bombay edition, 1892, p. 195). The learned translators of the *Harṣacarita* find an allusion to him in the word Śaśāṅkamaṇḍala (*Hc. C. T.*, Preface, p. x). According to one *MS*. of the *Harṣacarita* he is called Narendragupta (*Ep Ind.*, I, p. 70).

[4] The capital of Karṇasuvarṇa has been identified by Beveridge with Rangamati, near Berhampur, in Bengal (*J. A. S. B.*, LXII, p. 315). See also N. L. Dey's *Geographical Dictionary* (1927), p.

secuted the Buddhists[1] and uprooted the sacred Bodhi Tree.[2] Probably it is with regard to the Gauḍa king's treachery that the Madhuban and Banskhera inscriptions say that he (Rājya) "in consequence of his adherence to his promise (satyānurodhena) gave up his life in the mansion of his foe."[3] And this inveigling of the rescuer of Kanauj into the death-trap is further explained by the commentator on the *Harṣacarita*, who informs us that "Śaśāṅka threw Rājya off his guard by his offer to marry his daughter to him as a token of submission and friendship."[4] Whatever the means that were employed to perpetrate the foul deed, it is certain that after Rājya's death the outlook for both the allied houses of the Vardhanas and the Maukharis became gloomy in the extreme. Thanesvar was deprived of its young ruler; and Kanauj, having lost its sovereign as well as the timely support of the former kingdom, passed under the occupation of the king of Gauḍa, who, in order to divert the attention of Bhaṇḍi or his adversary's army, released Rājyaśrī, the widowed queen of Kanauj, from detention in that city.

Bāṇa says that instantly on hearing the tragic news of his brother's assassination, Harṣa's "aspect became terrific in the extreme," and "his wrathful curling lip seemed to drink the lives of all kings"[5] as he cursed

94; the Vappaghoṣāvaṭa grant of Jayanāga, edited by Dr. Barnett, *Ep. Ind.*, XVIII (April, 1925), p. 62.

[1] Watters, I, p. 343.

[2] *Life*, p. 171. Śaśāṅka's animosity against Buddhism is explained by his Śaivite tendencies (see Allan, *Gupta Coins*, p. 147).

[3] *Ep. Ind.*, I, pp. 72, 74; *Ibid.*, IV, p. 210. Cf. Prāṇānujjhitavānārāti bhavane satyānurodhena yaḥ."

[4] Compare the original : Tathā hi tena Śaśāṅkena viśwāsārthaṁ kanyāpradānaṁ uktvā pralobhito Rājyavardhanaḥ svagehe sānucaro bhunjān eva chadmanā vyāpāditaḥ.

[5] *Hc. Ç. T.*, p. 178.

the "vilest of Gauḍas" with his fiery spirit. Thereupon the general Siṁhanāda exhorted Harṣa to punish the miscreant, and assume the burden of sovereignty, in these words: "Now that the king has assumed his godhead and Rājyavardhana has lost his life by the sting of the vile Gauḍa serpent, you are, in the cataclysm which has come to pass, the only *śeṣa* left to support the earth. Comfort your unprotected people. Like the autumn sun, set your forehead-burning footsteps upon the heads of kings."[1] Harṣa forthwith replied to the advice of the general: "My heart would force chowries upon even the sun's presumptuously bright hands. *Enraged at the title of king*, my foot itches to make footstools of even the kings of beasts."[2] And he registered his determination to wreak vengeance with the following vow: "By the dust of my honoured lord's feet I swear that, unless in a limited number of days I clear the earth of Gauḍas, and make it resound with fetters on the feet of all kings who are excited to insolence by the elasticity of their bows, then will I hurl my sinful self, like a moth, into an oil-fed flame."[3]

Thus, according to Bāṇa, Harṣa immediately after the murder of his elder brother ascended the paternal throne of Thanesvar, and began to devise measures to retrieve the disaster that had overtaken the Vardhanas and the Maukhari house of Kanauj. There is absolutely no trace in the *Harṣacarita* of his displaying any hesitation in assuming the crown. Here we must pause to consider a passage occurring in the *Harṣacarita* on the strength of which scholars try to detect some scruples or reluctance on the part of Harṣa.[4] It runs thus:

[1] *Ibid.*, pp. 185-86.

[2] *Ibid.*, p. 187. Cf. "Rājaśabdaruṣā mṛigarājānāmapi śirānsi vāñchati pādaḥ pādapīṭhīkartuṁ" (*Hc.* Cal. ed., p. 460).

[3] *Ibid.*

[4] *Ibid.*, preface p. x; Dr. R. K. Mookerji, *Harṣa*, p. 20.

"He was embraced by the goddess of the Royal prosperity, who took him in her arms and, seizing him by all the royal marks on all his limbs, forced him, *however, reluctant*, to mount the throne,—and this though he had taken a *vow of austerity* and.did not swerve from his vow, hard like grasping the edge of a sword."[1] To me, however, it appears only a poetic way of describing that the wheel of Destiny was revolving in favour of Harṣa, and although he had not the prior claim to succeed his father—on account of his being younger—circumstances so conspired that he suddenly found himself elevated to the throne. Sanskrit literature is replete with such "poetic mannerisms," and we may in this connection also recall an almost parallel expression used in the Junagaḍh Rock inscription for Skandagupta: "Lakṣmīḥ svayaṁ yaṁ varayāṁ cakāra," meaning "whom the goddess of Fortune, of her own accord, selected as her husband."[2]

As regards Harṣa's previous reluctance and vow of austerity, the *Harṣacarita* may refer to one of these circumstances:

(*a*) Probably it alludes to his reluctance to avail himself of his father's preference for him, which Prabhākaravardhana seems to have indicated on his death-bed in these words: "Succeed to this world; appropriate my treasury; make prize of the feudatory kings; support the burden of royalty; protect the people; guard well your dependants."[3] There was nothing incongruous in passing over the claims of the elder son, Rājyavardhana, for such selections appear to have

[1] *Hc. C. T.*, p. 57. Cf. "Anicchantaṁ balāt āropayitumiva siṁhāsanaṁ sarvāvayaveṣu sarva-lakṣaṇaiḥ gṛihītaṁ gṛihīta brahmacaryaṁ āliṅgitaṁ Rājalakṣmyā pratipannāsidhārā dhāraṇavrataṁ" (Hc., Cal. ed., p. 159).

[2] *C. I. I.*, Vol. III, No. 14, line 5, pp. 59, 62.

[3] *Hc. C. T.*, p. 156.

been common in the Gupta times as well. Samudragupta was chosen to succeed his father to the distress of "others of equal birth," and with the consent of the state council (sabhyeṣūchvasiteṣu). Similarly Samudragupta also chose his successor (tatparigrihītena). But Harṣa was too noble-minded to take advantage of his brother's absence, and instead of striking while the iron was hot, he is represented to have thought thus: "Let sovereign glory flee to a hermitage;"[1] and "let valour mortify herself in forest seclusion, let heroism put on rags."[2]

(*b*) Secondly, the passage may refer to Harṣa's previous vow not to accept the crown when Rājya, overwhelmed by grief, wanted to abdicate in his favour and retire to the forest. Harṣa had also resolved to follow in his brother's train, if he persisted in renouncing the throne, thinking within himself: "And the sin involved in transgressing my elder's commands austerity in fine shall dispel in a hermitage."[3] But his subsequent accession to the throne without any hesitation meant no swerving from his original vow of renunciation, taken under certain conditions, as after his brother's death Harṣa was the only *Śeṣa* left to come to the succour of both the Thanesvar and Kanauj kingdoms.

And, besides, there was no other reason why Harṣa should refuse to assume the royal duties. Watters' statement that Harṣa "in the early part of his life had joined the Buddhist church and perhaps taken the vows of a Bhikṣu, or at least a lay member of the communion,"[4] merits no credence. Harṣa began as a Śaivite and continued to be so till late in his life, as the Banskhera inscription of the year 22, and Madhuban plate dated year 25,

[1] *Ibid.*, p. 158.
[2] *Ibid.*, p. 159.
[3] *Ibid.*, p. 173.
[4] Watters, I, p. 346.

which call him a "Paramamāheśvara," definitely show.[1] Moreover, it was probably due to his original Śaiva tendencies that he complimented the king of Assam through the latter's envoy, saying, "to whom save Śiva need he pay homage? This resolve of his increases my affection."[2] Vincent Smith thinks that "the nobles seem to have hesitated before offering the crown to his (Rājyavardhana's) youthful brother."[3] K. M. Panikkar also conjectures that the inheritance was not "a comfortable one," as the feudatories had shown themselves "refractory and rebellious;" or perhaps Rājya had "left an heir,"[4] in which case Harṣa scrupled to disinherit him. But I humbly submit that such assumptions are quite unwarranted. C. V. Vaidya is doubtful if Rājya was married,[5] and even supposing it was a fact, there is nothing to prove that he left a son. Besides, from Bāṇa's description we know it for certain that the feudatories were loyal to Harṣa. When Kuntala delivers the tidings of Rājya's murder in the audience-hall, the feudatories are represented as being in attendance on Harṣa. We are further told that "at the hour of marching the front of the king's residence became full of chieftains from every side."[6] Thus, if they had been turbulent from the beginning, they would have given greater trouble to young Harṣa after his brother's murder. But instead of revolting or creating disturbance they gave their unstinted help and loyal support to their royal master, who was now confronted with the difficult task of bringing the culprit to book.

Having fully discussed Harṣa's political status in

[1] See *Infra*.
[2] *Hc. C. T.*, p. 219.
[3] *Early Hist. of India*, 4th ed., p. 350.
[4] *Śrī Harṣa of Kanauj*, (Bombay, 1922), p. 15.
[5] *H. M. H. I.*, I, p. 7.
[6] *Hc. C. T.*, p. 202.

Thanesvar after his brother's death, let us now resume the thread of the narrative. With the resources of Thanesvar at his command Harṣa's immediate and pressing duties were to recover his sister, the widowed queen of Kanauj, from distress; relieve Kanauj from foreign occupation; and punish the treacherous murderer of his brother. Without losing any time he advanced with a huge army to realise these objectives, and on the way was met by Haṁsavega, who had come with precious presents as "confidential messenger" of the king of Prāgjotiśa (Assam) to seek an "undying alliance."[1] Harṣa readily accepted, being in dire need of staunch allies to help him in his "first expedition" undertaken, when he was yet young and inexperienced in the methods of war. Then permitting Haṁsavega to depart with return gifts Harṣa advanced against the enemy. Soon he came across Bhaṇḍi, who was in charge of the "Malwa king's whole force, conquered by the might of Rājyavardhana's arm,"[2] and learned from him that Rājyaśrī had been released—or as the poet puts it, "she had burst from her confinement, and with her train entered the Vindhya forest,"[3] where in spite of numerous searchers her whereabouts remained unknown. This news being extremely alarming, Harṣa, in fondness for his distressed sister, bade his army halt by the Ganges, and for the present postponed his march against the Gauḍa king, who was in occupation of Kanauj. Thenceforth, in conjunction with Mādhavagupta and a few tributary kings, Harṣa under-

[1] *Ibid.*, p. 211f. This was perhaps due to the fact that Bhāskaravarman was afraid of the growing strength of the adjacent kingdom of Śaśāṅka.

[2] *Ibid.*, p. 223.

[3] *Ibid.*, p. 224. It is difficult to make out which part of the Vindhyas is exactly meant here. Does the *Hc.* refer to its eastern spurs?

took in all haste the urgent task of finding his sister. He plunged into the depths of the Vindhya forest, and chanced to meet the Buddhist sage Divākaramitra, the "boy-friend of the deceased Grahavarman."[1] Through his good offices Harṣa succeeded in tracing Rājyaśrī, who, despairing of help and prostrate with grief, was just at the point of putting an end to her life by "mounting the funeral pile, surrounded by a troop of women."[2] After rescuing his sister, Harṣa desired to take leave of Divākaramitra, but Rājyaśrī was so overwhelmed by the heavy burden of successive misfortunes, and so impressed by the tranquil atmosphere of the hermitage, that she expressed a wish to assume the "red garments." The sage would not, however, approve of the idea and Harṣa added: "My sister, so young and so tried by adversity, must be cherished by me for a while, even if it involves the neglect of all my duties;"[3] and "at the end when I have accomplished my design, she and I will assume the red garments together"[4].

Harṣa then "went back in a few marches to his camp stationed along the bank of the Ganges," and at this point the *Harṣacarita* comes abruptly to an end. But in the meantime it appears that on the approach of Harṣa's army Śaśāṅka thought discretion was the better part of valour, and instead of facing an open conflict he withdrew from Kanauj, as after the conclusion of a treaty between Harṣa and Bhāskaravarman he was exposed to serious danger both from the front

[1] *Ibid.*, p. 233.

[2] *Ibid.*, pp. 240-41. It would thus appear that the custom of *Satī* or voluntary self-immolation of widows was then known. Bāṇa also describes Queen Yaśovatī as becoming a *Satī*, despite Harṣa's dissuasion against her resolve to "die while still unwidowed" (*Ibid.*, pp. 149-155).

[3] *Ibid.*, p. 257.

[4] *Ibid.*, p. 258.

and the rear.[1] Bhaṇḍi had already cut off the support of the Malwa army after the defeat and death of its leader, and in the face of the new odds arrayed against Śaśāṅka strategy certainly demanded that he should beat a masterly retreat.

Thus Kanauj was left in a hopeless state of confusion deprived as it was of its young Maukhari ruler. The kingdom, however, needed at this time the protection of a strong and guiding hand to inaugurate an era of growth and prosperity, and to ensure immunity from future attack or aggression from any hostile quarter. Grahavarman had left no heir as the following statement by Patralatā on behalf of Rājyaśrī shows: "A husband or a son is a woman's true support; but to those who are deprived of both, it is immodesty even to continue to live."[2] Besides, the *Harṣacarita* also hints at the "disappearance of all her other relatives,"[3] which expression probably means that the younger brothers of Grahavarman, for he was Avantivarman's eldest son (Sūnuragrajaḥ), had either been killed, or had fled away during the Gupta-Gauḍa disturbance. Should the crown, therefore, devolve upon the widowed queen Rājyaśrī, or was she to be doomed to obscurity, and her claims altogether ignored? But perhaps Rājyaśrī herself was unwilling to undertake the responsibilities and onerous duties of rulership. She was a young and inexperienced woman, and she was under the shadow of a great bereavement and affliction. Besides, she was

[1] See *Infra*. According to the Ganjam Plate (*Ep. Ind.*, VI, p. 141) Śaśāṅka was flourishing as late as the year 619 A. D. Besides, such an assumption would be quite in keeping with the Gauḍa monarch's cowardly stratagems as shown in his successful schemes against Rājyavardhana.

[2] *Hc. C. T.*, p. 254.

[3] *Ibid.*, p. 244. Cf. "Braṁśena ca śeṣasya bāndhavávargasya" (*Hc.*, Cal. ed., p. 651).

by nature inclined to the quietist teachings of Buddhism; hence there was little chance of her governing with vigour and success at this crisis.

In the absence of any other Maukhari claimant, should Harṣa then be asked to assume the burden and cares of the state on behalf of Rājyaśrī? Both he and his elder brother had rendered signal service to Kanauj during the political whirlpool that had threatened to engulf the kingdom. He had rescued its queen and between the brother and the sister the greatest fondness and attachment prevailed. Harṣa had further declared his intention of cherishing her "for a while," even though it meant the neglect of royal duties, which expression probably implies that he was prepared to stay in Kanauj for some time in order to settle its affairs, before he could undertake the fulfilment of his vow to punish those who had become inimical by the "elasticity of their bows." Accordingly the statesmen offered the crown to Harṣa, and Poni[1], whose power and reputation were high and of much weight, addressed the assembled ministers thus: "The destiny of the nation is to be fixed today...... I propose that he assume the royal authority; let each one give his opinion on the matter, whatever he thinks."[2] The Chief Ministers and Magistrates signified their full consent, exhorting Harṣa in these words: "Reign, then, with glory over the land, conquer the enemies of your country; wash out the insult laid on your kingdom"[3].

[1] The name Poni or Bāni is usually identified with Bhaṇḍi (Hoernle, *J. R. A. S.*, 1903, p. 560; Dr. R. K. Mookerji, *Harṣa*, p. 17, note 1), although beyond the similarity in sound there is hardly any justification for it, as we have already shown that the latter was a leading figure in the Thanesvar court, and not in Kanauj.

[2] Beal, I, p. 211; Watters, I, p. 343.

[3] *Ibid.*

But tempting though the offer was, Harṣa hesitated to accept it, for it not only implied taking upon himself an additional burden and responsibility, but also permanent residence in Kanauj to the neglect of the affairs of his paternal kingdom. Besides, it may be possible that he was not quite sure of the support that he would receive from the people of Kanauj, if he acceded to the requests of their statesmen. Harṣa, therefore, decided to refer the matter to the Bodhisattva Avalokiteśvara, who had "evidenced many spiritual wonders," in order probably to see if the omens were favourable to him.[1] The Bodhisattva promised him secret power, so that none of his neighbours should be able to triumph over him; but he further gave the warning "Ascend not the Lion-throne, and call not yourself Mahārāja."[2] After getting these instructions Harṣa assumed the royal office with the title "Śīlāditya," and calling himself a mere king's son or "Kumāra."[3] Now, this unostentatious title of Kumāra definitely suggests that although, according to Bāṇa, Harṣa was already king of Thanesvar, in Kanauj he was merely charged with the duty of keeping the machinery of the government running, and his political status there was originally no better than that of a guardian or, as Mr. N. Ray says, "Regent."[4] Indeed this fact is even corroborated by a Chinese work, entitled *Fang-chih*, which testifies that Harṣa "administered the kingdom in conjunction with his widowed sister."[5] But it would appear that with

[1] C. V. Vaidya was the first to suggest that this hesitation of Harṣa, referred to by Yuan Chwang, should not be confused with the passage of the *Harṣacarita* discussed above at length (*H. M. H. I.*, Vol. I, pp. 7-9).

[2] Beal, I, p. 213.

[3] Beal, I, p. 213; Watters, I, p. 343.

[4] *Ind. Hist. Quart.*, Dec. 1927, p. 773.

[5] Watters, I, p. 345; *Early Hist. of India.*, 4th ed., p. 351.

the lapse of time, when Harṣa had thoroughly made his position secure, and laid opposition, if any, to rest, he formally transferred his capital from Thanesvar to Kanauj, and declared himself sovereign ruler of the latter kingdom also by assuming the Imperial titles, which appear in his inscriptions. Thus beginning with a modest guardianship or regency, Harṣa's imposition of his authority over Kanauj was a sort of quiet usurpation in which the people acquiesced owing to the chaotic conditions rampant in the kingdom after Grahavarman's assassination. This dexterous stepping into the shoes of the Maukharis placed the entire resources of Kanauj at the disposal of Harṣa. Moreover, being already king of Thanesvar by succession, the amalgamation of the two powerful northern kingdoms resulted, which helped Harṣa greatly in extending the sphere of his influence and jurisdiction over the numerous warring states that continually disturbed the political equilibrium of the north.

PART II

CHAPTER IV

EXTENT OF THE KANAUJ EMPIRE

Under Harṣa

In discussing the knotty problem of the extension of the suzerainty of Kanauj during the time of Harṣa, we must consider first the limits of his paternal dominion, which with the transference of his seat of government to Kanauj had become united with his new territorial acquisition; and secondly his own campaigns and conquests. Lastly, we have to determine what relation the contemporary kingdoms bore to Kanauj, taking into consideration Yuan Chwang's testimony as to their political conditions and status.

The kingdom of Thanesvar, which had a modest beginning,[1] appears to have been augmented to a certain extent, both in territory and influence, under Prabhākaravardhana, as he is the first to be styled Mahārājādhirāja and Paramabhaṭṭāraka in the family inscriptions (e.g., the Madhuban plate). The *Harṣacarita* calls him "a lion to the Hūṇa deer, a burning fever to the king of the Indus land, a troubler of the sleep of Gujarat (? Gurjaras), a bilious plague to that

[1] This is evident from the fact that in the Banskhera and Madhuban plates the two immediate predecessors of Prabhākara are called simply Mahārājas.

scent-elephant the lord of Gāndhāra, a looter to the lawlessness of the Lāṭas, an axe to the creeper of Malwa's glory."[1] This passage, although significant with regard to the different powers existing at the time, however, hardly warrants our concluding, as has been done by Mr. C. V. Vaidya,[2] that these states had been actually conquered and annexed by Prabhākaravardhana. On the other hand, there is evidence that the "Hūṇa deer," instead of being overawed and cowed, was trying to pounce upon the "lion" himself for towards the close of his reign the kingdom was seriously disturbed by the Hūṇa menace, and Prabhākara had to despatch the crown-prince at the head of a strong force to cope with the danger. Hence making allowance for exaggeration, it apears that in the above passage of the *Harṣacarita* we have only a poetical description of Prabhākaravardhana's excellence and greatness as compared with the other contemporary rulers.[3] According to Bühler,[4] Prabhākara's possessions did not go beyond the limits of the kingdom of Thanesvar, described by Yuan Chwang, which, as Sir Alexander Cunningham suggests, probably included portions of southern Punjab and of

[1] *Hc. C. T.*, p. 101. Cf. "Hūṇahariṇakesarī Sindhurājajvaro Gurjara-prajāgaraḥ Gāndhārādhipagandhadvipa-Kūṭapākalaḥ. Lāṭapāṭavapāṭaccaraḥ Mālavalakṣmīlatāparaśuḥ" (*Hc.*, Calcutta ed., pp. 243-44).

[2] *H. M. H. I.*, I, p. 1f. See also Dr. R. K. Mookerji, *Harṣa*, p. 11, where Prabhākara is said to have attained the position of an emperor.

[3] The following remark of Dr. Fitz-Edward Hall seems to be very pertinent in this connection : "Unquestioning confidence in the representations of Indian panegyrists would entail the conclusion that, in the by-gone days of this country, everybody—above all if a patron—was constantly vanquishing everybody else." (*J. A. S. B.*, XXXI, p. 3).

[4] *Ep. Ind.*, I, p. 69.

eastern Rajputana. "A state, the circuit of which amounted to 7,000 *li* or 1200 miles, might exercise a considerable influence, keep its neighbours in fear, and afford to a very talented king the means for greater conquests."[1] We may thus conclude that the North-western frontiers of Thanesvar were limited by the Hūṇa territories in the Punjab, and in the north it probably extended upto the hills. In the east it was conterminous with the Maukhari kingdom of Kanauj;[2] and on the west and south it probably did not go much beyond the Panjab and the Rajputana desert.

Regarding the conquests of Harṣa, we do not seem to stand on certain ground for want of definite details. We admittedly have some vague generalities in the accounts of the admiring Yuan Chwang, e.g., "Proceeding eastward, he invaded the states which had refused allegiance; and waged incessant warfare until in six years he fought the "Five Indias" (according to the other reading: "had brought the Five Indias under allegiance").[3] Again, we are told : "He was soon able to avenge the injuries received by his brother, and to make himself *Master of India*. His renown was spread abroad everywhere, and all his subjects reverenced his virtues."[4] And lastly, speaking of Mahārāṣṭra Yuan Chwang says: "At the present time Śilāditya Mahārāja has conquered the nations from east to west, and carried his arms to remote districts".[5] But nowhere does the

[1] *Ibid.*

[2] We have fixed the limits of the Maukhari kingdom in the previous chapter; and we have to bear in mind that Harṣa became master of all these territories subsequently, although it may be possible that he had to fight again and bring to subjection any unruly or malcontent parts that had seized the opportunity to assert themselves during the Gauḍa-Malwa disturbance.

[3] Watters, I, p. 343; Beal, I, p. 213.

[4] *Life*, p. 83.

[5] Beal, II, pp. 256-57; Watters, II, p. 239.

worthy pilgrim specifically mention how, when and what kingdoms were conquered by Harṣa.

Nor is the evidence of Bāṇa more helpful on this point. We have noted that his account abruptly comes to a stop, and he does not even inform us how Harṣa proceeded against the Gauḍa king, who was the immediate object of his wrath. True, Bāṇa alludes to riders "intently occupied in rehearsing the approaching Gauḍa war."[1] And the learned translators of the *Harṣacarita* detect an indirect reference to the campaign in the concluding paragraph, in which "the sunset is described in terms suggesting bloody wars and the fall of Harṣa's enemy, followed by the rising of the moon of Harṣa's glory."[2] But there are evidences—to be discussed below—which preclude our drawing any such inference. Śaśāṅka evaded Harṣa's grasp, and continued to flourish till a considerably late date.

We are further informed by Bāṇa that Harṣa, "the greatest of all men, having pounded the king of Sindh, made his wealth his own,"[3] and also "taken tribute from an inaccessible land of the snowy mountains."[4] What these statements are worth, we shall consider in connection with the testimony of Yuan Chwang regarding the status of the different kingdoms that he visited.

Lastly, we may note the imperial titles given to Harṣa, which may indicate his widespread power and suzerainty. Bāṇa calls him: "king of kings, sovereign of all continents,"[5] and "Śrī-Harṣa, the king of kings, the lord of the four oceans, whose toe-nails are burnished

[1] *Hc. C. T.*, p. 209.

[2] *Ibid.*, p. 260, Note 4.

[3] *Ibid.*, p. 76. Cf. "Atra Puruṣottamena Sindhurājaṁ pramathya Lakṣmīḥātmī-kritā" (*Hc.* Cal. ed., pp. 210-11).

[4] *Ibid.* Cf. "Atra Parameśvareṇa tuṣāraśailabhuvo durgáyā grahītaḥ karaḥ."

[5] *Ibid.*, p. 75; see also *Ibid.*, pp. 66, 97, etc.

by the crest gems of all other monarchs, the leader of all emperors."[1] Far from urging that these pompous expressions argue Harṣa's paramount status, we might say that these high-sounding titles were sometimes conventional among the courtly panegyrists, and were used in a very loose way.

As the *Harṣacarita* stubbornly refuses to give any better clue to the suzerainty of Harṣa, we must now turn to our next guide, the indefatigable Chinese pilgrim, for help in unravelling the apparent indefiniteness of the power and influence of Kanauj over the surrounding territories. It may be noted here that the *Records* of Yuan Chwang are no political gazetteer. He came to India, defying the difficulties and hardships presented in his progress by both nature and man, on a mission that was primarily Buddhistic in its outlook and purpose. He makes only incidental references to the political status and government of different states, and as such they are all the more valuable and trustworthy. We should, therefore, analyse the testimony of Yuan Chwang in conjunction with that of the *Life* and indigenous epigraphs, and try to deduce conclusions as to the extent of the kingdom of Kanauj after learning the exact political conditions and status of the kingdoms of the North which Yuan Chwang visited, or of which he had heard. Extravagant claims about Harṣa's jurisdiction have been made; so we make no apologies for this detailed discussion regarding all the kingdoms of the north, beginning from the extreme north-western frontiers.

I. *Lan-p'o* or Lampa: Yuan Chwang begins his description from Lan-p'o (modern Lughman), although

[1] *Ibid.*, p. 40. Cf. "Devadevasya catuḥsamudrādhipateḥ sakalarājacakracūḍā-mani - śreni - śāṇa - koṇakaṣana - nirmalīkṛita - caraṇa nakhamaṇeḥ sarvacakravartinām dhaureyasya mahārājādhirāja parameśvara-śri Harṣadevasya" (*Hc.* Cal. ed., p. 112).

the countries described by him from Lan-p'o to Rajpur (Rajauri), both inclusive, were regarded by the people of India as "border lands" inhabited by "barbarians" and not part of their country. Regarding the political position of this region at the time of his visit the pilgrim says : "For several centuries the native dynasty had ceased to exist, great families fought for pre-eminence, and the state had recently become a dependency of Kapiśa."[1]

II. *Na-ka-lo-ho* or Nagar : This is represented by the tract called in modern times Nungnehar, and includes the present district of Jelalabad and the valley of the Kabul river. At that time "there was no king and the State was a province of Kapiśa."[2]

III. *Kan-t'o-lo* or Gāndhāra : "The royal family was extinct and the country was subject to Kapiśa. The towns and villages were desolate and the inhabitants were very few; in one corner of the city there were above 1,000 families."[3]

IV. *Fa-la-na* or Varana : The identification is doubtful. According to St. Martin it corresponds to modern Vanih, whereas Cunningham identifies it with Bannu : "It was well populated and was subject to Kapiśa."[4]

Thus *Kia-pi-shi* or Kapiśa was a strong and important kingdom in the north-west with several dependencies. We are unable to ascertain who was the king, but we are informed that he was a Kṣatriya and an adherent of Buddhism. As we are further told that "his power extended over more than ten of the neighbouring lands,"[5] we may be sure that Kapiśa was absolutely

[1] Watters, I, p. 181; Beal, I, p. 90.
[2] Watters, I, p. 183; Beal, I, p. 91.
[3] Watters, I, p. 199; Beal, I, p. 98.
[4] Watters, II, p. 262; Beal, II, p. 281.
[5] Watters, I, p. 123.

independent, and had nothing to do with the sovereignty of Kanauj.

V. *Ta-ch'a-shi-lo* or Takṣaśilā : Cunningham placed the site of the old city at the modern Shah-Dheri, just one mile to the north-east of Kāla-ka-serai.[1] Its ruins cover an extensive area. About its government the pilgrim says: "The chiefs were in a state of open feud, the royal family being extinguished; the country had formerly been subject to Kapiśa but now it was a dependency of Kashmir."[2]

VI. *Seng-ha-pu-lo* or Siṁhapura : identified with Narasiṁha or Ketas "situated on the north side of the Salt Range."[3] "There was no king and the country was a dependency of Kashmir."[4]

VII. *Wu-la-shih* or Uraśa : Corresponding with modern Hazara. "There was no ruler and the country was a dependency of Kashmir."[5]

VIII. *Pan-nu-ts'o* : equivalent with modern Punch.[6] "The country was a dependency of Kashmir."[7]

IX. *Ho-lo-she-pu-lo* or Rājapura : identical with the petty chieftainship of Rajori to the south of Kashmir.[8] Like Punch, "it had no sovereign of its own and was subject to Kashmir."[9]

Thus *Kia-shi-mi-lo* or Kashmir was anotner powerful state in Northern India holding sway over many outlying kingdoms. Unfortunately the *Life* and the

[1] *Anc. Geo. of India* (Calcutta, 1924), pp. 121, 681; see also Marshall's *Guide to Taxila*, pp. 1-4.

[2] Watters, I, p. 240; Beal, I, p. 136.

[3] *Anc. Geo. of India.*, p. 144.

[4] Watters, I, p. 248; Beal, I, p. 143.

[5] Watters, I, p. 256; Beal, I, p. 147.

[6] *Anc. Geo. of India.*, p. 147.

[7] Watters, I, p. 283: Beal, I, p. 163.

[8] *Anc. Geo. of India.*, p. 148.

[9] Watters, I, p. 284; Beal, I, p. 163.

Records of Yuan Chwang's Travels are both silent regarding the name of its king, who treated the pilgrim with marked ceremonious respect and hospitality, and "gave him twenty clerks to copy out manuscripts and five men to act as attendants."[1] The *Rājataraṅgiṇī*, however, affords us a clue, for, according to Kalhaṇa, Durlabhavardhana, who inaugurated the Karkoṭa dynasty, came to the throne in 3677 of the Laukika era or 601 A. D. He ruled for 36 years, which makes him exactly contemporary with Harṣa. Dr. R. K. Mookerji, on the other hand, tries to show on the supposed authority of the *Life* that Kashmir "in a way acknowledged the suzerainty of Harṣa."[2] To quote its testimony, we are told that "Śīlādityarāja, hearing that Kashmir possessed a tooth of the Buddha, coming in person to the chief frontier, asked permission to see and worship it."[3] The congregation was unwilling to accede to this request, and concealed the tooth, but the king of Kashmir fearing the exalted character of Harṣa, had the tooth unearthed and presented to him. Then "Śīlāditya seeing it was overpowered with reverence, and exercising force, carried it off to pay it religious offerings."[4] The episode, as narrated in the *Life*, will hardly bear the interpretation put upon it; and the expression that Śīlāditya carried off the tooth by "exercising force" probably means nothing more than that he brought it to Kanauj much against the wish of the people of Kashmir, who were even unwilling to allow Harṣa to see and worship the relic. There could be no question of any fight with the king of Kashmir, as the latter presented the sacred tooth to Harṣa of his own accord.

[1] Watters, I, p. 259.

[2] R. K. Mookerji, *Harṣa*, p. 40; C. V. Vaidya, *H. M. H. I.*, Vol. I, pp. 17, 206.

[3] *Life*, p. 183; see also Watters, I, p. 279.

[4] *Life*, p. 183.

Presumably a display of force, or a mere threat helped Harṣa to obtain the prized object; but any conclusions as to his authority being recognised in the valley are totally unwarranted.

We may here also consider a passage occurring in the *Rājataraṅgiṇī*, which runs as follows :—

Idaṁ svabhedavidhuraṁ Harṣādīnāṁ dharābhujāṁ, Kañcit kālam abhūd bhojyaṁ tataḥ prabhriti maṇḍalaṁ, i.e. "From that period onwards this country, which had suffered from internal dissensions, was for some time subject to Harṣa and other kings."[1]

Tempting as the identification might seem, this Harṣa should not be confused with the Harṣa of Kanauj, as has been done by Mr. N. Ray.[2] Firstly, the "chronological aberration," as noted by Stein,[3] should preclude any such supposition; and secondly, this Harṣa had a son, who is reputed to have ruled after him, whereas the Harṣa of Kanauj left no successor, and this was probably one of the reasons why the empire collapsed soon after his death. It would thus appear from the foregoing discussion that we have no grounds for believing that Kashmir owed allegiance to Harṣa.

X. From Rājapura the pilgrim proceeded to the *Cheh-ka* (Ṭakka) country, lying between the Indus and the *Pi-po-she* (Beas). It is said to have possessed numerous *Puṇyaśālas* or free rest-houses, where medicine and food were distributed, and where bodily wants and conveniences were looked after.[4] It had two dependencies, *Mou-lo-san-pu* or Multan (?),[5] and *Po-fa-to*,[6] identified with Parvata (Pavvata). *Cheh-ka* was thus another flourish-

[1] Vol. I, Bk. II, verse 7, (Stein, p. 56).
[2] *Ind. Hist. Quart.*, Dec., 1927, p. 780.
[3] Stein's *Rājataraṅgiṇī*, p. 56, Note 7.
[4] Watters, I, p. 286; Beal, I, pp. 165-166.
[5] Watters, II, p. 254; Beal, II, p. 274.
[6] Watters, II, p. 255; Beal, II, p. 275.

ing kingdom outside the pale of Harṣa's jurisdiction.

XI. The next important kingdom noticed by Yuan Chwang was *She-lan-ta-lo* or Jalandhara. We are told of a former king of this country, who learning Buddhism from an *arhat*, became a zealous believer. Thereupon the king of "Mid India," appreciating his sincere faith gave him sole control of matters relating to Buddhism in all India. He also travelled throughout India, and erected topes or monasteries at all sacred places.[1] The king of "Mid India" may or may not be identified with Harṣa, but it is certain that the latter did exercise some measure of influence over this kingdom, as we learn from the *Life*[2] that he charged the king of Jalandhara (named Wu-ti = Wuddhi or Buddhi)[3] to escort the pilgrim in safety to the frontiers.

XII. Leaving Jalandhara Yuan Chwang visited the *Ku-lu-to* or the Kuluta kingdom, corresponding "exactly with the position of Kullu in the upper valley of the Byas river."[4] The pilgrim is silent concerning its government.

XIII. *She-to-t'u-lu* or the Śatadru country, which, according to Cunningham is represented by modern Sirhind.[5] The pilgrim does not name any ruler.

XIV. *Po-li-ye-ta-lo* : Reinaud identifies this district with Pāryātra or Bairat, and Cunningham subscribes to this view.[6] Yuan Chwang says : "The king, who was of the *Fei-she* (Vaiśya) stock, was a man of courage and military skill."[7]

[1] Watters, I, p. 296; Beal, I, p. 176.

[2] *Life*, pp. 189-190.

[3] Watters restores the name *Wu-ti* or *Wu-ti-to* as Udito (See Vol. I, p. 297).

[4] *Anc. Geo. of India.*, p. 163.

[5] *Ibid.*, p. 166.

[6] *Ibid.*, p. 387.

[7] Watters, I, p. 300; Beal, I, p. 179.

XV. *Mo-tu-lo* or Mathura: The king is not named, but we are told that "the king and his statesmen devote themselves to good works."[1]

XVI. *Sa-t'a-ni-ssū-fa-lo* or Sthānvīśvara, identical with modern Thanesvar in the Ambala district.[2] Curiously enough, Yuan Chwang is silent as to its ruler and makes no reference to the Vardhanas.

XVII. *Su-lu-k'in-na* or Srughna, identified with the modern village of Sugh[3]. The king is not mentioned, and the capital is said to have been "in a ruinous condition."[4]

XVIII. *Mo-ti-pu-lo* or Matipura: identified by St. Martin and Cunningham with Madawar or Mandawar, a large town in Western Rohilkhand, near Bijnor.[5] "The king," says Yuan Chwang, "who was of the Śūdra stock, did not believe in Buddhism, and worshipped the Devas."[6]

XIX. *Po-lo-hih-mo-pu-lo* or Brahmapura: It denoted the hill-country between the Alakananda and Karnāli rivers, "which is now known as British Garhwal and Kumaon."[7] Yuan Chwang does not give us any information regarding its administration.

XX. *Su-fa-la-na-kiu-ta-lo* or the Suvarṇagotra country: It was said to lie to the north of Brahmapura in the great snow mountains, and was called "the eastern woman's country," because it was ruled by a succession of women. The husband of the queen was king, but he did not administer the government. The men attended only to the suppression of revolts

[1] Watters, I, p. 302; Beal, I, p. 181.
[2] *Anc. Geo. of India.*, p. 377f.
[3] *Ibid.*, p. 396.
[4] Watters, I, p. 318; Beal, I, p. 187.
[5] *Anc. Geo. of India*, p. 399.
[6] Watters, I, p. 322; Beal, I, p. 190; *Life*, p. 79.
[7] *Anc. Geo. of India*, p. 408.

and the cultivation of the fields.[1]

XXI. *Ku-pi-sang-na* or Goviśana : According to Cunningham this "corresponded very nearly with the modern districts of Kashipur, Rampur, and Pilibhit."[2] Its capital is said to have been a natural stronghold, but no king is mentioned.[3]

XXII. *Ngo-hi-ch'i-ta-lo* or Āhicchatra : occupying the eastern part of Rohilkhand. Vincent Smith thinks that modern Ramnagar in Bareilly district marks the site of its ancient capital.[4] We have no mention of any king, but we know from the evidence of the Banskhera inscription that Āhicchatra formed a *bhukti* or division under the direct control of Harṣa.[5]

XXIII. *Pi-lo-shan-na* : identified with the ruins called Atranji-Khera on the Kālīnadī. Yuan Chwang does not mention any ruler, but its proximity to Kanauj would argue that it must have been under Harṣa.

XXIV. *Kah-pi-t'a* (Kapitha) or Sankāśya, i.e., modern Sankisa. No king is mentioned. The vicinity of Kanauj may, however, point to its inclusion within that kingdom.

XXV. *Ka-no-kü-she* or Kanyākubja i.e., modern Kanauj. It was by far the most important city at that time, and the centre of the empire which the genius of Harṣa had built up.

XXVI. After visiting *Na-fa-t'i-p'o-ku-lo* or Navadevakula (modern Nobatganj), the pilgrim reached *A-yu-t-'e* or Ayodhyā. Yuan Chwang is silent as to

[1] Watters, I, p. 330; Beal, I, p. 199. This country is probably identical with the Suvarṇabhū in the north-east division of the *Brihat-Saṁhitā*, which Kern regards as "in all likelihood a mythical land." (*Ind. Ant.*, XXII, p. 190).

[2] *Anc. Geo. of India*, p. 412.

[3] Watters, I, p. 330; Beal, I, pp. 199-200.

[4] *Early Hist. of India*, 4th ed., pp. 391-92.

[5] *Ep. Ind.*, IV, pp. 210, 211.

its government, but if the coins found in Bhitaura (Fyzabad district) are attributable to Harṣa in accordance with Sir Richard Burn,[1] we have then direct evidence that it was under Kanauj.

XXVII. *A-ye-mu-k'a* or Hayamukha : identified with Daundia-Khera on the northern bank of the Ganges.[2] We have no information respecting its political relations; since Harṣa's authority extended much further, as we shall presently see, it may be included within his domains.

XXVIII. *Po-lo-ya-ka* or Prayāga, i.e., modern Allahabad. The "customary quinquennial great distribution of gifts," which Harṣa used to hold there, proves beyond doubt that it was within his direct sway and an important centre of the empire.

XXIX. *Kiao-shang-mi* or Kosambi : Dr. Vincent Smith thinks that the Satna railway station marks the approximate position of the capital of this country.[3] Better opinion, however, regards Kosam on the Jumna as its modern representative[4]. Yuan Chwang is silent about its political relations, but probably its destinies were bound up with Prayāga.

XXX. *P'i-sho-ka* or Viśoka : It has not yet been satisfactorily identified. The pilgrim omits to mention its government.

XXXI. *Shi-lo-fa-si-ti* or Śrāvasti, i.e., modern Sahet-Maheṭh.[5] Yuan Chwang is reticent regarding its political status, but we know from the Madhuban inscription that like Ahicchatra it formed a *bhukti* of Harṣa's kingdom[6].

[1] *J. R. A. S.*, 1906, pp. 843-50.
[2] *Anc. Geo. of India*, p. 443.
[3] *J. R. A. S.*, 1898, pp. 503-19.
[4] See Daya Ram Sahni, *Ibid.* 1927, p. 689.
[5] *Ibid.*, 1898, pp. 520-31.
[6] *Ep. Ind.*, I, pp. 72, 74.

XXXII. *Kie-pi-lo-fa-su-tu* or Kapilāvastu[1] : The "royal city" was a complete waste, and as the district had been left desolate for a very long time, it was sparsely inhabited. "The country was without a sovereign, each city having its own chief."[2]

XXXIII. *Lan-mo* or Rāma or Rāmagrāma : "This had been waste and wild for a long time, and its area was not defined : its towers were heaps of ruins, and there was a very scanty population".[3] We are not told anything about the rule of the country.

XXXIV. *Kou-shih-na-ka-lo* or Kuśinagara (modern Kasia).[4] "The city walls were in ruins, and the towns and villages were deserted."[5]

XXXV. *Po-lo-na-se* or Vārāṇasi, i.e., modern Benares. "The inhabitants were very numerous and had boundless wealth, their houses being full of rare valuables," but they cared little for Buddhism.[6] There is no mention of its political status.

XXXVI. Passing then through the *Chan-chu* country, which has not been satisfactorily identified,[7] the pilgrim arrived in *Fei-she-li* or Vaiśāli country. The pilgrim is silent about the nature of its government.

XXXVII. *Fu-li-chih* or the Vriji country : "The chief city was called *Chan-shu-na*; it was in a ruinous state and the old walled city, which was like a country town, had a population of over 3,000 families."[8] The name of the ruler is not recorded.

[1] See N. L. Dey's *Geographical Dictionary of Ancient and Mediæval India* (1927), pp. 90-91 for its identification.

[2] Watters, II, p. 1; Beal, II, p. 14.

[3] Watters, II, p. 20; Beal, II, p. 26.

[4] *Arch. Surv. Ind. Rep.*, XVIII, Pref. and p. 55f.

[5] Watters, II, p. 25; Beal, II, p. 32.

[6] Watters, II, p. 47; Beal, II, p. 44f.

[7] Beal identifies it with Ghazipur (Vol. II, p. 61; see also Cunningham, *Anc. Geo. of India*, p. 503).

[8] Watters, II, p. 81; Beal, II, p. 78.

XXXVIII. *Ni-po-lo* or Nepal : This is the next important kingdom, about which the pilgrim has unhappily just a few words only to say. "The kings of Nepal were Kṣatriya Licchavis, and they were eminent scholars and believing Buddhists. A *recent king*, whose name is given as Ang-shu-fa-na or Aṁśuvarman .... had composed a treatise on etymology."[1] It has usually been assumed on the authority of Bühler, Bhagvan Lal Indraji,[2] Fleet, Vincent Smith that Nepal came under the suzerainty of Harṣa; but this view has also been called to question by Sylvain Lévi, Ettinghausen and others. The problem being so controversial, we must critically examine the available evidence before coming to any conclusion. To begin with the arguments adduced in support of Harṣa's conquest of Nepal :—

(*a*) Certain Nepalese inscriptions[3] have been discovered, and among them there are some that refer to a king named Aṁśuvarman; these are dated in the years 34, 39 and 45. He is described in these inscriptions as a mere *Sāmanta* or *Mahāsāmanta*; and since "it is an indisputable axiom that nobody but an anointed king can initiate a *Saṁvat* of his own",[4] Aṁśuvarman has been ruled out as a possible originator of the era in which they are dated. Yuan Chwang calls Aṁśuvarman a "recent king"; and the characters of the inscriptions are also said to belong to the close of the sixth, or the early part of the seventh century A. D.[5] Hence, the dates have with some plausibility been referred to the

[1] Watters, II, p. 84; Beal, II, p. 81.

[2] *Ind. Ant.*, XIII, p. 411f.

[3] See *Ibid.*, IX, p. 169f. Nos. 6, 7 and 8 : Kielhorn's Nos. 531-33. The numbers quoted hereafter refer to the list of Indraji and Bühler, *Ind. Ant.*, IX, p. 168.

[4] *Ibid.*, XIII, p. 420.

[5] *Ibid.*, p. 418.

Harṣa era, as at this period it was "in widest use"; and "no other known Indian era can meet the requirements of the case."[1] Granting this circumstance, it necessarily implies the subordination of Nepal to Kanauj, for no other independent monarch would use the era started by another.[2]

(*b*) That the Harṣa era was used in Nepal is further maintained on the evidence of inscription No. 15, dated *Saṁvat* 153,[3] which states that Jayadeva's mother, Vatsadevī, was the daughter of a Maukhari prince or chief, Bhogavarman, and the grand-daughter of "the great Ādityasena, the illustrious lord of Magadha." We know Ādityasena of Magadha from the Shahpur stone image inscription,[4] dated year 66 of an unspecified era, which "from the known facts of Ādityasena's history .... is that of Harṣavardhana of Kanauj."[5] Now, the distance between this date and that of his grandson Jayadeva is 87 years, or slightly above the duration of three Indian generations, which amounts to 78 years approximately[6]. "Under these circumstances," it is asserted that "it is not in the least doubtful that the great-grandfather and great-grandson used the same era,"[7] viz. that of Harṣa.

[1] *Ibid.*, p. 421.

[2] The following remark seems apposite here: "If an Indian prince adopts a new foreign era, especially one founded by a contemporary, that may be considered as almost a certain proof that the borrower had to submit to the *Śaka-kartri*, or establisher of the era" (*Ibid.*, XIX, pp. 40-41).

[3] *Ibid.*, IX, pp. 178, 181.

[4] *C. I. I.*, Vol. III, pp. 209-10.

[5] *Ibid.*, p. 210.

[6] Bhagvan Lal Indraji and Bühler assure us that "in India the duration of a generation amounts, as the statistical tables of the life-insurance companies show, at the outside to only 26 years" (*Ind. Ant.*, XIII, p. 417).

[7] *Ibid.*, p. 421.

(*c*) The *Vaṁśāvalī* informs us that immediately before the accession of Aṁśuvarman, Vikramāditya came to the country, and established his era there. It is argued that this statement preserves a reminiscence of Harṣa's conquest of Nepal, as at this period the name Vikramāditya could have reference to Harṣa only among Indian kings.

(*d*) A "much stronger argument" is found in the existence of the Bais Rajputs in Nepal according to the testimony of the *Vaṁśāvalī*. "Since it is an almost universal rule with Indian princes that on the occasion of conquests they grant a portion of land to their clansmen,"[1] probably we have here a direct proof that Nepal was once in the power of a Bais king, who could be nobody else but Harṣa of Kanauj, as we know on the authority of Yuan Chwang that he belonged to the *Feishe* caste, identified by Sir Alexander Cunningham with the Bais Rajputs.[2]

(*e*) Lastly, we might mention the oft-quoted passage of Bāṇa that Harṣa "exacted tribute from an inaccessible country of snowy mountains," which has been construed as referring to Nepal.

Apparently, there is some force in these arguments, but they are open to serious objections. First, if the dates of the inscriptions of Aṁśuvarman be accepted as referring to the Harṣa era, the last known date for him according to inscription No. 8 would be A. D. 606 + 45 = 651 A. D. The *Records* on the other hand imply by the word "recent" that Aṁśuvarman's reign had terminated shortly before the pilgrim's visit in about 637 A. D. And we have, therefore, a discrepancy of about 14 years between the two testimonies. Scholars

[1] *Ibid.*

[2] *Anc. Geo. of India*, pp. 432-33; See also Bühler, *Ep. Ind.*, I, p. 68, note 4; Hoernle, *J. R. A. S.*, 1903, p. 557.

try to overcome this difficulty by suggesting that the pilgrim did not himself go to Nepal, and his evidence was "mere hearsay liable to be coloured and distorted by misunderstanding or misrepresentation." The assumption, however, is quite gratuitous, for Yuan Chwang was a careful and trustworthy writer, who invariably tried to ascertain facts and note them down correctly. He moved in the highest circles, among powerful potentates and celebrated monks, who could certainly be relied upon to supply correct information.[1] Besides, Yuan Chwang mentions the countries that he did not visit, and as an instance we may cite the case of the six countries beyond Samataṭa, regarding which he speaks only on information gained here and there.[2] Thus there can be no doubt about the pilgrim's testimony, and so to reconcile the conflicting evidence we must refer the dates in the inscriptions to some other era instead of that of Harṣa. Yuan Chwang's visit to those parts has been fixed at about 637 A. D. We also know from inscriptions Nos. 8 and 9 that Aṁśuvarman died, and his successor was on the throne between *Saṁvat* 45 and 48. Hence, assuming that Aṁśuvarman was dead a couple of years before the pilgrim's visit, and that the date 45 denotes the last year of his reign, we come to the conclusion that the reckoning in the inscriptions began in the year 590 A. D. approximately. The fact that Aṁśuvarman was a mere *Sāmanta* or *Mahāsāmanta* need not present any obstacle in adopting this view. Probably he did not start any era formally soon after his accession, but at first dated the inscriptions in the years of his reign. Later on, when he

[1] See also *Journal of the Mythic Society*. Unfortunately I have lost the exact reference to this article, which was available to me in the British Museum, and to which I owe some suggestions.

[2] Watters, II, p. 187.

assumed the supreme power in the land, he converted it into an era dating back to the beginning of his rule, and the same reckoning was continued by his successors. Aṁśuvarman's earliest inscription is dated *Saṁvat* 34, and *Saṁvat* undoubtedly indicates an era.

At this point we may be called upon to explain how he could commence an era, when his master was alive in *Saṁvat* 39. It would appear that Śivadeva was only the nominal ruler, whereas the real power was vested in Aṁśuvarman, who is referred to in inscription No. 5 of Śivadeva as one "who has destroyed the power of all (my) enemies by his heroic majesty" .... and "whose brilliant fame, gained by the trouble of properly protecting the subjects, pervades the universe."[1] Besides, inscriptions Nos. 6 to 8 of Aṁśuvarman do not mention any superior lord; and as he himself assumed sovereign powers (for example, appointing Udayadeva as his chief executive officer) we may infer that he had become powerful and independent even during his master's lifetime. That he called himself "*Mahāsāmanta*" was probably due to habit or out of respect for his old lord alive in *Saṁvat* 39. We may recall in this connection the case of Puṣyamitra, who calls himself "*Senāpati*" even after becoming king[2] or of Rudradāman mentioned as a mere "*Mahākṣatrapa*" after the assumption of sovereign status.[3] The subordinate titles are dropped in Aṁśuvarman's inscription

[1] *Ind. Ant.*, IX, p. 169.

[2] *Mālavikāgnimitra* Act V, p. 131 (S. P. Pandit's Edition, 1889); Cf. also the Ayodhyā inscription (*J. B. O. R. S.*, 1924, pp. 202-08).

[3] Junagaḍh Rock Inscription of Rudradaman, *Ep. Ind.*, VIII, pp. 40, 44, 45. An analogy to the retention of the feudatory title may also be found in the use of the epithet "Peshwa" by the Mahratta rulers of the Deccan, who instead of being the Peshwas or Ministers of the descendants of Śivāji were in reality their masters.

of the year 45,[1] and in that of Jiṣṇugupta of *Saṁvat* 48, in which he is referred to as "Bhaṭṭāraka Mahārājādhirāja Sri Aṁśuvarmapādaḥ."[2] There is thus nothing to militate against the view propounded above that the inscriptions are dated in an independent era.

Secondly, argument (*b*) loses its entire force if it be granted that the reckoning of Aṁśuvarman's inscriptions began sometime in 590 A. D. Adding 153 to 590 A. D., we get 743 A. D. as the date of Jayadeva's inscription No. 15. If the date 66 of the Shahpur inscription is to be referred to the Harṣa era—as has been done by Fleet—the difference between Ādityasena and his great-grandson Jayadeva would be only 743-672 A. D.=71 years, or slightly less than the duration of three Indian generations, which as mentioned above, amounts to roughly 78 years. Thus, according to this proposition also the dates would tally remarkably well.

Thirdly, the *Vaṁśāvalī* is worthless for purposes of history, as a few instances will show. It says that Aṁśuvarman came to the throne in Kali 3000=101 B. C.,[3] which is in violent conflict with the testimonies of both Yuan Chwang and the inscriptions. Again, Aṁśuvarman's seventh successor, Vīradeva, is said to have ruled in Kaliyuga 3623 or 522 A. D.,[4] and thus we have the absurdity of seven generations for six hundred years.

Besides, Harṣa was never known as Vikramāditya (even Bāṇa or the inscriptions do not bestow on him this title, although it is so commonly adopted by powerful Hindu potentates); and it is stretching the point to say that he was called Vikramāditya by confusion. Pro-

[1] No. 8, *Ind. Ant.*, IX, p. 171.
[2] *Ibid.*, No. 9, p. 172.
[3] *Ibid.*, XIII, p. 418.
[4] *Ibid.*

bably by using the expression "Vikramāditya came and established his era" the authors of the *Vaṁśāvali* simply tried to connect the current era in Nepal with the renowned name of Vikramāditya, the founder of the Vikrama era.

Fourthly, the force of argument (*d*) above lies in the correct identification of the *Fei-she* caste with the Bais Rajputs. It was a casual suggestion of Sir Alexander Cunningham, but we venture to say that it is far from conclusive, as the family suffix Vardhana (usually used after Vaiśya names only) itself would show.[1]

Fifthly, the passage in the *Harṣacarita* is not such as to warrant our drawing any definite conclusions. "The inaccessible land of snowy mountains" may not refer to Nepal. Ettinghausen[2] thought that it referred to some Tukhāra country. Moreover, it is capable of bearing more than one interpretation. "Atra parameśvareṇa tuṣāra śailabhuvo Durgāyā grihītaḥ karaḥ," might as well mean without violence to the context: "Here the supreme lord has obtained the hand of Durgā born in the snowy mountains," which in all probability alludes to Harṣa's marriage with some hill-princess belonging to a very powerful family. That he was married is evident from the following passage put by Bāṇa into the mouth of Harṣa: "Kalatraṁ rakṣatu iti śrīste nistriṁsedhivasati," i.e., "if you would have me watch over my wife, glory resides in your steel."[3]

[1] See *Ante*.

[2] *Harṣavardhana*, p. 47.

[3] *Hc. C. T.*, p. 175. Although, as we have seen above, Bāṇa is quite explicit about Harṣa's marriage, it is strange that Dr. Beni Prasad observes: "Neither Bāṇabhaṭṭa nor Yuan Chwang nor any of the contemporary inscriptions refers to any wife of Harṣavardhana, or to the fact of his marriage" (*The State in Ancient India*, Chap. XIV, p. 385). Moreover, Yuan Chwang definitely informs us that Dhruvabhaṭṭa, the king of Valabhi, was Harṣa's

The upshot of this lengthy but necessary discussion is that we have no certain evidence pointing to Harṣa's interference in the affairs of the valley, or to the introduction of his era there.[1] It will, therefore, be safer to exclude Nepal from the sphere of the suzerainty of Kanauj.[2]

son-in-law, and this obviously he could not become without the latter's marriage.

[1] See also *J.B.O.R.S.*, Septr., 1936, p. 161 f. Mr. K.P. Jayasval, however, considers 595 A. D. to be the initial year of Aṁśuvarman's era.

[2] We may also note here that at this time Tibet wielded supreme influence over Nepal, which gave its full support to the mission of Wang-hiuen-tse in its punitive expedition against the usurper of Harṣa's throne. Both Watters (Vol. II, p. 85), and Vincent Smith (*Early Hist. of India*, 4th ed., pp. 366, 375) admit this, but in the description of Harṣa's kingdom the latter includes Nepal (see *Ibid.*, p. 354).

PART II

CHAPTER V

Extent of the Empire (continued)

We shall now describe the political conditions of the eastern parts of India visited by the Chinese pilgrim.

XXXIX. *Mo-kie-to* or Magadha: Yuan Chwang does not mention in what relation this ancient kingdom stood to Kanauj, nor does he note the nature of its government. All the information he gives is that "in recent times" Śaśāṅka cut down the Bodhi Tree; and "a few months afterwards Pūrṇavarman, the last descendant of Aśoka on the throne of Magadha, brought the Tree back to life."[1] This Pūrṇavarman[2] must have lived in the beginning of the 7th century A. D., since he is represented here as the contemporary of Śaśāṅka, whose last date according to the Ganjam plate was 619 A.D. After Pūrṇavarman's death, probably Magadha passed under the jurisdiction of Harṣa, as the Chinese documents connected with his embassy to that country seem to style him "king of Magadha."[3] Support for this view may further be found in the discovery of Harṣa's seals at Nalanda[4] and from Yuan Chwang, who, describing the establishments around the

[1] Watters, II, p. 115; Beal, II, p. 118.

[2] It is possible that Pūrṇavarman was a Maukhari acting as governor of Magadha on behalf of the penultimate or the last Maukhari king of Kanauj who ruled over it since the days of Sarvavarman. (See chapter II).

[3] Watters, I, p. 351.

[4] Ep. Ind., XXI (April, 1931), pp. 74-76.

Nalanda convent, records "a bronze temple in course of construction by king Śīlāditya,"[1] and we may be sure that this name could only have reference to the great king of Kanauj at this period.

XL. *I-lan-na-po-fa-to* country: identified with the modern district of Monghyr. The pilgrim says: "in recent times the king of a neighbouring State had deposed the ruler and given the capital to the Buddhist brethren".[2] Its proximity to Magadha perhaps justifies our identifying this generous king of the "border country" with Harṣa.

XLI. *Chan-po* (Campa) or modern Bhagalpur. Yuan Chwang is reticent about its political relations.

XLII. *Ka-chu-wen* (?) Ki-lo (or Kajangala) : identified by Cunningham with the modern Rajmahal. We are told that "the native dynasty had been extinguished some centuries before the time of the pilgrim's visit, and the country had come under a neighbouring State, so the capital was deserted and the people lived in towns and villages. Hence when king Śīlāditya in his progress to "East India" held his court here, he cut grass to make huts and burned these when leaving."[3] The fact of Harṣa having held his court there proves beyond doubt that it was included within his wide dominions. That the king's temporary residence was burnt after his departure should not lead us to the belief that Harṣa merely "carried on a military raid in this direction," as supposed by Dr. R. C. Majumdar,[4] for Yuan Chwang himself informs us that the sovereign "made visits of inspection throughout his dominions .... having temporary buildings erected for his residence at each place of sojourn."

[1] Watters, II, p. 171; *Life*, p. 119.
[2] Watters, II, p. 178; Beal, II, p. 187.
[3] Watters, II, p. 183; Beal, II, p. 193.
[4] *J. B. O. R. S.*, 1923, p. 314.

XLIII. *Pun-na-fa-tan-na* (or Puṇḍravardhana): identified with modern Pabna. *San-mo-ta-t'a* or *Samataṭa*, regarded as lying in the district of modern Faridpur, south of Dacca.[1] *Tan-mo-lih-ti* (Tāmralipti), corresponding to the modern Tamluk. *Kie-lo-na-su-fa-la-na* i.e., *Karṇasuvarṇa*, equivalent to the modern districts of Burdwan, Bīrbhum, and Murshidabad.[2] These constituted in those days the several divisions of Bengal. The king of these regions shortly before the visit of Yuan Chwang was *She-shang-kia* or Śaśāṅka, the enemy and oppressor of Buddhists, who had treacherously murdered Rājyavardhana.[3] A king with the same name is known to have been in power about the year 619 A. D., for the Ganjaṁ copper plate of the Gupta year 300 refers to him in pompous expressions: "While the Mahārājādhirāja, the glorious Śaśāṅkarāja, was ruling over the earth, surrounded by the girdle of the waves of the water of the four oceans, together with islands, mountains and cities."[4] If the Śaśāṅkas of the *Si-yu-ki* and the Ganjam inscription are identical as has been accepted on all hands, it is certain that Harṣa was unable to make any headway against his adversary for at least thirteen years after the murder of Rājya. Yuan Chwang, however, does not mention any reigning king during his visit to these parts, and the manner in

[1] Watters, II, p. 188.

[2] *Ibid.*, p. 193.

[3] Yuan Chwang calls Śaśāṅka king of Karṇasuvarṇa; and Bāṇa refers to him as the king of Gauḍa, which designated Bengal in a loose way. Putting these two testimonies together with the Ganjam plate, we know that Śaśāṅka was ruler of a pretty extensive territory, comprising Bengal proper and portions of the eastern-coast line.

[4] Śaśāṅka's sovereign status about 619 A. D. is known not only by the title Mahārājādhirāja, but also by the fact that Mahārāja Mādhavarāja, who issued the grant, calls himself a Mahāsāmanta, and was evidently a feudatory of Śaśāṅka.

which he speaks about Śaśāṅka shows that he had lived not very long before his itinerary. This agrees admirably with the testimony of the Ganjam inscription. We must, therefore, explain what happened to Śaśāṅka's kingdom after his death, which may be tentatively fixed in the year 620 A. D. with a slight margin for error.

It has been conjectured that the Nidhanpur inscription celebrates the triumphant entry of Bhāskaravarman of Assam into the capital of Karṇasuvarṇa after his victory, for it describes him as a vanquisher of "hundreds of kings" and records a grant made from his camp there.[1] This must have happened after the tumult following Aruṇa's usurpation and Bhāskara's siding with Wang-hiuen-tse, as in spite of the "imperishable alliance" there seems little likelihood that Harṣa would allow him to appropriate those fertile provinces to himself, and thus gain an immense accession of strength. Politics is a game that hardly knows any magnanimity; and especially in ancient India, dominated by the theories of the *Arthaśāstra* and the *Mahābhārata*, which advocate that a king, although apparently showing friendly feelings, should always entertain a deep suspicion of an ally, such growth in the power of a contemporary kingdom would never have been tolerated. Hence, from the silence of Yuan Chwang we may conclude that Harṣa, who was waiting for a favourable opportunity to fulfil the vow taken at the start of his career, gratified his ancient grudge against Gauḍa when the backbone of strength and resistance was broken by the death of Śaśāṅka. Dr. R. G. Basak has, however, brought out a piece of evidence from the *Mañjuśrīmūlakalpa* (pp. 634-35), according to which Harṣa defeated Śaśāṅka and "caused a great havoc among the Bengali people." But this campaign does not appear to have

[1] *Ep. Ind.*, XII, p. 66.

resulted in the establishment of Harṣa's supremacy over Gauḍa, and Dr. Basak rightly says that "it was probably after Saśāṅka's death that Harṣa could take entire possession of his enemy's kingdom."[1]

XLIV. *Ka-mo-lu-po* or Kāmarūpa, i.e., modern Assam. Yuan Chwang informs us that "the reigning king, who was a Brahman by caste, and a descendant of Nārāyaṇadeva, was named Bhāskaravarman, his other name being Kumāra. The sovereignty had been transmitted in the family for one thousand generations."[2] He was in great fear of his powerful neighbour, Śaśāṅka, and this was probably the reason why he so readily extended the hand of friendship to Harṣa at the initial stage of his campaigns. Dr. R. K. Mookerji, on the other hand, affirms that "the king of distant Kāmarūpa (Assam) offered him allegiance of his own accord and was anointed king by his liege lord."[3] But I find no authority whatsoever for this assertion. Can the conclusion of a treaty by any stretch of imagination be interpreted as "offering allegiance of his own accord"? The learned Professor finds support for the second part of his statement in a dubious passage occurring in the *Harṣacarita*, viz., "Atra devena abhiṣiktaḥ Kumāraḥ."[4] To my mind, however, it seems to have no bearing upon Bhāskaravarman, for Bāṇa calls him "*Prāgjyotiṣeśvara*" or king of Assam,[5] at the time when negotiations were

[1] *History of North-Eastern India* (Calcutta, 1934), p. 152; *Ind. Hist. Quart.*, March 1932, pp. 14-15.

[2] Watters, II, p. 186; Beal, II, p. 196. Strange to say, in some of the family names Yuan Chwang is remarkably confirmed by Bāṇa and the inscriptions. See *Hc. C. T.*, p. 217; *J. B. O. R. S.*, 1919, p. 302; also 1920, p. 151.

[3] *Harṣa*, p. 44. See also p. 48, where the author calls Bhāskara "a vassal chief."

[4] Hc. C. T., p. 76; Hc. *Cal. ed.*, pp. 210-11.

[5] By some slip the term has unfortunately been translated as

opened by his messenger Haṁsavega. I venture to suggest that the passage most probably refers to Mādhavagupta,[1] the youthful friend of Harṣa, to whom he delegated his authority over Magadha. This is evident if the testimony of Bāṇa is taken in conjunction with that of the Aphsad inscription.[2] This devolution of political power was perhaps a reward for the services that Mādhavagupta had rendered to Harṣa during his early troubles. Or, he was stationed there as a bulwark against any possible encroachment by Śaśāṅka, who had escaped without being punished and was yet powerful.

The episode of the forced visit of Yuan Chwang would hardly lead us to any conclusion. It is said that when Harṣa sent for the Chinese pilgrim, who was then staying with Bhāskaravarman, he got the reply that Harṣa could have his head, but not his guest—an expression which undoubtedly stressed his reluctance to part with the illustrious visitor. Receiving an unfavourable reply Harṣa is represented to have made the bold demand to "send the head,"[3] and ultimately the threat had the desired effect. Obviously it cannot follow from this yielding to the pressure of a valued ally that the king of Assam accepted the suzerainty of Harṣa.

The circumstance of attending both the assemblies at Kanauj and Prayāga also does not help us to determine the political relations of the two potentates. Bhāskara witnessed their proceedings as a friend on an equal footing with Harṣa,[4] and there is no evidence that it

"Heir-Apparent of Assam" by the learned translators (see *Hc.C.T.*, p. 211).

[1] The term "Kumāra" has probably been used by Bāṇa in its general sense of "prince" without reference to any particular name.

[2] See *Infra.*

[3] *Life*, p. 172.

[4] Compare in this connection the installation ceremony of

involved a compromise of his independence.

XLV. *Wu-tu* (Odra) or modern Orissa, and *Kung-yu(gu* or *ya)-to* or Kongodha, identical with the modern Ganjam district[1]. Yuan Chwang is silent about the government of both, but he describes the latter as a great military country: "As the towns were naturally strong there was a gallant army, which kept the neighbouring countries in awe, and so there was no powerful enemy."[2] At the time of the pilgrim's arrival in these parts, as we know from the *Life*,[3] this country had been attacked and subjugated by the king of Kanauj. It was then "apparently a part of that great sovereign's kingdom." Thus it appears that Harṣa made this region a strong military outpost of his far-flung empire, probably with a view to preventing any foreign incursions on the borders, threatened as they were by the eastward advance of Pulakeśi II, who is credited with the conquest of Kośala and Kalinga in the Aihole inscription.[4] Regarding Orissa, there are grounds to infer that it came within the pale of Harṣa's sovereignty. For the *Life* tells us that after the subjugation of Kongodha Śilāditya camped in Orissa for a time,[5] and made a munificent gift of "the revenue of eighty large towns of Orissa" to Jayasena, "the admiration of the period," who in his characteristic other-worldliness declined the king's repeated offers.[6]

Having dealt with those portions of the north and east that lay in the pilgrim's route, we now come

Cakrāyudha, which was attended by nine independent powers (See *Infra.*).

[1] See also *J. B. O. R. S.*, Dec. 1926, pp. 585-86.

[2] Watters, II, p. 197; Beal, II, p. 207.

[3] *Life*, pp. 159, 172.

[4] *Ind. Ant.*, VIII, pp. 242, 245.

[5] *Life*, p. 159.

[6] *Ibid.*, p. 154.

to the kingdoms of the south-west and west.

XLVI. *Mo-ha-la-ch'a* or Mahārāṣṭra. Yuan Chwang gives us a very reliable description of this kingdom. The king, we are told, was "a Kṣatriya by birth, and his name was Pu-lo-ki-she (Pulakeśi). The benevolent sway of this king reached far and wide, and his vassals served him with perfect loyalty. The great king Śīlāditya at this time was invading east and west; and countries far and near were giving in allegiance to him, but *Mo-ha-la-ch'a* refused to become subject to him."[1] Additional information is furnished by the *Life*[2] that Śīlāditya "boasting of his skill and invariable success of his generals filled with confidence himself, marched at the head of his troops to contend with this prince." But even his supreme and masterful command did not enable him to subjugate or prevail over his powerful southern rival, who had by his extensive conquests in the south justly won the proud title of "Dakṣiṇāpatha prithivyāḥ svāmī" or "lord of the whole region of the south."[3]

The pilgrim's account of this clash between the two great rivals is remarkably confirmed by the testimony of the Cālukya inscriptions also. The Aihole Meguṭi inscription of A. D. 634, containing a description of Pulakeśī's exploits, refers to the event as follows: "Envious because his troops of mighty elephants were slain in war, Harṣa, whose lotuses, which were his feet, were covered with the rays of the jewels of the chiefs that were nourished by his immeasurable power .... was caused by him to have his joy melted away by fear."[4] Further references to the same event

[1] Watters, II, p. 239; Beal, II, p. 256.

[2] *Life*, p. 147.

[3] Yekkeri inscription, *Ep. Ind.*, V, pp. 7, 8.

[4] Cf. "Aparimita-vibhūti-sphīta-sāmanta-senā makuṭa-maṇi-mayūkh-ākkrānta-pādāravindaḥ ı yudhi patita-gaja(je)ndra-ānīka-vī(bī)

occur in the Nirpan,[1] Karnul,[2] and Togarcedu grants,[3] which testify that the Cālukya monarch acquired the title of "Parameśvara" or "supreme lord" by defeating Harṣavardhana "the warlike lord of all the region of the north" (Sakalottarāpathanātha).[4] This reverse was perhaps due not only to the proud spirit and warlike character of the Mahrattas, but also to Pulakeśī's superior and carefully equipped troops—cavalry and elephants. It may be interesting to note in passing that his was the first great military achievement of the South against a northern power; and henceforth history will present examples of southern potentates, like the Rāṣṭrakūṭa Indra III, carrying their arms northwards and bringing destruction on Kanauj.

XLVII. *Po-lu-ka-cha-po* (Bhrigukacchapa or Bhrigukaccha, i.e., Broach): identified with the kingdom founded by Dadda. It was doubtless independent of Kanauj, as its ruler gave protection to one of Harṣa's vanquished adversaries.[5]

XLVIII. *Mo-la-po* or Western Malwa, with its dependencies of *Kita*, identified with Cutch or Kheḍa; *Ānandapura* and *Su-la-cha* or Surat. Regarding Malwa, Yuan Chwang informs us that the local records told of a king, by name Śīlāditya, who had reigned over the country sixty years before the pilgrim's arrival, a monarch of great administrative ability, and of rare kindness and compassion."[6] This Śīlāditya has been

bhatsa-bhūto bhaya-vigaḷita-harṣo yena c-ākāri Harṣaḥ", *Ep. Ind.*, VI, pp. 6, 10, verse 23; *Ind. Ant.*, VIII, pp. 242, 244.

[1] *Ind. Ant.*, IX, pp. 124-25.

[2] *Ibid.*, XI, p. 68.

[3] *Ibid.*, VI, pp. 84-87.

[4] Also see in this connection: (*a*) a grant of the Yuvarāja Śīlāditya Śryāśraya (*Ind. Ant.*, XIII, p. 74); (*b*) the Kauṭhem grant of Vikramāditya II (*Ibid.*, XVI, p. 22).

[5] See *Infra*.

[6] Watters, II, p. 242; Beal, II, p. 261; *Life*, p. 148.

identified with Śīlāditya Dharmāditya of the Valabhi dynasty, whose nephew Dhruvabhaṭa was ruling over Valabhi at the time of Yuan Chwang's visit. We may, therefore, infer that Śīlāditya Dharmāditya was the original ruler of Valabhi, to which he annexed Western Malwa (or *Mo-la-po*); and that his nephew Dhruvabhaṭa II, a contemporary of Yuan Chwang, was also in possession of Malwa with its three dependencies.

XLIX. About *Falapi* or Valabhi Yuan Chwang records: "The reigning sovereign was of Kṣatriya birth, a nephew of Śīlāditya the former king of Malava, and a son-in-law of the Śīlāditya reigning at Kānyakubja; his name was *Tu-lo-po-po-ta* (i.e., Dhruvabhaṭa); he was of a hasty temper, and of shallow views, but he was a sincere believer in Buddhism."[1]

It is usually assumed that Valabhi was a feudatory state of Harṣa. Dr. Vincent Smith discussing his campaigns remarks that after the flight Dhruvabhaṭa "was compelled to sue for peace, to accept the hand of the victor's daughter, and to be content with the position of a feudatory vassal."[2] He further adds: "The same campaign may be presumed to have involved the submission of the kingdoms or countries of Ānandapura, Kicha or Cutch (?), and Soraṭha or Southern Kathiawar, all of which in A. D. 641 were still reckoned to be dependencies of Mo-la-po, or Western Malava, formerly subject to Valabhi."[3] The latest follower of Smith is Dr. R. K. Mookerji,[4] and as this view is rather common among scholars, we proceed to examine how far the facts at our disposal justify it.

There is an interesting passage in the Nausari copper-plate grant, which contains a reference to Harṣa's

[1] Watters, II, p. 246; Beal, II, p. 267; *Life*, p. 149.

[2] *Early Hist. of India* 4th ed., p. 354.

[3] *Ibid.*

[4] *Harṣa*, pp. 30-31.

fight with the king of Valabhi. We are told of "the illustrious Dadda .... over whom, with the grace of a white cloud, there hung ceaselessly a canopy of glory, gained by protecting (or rescuing ?) the lord of Valabhi, who had been overpowered by the great lord, the illustrious Harṣadeva."[1] The Valabhi king, contemporary with Dadda II of Broach was Dhruvasena II, but Yuan Chwang calls the then monarch of this kingdom Tu-lo-po-pa-ta, or Dhruvabhaṭa, so that we may suppose both the names to refer to one and the same person. Putting together the evidence of the Nausari inscription and of Yuan Chwang, we may further infer that Dhruvabhaṭa or Dhruvasena II first sought the protection of Dadda II of Broach after meeting with a reverse against Harṣa, and later on regained his power, being on the throne during the pilgrim's visit. We are, therefore, called upon to explain how a minor king—a mere *Sāmanta*—like that of Broach, could afford protection to Dhruvabhaṭa against the forces of Harṣa, and what was his status after the restoration. The answer to this query probably lies in the Aihole inscription, which informs us that "subdued by his (Pulakeśi's) splendour, the Lāṭas, Mālavas, and Gurjaras became, as it were, teachers of how feudatories subdued by force ought to behave."[2] Commenting on this passage, Dr. Kielhorn remarked that the powers[3] mentioned above, being "impressed by the majesty and power of Pulakeśi had voluntarily submitted to him, or sought his protection."[4] This must surely have been when they were

[1] Parameśvara-śrī-Harṣa-devābhibhūta Valabhī-pati (ri) trānopajāta bhramad adabhra subhrābhra vibhrama yaśovitānaḥ Śrī Daddaḥ (*Ind. Ant.*, XIII, pp. 77-79).

[2] *Ep. Ind.*, VI, pp. 6, 10, verse 22.

[3] They are obviously to be identified with the Broach and Valabhi kingdoms.

[4] *Ibid.*, note 5.

threatened by the aggressions of the Kanauj king. Pulakeśi lent a willing ear to their appeal for succour, and as well pointed out by Dr. R. C. Majumdar,[1] the confederacy thus formed was a formidable one, "resulting in Harṣa's complete discomfiture." The fact that the Cālukya inscriptions do not mention any such joint action would not militate against this view, for the inscriptions represent those powers as feudatories, and they would naturally give the whole credit to a ruler of the dynasty. Harṣa gave way against these tremendous odds, and a treaty was arranged, stipulating the restoration of Dhruvabhaṭa II, who (perhaps as a mark of the termination of hostilities) further accepted the hand of Harṣa's daughter.'[2] This matrimonial arrangement was undoubtedly a masterly stroke of diplomacy, as it procured for Harṣa the alliance of his quondam foe, who could henceforth be relied upon to restrain the northern ambitions (if any) of his great southern neighbour Pulakeśi II. But even supposing the suggestion, offered above, to be utterly untenable, we have no grounds for inferring the subordination of Valabhi to Kanauj. There is no trace of it in Yuan Chwang's account, and it is also certain that Dhruvabhaṭa II was on the throne during the time of the pilgrim's visit. He must have, therefore, regained his position by the might of his sword, and his previous defeat, referred to in the Nausari inscription, was no proof of feudatory rank. It might as well be said that by

[1] See *J. B. O. R. S.*, 1923, p. 319 f., to which I owe some suggestions.

[2] Such diplomatic marriages after a trial of strength were not unknown in ancient India. For instance, we are told that Seleukos Nikator ratified the peace with Candragupta Maurya by a "matrimonial alliance," although the expression used does not justify the current assumption that Seleukos "gave his daughter in marriage" to his Indian rival (see also Smith's *Aśoka*, 3rd ed., p. 15 and note).

his failure against Pulakeśi, Harṣa was compelled to recognise the southern monarch as his suzerain and overlord. But how utterly wide the mark such a statement would be.

The fact that Dhruvabhaṭa attended the religious assembly at Prayāga does not prove anything about his status. He went there as Harṣa's son-in-law, and as an independent prince like Bhāskaravarman. There was no "element of political obligation" in his attendance. Moreover, Dhruvabhaṭa himself used to hold such gatherings in his realm, and this circumstance must have also prompted him to witness the proceedings of a grander assembly. The *Life* says: "He is faithfully attached to the three treasures, and every year he assembles a great gathering and for seven days he entertains priests from all countries and bestows on them food of the best description, choice jewels, bedding and clothes, with varieties of medicaments and other things of different kinds."[1] Lastly, in the same connection the *Life* gives Dhruvabhaṭa the significant title of "King of South India,"[2] which speaks for itself and needs no comment. Thus, the available evidence does not justify the current assumption that Valabhi was a feudatory state of Kanauj.

L. *Ku-che-lo*, or the Gurjara kingdom: "The king, who was a Kṣatriya by birth, was a young man, celebrated for his wisdom and valour, and he was a profound believer in Buddhism, and a patron of exceptional abilities."[3]

LI. *Wu-she-yen-na* or Ujjain: We are told that "the king was of the Brahman caste; he was well-learned in the heterodox lore, but he was not a Buddhist."[4]

[1] *Life*, pp. 149-150.
[2] *Ibid.*, p. 185.
[3] Watters, II, p. 249; Beal, II, p. 270.
[4] Watters, II, p. 250; Beal, II, p. 271.

LII. *Chih-chi-to*: identified with the kingdom of Jajhoti, the capital of which was Khajuraho, which corresponds with the modern region of Bundelkhand. As regards its government, the pilgrim informs us: "The king, who was a Brahman, was a firm believer in Buddhism, and encouraged men of merit, and learned scholars of other lands collected here in numbers."[1]

LIII. *Mo-hi-ssu-fa-lo-pu-lo* or Maheśvarapura: corresponding with the region round about Gwalior between the Cambal and the Sindhu rivers.[2] Yuan Chwang says: "The king was a Brahman, and was not a believer in Buddhism."[3]

LIV. *Sin-tu*: Sindh was under a vigorous government, and it had then at least three dependencies, viz. (*a*) *Atien-po-chih-lo* or Atyanabakela: "The country had latterly been without a sovereign and was under Sindh."[4] (*b*) *Pi-to-shih-lo*, identified by Cunningham with Haidarabad or Nirankot, and by General Haig with the Thar and Parker district of West India. "It had no government of its own, and was subject to Sindh."[5] (*c*) *A-fan-tu*, identical with Brahmanabad or the Khairpur territory. "It had no sovereign and was under Sindh."[6]

Bāṇa, on the other hand, would have us believe that Harṣa pounded a king of Sindh, and appropriated the *Rājalakṣmī* or fortune of that monarch.[7] Probably

[1] Watters, II, p. 251; Beal, II, p. 271.

[2] See Map of India at the end of Watters, Vol. II. According to Cunningham it was identical with Māhiṣmatīpura or Māndhāta on the upper Narbada (*Anc. Geo. of India.* pp. 559-60).

[3] Watters, II, p. 251; Beal, II, p. 271.

[4] Watters, II, p. 256; Beal, II, p. 276. Watters restores the name of the capital as Kaccheśvara.

[5] Watters, II, p. 258; Beal, II, p. 279.

[6] *Ibid.*, p. 259; *Ibid.*, p. 280.

[7] Compare *Harṣacarita* 'Atra puruṣottamena Sindhurājaṁ pramathya Lakṣmīḥātmī-kritā.

what happened was that sometime during his reign Harṣa came into collision with the king of Sindh, and it resulted in the defeat of the latter. But the victory was no more than a brilliant conclusion of hostilities, as in the case of Pulakeśi II, for we know definitely on the authority of Yuan Chwang that Sindh continued to be ruled by a king of the Śūdra caste, who was a sincere believer in Buddhism.[1]

Conclusion

We have now finished our critical survey of Yuan Chwang's description of contemporary kingdoms, along with the evidence of other relevant authorities, in regard to their government and the nature of their political status. There are indeed some very striking features in the narrative of the pilgrim. It is to be noticed that he is very careful to mention the governments of the countries he visited, and to name the dependencies of certain kingdoms, like Kapiśa, Kashmir, Mālava and Sindh. In case of certain countries he even notes the transfer of allegiance, as we learn about Taxilla that it "had been formerly subject to Kapiśa, but now it was a dependency of Kashmir."[2] About *Lang-kie* (*ka*)-*lo* he observes: "It had no supreme government, each valley having a separate government of its own, but it was subject to Persia."[3] Again, in the case of *A-tien-po-chih-lo* the pilgrim notes: "The country had latterly been without a sovereign and was under Sindh."[4]

[1] Watters, II, p. 252; Beal, II, p. 272. The Buddhist king of the Śūdra caste at the time of Yuan Chwang must have been Sihas-rai, son of Divājī, who was succeeded by his son Sāhasī. This dynasty seems to have preceded the one founded by the Brahman Cach according to the *Cachnāmā*.

[2] Watters, I, p. 240; Beal, I, p. 136.

[3] Watters, II, p. 257; Beal, II, p. 277.

[4] Watters, II, p. 256; Beal, II, p. 276.

Similarly, as regards Lampa or *Lan-po* he says: "For several centuries the native dynasty had ceased to exist, great families fought for pre-eminence, and the state had recently become a dependency of Kapiśa;"[1] but he does not, strange to say, name one kingdom or territory as being subject to Kanauj, although he generally calls its king "lord of the Five Indias," and one who had "conquered all the nations from east to west, and carried his arms to the remote districts."[2] Thus, if we take Yuan Chwang's account too literally we shall have to say with Dr. R. C. Majumdar that "so far at least as these accounts are concerned, Harṣavardhana was merely king of Kanauj."[3]

But such a conclusion would indeed be entirely wide the mark as Yuan Chwang himself credits Harṣa with extensive conquests and protracted military campaigns. The *Life* also describes him as a powerful monarch attended by numerous feudatories during the assemblies at Kanauj and Prayāga. Hence, however difficult it might be to determine the exact limits of the kingdom during his time, it is clear that by his military skill Harṣa enlarged them, thus winning for himself a high reputation for valour, to which the pilgrim bears eloquent testimony. Is it then to be assumed that the territories in Northern India, about the governments of which Yuan Chwang maintains silence, were included within Kanauj? Probably he thought that Harṣa's dominions were too well-known to need any explicit mention, and relying on this assumption we may well suppose that the following parts were under his authority :—

[1] Watters, I, p. 181; Beal, I, p. 90.
[2] Beal, II, pp. 256-7; *Life*, p. 83.
[3] *J. B. O. R. S.*, 1923, p. 318.

Ku-lu-to or Kullu.
She-to-t'u-lu or Śatadru country, i.e., modern Sirhind.
Sa-ta-ni-ssu-fa-lo or Sthānvīśvara (Thanesvar).
Su-lu-kin-na or Srughna (Sugh).
Po-lo-hih-mo-pu-lo or Brahmapura.
Ku-pi-sang-na or Govisāna (modern districts of Kashipur, Rampur and Pilibhit).
Ngo-hi-chi-ta-lo or Ahicchatra (eastern part of Rohilkhand).
Pi-lo-shan-na or Atranjikhera.
Kah-pi-t'a (Kapittha) or Sankāsya, i.e., modern Sankissa.
A-yu-te or Ayodhyā.
A-ye-mu-k'a (Hayamukha) i.e, Daundiakhera.
Po-lo-ya-ka or Prayāga.
Kiao-shang-mi or Kosambi.
Pi-sho-ka or Viśoka (?)
Shi-lo-fa-si-tu or Srāvasti.
Lan-mo (Rāma) or Rāmagrāma.
Kou-shih-na-ka-lo or Kuśinagara.
Po-lo-na-se or Vārāṇasī.
Chan-chu country or Ghazipur district (?).
Fei-she-li or Vaisali.
Fu-li-chih or the Vriji county.
Mo-kie-t'o or Magadha.
I-lan-na-po-fa-to or Monghyr.
Chan-po (Campa) i.e., Bhagalpur.
Ku-chu-wen (Kajangala) i.e., Rajmahal.
Pun-na-fa-tan-na or Pauṇḍravardhana.
San-mo-ta-ch'a or Samataṭa.
Tan-mo-lih-ti or Tāmralipti.
Kie-lo-na-su-fa-la-na or Karṇasuvarṇa.
Wu-tu (Odra) or Orissa.
Kung-yu-to (Kongodha) i.e., modern Ganjam.

That some of these portions were actually within the empire of Harṣa can be proved by means of independent evidence. We have already discussed above that his ancestral kingdom comprised Sthānvīśvara (Thanesvar), the valley of the Saraswati river and parts of eastern Rajputana. The findspots of the Banskhera,[1] and Madhuban plates,[2] recording grants of land, show that Ahicchatra and Śrāvastī formed *bhuktis* or divisions of his empire. If the Śīlāditya coins found in the Bhitaura hoard (Fyzabad district) are to be attributed to Harṣa, as has been done by Sir Richard Burn,[3] we have then direct proof that Ayodhyā was under Harṣa. Likewise, Prayāga was certainly included, since it was the scene of his great charitable distribution. We may also add that Harṣa's title "King of Magadha," found in the Chinese documents connected with his embassy, un-

[1] *Ep. Ind.*, IV, pp. 208-11.

[2] *Ibid.*, I, pp. 71-74.

[3] *J. R. A. S.*, 1906, pp. 843-50. See also Dr. R. K. Mookerji's *Harṣa*, pp. 116-17 for this ascription. Dr. Hoernle, however, doubts this attribution, although the views of Sir Richard Burn were evidently known to him (*J. R. A. S.*, 1909, pp. 446-48). He bases his opposition on the following grounds :

(*a*) Śīlāditya was not the official title of Harṣa, as both the inscriptions and Bāṇa are unaware of it. He thinks that Harṣa was known by this title among Buddhist monks only, from whom Yuan Chwang adopted it.

(*b*) The *Rājataraṅgiṇī* (Vol. I, Bk. III, verse 330, Stein's Trans., p. 98) knows of another Pratāpaśīla, surnamed Śīlāditya. Speaking of Pravarasena it says that "he replaced Pratāpaśīla, also called Śīlāditya, the son of Vikramāditya, who had been dethroned by enemies, in the kingdom of his father." This Vikramāditya is identified with Yaśodharman of Malwa, who is credited in the Mandasor inscription (*C. I. I.*, III, No. 33, pp. 145, 148) with extensive conquests as far as the Himalayas; and Śīlāditya with his son of the same name (See *J. R. A. S.*, 1903, pp. 545 f.).

mistakably points to the same conclusion. Again, the fact that Śilāditya held his court at Kajangala in his progress to East India is conclusive proof, as has been shown above, that his empire extended so far. We further know that Harṣa was carrying on military operations in Kongodha as late as the year 643 A. D. Lastly, regarding Orissa it is clear from the *Life*[1] that he exercised his authority there.

Negatively, the Chinese pilgrim indicates what states lay beyond the pale of Harṣa's jurisdiction by mentioning the ruling sovereigns of each. These were:—

Kia-pi-shi or Kapiśa;
Kia-shi-mi-lo or Kashmir;
She-lan-ta-lo or Jālandhara;
Po-li-ye-ta-lo or Bairāt;
Mo-tu-lo or Mathurā;
Mo-ti-pu-lo (Matipura);
Su-fa-la-na-kiu-ta-lo or the Suvarṇagotra country;
Kie-pi-lo-fa-su-tu or Kapilāvastu;
Ni-po-lo or Nepal;
Ka-mo-lu-po or Kāmarūpa;
Mo-ha-la-ch'a or Mahārāṣṭra;
Po-lu-ka-cha-po (Bhrigukacchapa) or Broach;
Fa-la-pi or Valabhī;
Ku-che-lo or Gurjara country;
Wu-she-yen-na or Ujjain;
Chih-chi-to (Jajhoti) or Bundelkhand;
Mo-hi-ssu-fa-lo-pu-lo or Māheśvarapura;
Sin-tu or Sindh.

We may, therefore, on the strength of Yuan Chwang's testimony and other epigraphic and literary evidences, roughly define the Kanauj kingdom of Harṣa in modern geographical terminology as consisting of portions of Eastern Panjab, almost the whole of the

[1] *Life*, p. 154; see *Supra*.

present United Provinces (excepting Mathura and Matipura), Bihar, Bengal and Orissa including Kongodha or the Ganjam region.

That this was the view of Yuan Chwang is further evident from the fact that all the places mentioned in connection with Harṣa's tours of inspection lie eastward;[1] and moreover he calls Harṣa "lord of the five Indias," which has been explained as comprising Svarāṣṭra or the Panjab (i.e., eastern parts of the Panjab in this case), Kānyakubja, Mithila or Bihar, Gauḍa or Bengal, and Utkala or Orissa.[2]

Thus the whole evidence harmonises remarkably well, and it is high time to give up all exaggerated notions of Harṣa's sovereignty or political jurisdiction extending up to Kashmir and Sindh, Gujrat and even the far South, Kāmarūpa (Assam) and Nepal. Such a view is flagrantly opposed to the unimpeachable contemporary testimony of Yuan Chwang. Besides, there is nothing in the inscriptions or literature to support it. These territories themselves were of sufficiently imposing dimensions, being much larger than any other individual state in Northern India; and this was the reason why the power and majesty of Harṣa made such a deep impression upon the illustrious Master of the Law.[3]

[1] See *Infra.*

[2] Havell, *Aryan Rule in India*, p. 191, note 1; D. C. Sen, *History of Bengali Language and literature*, p. 385; Smith, *Early History of India*, 4th ed., p. 353.

[3] Before concluding we must note the phenomenon of small kingdoms like Matipura, Maheśvarapura, and Jejākabhukti etc., almost adjacent to Kanauj. Several explanations may be postulated for this circumstance.

(*a*) These states in order to save themselves from being swept away by the war-frenzy of Harṣa must have offered their alliance at the very beginning. And Harṣa, who stood in dire need of allies then, astutely tolerated their continued existence. We may cite Jalandhara here as an

Note A

An objection

A possible objection to our view may be raised in the title "Sakalottarāpathanātha," given to Harṣa in the southern inscriptions. This has been interpreted as implying that Harṣa "achieved the proud position of being the paramount sovereign of the whole of Northern India."[1] But there are grounds for supposing that the epithet does not bear any geographical significance. There is mention of another "Sakalottarāpathanātha" in the inscriptions of Cālukya Vinayāditya,[2] and the sug-

instance. The *Life* informs us that Harṣa charged its king, Wu-ti, to escort Yuan Chwang in safety to the frontiers, whereas from the *Records* we learn that a former ruler of Jalandhara was on terms of close friendship with the king of "Mid-India" (See *ante*).

(*b*) The kings of these territories may have been conquered and subsequently reinstated by Harṣa, having accepted his nominal suzerainty. Similarly, we are told in the Allahabad pillar inscription (*C. I. I.*, III, No. I, p. 14) that Samudragupta "established (again) many royal families, fallen and deprived of sovereignty."

(*c*) The existence of certain kingdoms on the southern route at the time of Yuan Chwang is also in no way incompatible with Harṣa's southern campaigns. They must have given a passage to the latter's forces through their territories to escape incurring his wrath. Or, if they had submitted to his yoke previously, they may have taken advantage of Harṣa's discomfiture when warring against Pulakeśi II. Yuan Chwang visited these parts after this event, and it is certain from his description that these territories were then under their native rulers.

[1] *Harṣa*, p. 43.

[2] Compare for example : "Vinayāditya Satyāśraya had acquired the insignia of supreme dominion by crushing the lord of all the region of the North" (Sakal-ottarā-patha-nātha-mathanopārjjita)—*Ind. Ant.*, IX, p. 129; *Ibid.*, VII, pp. 107,111.

gested identification is that in all probability he was one of the successors of Mahārājādhirāja Ādityasena in the Later Gupta line of Magadha. In this case, however, it is known beyond doubt that his dominions did not comprise the whole of Northern India. It is thus evident that the expression "Sakalottarāpathanātha" was used in a vague and loose way, and did not necessarily connote the whole of the region extending from the Himalayas to the Vindhya ranges.

Note B

Harṣa and the Far South

In connection with the topic of the extent of the Kanauj kingdom, we may also take notice of the following lines in praise of Harṣa, attributed to Mayūra, who is reputed to have been the father-in-law of Bāṇa :

"Bhūpālāḥ Śaśibhāskarānvayabhuvaḥ ke nāma nāsāditaḥ,
Bhartāraṁ punar ekaṁ eva hi bhuvas tvāṁ deva manyāmahe,
Yenāṅgaṁ parimṛṣya Kuntalaṁ athākṛṣya vyudasyāyataṁ,
Colaṁ prāpya ca Madhyadeśaṁ adhunā Kāñcyāṁ karaḥ pātitaḥ."[1]

It is thought that reference is here made to the southern conquests of Harṣa as far as Kuntala, Coḷa, and Kāñcī.

Support for this view is further found in the Gaddemane inscription, in which we come across the following passage in characters of the 7th century :

[1] Vallabhadeva's *Subhāṣitāvali*, ed, Peterson, (Bombay, 1886), stanza 2515, p. 429; *J. R. A. S.*, 1926, p. 487; *Ind. Hist. Quart.*, Dec., 1927, p.788.

"Svasti Śrī Śila-ādityan diśāṁ-bharggan ākevaḷan aggaḷakaṇtakan,
Péraḷke vare Pettaṇi Satyāṅkan aṭṭuḷabhataṁ bedare Mahendran,
Beḍara rāyara Malappara Kalegaduḷe vividu svarggālaya
Kkeridan beḷeya maḷa kādon kalyānaṁ akke aḷivon pañc-ma."

It mentions the death of one Peṭṭani Satyāṅka, while engaged in a fight against some Beḍa chiefs, when Śīlāditya invaded the south, and Mahendra took to flight. It is supposed that the name Śīlāditya refers to Harṣa of Kanauj, and Mahendra to his Pallava contemporary Mahendravarman I.[1]

The theory of Harṣa's invasion of the south does not, however, seem to rest on solid foundations. Firstly, the identification of Śīlāditya with Harṣa is far from certain. Dr. R. C. Majumdar identifies him with Yuvarāja Sryāśraya Śīlāditya, who lived in the second half of the 7th century A. D., and Mahendra with Mahendravarman II, on the ground that there was "constant hostility between the Cālukyas and the Pallavas" about this period.[2] Secondly, it does not seem probable that Harṣa could play the rôle of a second Samudragupta, or that his victorious arms could penetrate so far south, when at the very frontiers of the Deccan he had to bear the humiliation of an ignominious defeat at the hands of Pulakeśi II, who also claims to have won a victory against the Pallava king. Thirdly, the passage of Mayūra has hardly any air of reality and appears as "praise in the conventional exaggerated style of a

[1] *Ann. Rep. Mysore Arch. Dept.*, 1923, p. 83; *Ind. Hist. Quart.* Dec., 1927, pp. 788-89.

[2] *Ind. Hist. Quart.*, V, 1929, p. 235.

poet, given to punning, and without any reference to historical accuracy."

Note C

The Harṣa era

The findspots of the inscriptions supposed to be dated in the Harṣa era also do not militate against the view set forth above. These records may be classified as follows:

(*a*) Two inscriptions of Harṣa himself, Nos. 528 and 529.[1]

(*b*) An inscription of Ādityasena of Magadha, No. 535.

(*c*) Four miscellaneous inscriptions, Nos. 543, 545 to 547.

(*d*) Ahar stone inscription[2] and Pāṇḍava-kā-kilā fragmentary stone inscription.[3] The two inscriptions of Harṣa come from Banskhera and Madhuban in the Shahjahanpur and Azamgarh districts of the present United Provinces respectively. The inscription of Ādityasena was discovered in Shahpur in the

[1] The numbers refer to Kielhorn's list (*Ep. Ind.*, V, Appendix, pp. 73-75). We have omitted here the two Pratīhāra inscriptions Nos. 542 and 544, which have been successfully demonstrated by Dr. D. R. Bhandarkar to be dated in the Vikrama era (*J. B. B. R. A. S.*, XXI, pp. 405f); also the eleven Nepalese inscriptions Nos. 530-534 and 536-541, which are dated in some local era, as discussed elsewhere. It is to be observed that Dr. Kielhorn also doubted this ascription, and he put a query mark against each of them (*Ep. Ind.*, V, Appendix, pp. 73-74). See also Dr. R. C. Majumdar, *J. B. O. R. S.*, 1923, pp. 322-23, on this point.

[2] *Ep. Ind.*, XIX, pp. 52-62.

[3] *Rajputana Museum Report*, 1924, p. 3.

district of Patna. Those of the third category have been found in different localities. One comes from Nirmand in the Sutlej district; one from Khajuraho, not far from the borders of modern United Provinces; the third from Pehoa in the Karnal district; and the last from Panjaur in Thanesvar. Lastly, Ahar is in the Bulandshahr district, U. P., and Pāṇḍava-kā-kilā is in Delhi. Thus excluding the records of Harṣa there are only seven which are said to use the Harṣa era, although none of them refers to the era as such; and it is remarkable that all of them come from places that were within the limits of the Kanauj kingdom at this time. Hence even if it be held that an era could be employed in those territories only, which were once within the jurisdiction of its originator, the evidence of the findspots of these inscriptions is fully in accord with our conclusions.[1]

Note D

Chronology of Harṣa's Campaigns

There is a remark of Yuan Chwang that "Harṣa waged incessant warfare until in six years he had brought the Five Indias under allegiance,"[2] which has unfortunately been the source of some error in history. Relying on it Dr. R. K. Mookerji states that "we may assume that all his (Harṣa's) conquests were over by about

[1] Alberuni, too, notes that the Harṣa era was used in his time in "Mathura and the country of Kanauj" (Sachau, Eng. Trans., II, p. 5).

[2] Watters, I, p. 343; Beal, I, p. 213.

A. D. 612, and that he had become king six years earlier (the period of his conquests) in A. D. 606."[1] He adds further : "it is thus reasonable to conclude... that Harṣa's wars with Valabhi and Pulakeśi took place within A. D. 612." This assumption, however, seems gratuitous and open to several objections. First, it is quite needless and baseless to suppose that Yuan Chwang's "six years" began in A. D. 606, the year of Harṣa's accession, and ended in A. D. 612. Secondly, it would involve a discrepancy since the term "Five Indias," as explained above, implies sovereignty over Gauḍa and Orissa also, but we have on the other hand positive evidence in the Ganjam inscription that his inveterate enemy Śaśāṅka was flourishing in these regions as late as the year 619 A. D. Thirdly, we know that Pulakeśi II came to the throne about the year 609-10 A. D., and it would indeed be almost a miracle if at the very start of his career and with his position still unconsolidated at home, the Cālukya monarch inflicted a crushing defeat on Harṣa, who already had—as alleged—become "lord of the Five Indias."

The learned Professor cites the authority of Dr. Fleet who was of opinion that the Haidarabad grant, dated in the third year of Pulakeśi's *Rājyābhiṣeka* or installation in the sovereignty in the Śaka *saṁvat* 534 expired or 612 A. D., implied "by the title which Pulakeśi acquired by his victory over him (Harṣa), that that victory had then already been achieved."[2] Now, what does the Haidarabad grant testify? It informs us that Pulakeśi II acquired the title of Parameśvara "by defeating hostile kings, who had applied themselves (or a hostile king who had applied himself) to

[1] *Harṣa*, p. 36, Note I; see also C. V. Vaidya, *H. M. H. I.*, I, p. 13.

[2] Fleet, *Dynasties of the Kanarese Districts*, pp. 351, 356.

the contest of a hundred battles."[1] Since the subsequent records state more specifically that he acquired it "by defeating the glorious Harṣavardhana, the warlike lord of all region of the North," it is with some plausibility argued that the conflict, which according to the Haidarabad grant won this title for Pulakeśi, was against Harṣa himself, and that it occurred about A. D. 612, the date of the epigraph. If this, however, were a fact, would it not be inexplicable why Harṣavardhana's name is not mentioned in the earlier Haidarabad grant, and finds specific mention—with legitimate pride too—in the Aihole inscription of A. D. 634-35, and other later documents. In my opinion this omission goes against Dr. Fleet's theory, for it appears hard to believe that any of Pulakeśi's earlier inscriptions would ignore the name of so great and formidable an adversary, and particularly when the victory was achieved just at the start of the Cālukya monarch's career.

The title Parameśvara was very commonly assumed by kings in those days after gaining the paramount or the imperial status. It was; for instance, adopted by Sarvavarman and Avantivarman Maukhari,[2] Dharasena of Valabhi,[3] and a host of other rulers. Presumably Pulakeśi II at first assumed it as a regal title only after certain preliminary successes against his rivals and the consolidation of his power at Badami. But when he subsequently scored a brilliant triumph over Harṣa he felt special pride in its possession, and thenceforth it became a sort of a secondary name or a substitute for a name to him (aparanāmadheyaḥ).

At this point we must also explain the other statement of Yuan Chwang that Harṣa "reigned in peace

[1] *Ibid.*
[2] Deo-Baranark inscription, *C. I. I.*, III, pp. 214-18.
[3] *Ibid.*, Introduction, p. 41; *J. B. B. R. A. S.*, X, p. 79.

for thirty years without raising a weapon."[1] This is how Watters has translated the passage, but the text does not appear to be quite clear, as Beal renders it thus : "*After* thirty years his arms reposed, and he governed everywhere in peace."[2] If Beal's interpretation were accepted, it would convey the sense that Harṣa carried on warfare for thirty years, after which his authority was established and he reigned in peace. If Watters' rendering be correct, how are we to reconcile this statement of Yuan Chwang with his other information that Harṣa had made an attack on the Kongoda (Ganjam) region as late as A. D. 643? I, therefore, venture to throw out a suggestion. The Chinese pilgrim probably meant that at the time of his visit Harṣa's reign had been peaceful internally, and the home-provinces had enjoyed the blessings of orderly government for thirty years. We know that when Harṣa was called upon to occupy the throne, both the kingdoms of Thanesvar and Kanauj were passing through an acute crisis. Prabhākara and Rājyavardhana had died within a short space of time, and there were perhaps some fears of a recrudescence of the Hūṇa danger. The Maukhari dominions had also suffered serious losses and reverses owing to the combined attack of Devagupta of Malwa and Śaśāṅka of Gauḍa. Kanauj itself had fallen and the political conflagration threatened even to consume his ancestral kingdom. Harṣa, however, instead of losing nerve at that juncture acted promptly and decisively, and by his energy and military courage succeeded in overawing Śaśāṅka and recovering the lost ground. Soon the storm subsided and Harṣa established internal security and stability of government within a comparatively short period. It was

[1] Watters, I, p. 343.
[2] Beal, I, p. 213.

to this protracted quiet in the kingdom that Yuan Chwang makes pointed reference, since we also know on his authority that rebellions and internal upheavals were not of rare occurrence in those days.[1] But the success of his internal government did not mean any peace to him in his foreign relations. He was frankly imperialistic in his outlook, and the Kongoda campaign in 643 A. D. proves beyond doubt that he had to undertake military expeditions intermittently almost till the close of his momentous reign. It is difficult to determine with certitude how long he took to annex Orissa and Bengal, but from the fact that Śaśāṅka was in power till A. D. 619, it seems reasonable to conclude that the event must have occurred after that date—say, sometime between 620 A. D. and 625 A. D., the exact year of Śaśāṅka's death being unknown.[2]

Regarding the date of Harṣa's conflict with the mighty southern monarch, we stand on no less uncertain ground. It must have, however, happened before 634-35 A.D., the date of the Aihole inscription in which the great clash finds unmistakable mention.[3] Yuan Chwang's statement that the engagement took place when Harṣa

[1] Watters, I, p. 170. Cf. "Rebellion and regicide have occasionally arisen."

[2] Cf. also Ma-twan-lin, the Chinese encyclopædist; "In the years 618 and 627 there were great troubles in the kingdom. The king Śilāditya made war and fought such battles as had never been before" (*J. R. A. S.*, N. S. IV, (1869-70), p. 86; see also *J. A. S. B.*, VI, p. 68).

[3] Curiously enough, Prof. Jouveau Dubreuil does not detect any allusion to the repulse of Harṣa by Pulakeśi II in the Aihole inscription. He says, "It is noteworthy that the Aihole inscription, which bears the date 634 A. D., makes no mention of king Harṣavardhana" (*Anc. Hist. of the Deccan*, Eng. Trans., p. 113; see also K. M. Panikkar, *Śrī Harṣa of Kanauj*, p. 23). But this view is clearly erroneous (see Kielhorn, *Ep. Ind.*, VI, p. 6, verse 23, line 11).

was invading remote countries further shows that it was probably after his eastern campaigns and conquests. Thus the earliest and the latest limits may be fixed between 625-634 A. D., and we may, therefore, take in round numbers the year 630 A. D. as the date of the event.[1]

[1] See also Dr. A. S. Altekar, *Ann. Bhand. Res. Inst.*, XIII (1932), pp. 300-06. Dr. Vincent Smith, however, conjectures 620 A. D. to be the approximate date for the fight (*Early Hist. of India*, 4th ed., p. 353; see also C. V. Vaidya, *H. M. H. I.*, I, p. 13). On the strength of the supposed omission in the Aihole inscription, Prof. Jouveau Dubreuil wrongly assigns the date 637-38 for this event (*Anc. Hist. of the Deccan*, Eng. Trans., p. 113).

PART II

CHAPTER VI

Glimpses of Harṣa's Government

It is evident from the foregoing account that the Kanauj kingdom under Harṣa mostly extended towards the east, and it was probably natural too that he should aspire to control the territories lying on this side, since the southern routes were already blocked by the mighty arms of Pulakeśi II. In those early times the Ganges was the highway of traffic linking up all the country from Bengal to "Mid India", and it was therefore necessary for the commerce and prosperity of the kingdom that Kanauj should be supreme over this vast Gangetic region. Indeed, the tendency of its kings to conquer Magadha and even the territories beyond it is noticeable throughout the course of its chequered history. Harṣa succeeded in bringing nearly the whole of the Gangetic plain under his yoke, and the kingdom having thus developed into gigantic proportions the task of its successful governance became all the more complicated and difficult. It was an age of mutually repellent and warring states engaged in petty internecine jealousies, and hence statesmanship and military skill of a high order were called forth to hold the empire together, and ensure its peaceful and orderly progress.

Military Strength

The first thing that Harṣa did was to increase his military strength, both to keep the unsubdued kingdoms overawed and to fortify his own position against internal upheavals and foreign aggressions. Yuan Chwang informs us : "Then having enlarged his territory he increased his army bringing the elephant corps upto 60,000 and the cavalry to 100,000."[1] It was thus on this large and strong force that the empire ultimately rested.[2] These high figures might at first appear incredible, but there are grounds for supposing that the maintenance of an unwieldy force was quite usual with an ambitious Indian potentate. The force at the command of Mahāpadma Nanda is said to have numbered 80,000 horse; 200,000 foot; 8,000 chariots and 6,000 fighting elephants. This huge force was greatly augmented by Candragupta Maurya, who raised the numbers of the infantry to 600,000 and also had 30,000 horse, and 9,000 elephants, besides chariots.[3] In the 16th century (1509-30 A. D.) Kriṣṇa-deva, the Rājā of Vijayanagar, led against Raicur an army consisting of 703,000 foot, 32,600 horse, and 531 elephants, besides camp followers.[4] Thus, as compared with these huge numbers Harṣa's army was small, and it speaks much for the effectiveness of his government.

[1] Watters, I, p. 343 ; Beal, I, p. 213. Bāṇa says that horses were recruited "from Vanāyu, Āraṭṭa, Kamboja, Bharadvāja, Sindh and Persia" (*Hc. C. T.*, p. 50). It is significant that both Bāṇa and Yuan Chwang omit to make any mention of chariots in Harṣa's army, although the latter authority speaks of the four traditional elements of the army in his general description (Watters, I, p. 171). At one place Bāṇa refers to "troops of camels" also (*Hc. C. T.*, p. 46).

[2] We are told that "the military guard the frontiers, or go out to punish the refractory. They also mount guard at night round the palace" (Beal, I, p. 87).

[3] *Early Hist. of India*, 4th ed., p. 132.

[4] Sewell, *A Forgotten Empire*, p. 147. Compare also the remark of Sewell : "I can only call attention to the fact that large armies seem to have always been the rule in India."

Alliances

But the army is merely an arm of policy. Harṣa secured and strengthened his position by other means as well. He concluded an "undying alliance" with the king of Assam at the very beginning, which gave Harṣa the help and co-operation of a powerful ruler both in his external and internal affairs. In ancient India, as in mediæval Europe, royal marriages played a very important part in the politics of the country. Harṣa, therefore, cemented his alliance with Valabhi after the termination of hostilities by giving the hand of his daughter to its king. Thereby he not only gained a valued ally, but it must have also meant the opening of the southern routes for him. Further, he maintained diplomatic intercourse with the Chinese empire. A Brahman envoy, whom he had sent to the Tang Emperor of China, Tai-Tsung, in 641 A. D. returned in 643 A. D., accompanied by a Chinese mission bearing a reply to Harṣa's dispatch.[1] His diplomatic relations with China were probably meant as a counterpoise to the friendship that Pulakeśi II, his southern rival, cultivated with the king of Persia about which we are informed by the Arab historian Tabari.[2]

Harṣa's exertions

In an oriental despotism the sovereign being the centre of the state much of the success in administration necessarily depends on his benevolent example. He must needs pay laborious attention to details in order to infuse life into the governmental machinery, and to check the corruption and laxity of officers placed in authority over distant areas. With this end in view Harṣa appears to have essayed the difficult task of supervising personally

[1] *Early Hist. of India*, 4th ed., p. 366.
[2] *J. R. A. S.*, N. S., XI (1879), pp. 165-66.

the affairs of his wide dominions. Yuan Chwang informs us that "the king's day was divided into three periods, of which one was given up to affairs of government, and two were devoted to religious works. He was indefatigable and the day was too short for him."[1] But in spite of this overwork Harṣa was not content to rule from the luxurious surroundings of the palace only. He freely went in the midst of the populace, albeit to make the imperial decrees more effective. "If there was any irregularity," observes the pilgrim, "in the manners of the people of the cities, he went amongst them."[2] Except during the rainy season when it was not possible to keep on moving with a huge retinue, camping out being also prohibited by the Buddhist rule at this time of the year, Harṣa insisted on going about from place to place to "punish the evil doers and reward the good." We are told by Yuan Chwang that "the king made visits of inspection throughout his dominions, not residing long at any place but having temporary buildings erected for his residence at each place of sojourn, and he did not go abroad during the three months of the rain-season retreat. At the royal lodges every day viands were provided for 1,000 Buddhist monks and 500 Brahmans."[3] During the course of these tours the subjects must have been afforded opportunities to ventilate their grievances to the king. At any rate Bāṇa informs us that during the course of his march against the Gauḍa king the country folk approached Harṣa, "bringing to light imaginary wrongs of former governors, lauding hundreds of past officials, reporting ancient misdeeds of knaves."[4] While

[1] Watters, I, p. 344; Beal, I, p. 215.
[2] *Ibid.*
[3] *Ibid.*
[4] *Hc. C. T.*, p. 208.

Harṣa halted in extremely unassuming constructions built of grass—which were burnt when leaving—[1] his progress was marked by pomp and circumstance. The *Life* records that as Śīlāditya marched, he was accompanied by several hundred persons with golden drums, who beat one stroke for every step taken, and this was called "music-pace-drums."[2] This method was reserved for Harṣa only, and no other king was permitted to adopt it. It would perhaps be interesting to note here some of the places where Harṣa appears to have camped. The *Life* tells us that when Yuan Chwang first met Harṣa, he was visiting different parts of the empire, and was camping as far distant from Kanauj as *Kie-shu-ho-ki-lo* (Kajughira or Kajangala) in Bengal[3]. The Banskhera and Madhuban plates issued from Vardhamānakoṭi and Kapitthika (Yuan Chwang's Kapitha or Sankasya) respectively give us two more camps. Among his other places of sojourn were Prayāga, Maṇitāra (Oudh) along the Ajirāvatī river[4], and Orissa[5]. Thus denying himself the comforts of the palace, Harṣa toured round his far-flung empire to promote the weal and well-being of the subjects, halting in simple structures of grass and boughs raised for the occasion, and known as "travelling palaces" or "pavilions of travel."[6]

[1] Watters, II, p. 183.

[2] *Life*, p. 173.

[3] *Ibid.*, p. 172; Watters, II, p. 183.

[4] *Hc. C. T.*, p. 46.

[5] The fact that all these places where Harṣa is known to have camped lie eastward or in the U. P. probably further tends to confirm our view about the limits of the Kanauj kingdom under Harṣa. To the other places in the south he went in the capacity of an unwelcome invader, and not as a ruler anxious to relieve the distress of his subjects.

[6] *Life*, p. 173.

Civil administration

Our authorities on Harṣa unfortunately yield us very meagre data for the then existing system of government. Probably Harṣa was assisted in the task of administration by an advisory council as favoured and advocated by ancient Indian political thinkers.[1] According to Yuan Chwang, Harṣa was invited to accept the crown of Kanauj by the statesmen and ministers of that kingdom, led by Poni; and it does not seem unreasonable to believe that they may have continued to wield some sort of control even during the palmy days of Harṣa's power. The pilgrim even goes so far as to assert that "a commission of officers held the land."[2]

Further, owing to the large extent of territory and the scanty and slow means of communication, it was necessary to establish strong centres of government in order to keep the loosely-knit parts of the empire together. The outlying provinces were, therefore, put in charge of governors, as we are informed by the following passage in the *Harṣacarita*: "Atra lokanāthena diśāṁ mukheṣu parikalpitāḥ lokapālāḥ," i.e., "he, the protector of all people, appointed protectors in the several directions."[3] They were sometimes also known

[1] See e.g., Kauṭilya's *Arthaśāstra*, Bk. I, ch. VII, p. 13 : "Sovereignty is possible only with assistance. A single wheel can never move. Hence, he shall employ ministers and hear their opinion."

[2] Beal, I, p. 210.

[3] *Harṣacarita* (Cal. ed.), p. 211. Compare also the Junagaḍh rock inscription of Skandagupta, which speaks of similar appointments : "Sarveṣu deśeṣu vidhāya goptṛīn," i.e., "having appointed protectors in all countries." (*C. I. I.*, III, No. 14, pp. 59, 62). It may, however, be remarked that the above passage in the *Harṣacarita* does not admit of an unambiguous interpretation. There is evidently a play on words, and Bāṇa also compares Harṣa with a great god, who appoints regents of the several quarters.

as Sāmantas and Mahāsāmantas. They maintained law and order in the distant parts of the empire, and must have been invested with considerable power. Probably Mādhavagupta was one such governor or local ruler. This assumption seems irresistible if the testimonies of the *Harṣacarita* and the Aphsad inscription are considered in conjunction. The former mentions Mādhavagupta, Prince of Malwa, as a youthful companion of Harṣa at the Thanesvar court; whereas from the latter it is evident that he was ruling over the Magadha region, and is further credited "with the desire to associate himself with the glorious Harṣadeva."[1] This political arrangement was perhaps made by Harṣa either to reward his services rendered during the initial crisis, or to make him a bulwark against the aggressions of Śaśāṅka, who was in power at least till 619 A.D. Or, it may be that by the appointment of a strong lieutenant in Magadha, Harṣa was only manœuvring to further his designs against Śaśāṅka's territories in Bengal and the coastal regions. Mādhavagupta's family, however, declared the independence of Magadha in the confusion following Harṣa's death, as we shall see later on.

"Since administration means many functions and not one, which are moreover not restricted to a single place," success in government must largely depend upon the efficient organisation of a Bureaucracy. We may, therefore, indicate some of the state-functionaries, civil and military, that are mentioned in the *Harṣacarita* and the inscriptions :—

I. *Mahāsandhivigrahādhikrita*, or the "supreme minister of peace and war," who also probably accompanied the king to the battlefield. Bāṇa mentions Avanti as the incumbent of this office.

[1] *C. I. I.*, III, No. 42, pp. 204, 207. Cf. "Śrī-Harṣadeva nija-saṁgama-vāñcchayā."

II. *Mahābalādhikrita*, or officer in supreme command of the army.

III. *Balādhikrita*, or commander.

IV. *Senāpati*, literally "lord or chief of the army," i.e., a general.[1] The *Harṣacarita* gives his name as Siṁhanāda.

V. *Brihadaśvavāra*, or the head-cavalry officer. He is called Kuntala in the *Harṣacarita*.

VI. *Kaṭuka*, or commandant of the elephant force. Bāṇa names him Skandagupta. Mr. Y. R. Gupte, on the other hand, says that *Kaṭukas* "apparently mean any persons (officers, members of a religious assembly not generally held in respect at the time, etc.) who are disagreeable to the public."[2]

VII. *Pātī (Pāṭhī)-pati*, or "superintendents of soldiers' barracks."

VIII. *Cāṭa-bhaṭa*, or irregular and regular soldiers.[3] Vogel, however, thinks that *Cāṭa* is equivalent to modern *Cār* or "head of a pargana responsible for the internal management of a district for the collection of revenue and the apprehension of criminals." According to the same scholar *bhaṭa*, which is usually compounded with *Cāṭa*, should be taken to mean "an official subordinate to the head of a pargana."[4]

IX. *Yāma-ceṭis* or *Yāmakinyaḥ* or "women-watchers of the night."

X. *Dūta*, i.e., Envoy or Ambassador. His duty was to promote and foster friendly relations between different states. For instance, we learn from the

[1] *C. I. I.*, III, p. 167.

[2] *Ep. Ind.*, XIII, p. 117, Note 9.

[3] Bühler, *Ind. Ant.*, (V), 1876, p. 115 Note; Fleet, *C. I. I.*, III, p. 98, Note 2.

[4] *Antiquities of the Camba State*, Part I, pp. 131-32. Indraji translates the term as "Cātān prati bhaṭaḥ," i.e., soldiers against robbers (*Ind. Ant.*, IX, p. 175, Note 41).

18

Harṣacarita that the king of Assam sent one Haṁsavega to conclude an "imperishable alliance" with Harṣa.

XI. *Rājasthānīya*, literally it denotes an officer who had to deal with other *Rājasthānas* or kingdoms, i.e., Foreign Secretary[1]. A better meaning would be a Viceroy or Governor, since in the Mandasor inscription (Fleet, *C. I. I.*, No. 35) the term "Rājasthāna" is used in the sense of a province. The explanation of the word in the *Lokaprakāśa* (iv), as given by Bühler, is : "Prajā pālanārthaṁ-udvahati rakṣayati ca sa rājasthānīyaḥ," i.e., "He, who carries out the object of protecting subjects and shelters them, is called a Rājasthānīya."[2] From this description it is clear that this office must have been an important one and invested with considerable authority. It is, however, curious that in the Maliya grant of Dharasena II (Fleet's No. 38) and in the Deo-Baranārk inscription (No. 42) the Rājasthānīya is mentioned rather low down in the list of officials.

XII. *Kumārāmātya*, literally a counsellor of the prince.[3] But it may also be explained as "*Kaumārād ārabhya amātyaḥ*," or "one who was in the service of the king from the time when he was a boy."[4] This office frequently occurs in Gupta records, and so some scholars interpret it as referring to the princes of the blood royal "who formed a council of the nobles, and who were consulted by the ruling chiefs on points of imperial importance."[5]

XIII. *Uparika*. This, along with Mahārāja, was

[1] Indraji, *Bom. Gaz.*, Vol. I, pt. I, p. 82.

[2] *Ind. Ant.*, V, p. 207. According to Dr. Stein, this officer was equivalent to a modern chief justice (*Rājat.*, Trans. Bk. VII, p. 316, Note).

[3] *C. I. I.*, III, p. 16, Note 7.

[4] Bloch, *Ep. Ind.*, X, p. 50, Note 2.

[5] *Ibid.*, XI, p. 176. Bühler translated it as "princes and ministers" (*Ind. Ant.*, IV, p. 175).

an official title of the Governor of a province;[1] hence its holder may be considered equivalent to a provincial governor. Probably the Emperor himself appointed this exalted functionary. At any rate, such was the case in the Gupta times, as is clear from the expression "tatpāda-parigrahīta."

XIV. *Viṣayapati*, i.e., the head of a Viṣaya corresponding roughly to a modern district. We do not know who appointed them during the reign of Harṣa, but some light with regard to their position may be thrown on the basis of the Gupta records. It appears from the Damodarapur copper plates that the Viṣayapatis were known as "tanniyuktakas," and were directly responsible to the provincial governors. They had their headquarters in Adhiṣṭhānas (towns), where their offices (adhikaraṇas) were located. These grants also reveal to us another interesting fact that these District officers were assisted in their administration (saṁvyavahāra) by a Board of four Advisers representing the principal local interests of those times, viz.,

(*a*) Nagara-Śreṣṭhin, who probably represented the upper ten of the urban population.

(*b*) Sārthavāha—the chief merchant, perhaps representing the trade-guilds.

(*c*) Prathama-Kulika—the chief artisan, who was the spokesman of the artisan classes.

(*d*) Prathama-Kāyastha—the chief scribe, probably a representative of the scribes as a class.

XV. *Mahattara*, literally meaning one high in rank, from which it presumably came to connote those who were the recognised headmen of the village.[2] They

[1] *Ep. Ind.*, XV, pp. 114, 127, etc.

[2] *Ep. Ind.*, XV, p. 136; *Ind. Ant.*, 1910, p. 213. The *Life* informs us that *Ta-kwan* or official guides also bore the designation *Mo-ho-ta-lo*, (see p. 189).

were prominent by either ability, age, experience, or wealth.

XVI. *Pramātri*, literally "a person fit to perceive or judge" from root *mā*; hence it may mean an officer entrusted with justice. Some scholars think it denoted an officer whose work was to make a survey of the land. Bühler, on the other hand, translates it as "spiritual councillor."[1]

XVII. *Daussādhanika*, literally one who undertook difficult tasks. If, however, this term is identical with "Daussādhika" or "Dauḥsādhasādhanika," we may with Dr. R. G. Basak render it as "porter or superintendent of villages."[2]

XVIII. *Bhogika or Bhogapati*, i.e., one responsible for the collection of the *bhoga* or the state share of the land produce taken in kind, as a rule one-sixth. Fleet, however, was of opinion that "in the inscriptions it is a technical official title, possibly connected with the territorial terms Bhoga and Bhukti."[3] Another scholar, Dr. R. G. Basak, explains the word by "groom."[4]

XIX. *Āynktaka*, literally meaning appointed. This term was probably applied to minor officials of the government. The word "āyukta" or "āyuktaka" occurs in Pāṇini's *Aṣṭādhyāyī* (II, 3, 40) where it denotes a person appointed to some small work of a special character. Dr. Thomas has also pointed out that in the *Arthaśāstra* "yukta" or "yuktaka" occurs in the sense of a minor official.[5] It may further be held that the Āyuktakas were identical with the "Āyuktapuruṣas" mentioned in the Allahabad pillar inscription of Samu-

[1] *Ep. Ind.*, I, p. 118, Note 56.
[2] *Ibid.*, XII, pp. 43, 141.
[3] *C. I. I.*, III, p. 100, Note 2.
[4] *Ep. Ind.* XII, p. 43; see also Monier-Williams' *Sanskrit Dictionary*.
[5] *J. R. A. S.*, 1909, p. 467.

dragupta (line 26).

XX. *Mahāpratihāra*, i.e., Chief warder or Usher. This officer invariably finds mention in records, which shows that he must have been an important figure in the states of ancient India. According to the *Harṣacarita*, Pāriyātra was Harṣa's "chief of the doorkeepers."

XXI. *Pratihāra* or Chamberlain.

XXII. *Mīmāṁsakas*, or justices. Or, were they interpreters of *Mīmāṁsā* or sacred philosophy?[1]

XXIII. *Dīrghādhvaga*, i.e., express couriers,[2] who "continually went and returned."[3] They used to deliver messages pretty quickly, as for instance, we learn from the *Life* that a messenger sent by Kumārarāja of Kāmarūpa (Assam) was able to present a letter to Śīlabhadra at Nalanda after two days only.[4]

XXIV. *Lekhahāraka*, or letter-carrier. This term is also found in the *Harṣacarita*,[5] but we do not know with certainty whether it was synonymous with *Dīrghādhvaga* or denoted a separate class of couriers.

XXV. *Sarvagatāḥ*,[6] literally denoting going everywhere. They were probably officers of the secret service.

XXVI. *Grāmākṣapaṭalika*, or the village notary. It may be noted that it was the village notary who presented to Harṣa "a new-made golden seal with a bull for its emblem" on the occasion of his first halt.[7]

XXVII. *Akṣapaṭalika*, or keeper of records. Yuan Chwang also mentions that there are separate custodians for the archives and records. "The official annals and

[1] *Ep. Ind.*, XIV, p. 325.
[2] *Hc.*, ed. by Führer (Bombay, 1909), p. 223; *Hc. C. T.*, p. 145.
[3] Beal, I, p. 215.
[4] *Life*, p. 169.
[5] *Hc.*, (Calcutta edition), p. 600; *Hc. C. T.*, p. 223.
[6] *Hc.*, (Bombay, 1909), p. 57; *Hc. C. T.*, p. 27.
[7] *Hc.*, p. 274; *Hc. C. T.*, p. 198.

state papers are called collectively *Ni-lo-pi-tu* (or *ca*); in these good and bad are recorded, and instances of public calamity and good fortune are set forth in detail."[1]

XXVIII. *Mahākṣapaṭalādhikaraṇādhikrita*, i.e., office of "one appointed to the post of notary-in-chief. This expression occurs in the Banskhera and Madhuban copper plates, which respectively name this officer Mahāsāmanta Mahārāja Bhānu and Sāmanta Mahārāja Īśvaragupta.

XXIX. *Pustakakrit* or *Pustakrit*.[2] In the Damodarapur copper plates the term "Pustapāla" occurs. According to Dr. R. G. Basak they were "those who were made aware of the title to all lands. The Govt. sanctioned land-sales only after these record-keepers had, on receipt of application from purchasers, determined the title to the land under proposal of transfer and sent in their report to the government." (*Ep. Ind.*, XV, p. 128).

XXX. *Lekhaka*, or writer[3].

XXXI. *Karaṇi* or *Karaṇika*, i.e., clerk.[4] He was probably responsible for drafting documents (Karaṇa). It is worth noticing that certain Candrāsenīya Kāyastha Prabhus of the Deccan, who are supposed to have migrated from Oudh in the United Provinces, still bear the surname Karṇika or Karaṇika.[5]

XXXII. *Dūtaka*. This was the designation of an officer employed in connection with formal grants. His duty, as remarked by Fleet, "was to carry, not the actual charter itself, for delivery into the hand of the grantee but the king's sanction and order to the local

[1] Watters, I, p. 154.
[2] *Hc.*, ed. by Führer (Bombay, 1909), p. 67; *Hc. C. T.*, p. 33.
[3] *Ibid.*
[4] *Hc.*, p. 274; *Hc. C. T.*, p. 198.
[5] *Ep. Ind.*, XVIII, p. 224, Note 1.

officials, whose duty it then was to have the charter drawn up and delivered."[1] The *Dūtaka* of the Banskhera copper plate was Mahāpramātā Mahāsāmanta-Śrī-Skandagupta. It was signed by Harṣa himself, as is clear from the expression "Svahasto mama Mahārājādhirāja Śrī-Harṣasya" i.e., "given under my own hand and seal."

XXXIII. Bāṇa also mentions the *Adhyakṣas*, which shows that probably the subordinate officials were under their departmental superintendents.

XXXIV. *Sevaka.* This term occurs in the Banskhera and Madhuban charters, and perhaps denotes any menial servant in state employ.

Territorial divisions

According to the inscriptions of Harṣa the country was divided for administrative purposes into the following divisions :—

(*a*) *Bhukti*, i.e., province or division, as for instance the Śrāvasti *Bhukti*, or the Ahicchatra *Bhukti* mentioned in the Madhuban and Banskhera grants respectively.

(*b*) The *Bhukti* was further subdivided into *Viṣayas* corresponding to modern districts. The Madhuban record gives us the name of Kuṇḍadhāni *Viṣaya*, whereas the Banskhera copper plate mentions the Angadīya *Viṣaya*

(*c*) *Paṭhaka.*[2] This was a still smaller territorial term perhaps of the size of the present day Tahsil or Talukā.

(*d*) *Grāma* or village. This was the lowest unit of administration in ancient times, as it is even

[1] *C. I. I.*, III, p. 100, Note 3.
[2] See the Banskhera inscription.

now. We have for example the Soma-Kuṇḍa-kā-grāma in the Madhuban charter.

Regarding the general features of the government, it appears that it was founded on benign principles. Yuan Chwang was impressed favourably, and he observes : "As the Government is generous official requirements are few. Families are not registered, and individuals are not subject to forced labour contributions.............. Taxation being light, and forced service being sparingly used, every one keeps to his hereditary occupation and attends to his patrimony"[1] The people were thus left to grow in their own surroundings free and unfettered by the shackles of over-government. Harṣa being "just in his administration, and punctilious in the discharge of his duties,"[2] society was not choked by a grinding bureaucracy, or overburdened by a heavy system of taxation. The main source of revenue was the traditional one-sixth of the produce,[3] and "light duties at ferries and barrier stations,"[4] paid by tradesmen, who went to and fro bartering their merchandise. The Madhuban and Banskhera grants tell us of other dues, viz., the *Tulya-meya* (taxes depending on the weight and measure of the commodities); *Bhāgabhogakarahiraṇyādi* (share of the enjoyment or produce, payments in cash, and other kinds of income.[5]

The enlightened nature of Harṣa's government may further be judged by its expenditure. It is indeed remarkable that besides other items, liberal provision

[1] Watters, I, p. 176. Yuan Chwang does not mention these conditions in relation to any particular kingdom, but probably he had Kanauj—the leading state of that time—in view.

[2] *Ibid.*, p. 343.

[3] *Ibid.*, p. 176; cf. also *Manusmriti*, VII, 130-31; VIII, 308.

[4] Watters, I, p. 176.

[5] *Ep. Ind.*, I, pp. 73, 75; *Ibid.*, IV, p. 211. See also *Infra.*

was made for charity to various religious communities. "Of the royal land," says Yuan Chwang, "there is a four-fold division. One part is for the expenses of government and state-worship, one for endowment of great public servants, one to reward high intellectual eminence, and one for acquiring religious merit by gifts to various sects"[1] With regard to payment of officials we are told that "ministers of state and common officials all have their portion of land, and are maintained by the cities assigned to them," but "those who are employed in the government service are paid according to their work."[2]

Criminal administration

Owing to the well-organised character of the government there do not seem to have been many instances of violent crime. Yuan Chwang testifies to this rather amazing fact : "As the government is honestly administered and the people live together on good terms the criminal class is small."[3] But the roads and river routes were by no means immune from bands of brigands, Yuan Chwang himself being stripped by them more than once. At one time, when the pilgrim had proceeded eastward from Ayodhyā (not very distant from Kanauj) and was going down the Ganges with about eighty other fellow-passengers on board a ship, the robbers selected him on account of his handsome form as an offering to the goddess Durgā, whom they paid worship; and it was fortunately through the intercession of Nature that he escaped meeting a cruel death at their hands. We learn that all of a sudden a "black tempest" (typhoon) arose, which terrified the

[1] Watters, I, p. 176.
[2] *Ibid.*, pp. 176-77.
[3] Watters, I, p. 171.

pirates, and interpreting it as an indication of divine anger they sincerely felt repentance for their evil ways and not only spared Yuan Chwang's life but also "took on themselves the five obligations of a lay-believer."[1]

Once while he was in the Panjab, Yuan Chwang had similarly to encounter a band of fifty bandits in a great forest of *Po-lo-che* trees (Palāśas) near the town of *Che-kia-lo* (Śākala). He and his companions were deprived of all their clothes and goods, and hotly pursued by the gang with drawn swords. A Brahman peasant, who appeared on the scene with eighty armed men just at the right time, however, saved their lives and dispersed the robbers[2].

The law against crime appears to have been exceptionally severe. Imprisonment for life was the ordinary penalty for transgressions of the statute law and conspiracy against the sovereign, and we are informed that the prisoners were so cruelly treated that they were not at all considered as members of the community.[3] The *Harṣacarita* on the other hand refers to the custom of releasing prisoners on festive and joyous occasions. Thus Harṣa's birth saw "disorderly crowds of freed prisoners, their faces hairy with long matted beards."[4] The other punishments were more sanguinary than in the Gupta period : "For offences against social morality, and disloyal and unfilial conduct, the punishment is to cut off the nose, or an ear, or a hand, or a foot, or to banish the offender to another country or into the wilderness."[5] Minor offences could be "atoned for by a

[1] *Life*, pp. 86-90. This incident clearly proves that human sacrifices to propitiate the gods or goddesses were then not unknown. Bāṇa also at one place refers to them (*Hc. C. T.*, p. 92).

[2] *Life*, p. 73.

[3] Watters, I, p. 172.

[4] *Hc. C. T.*, p. 111.

[5] Watters, I, p. 172; Beal, I, pp. 83-84.

money payment." Ordeals by water, fire, weighing, or poison, were esteemed as efficient instruments to determine the innocence or guilt of an accused person, and the Chinese pilgrim apparently describesthem with approval.[1] The severity of the criminal administration was no doubt largely responsible for the infrequency of violations of the law, but it may also have been due to the character of the Indian people, who are described as of "pure moral principles." Yuan Chwang adds: "They will not take anything wrongfully, and they yield more than fairness requires. They fear the retribution for sins in other lives, and make light of what conduct produces in this life. They do not practise deceit and they keep their sworn obligations."[2]

Kanauj under Harṣa

The prosperity and importance of Kanauj, so well begun during the time of the Maukharis, grew tremendously under Harṣa; and it now easily became the premier city of Northern India supplanting Pāṭaliputra, the older centre, through which the main currents of political life had flowed since the days of the Buddha. To the observant eyes of a foreigner it must have appeared as a great cosmopolitan town, whose inhabitants were equally divided between orthodoxy and heterodoxy. There were one hundred Buddhist monasteries with more than 10,000 brethren who were students of both the "Vehicles." The Deva-temples amounted to more than two hundred, and the non-Buddhists were several thousands in number.[3] The

[1] Watters, I, p. 172; Beal, I, p. 84.

[2] Watters, I, p. 171; Beal, I, p. 83. For a discussion on Harṣa's administrative system, see also Dr. R. K. Mookerji, *Harṣa* (p. 84 f.) where the author has copiously supplemented it by the evidence of the Gupta inscriptions.

[3] Watters, I, p. 340; Beal, I, p. 207.

town itself had grown to enormous proportions. With the river Ganges flowing down its western base Kanauj was above twenty *li* in length and four or five *li* in breadth (i.e., about five miles long and $1\frac{1}{4}$ miles broad). According to the traditional practice the city was very strongly defended by quadrangular walls, broad and high, and had lofty structures everywhere. "There were beautiful gardens and tanks of clear water, and in it rarities from strange lands were collected".[1] Yuan Chwang is silent regarding further details of the appearance of the metropolis, but the following general description of the system of town-planning then in vogue may be of some interest in this connection: "The thoroughfares are narrow tortuous passages. The shops are on the highways and booths (or, inns) line the roads. Butchers, fishermen, public performers, executioners, and scavengers have their habitations marked by a distinguishing sign. They are forced to live outside the city and they sneak along on the left when going about in the hamlets".[2] Thus people following certain occupations were segregated, and these regulations must have doubtless been galling to them. As to the construction of houses in Kanauj, we must here refer to the general character of Indian buildings described by Yuan Chwang. "Their halls and terraced belvederes have wooden flatroofed rooms, and are coated with *chunam*, and covered with tiles burnt or unburnt. They are of extraordinary height." But the more modest dwellings "thatched with coarse or common grass are of bricks or boards; their walls are ornamented with *chunam*; the floor is purified with cow-dung and strewn with flowers of the season."[3] They were onthe whole

[1] Watters, I, p. 340; Beal, I, p. 206.
[2] Watters, I, p. 147; Beal, I, pp. 73-74.
[3] Watters, I, p. 147; Beal, I, p. 74.

comfortable and simple, or in the words of Yuan Chwang "sumptuous inside and economical outside." The houses of the rich were probably decorated and whitewashed on ceremonious occasions. Bāṇa at any rate informs us that at the time of Rājyaśrī's marriage painters "painted auspicious scenes" and workmen "mounted on ladders, with brushes upheld in their hands and plaster pails on their shoulders, whitened the top of the street wall of the palace"[1] at Thanesvar.

The wealth and prosperity of Kanauj was further manifest in the people who "had a refined appearance and dressed in glossy silk attire."[2] There were families with great wealth. Fruit and flowers were abundant. Yuan Chwang describes the usual clothing of the Indians thus: "The men wind a strip of cloth round the waist and up to the armpits and leave the right shoulder bare. The women wear a long robe which covers both shoulders and falls down loose."[3] It is, however, remarkable that the inner and outer dress had no tailoring. As to colour, the people preferred fresh white garments and did not at all esteem motley or embroidered. The inhabitants varied in their personal tastes. Some clipped their moustaches; others adopted fantastic fashions. They wore garlands on their heads and necklaces on their bodies.[4]

[1] *Hc. C. T.*, p. 124.

[2] Watters, I, p. 340; Beal, I, p. 207. Yuan Chwang mentions four kinds of cloths, viz., *Kiao-shê-ye* (Kauseya) or silk; *Ch'u-mo* (Kṣauma) or linen; *Han* (*Kan*)*-po-lo* (Kambala) or woollen texture; *Ho-la-li* (Ral ?) being a texture made from the wool of a wild animal (Watters, I, p. 148; Beal, I, p. 75). Bāṇa speaks of soft textures of linen, cotton, bark-silk, spider's thread, muslin, and shot silk(*Hc. C. T.*, p. 125).

[3] Watters, I, p. 148; Beal, I, p. 75.

[4] *Ibid.* Bāṇa mentions jewelled rings, earrings, necklaces, armlets etc. as ornaments (*Hc. C. T.*, pp. 92, 97).

Lastly we are told that the citizens were given to learning and the arts, while they were clear and suggestive in discourse. Thus says Yuan Chwang in praise of the people of "Mid India" (which term probably stands for Kanauj and adjacent territories) at this time: "They are pre-eminently explicit and correct in speech, their expressions being harmonious and elegant, like those of the Devas, and their intonation clear and distinct serving as rule and pattern for others."[1] The monasteries also at Kanauj were far-famed as repositories of learning. One such college was the Bhadravihāra, where Yuan Chwang stayed for three months studying under the direction of Vīryasena, a celebrated doctor of the Three Piṭakas.[2] In short, Kanauj was under Harṣa the centre of culture and crafts, power and politics, religion and riches; while its grandeur was apparently so great that according to the *Cach-Nāma* long afterwards the expression "you want Kanauj" passed into a proverb, meaning "you want the impossible."[3]

[1] Watters, I, p. 153; Beal, I, p. 77.
[2] *Life*, p. 84.
[3] English Translation, p. 52.

PART II

CHAPTER VII

HARṢA'S RELIGIOUS ACTIVITIES AND RELIGION

SECTION A

Assembly at Kanauj[1]

Great as was Harṣa as a ruler and conqueror, he was greater still in the arts of peace, which "hath her victories no less renowned than war." One of the latter class of events was the convocation of a grand assembly at Kānyakubja to give the utmost publicity to, and exhibit the refinements of, the doctrines of the Mahāyāna, which had captured the imagination of Harṣa on account of its lucid exposition by the illustrious pilgrim. He, therefore, sent "an order throughout the different kingdoms that all the disciples of the various schools should assemble in the town of Kanyākubja to investigate the treatise of the Master of the Law, of China."[2] Harṣa marched from his camp with his accustomed pomp and pageantry along the southern bank of the Ganges, accompanied by Yuan Chwang and an enormous multitude; while his chief friend and ally Bhāskara-varman, king of Assam, kept pace with him on the opposite bank. Advancing up the river in battle array with their staff and soldiers the two kings arrived at the rendezvous *viz.*, Kanauj, in the course

[1] This account is mainly based on the *Si-yu-ki* and the *Life*.
[2] *Life*, p. 176.

of ninety days when the second month of spring was passing.[1] On arrival they found there were already present for their reception "kings of eighteen countries of the Five Indias;[2] three thousand priests thoroughly acquainted with the Great and Little vehicle, besides about three thousand Brahmans and Nirgranthas and about a thousand priests of the Nalanda monastery."[3] Harṣa had previously ordered two thatched halls, each capable of seating one thousand persons,[4] to be erected at the place of the assembly for the accommodation of the vast concourse, and also a precious tower, about 100 feet high, in the middle of which was placed a golden statue of the Buddha, "of the same height as the king himself."[5] The proceedings of the assembly were opened by a huge and solemn procession starting from the king's resting-hall (palace of travel), constructed for the occasion, and the main object of attraction was a golden statue of the Buddha, about three feet high, which was carried on a gorgeously caparisoned elephant. This was accompanied by Harṣa in person, who attired as the god Śakra held a precious canopy or *cowrie*, whilst his friend and ally, Kumārarāja, was also in attendance with a white parasol in the guise of the god Brahmā.[6] Each of the two kings had an escort of two harnessed elephants, laden with jewels and flowers,[7] while the Master of the Law and the

[1] Beal, I, p. 218; *Life*, p. 176. According to the *Life* they reached the rendezvous "in the beginning of the last month of the year" (*Life*, p. 176).

[2] *Life*, p. 177. The *Si-yu-ki* states that there were kings of twenty countries present (Beal, I, p. 218).

[3] *Life*, p. 177.

[4] *Ibid.*

[5] Beal, I, p. 218.

[6] *Ibid.*, *Life*, p. 177.

[7] *Life*, pp. 177-78. According to the *Si-yu-ki* the escort

chief state-officials were severally mounted on a great elephant. There were, moreover, three hundred other great elephants reserved for the princes, ministers, and chief priests of the different countries who rode in double file on each side of the procession course.[1] As the procession wended its way Harṣa scattered on every side pearls, gold, and silver flowers, and various precious substances in honour of the three objects of worship—the Buddha, the Dharma, and the Sangha. On reaching their destination Śīlāditya first washed the image at the altar, and then himself bore it on his shoulder to the western tower, where he offered to it thousands of silken garments embroidered with gems.[2] Then in order were allowed to enter the Hall the princes of the eighteen countries, one thousand renowned priests, and five hundred distinguished Brahmans and heretics with two hundred great ministers of the different kingdoms, while the unbelievers and secular people were seated outside the gate of the hall.[3] These ceremonies were followed by a public dinner, of which all the people present, within and without, partook. This being over, Harṣa opened the conference by inviting the Chinese pilgrim to take his seat as "Lord of the discussion."[4] Yuan Chwang began the proceedings by dwelling on the merits of the "Great Vehicle," and having fixed a subject for discussion he called upon Ming-hien, a *shaman* of the

consisted of five hundred war elephants clad in armour. (Beal, I, p. 218).

[1] *Life*, p. 178. The *Si-yu-ki* says : "In front and behind the statue of the Buddha went one hundred great elephants, carrying musicians, who sounded their drums and raised their music" (Beal, I, pp. 218-19).

[2] Beal, I, p. 219. According to the *Life* (p. 178) "the king and the Master of the Law, in succession, presented it with offerings."

[3] *Life*, p. 178.

[4] *Ibid.*

Nalanda monastery, to give his discourse. The Master of the Law, anticipating Martin Luther, announced the subject to the assembled people by a placard nailed outside the hall, which stated: "If there is any one who can find a single word in the proposition contrary to reason, or is able to entangle (the argument) then at the request of the opponent, I offer my head as a recompense."[1] There was none to take up the challenge and Yuan Chwang remained in undisputed possession of the field until night, when very well satisfied at the event Harṣa retired with others, having declared the assembly adjourned. The next morning they again escorted the image as before, and thus five days elapsed when the "unbelievers of the Little Vehicle," mortified at the overthrow of their system of beliefs, entered into a conspiracy to take the life of the Chinese pilgrim. Scenting that his celebrated guest's life was in danger at the hand of theological rivals, the royal patron at once issued a threatening proclamation that "if any one should hurt or touch the Master of the Law, he shall be forthwith beheaded; and whoever speaks against him, his tongue shall be cut out; but all those who desire to profit by his instruction, relying on my goodwill, need not fear this manifesto."[2] This stern announcement had the desired effect; and we are frankly told by the pilgrim's biographer that "from this time the followers of error withdrew and disappeared, so that when

[1] *Life*, p. 179. It appears that such a formula was a part of the tradition of these public disputations. We may, as an instance, also cite the challenge issued by "a heretic of the '*Shun-si*' sect (Lokātiya)" to the monks of Nalanda: "If anyone within can refute these principles, I will then give my head as a proof of his victory" (*Life*, p. 161). Yuan Chwang emerged triumphant from the discussion, but instead of demanding the head of his vanquished opponent he made him his disciple (*Ibid.*, pp. 161-64).

[2] *Life*, p. 180.

eighteen days had passed there had been no one to enter on the discussion."[1]

Thus though according to the *Life* the programme was gone through successfully to the utter confusion of all heretics and the joy of the Mahāyānists, the account preserved in the *Si-yu-ki* avers that the convocation terminated by startling incidents. It is stated that on the day of separation a great fire suddenly broke out in the tower and the pavilion over the gate of the hall erected at an immense cost. They were partly destroyed by the flames, when at the prayerful intervention of the king the fire was extinguished and the smoke disappeared making pious hearts thereby recognise a miracle.[2] Harṣa then ascended the top of the great tower in company with the assembled kings to survey the scene. As he was coming down the steps a fanatical heretic, knife in hand, suddenly tried to attack him. The attempt, however, was frustrated by the alertness of the king, who promptly seized the culprit. The princely train demanded the would-be assassin's immediate death, but Harṣa, instead of giving any such decree, with unruffled countenance questioned his assailant about his intentions. At the royal interrogation the criminal openly confessed, "Great king! you have assembled the people of different countries, and exhausted your treasury in offerings to the Śramaṇas, and cast a metal image of Buddha; but the heretics who have come from a distance *have scarcely been spoken to*. Their minds, therefore, have been affected with resentment, and they procured me, wretched man that I am! to undertake this unlucky deed."[3] Five hundred Brahmans, "all of singular talent," were then arrested on the strength of

[1] *Ibid.*
[2] Beal, I, p. 219.
[3] Beal, I, p. 221.

this confession, and being "straitly questioned" by the king they admitted that, inspired by jealousy against the Śramaṇas, whom he "had reverenced and exceedingly honoured," they had fired the tower by shooting into it burning arrows, and had purposed to kill him in the resulting confusion. Their attempt having miscarried, they had hired this miscreant to lay in wait for the king in a narrow passage to assassinate him.[1] Although the ministers and the kings "demanded the extermination of the heretics", Harṣa punished only the alleged principals in the plot, sending the five hundred Brahmans into exile and extending his royal mercy to the rest.

Whichever of the two accounts may be true, it is certain that the victory of Yuan Chwang in this assembly of public disputation considerably enhanced his prestige and influence over Harṣa, who reverencing him more than ever, lavishly bestowed on him 10,000 pieces of gold, 30,000 pieces of silver, and 100 garments of superior cotton. All the princes of the eighteen kingdoms, moreover, presented him with rare jewels.[2] But the generosity of the royal patrons was baffled by the extreme abnegation of the pilgrim, who in a rare bnt truly religious spirit declined to accept any of these gifts. Harṣa then requested the Master of the Law to mount a great elephant and go round the city in company with the ministers of state, so that proclamation might be made among the crowds that "he had established the standard of right doctrine, without gainsaying."[3] Yuan Chwang with his usual modesty desired to waive this mark of distinction, but the king said, "it has ever been the custom, the matter cannot be passed over."

[1] *Ibid.*
[2] *Life*, p. 180.
[3] *Ibid.*

Accordingly it was proclaimed throughout Kanauj that "the Master of the Law from the kingdom of China has established the principles of the Great Vehicle and overthrown all opposing doctrines; for eighteen days no one has dared to enter on the discussion."[1] The whole multitude was immensely delighted by his success; some designated him "Mahāyāna Deva," whilst others called him "Mokṣa Deva."[2]

SECTION B

Quinquennial distributions at Prayāga[3]

When the special assembly at Kanauj broke up, Yuan Chwang began to make preparations for his homeward journey, but Harṣa invited him to attend another imposing ceremony, which the sovereign used to hold every five years at Prayāga at the confluence of the Ganges and the Jumna. The ultra-sacredness of this site "due to the crescent-shaped formation of the land, where the two holy rivers united, went back to the earliest vedic times;"[4] and as it was thought "more advantageous to give one mite in charity in this place than a thousand in any other place,"[5] this spot had come to be known as the "Arena of Charitable Offerings."[6] Harṣa explained to his illustrious guest that during the last thirty years he had celebrated five of these great quinquennial distributions of alms called the *Mahā-mokṣa Pariṣad*, and it was now time to hold the

[1] *Ibid.*, p. 181.

[2] *Ibid.*

[3] The account of the Prayāga assembly is based on the *Life* (pp. 183-87).

[4] E. B. Havell, *Aryan Rule in India*, p. 204.

[5] *Life*, p. 184.

[6] It was also called the "Field of great Beneficence" (*Life*, p. 90), or "the Grand Arena of Largesse" (Watters, I, p. 364).

sixth. Yuan Chwang, although homesick, was too religiously-minded to refuse Harṣa's invitation to witness this display of charity wherein the accumulated treasure would be freely distributed to the poor and needy, as well as to the devout of all denominations. He, therefore, agreed to be present at that unique function saying, "if Your Majesty does not grudge his treasure for the good of others, how can Yuan Chwang grudge a short delay (in his departure)."[1] Attended by the "kings of eighteen kingdoms" and by Yuan Chwang, Harṣa then arrived in *Po-lo-ye-kia* or Prayāga to find already assembled there a huge concourse of people amounting to about 500,000—Śramaṇas, heretics, Nirgranthas, the poor, the orphans, and the solitary (bereaved) of the Five Indias who had been summoned by an imperial decree.[2] The "Great Distribution Arena" was the vast sandy plain, fourteen or fifteen *li* in circuit, bounded on the north by the Ganges (*King-kia*), and on the south by the Jumna (*Yen-mu-na*). The arrangements for the solemn ceremonial were completed before the arrival of the royal cortége. A great square space was marked off by a bamboo hedge 1,000 paces on each side, and in the middle "many scores of thatched buildings" were erected to deposit all the treasures (intended for distribution); to wit, gold, silver, fine pearls, red glass, and other valuables; while the less costly articles such as silk and cotton garments, the gold and silver money, were placed in "several hundred store-houses" constructed by the side of the above. Outside this quadrangle were pavilions for refreshments, and there were also constructed "some hundred or so long buildings ...in which some thousand people might sit down for

[1] *Life*, p. 184.
[2] *Ibid.*, p. 185.

rest."[1] Besides these numerous erections, there was the tent of Harṣa pitched on the north bank of the Ganges, and that of *Tu-lu-po-pa-cha* (Dhruvabhaṭa), "king of South India," who had located himself on the west of the junction of the two mighty rivers. The camp of the king of Assam was on the south side of the Jumna, whereas the space lying to the west of the Valabhi camp was occupied by the numerous people who had collected there to receive the royal bounty. The proceedings of this grand assembly lasted for seventy-five days, commencing with a military procession of the followers of Harṣa and of Kumārarāja, embarked in ships, and the attendants of Dhruvabhaṭa mounted on elephants, which proceeded in an impressive array to the scene of the distribution. The "Kings of the eighteen countries" followed in the order previously arranged.

The religious services were of the curiously eclectic kind so characteristic of Hindu society and worship. On the first day the image of the Buddha was set up in one of the temporary shrines built upon the sands; flowers were offered, and vast quantities of precious articles and clothing of the finest quality were lavishly distributed. On the second day the image of Ādityadeva (Sun) was worshipped with similar rites; and on the third day the image of Īśvara-deva (Śiva) received adoration, but in each case the gifts bestowed were of only half the value of those consecrated to the Buddha on the opening day. On the fourth day began the distribution of the stupendous treasures thus dedicated to the service of the divinity. To each of the selected ten thousand of the "religious community" (Buddhist monks probably) were given one hundred pieces of gold, one pearl, one cotton garment, various drinks and meats; flowers and perfumes. During the next twenty

[1] *Life*, p. 185.

days the Brahmans were the recipients of generous gifts. The next ten days were reserved for the bestowal of largess on those described in the *Life* as "heretics," i.e., probably Jains and members of other sects.[1] The same number of days were spent on bestowing alms upon those mendicants who had come from distant countries, whilst it took a month to distribute charity to the poor, the orphans, and the destitute. By this time nothing was left of all the surplus of the imperial coffers that had accumulated in the previous five years. There now remained only the horses, elephants, and military accoutrements of the imperial forces, "which were necessary for maintaining order and protecting the royal estate."[2] Then in imitation of the Prince Siddhārtha Gautama at the hour of his great Renunciation, Harṣa freely and without stint gave away his gems and goods, his clothing and necklaces, earrings and bracelets, chaplets, neck-jewel, and bright head-jewel.[3] The Chinese author, Hwui-li, informs us in conclusion that "all being given away, he (Harṣa) begged from his sister (Rājyaśrī) an ordinary second-hand garment, and having put it on he paid worship to the Buddhas of the ten regions," and rejoiced that his treasure had thus been exhausted in the "field of religious merit."[4] At the close of the "magnificent convocations" the assembled kings redeemed by their money Harṣa's regalia, court vestments, and other costly presents from the persons on whom they had been bestowed, and restored them to the king. Harṣa, however, after the lapse of a few days again distributed them, and thus

[1] For an idea of the variety of religious sects, see Appendix I.

[2] *Life*, p. 186.

[3] *Ibid.*, p. 187.

[4] *Ibid.*

established a record in individual charity and liberality hardly equalled in history.[1]

Yuan Chwang's departure

After the successful termination of the proceedings of the Prayāga convocation Yuan Chwang begged leave to depart, and his request was granted on condition that he would stay yet another ten days as the state guest of the king of Kanauj. Harṣa suggested to the Chinese pilgrim that if he selected the southern sea-route,[2] i.e., by way of Java or Sumatra, he should be accompanied by official attendants, but Yuan Chwang preferred to return by the northern road. Both the sovereigns of Kanauj and Assam offered the Master of the Law every sort of valuable gift; he, however, declined to accept anything except a cape called *ho-la-li* of coarse skin designed as a protection from rain. Thus he took his departure, and Harṣa saw him off with a large retinue for a long distance. He also provided his honoured guest with a military escort of "a king of North India called Udhita" to carry the books and images on horseback, but the advance being slow king Śīlāditya afterwards "attached to the escort of Udhitarāja a great elephant, with three thousand gold pieces and ten thousand silver pieces"[3] to meet the necessary expenses of the pilgrim's arduous journey overland to China. This separation from his spiritual instructor troubled Harṣa, and three days later he, in company with Kumārarāja, Dhruvabhaṭa, and several hundred horsemen, overtook

[1] But this sort of munificence must have been a heavy drain on the treasury. Was it, therefore, responsible for the sudden collapse of the kingdom after Harṣa's death?

[2] This was the route followed by Fa-hian on his return journey home. It also shows that sea-voyages were common, and Harṣa's administration was quite familiar with the sea-route to China.

[3] *Life*, p. 189.

Yuan Chwang in order to spend a little more time with him before taking final leave. The great sovereign of Kanauj then commanded four *Ta-kwan* (official guides) called *Mo-ho-ta-lo* (Mahattaras), giving them letters on "fine white cotton stuff and sealed with red wax," which they were ordered to present "in all countries through which they conducted the Master, to the end that the princes of these countries might provide carriages or modes of conveyance to escort the Master even to the borders of China."[1] Thus the fame and influence of the Kanauj monarch had extended to far-off lands, and their rulers were ready to comply with his wishes.

SECTION C

Harṣa's religion and devotion

From an account of Harṣa's benevolent activities we pass on to a consideration of his system of beliefs, which urged him to scorn delights incidental to his position, and work untiringly for the moral progress and material well-being of his subjects. It may at the outset be mentioned that Harṣa did not inherit Buddhism. His father, Prabhākaravardhana was an ardent devotee of the Sun, and "kneeling eastwards upon the ground in a circle smeared with saffron paste" he daily offered to that luminary "a bunch of red lotuses set in a pure vessel of ruby and tinged, like his own heart, with the sun's hue."[2] This fact is confirmed by the Sonpat seal and the Madhuban and Banskhera inscriptions, which apply the epithet "paramādityabhaktaḥ" to Prabhākara. We also learn from these epigraphs that Harṣa's grandfather Ādityavardhana, and great-grand-father Rājyavar-

[1] *Ibid.*, p. 190.
[2] *Hc. C. T.*, p. 104.

dhana were votaries of the Sun. The *Harṣacarita* further testifies that Harṣa's remote ancestor Puṣpabhūti "entertained a great, almost inborn, devotion towards Śiva the adorable."[1] We have even grounds to believe that Harṣa himself, was in his earlier days a devotee of the god Śiva. When he started on his campaign he "had with deep devotion offered worship to the adorable Nīlalohita," and "bestowed upon Brahmans sesamum vessels of precious stones, silver, and gold in thousands."[2] At the time of his first halt the golden seal presented to him by the village notary was inscribed with the emblem of a bull,[3] which is regarded in Hindu mythology as the *Vāhana* or carrier of Śiva. Similarly, there is the reclining Nandi symbol on the Sonpat copper seal of Harṣa. It was also probably due to his Śaiva tendencies that he complimented the king of Assam through the latter's envoy saying "to whom save Śiva need he pay homage? This resolve of his increases my affection."[4] But the most important testimony is that of the copper plates—Banskhera plate of the year 22 of his reign = 628 A. D., and Madhuban plate of the year 25 i.e., 631 A. D.—which definitely call Harṣa a "Paramamāheśvara" or a devout worshipper of the god Maheśvara or Śiva.[5]

In his latter years, however, Harṣa appears to have inclined towards Buddhism, and eventually adopted it with a coating of a curious sort of eclecticism. It is difficult to determine what inner feelings and compunctions of conscience brought about this mighty religious

[1] *Ibid.*, p. 84.

[2] *Ibid.*, p. 197.

[3] *Ibid.*, p. 198.

[4] *Ibid.*, p. 219. Cf. "Harāt-ṛite·kaṁ-anyaṁ namasyati. Saṁvardhitā me prītiḥ amunā saṁkalpena..." (*Hc.*, Cal. ed., p. 589).

[5] *Ep. Ind.*, IV, p. 211; I, pp. 72, 74. These documents record Harṣa's grants of villages to orthodox vedic Brahmans, thus pointing to his Brahmanist proclivities.

transformation; but there seems little doubt that his earlier repeated calamities, his protracted campaigns of violence and bloodshed, his fondness for his dead brother Rājyavardhana, a "paramasaugata," and his association with his sister Rājyaśrī, also an earnest Buddhist, stimulated his interest in the Buddha's gospel of peace and non-violence. Probably the philosophy of the Saṁmatīya school of Buddhism, of which Rājyaśrī was an exponent,[1] originally held the chief place in Harṣa's affections, but after meeting with Yuan Chwang and listening to his brilliant exposition of the doctrines of the Mahāyāna he transferred his allegiance to this "advanced" school. Thenceforward he stood as its redoubtable champion, and convoked a special assembly at Kānyakubja for the avowed purpose of exhibiting "the refinements of the great Vehicle" and of making "manifest the exceeding merit of the Master." On this occasion Harṣa also showed some amount of open partiality and narrow sectarian spirit for the Mahāyāna. He interdicted and stifled free discussion on the pretext that the Chinese pilgrim's life was in danger, and further offered a slight to the chief gods of the Brahmans—Śakra and Brahmā—by representing them as mere attendants on the Buddha during the celebrations. The *Si-yu-ki* even states that the assembled Brahmans, who "had scarcely been spoken to," felt so keenly insulted at their neglect that they hatched an unsuccessful plot to kill the king.[2] It must not, however, be understood that henceforth Harṣa became a sort of royal missionary, like Aśoka, preaching and propagating the Dharma with the aid of his vast resources. On the contrary, he maintained the eclectic character of his public worship, and officially honoured the Brahmanical deities

[1] *Life*, p. 176.
[2] See *supra*.

of Āditya (sun) and Śiva in the Prayāga gathering. He also made handsome gifts to the Brahmans, although it is true that the Buddhists had the first place in his scheme of charities. As proof of Harṣa's catholicity we may add here the information furnished by Yuan Chwang that the former was accustomed to provide viands every day for 500 Brahmans along with 1,000 Buddhists at the "royal lodges" during his tours.[1]

Among other activities of Harṣa which betray his special favour and marked leanings towards Buddhism, we may first mention his "forcible" appropriation of the tooth-relic of the Buddha from Kashmir, and its subsequent enshrinement in a *Saṅghārāma* in Kanauj[2]. Yuan Chwang also notes some of Harṣa's measures, calculated to promote the well-being of the Buddhist order and give an impetus to its propagation. We are told that "once a year he summoned all the Buddhist monks together, and for twenty-one days supplied them with the regulation requisites. He furnished the chapels and liberally adorned the common halls of the monasteries. He brought the Brethren together for examination and discussion, giving rewards and punishments according to merit and demerit[3]. Yuan Chwang adds further that the best and most learned of them were "advanced to the Lion's Throne" (i.e., promoted to the highest places), and Harṣa considered them as his spiritual guides. Those who were merely perfect in the observance of the ceremonial rules were "honoured with formal reverence." But others guilty of unbecoming conduct were "banished from his presence and from the country."[4] Indeed, Harṣa was so

[1] Watters, I, p. 344; Beal, I, p. 215.
[2] *Life*, pp. 181, 183.
[3] Watters, I, p. 344; Beal, I, pp. 214-15.
[4] *Ibid.*

interested in the right diffusion and dissemination of the Buddhist doctrine that at one time, having noticed the ascendancy of the Hīnayāna in Orissa, he sent for four eminent doctors from the Nalanda convent in order to overthrow in discussion the upholders of that system. In response to his message Śīlabhadra, "the treasure of the true doctrine," commissioned Sāgaramatī, Prajñārasmi, Siṁharasmi, and the Master of the Law; but before they could start on their mission Harṣa sent word to the effect: "There is no immediate pressure for my former request; let them wait, and afterwards come here."[1] Again, we are informed that Harṣa erected thousands of topes on the banks of the Ganges, and Buddhist monasteries at the sacred places of the Buddhists.[2] These structures, the construction and multiplication of which was so dear to the heart of every believing Buddhist in order to gain merit, were perhaps built of very flimsy materials, and so they have not been able to withstand the ravages of time and nature. Their disappearance may also be due to the fact that they lay in the track of the hosts of Islam, and were exposed to their iconoclastic zeal. In conclusion, we may mention some promulgations of Harṣa, which had a distinctly Buddhist flavour. The king of Kanauj is represented to have "practised to the utmost the rules of temperance" and "sought to plant the tree of religious merit to such an extent that he forgot to sleep or to eat."[3] He also prohibited the taking of life and the use of animal food under severe penalties.[4] Further, Harṣa copied the benevolent institutions of Aśoka, and "in all the highways of the towns and villages throughout

[1] *Life*, pp. 160-61.
[2] Watters, I, p. 344.
[3] Beal, I, p. 214; Watters, I, p. 344.
[4] *Ibid.*; *Ibid.*

India he erected hospices (*puṇyaśālas*), provided with food and drink, and stationed there physicians, with medicines for travellers and poor persons round about, to be given without any stint."[1] Thus Harṣa anticipated the deeds of modern Christianity,[2] and his lively sympathy with all creatures, human and animal, found powerful expression in the extensive provision of relief that he made throughout his dominions for the sick, the dumb, and the distressed. As a result of Harṣa's benevolent exertions and untiring attentions there was a marked growth of Buddhism in Kanauj, though it was visibly on the wane in other centres. While Fa-hian in the early quarter of the fifth century A. D. could find only two monasteries of small consequence in Kanauj, Yuan Chwang after the lapse of just over a couple of centuries notices as many as a hundred "with more than 10,000 Brethren who were students of both the "Vehicles."[3]

[1] Beal, I, p. 214.

[2] On the strength of a remark of Dr. Edkins, quoted in the *Athenaeum*, 3rd July, 1880, p. 8, Dr. R. K. Mookerji makes the statement that Harṣa "had some touch with Christianity too" (*Harṣa*, p. 145, Note 1). The learned Professor, however, has entirely misunderstood the sense. The passage referred to informs us that the same emperor who welcomed the pilgrim Yuan Chwang *on his return from India*, laden with Sanskrit manuscripts, "received with equal favour the Syrian Christians, Alopen, and his companions, who had arrived in A. D. 639." It is thus evident that we have here a distinct reference to the Emperor of China, and not to Harṣa (See also my article in *J. R. A. S.*, July, 1928, p. 629). The same misapprehension occurs in *Ind. Ant.*, XII, p. 232, Note 19; Max Müller's *India, What can it teach us?* p. 286, Note 4.

[3] See Appendix I.

APPENDIX I

Yuan Chwang gives the following information with regard to the condition of Buddhism and other religions in the different parts of the kingdom of Kanauj at the time of his visit:—

(i) *Ku-lu-to* or Kullu : "There were in the country twenty Buddhist monasteries with above 1,000 Brethren of whom the most were Mahāyānists a few adhering to the schools. Of Deva-Temples there were fifteen and the professed non-Buddhists lived pell-mell" (Watters, I, p. 298; Beal, I, p. 177).

(ii) *She-to-tu-lu* (Śatadru country) or Sirhind: "In and about the capital were ten monasteries, but they were desolate, and the Brethren were very few" (Watters, I, p. 299; Beal, I, p. 178).

(iii) *Sa-ta-ni-ssu-fa-lo* (Sthānvīśvara) or Thanesvar : "There were three Buddhist monasteries with above 700 professed Buddhists, all Hīnayanists. There were also above 100 Deva-Temples and the non-Buddhists were very numerous" (Watters, I, p. 314; Beal, I, pp. 183-84).

(iv) *Su-lu-kin-na* or Srughna : "There were five Buddhist monasteries and above 1,000 Buddhist ecclesiastics, the majority of whom were Hīnayānists, a few adhering to "other schools." There were 100 Deva-Temples, and the non-Buddhists were very numerous (Watters, I, p. 318; Beal, I, p. 188).

(v) *Po-lo-hih-mo-pu-lo* or Brahmapura : "There were five Buddhist monasteries, but there are very few Brethren : there were above ten Deva-Temples and the sectarians lived pell-mell" (Watters, I, p. 329, Beal, I, p. 198).

(vi) *Ku-pi-sang-na* or Govisāna : "There were two Buddhist monasteries with above 100 Brethren all Hīnayānists. Of Deva-Temples there were above 30, and the sectarians lived pell-mell" (Watters, I, p. 331; Beal I, p. 200).

(vii) *Ngo-hi-chi-ta-lo* (Ahicchatra) or eastern part of Rohilkhand : "There were above ten Buddhist monasteries, and more than 1,000 Brethren students of the Hīnayāna. Deva-Temples were nine in number, and there were above 300 professed adherents of the other systems Pāśupatas who worshipped Īśvara (Śiva)" (Watters, I, p. 331; Beal, I, p. 200).

(viii) *Pi-lo-shan-na* or Atranjikhera : "There were two Buddhist monasteries with 300 Brethren, all Mahāyāna students. There were five Deva-Temples and the sectarians lived pell-mell" (Watters, I, p. 332; Beal, I, p. 201).

(ix) *Kah-pi-t'a* (Kapittha) or Sankāsya : "There were four Buddhist monasteries and above 1,000 Brethren, all of the Saṁmatīya school. The Deva-Temples were ten in number and the non-Buddhists, who lived pell-mell, were Śaivites" (Watters, I, p. 333; Beal, I, p. 202).

(x) *Ka-no-kü-she* or Kanyākubja : "There were 100 Buddhist monasteries with more than 10,000 Brethren who were students of both the Vehicles. There were more than 200 Deva-Temples and the non-Buddhists were several thousands in number" (Watters, I, p. 340; Beal, I, p. 207).

(xi) *A-yu-te* or Ayodhyā : "There were above 100 Buddhist monasteries, and more than 3,000 Brethren who were students of both Vehicles. There were ten Deva-Temples, and the non-Buddhists were few in number" (Watters, I, p. 355; Beal, I, p. 225).

(xii) *A-ye-mu-k'a* (Hayamukha) i.e., Daundiakhera : "There were five Buddhist monasteries with above 1,000 Brethren who were adherents of the Saṁmatīya school, and there were more than ten Deva-Temples" (Watters, I, p. 359; Beal, I, p. 230).

(xiii) *Po-lo-ya-ka* or Prayāga : "There were only two Buddhist monasteries and very few Brethren, all Hīnayānists. There were some hundreds of Deva-Temples and the majority of the inhabitants were non-Buddhists"(Watters, I, p. 361; Beal, I, p. 230).

(xiv) *Kiao-shang-mi* or Kosambi : "There were more than ten Buddhist monasteries, but all in utter ruin; and the Brethren, who were above 300 in number, were adherents of the Hīnayāna system. There were more than fifty Deva-Temples and the non-Buddhists were very numerous" (Watters, I, p. 366; Beal, I, p. 235).

(xv) *Pi-sho-ka* (unidentified): "It had above twenty Buddhist monasteries and 3,000 Brethren who were all adherents of the Saṁmatīya school. There were above 50 Deva-Temples and the non-Buddhists were very numerous" (Watters, I, p. 373; Beal, I, pp. 239-40).

(xvi) *Shi-lo-fa-si-tu* or Sravasti : "There were some hundreds of Buddhist monasteries, of which the most were in ruins : the Brethren, who were very few, were Saṁmatīyas. There were 100 Deva-Temples and the non-Buddhists were very numerous" (Watters, I, p. 377; Beal, II, p. 2).

(xvii) *Lan-mo* (Rāma) or Rāmagrāma : Yuan Chwang does not give us any definite information excepting that there was a Śrāmanera monastery (Watters, II, p. 20 f.; Beal, II, p. 26 f.).

(xviii) *Kou-shih-na-ka-lo* or Kuśinagara : The pilgrim is silent about the condition of both Buddhism and Brahmanism, although he mentions a number of Buddhist topes.

(xix) *Po-lo-na-se* or Bārāṇasī : "There were above thirty Buddhist monasteries with more than 3,000 Brethren all adherents of the Saṁmatīya school. Of Deva-Temples there were above 100, and there were more than 10,000 professed adherents of the sects, the majority being devotees of Śiva; some of these cut off their hair; others made it into a top-knot; some went about naked and some besmeared themselves with ashes; they were persevering in austerities seeking release from mortal existence" (Watters, II, p. 47; Beal, II, pp. 44-45).

(xx) *Chan-chu* country (Ghazipur district ?): "There were above ten Buddhist establishments with nearly a thousand Brethren and attached to the system of the "Little Vehicle." There were twenty Deva-Temples, and the followers of the different non-Buddhist systems dwelt pell-mell" (Watters, II, p. 59; Beal, II, p. 61).

(xxi) *Fei-she-li* or Vaiśāli : "The Buddhist establishments, of which there were some hundreds, were, with the exception of three or four, dilapidated and deserted, and the Brethren were very few. There were some tens of Deva-Temples, the various sects lived pell-mell, and the Digambaras flourished" (Watters, II, p. 63; Beal, II, p. 66).

(xxii) *Fu-li-chih* or the Vriji country : "There were few Buddhists, and the monasteries were above ten in number, the Brethren of which, less than 1,000 in number were students and adherents of both the "Great and Little Vehicles." There were some tens of Deva-Temples and the non-Buddhists were very numerous" (Watters, II, p. 81; Beal II, p. 78).

(xxiii) *Mo-kie-to* or Magadha : "There were above fifty Buddhist monasteries, and more than 10,000 ecclesiastics, for the most part adherents of the Mahāyāna system. There were some tens of Deva-Temples, and the adherents of the various sects were very numerous" (Watters, II, pp. 86-87; Beal, II, p. 82).

(xxiv) *I-lan-na-po-fa-to* or Monghyr : "There were above ten Buddhist monasteries and more than 4,000 Brethren the most of whom were Hīnayānists of the Saṁmatīya school; there were above twenty Deva-Temples and the adherents of the various religions lived pell-mell" (Watters, II, p. 178; Beal, II, p. 186).

(xxv) *Chan-po* (Campa) i.e., Bhagalpur : "There were some tens of monasteries mostly in ruins, and there were above 200 Brethren all Hīnayānists" (Watters, II, p. 181; Beal, II, p. 192).

(xxvi) *Ka-chu-wen* (?) *K'ilo* (Kajangala) i.e., Rajmahal : "There were six or seven Buddhist monasteries and above 300 Brethren; the Deva-Temples were ten in number and the various systems lived pell-mell" (Watters, II, p. 183; Beal, II, p. 193).

(xxvii) *Pun-na-fa-tan-na* or Puṇḍravardhana : "There were twenty Buddhist monasteries and above 3,000 Brethren by whom the "Great and Little Vehicles" were followed; the Deva-Temples were 100 in number, and the followers of the various sects lived pell-mell; the Digambara Nirgranthas being very numerous" (Watters, II, p. 184; Beal, II, p. 194).

(xxviii) *San-mo-ta-cha* or Samataṭa : "It had more than 30 Buddhist monasteries and above 2,000 Brethren, all adherents of the Sthavira school. There were 100 Deva-Temples, the various sects lived pell-mell, and the Digambara Nirgranthas were very numerous" (Watters, II, p. 187; Beal, II, p. 199).

(xxix) *Tan-mo-lih-ti* or Tāmralipti : "Of Deva-Temples there were more than 50, and the non-Buddhists lived pell-mell. There were above ten Buddhist monasteries and more than 1,000 Brethren" (Watters, II, p. 190; Beal, II, p. 200).

(xxx) *Kie-lo-na-su-fa-la-na* or Karṇasuvarṇa : "There were more than ten Buddhist monasteries, and above 2,000 Brethren who were all adherents of the Saṁmatīya school; there were 50 Deva-Temples and the followers of the various religions were very numerous" (Watters, II, p. 191; Beal, II, p. 201).

(xxxi) *Wu-tu* (Oḍra) or Orissa : "There were 100 Buddhist monasteries, and a myriad Brethren, all Mahāyānists. Of Deva-Temples there were 50, and the various sects lived pell-mell" (Watters, II, p. 193; Beal, II, p. 204).

(xxxii) *Kung-yü-to* (Kongoda) or Ganjam : "The people were not Buddhists. Deva-Temples were above 100 in number, and of Tīrthikas there were more than 10,000" (Watters, II, p. 196; Beal, II, p. 206).

It would be evident from the above extracts that Buddhism, Brahmanism, and Jainism were the principal religions in Harṣa's empire. Of these the last was not so popular excepting in certain parts, viz., Vaisali, Puṇḍravardhana and Samataṭa, where the Digambaras were numerous. These along with the Svetāmbaras or Svetapaṭas, as Bāṇa calls them, formed the two great sections of the Jaina community. To Yuan Chwang, who mostly saw things through Buddhist spectacles, the religion of the Enlightened One appeared to be in quite a flourishing condition, although it had suffered decline in several localities like Kosambi, Srāvasti, and Vaisali. The monastic establishments, whose very existence depended upon the support and charity of the laity, were the centres of Buddhist life and activity. Of the two broad divisions of Buddhism, Mahāyāna and Hīnayāna, the former seems to have considerably gained ground. We must, however, be extremely cautious in accepting the figures supplied by Yuan Chwang, as it is very doubtful if a proper census of the adherents of the rival religions was ever taken; and moreover the accuracy of his information is marred by such vague statements as "myriad Brethren," "some tens," "few," or "several thousands in number." The pilgrim further says in his general description of India that there were 18 schools of Buddhism, which differed widely in their practices and claimed intellectual superiority over one another[1].

Such unseemly controversies among the various sects must have weakened the cause of Buddhism and reacted in favour of Brahmanism, which had been showing signs of revival and vigour since the glorious epoch of the Guptas. Indeed, at the time of Yuan Chwang its influence was so potent and marked that India itself had come to be known as "the country of the Brahmans (Po-lo-men-kuo)." The main strongholds of Brahmanism in the kingdom of Kanauj were Prayāga and Vārāṇasī. Like Jainism and Buddhism, which in its Mahāyāna form encouraged the worship of the Buddha and the Bodhisattvas, Brahmanism was frankly given to idolatry. The most popular Brahmanical deities then were Āditya, Śiva, and Viṣṇu, and their idols were installed in what Yuan Chwang calls "Deva-Temples," existing almost in abundance. The *Harṣa-carita* gives us an idea of how images were worshipped. We learn, for instance, that on the day fixed for his departure Bāṇa washed the image with milk and then "offered worship to Śiva, with lighted lamps, ointments, oblations, banners, perfumes, incense, and sweet flowers."[2] It may be pertinent to add here that this passage further informs us that the Brahmans were wont to kindle the sacrificial fire (Agni) and offer oblations by a profuse pouring of ghee "on certain auspicious occasions, if not daily. They also held the cow sacred, and believed in the efficacy of performing superstitious rites in order to bring good luck."[3] Another feature of Brahmanism was the multiplicity of philosophical schools and ascetic orders. Bāṇa mentions the followers of Kapila, Kaṇāda, Upaniṣads (i.e., Vedān-

[1] Watters, I, p. 162.
[2] *Hc. C. T.*, p. 44.
[3] *Ibid.*, pp. 44-45; see also pp. 71, 90, 130.

tins), believers in God as a creator (Aiśvara-kāraṇikas), and even athiests like the Lokāyatikas[1]. Similarly, there were different classes of recluses as those pulling out their hair (Keśaluñcakas), Pañcarātrikas (Vaiṣṇava ascetics), Parāsara mendicants, Pāsupatas or Śaivas, Varṇis (Brahmacāris), Bhāgavatas (followers of Kriṣṇa) etc.[2] The *Life* also gives us names like the Bhūtas, Kāpālikas, Jūtikas, Sāṅkhyas, Vaiṣesikas, Chingkias (Chūdinkas).[3] They differed not only in their observances and beliefs, but as Yuan Chwang tells us, even their garbs varied. "Some wear peacock's tail, some adorn themselves with a necklace of skulls; some are quite naked; some cover the body with grass or boards, some pull out their hair and clip their moustaches; some mat their side-hair and make a top-knot coil."[4] In this connection it is interesting to recall that Bāṇa also refers to distinguishing sectarial marks on the foreheads. Yuan Chwang speaks highly of such men as "promenaded through life away from human affairs" and devoted their time and energy to gain knowledge and spirituality. They were not moved by honour or reproach, but their fame was widespread and the rulers treated them with ceremony and respect. They got their food by begging and paid no attention whatsoever to their personal needs and comforts in the pursuit of what they considered Truth.[5]

[1] *Ibid.*, p. 236.
[2] *Ibid.*, pp. 33, 49, 236.
[3] *Life*, pp. 161-62.
[4] Watters, I, p. 148; Beal, I, p. 76.
[5] Watters, I, pp. 160-61.

PART II

CHAPTER VIII

HARṢA AS AN AUTHOR AND PATRON OF LETTERS

Harṣa's claim to the remembrance of history rests not merely on the fact that he considerably enlarged the boundaries of the Kanauj kingdom, but still more on the enlightened character of his government and his liberal patronage of learning. According to Yuan Chwang, Harṣa used to earmark a fourth of the revenue from the crown lands for rewarding high intellectual eminence, and another fourth for gifts to various sects.[1] This official honour and attention paid to men of genius or literary distinction doubtless stimulated and encouraged them to devote "themselves to a thorough acquisition of knowledge," as the pilgrim himself testifies elsewhere.[2] The *Life* further records Harṣa's generous assignment of "the revenue of eighty large towns of Orissa" to a noted Buddhist scholar named Jayasena, who had become the admiration of the age on account of his piety and encyclopaedic learning. But inspired as the latter was by a lofty spirit of sacrifice and self-abnegation, he declined even this tempting offer.[3]

[1] Watters, I, p. 176; Beal, I, p. 87. In this connection we may also recall Kauṭilya's scheme of assigning land to spiritual guides and learned Brahmans (*Arthaśāstra*, Bk. II, Chaps. 1-2, pp. 45, 48). Such grants of land are called in an inscription "Vidyādhana" (*Ind. Ant.*, XII, pp. 193-94).

[2] Watters, I, p. 161; Beal, I, p. 80.

[3] *Life*, p. 154.

Harṣa also made munificent endowments to Nalanda, the great centre of Buddhist culture. One of his gifts to this University consisted in the construction of a magnificent *Vihāra* or temple covered with brass plates by the side of the principal monastery, about one hundred feet in height[1]. Perhaps a few words about Nalanda may not be amiss here. It was at that time the most celebrated seat of learning, and the pride of the Buddhist world. Kings vied with one another in their liberality to patronise and endow this great institution. The *Life* tells us that its structures were added by no fewer than six rulers in connected succession, *viz.*, Śakrāditya, Budhagupta, Tathāgatagupta, Bālāditya, Vajra, and a king of "Mid-India."[2] The sovereign of the country (i.e., Harṣa) had also "remitted the revenues of about 100 villages for the endowment of the convent."[3] Further, we learn that even the village householders contributed their mite towards supplying the four requisites of clothes, food, bedding, and medicine to the resident students.[4] The whole establishment was surrounded on all sides by a lofty brick wall pierced by a big gate. The buildings inside were remarkable for their beauty and grandeur. To quote the picturesque language of the *Life*, "the richly adorned towers, and the fairy-like turrets, like pointed hill tops, are congregated together. The observatories seem to be lost in the vapours (of the morning) and the upper rooms tower above the clouds."[5] Nalanda counted on its rolls several thousand "Brethren" (according to the *Life* their number was 10,000),[6] some

[1] *Life*, p. 159; Watters, II, p. 171.
[2] *Life*, pp. 110-11.
[3] *Ibid.*, p. 112.
[4] *Ibid.*, pp. 112-13.
[5] *Ibid*, p. 111.
[6] *Ibid.*, p. 112.

of whom had even come from distant foreign countries "to put an end to their doubts."[1] This high figure is no doubt striking if we take into consideration the fact that the University was meant for advanced studies, and it was not an easy matter to get admission into its portals. Yuan Chwang informs us that each candidate's fitness and scholastic attainments were subjected to a searching examination by the method of discussion, on account of which many of them had often to return disappointed. Life at Nalanda was one of severe discipline and earnest endeavour. The "Brethren," we are told, were very strict in observing the precepts and regulations of their order; they were looked upto as models by all India; learning and discussing they found the day too short; day and night they admonished each other, juniors and seniors mutually helping to perfection.[2]

Lectures on various topics were delivered to them from about 100 pulpits every day, and these discourses were so important and instructive that none of the students ever thought of missing them "even for a minute."[3] There they studied the "Great Vehicle," and also (the works belonging to) the eighteen sects, and not only so, but even ordinary works, such as the Vedas and other books, the Hetuvidyā, Ṣabdavidyā, the Cikitsāvidyā, the works on magic (Atharvaveda), the Sāṅkhya; besides these they thoroughly investigated the "miscellaneous" works.[4] During his stay of five years at Nalanda Yuan Chwang himself received instruction in "all the collection (of Buddhist books), and the sacred books of the Brahmans."[5] Among the

[1] Watters, II, p. 165.
[2] Watters, II, p. 165; Beal, II, p. 170.
[3] *Life*, p. 112.
[4] *Ibid.*
[5] *Ibid.*, p. 125.

specific subjects, which he learnt under the guidance of Śīlabhadra, are mentioned the Yoga-Śāstra, the Nyāya-Anusāra-Śāstra, the Hetuvidyāśāstra, the Śabdavidyā, the Vyākaraṇa etc., besides such Buddhist works as Koṣa, Vibhāṣā and others.[1] Thus it appears from this comprehensive curriculum that the main object of the establishment was not so much to instruct the pupils in any barren and jejune system of dogmas and creeds, but to rouse them to mental activity and spiritual speculation. The success of Nalanda may best be shown by giving the names of some of its brilliant scholars—men "of model character and perspicacious intellect"—like Śīlabhadra, Jñānacandra, Dharmapāla, Candrapāla, Guṇamati, Sthiramati, Prabhāmitra and Jinamitra, the fame of whose abilities and learning had travelled abroad and attracted seekers after knowledge from all parts of the Buddhist world. Indeed, Nalanda had become so celebrated that "those who stole the name (of Nalanda Brother) were all treated with respect wherever they went."[2]

Harṣa's interest in literature is further evident from his patronage of authors of repute and merit. The most shining light in his literary coterie was undoubtedly Bāṇa or Bāṇabhaṭṭa, who composed the well-known *Harṣacarita* devoted to the laboured and fulsome panegyric of his royal patron. It belongs to the domain

[1] *Ibid.*, p. 121.

[2] Watters, II, p. 165; Beal, II, p. 170; see also "*The University of Nalanda*" by H. D. Sankalia, (Madras, 1934). Among other important centres of learning in the kingdom of Kanauj were the *Ti-lo-shi-kia* monastery where "scholars from distant countries flocked together in crowds" (Beal, II, p. 102); the *Lo-to-wei-chi* (Raktaviṭi) sanghārāma in Karṇasuvarṇa, the rendezvous of learned celebrities; and the Bhadravihāra in Kānyakubja itself, where Yuan Chwang studied for sometime under Vīryasena. (See *Supra*).

of a writer on Sanskrit literature to discuss his writings, but suffice it here to say that among Bāṇa's other works are (*a*) *Caṇḍīśataka*, (*b*) the *Pārvatīpariṇaya*,[1] (*c*) and the *Kādambarī*. Curiously enough, he left both the romances —the *Harṣacarita* and the *Kādambarī*—unfinished. The latter, however, was taken up by his son, Bhūṣaṇabhaṭṭa, in the midst of a speech in which Kādambarī's sorrows are told, and the style of this later addition fortunately is an exact and skilful imitation of the first portion. The next member of this distinguished circle was Mayūra, whose chief contribution to the literature of the day was the *Sūryaśataka*. Chronologically antecedent to this was perhaps the *Mayūraśataka*, since in the legend the latter is said to have caused the leprosy which the former cured.[2] That Mayūra was in the court of Harṣa may be substantiated by the following stanza occurring in Sārangdhara's *Paddhati* and other works :

> "Aho prabhāvo Vāgdevyā yan Mātanga Divākaraḥ,
> Śrī-Harṣasyābhavat sabhyaḥ samo Bāṇa-Mayūrayoḥ."

i.e., "So great is the power of Saraswati that even the outcaste Divākara became a courtier of Harṣa on equal terms with Bāṇa and Mayūra."[3] This remarkable passage reveals to us yet another poet named Divākara. Nothing tangible has so far been brought to light concerning this shadowy bard, but his literary excellences

[1] Its authorship is, however, doubtful.

[2] Some critics are of opinion that the *Sūryaśataka* and the *Mayūraśataka* are not separate works, but they are simply two different names of one and the same text. On the life and works of Mayūra see "*The Sanskrit Poems of Mayūra*," edited by Quackenbos (Columbia University Series, Vol. 9). See *Ibid.*, p. 60.

[3] Compare Peterson's edition, Vol. I, Stanza 139, p. 30 (Bombay Sanskrit Series, No. 37). Also Parab's *Subhāṣitaratnabhāṇḍāgāra* (5th ed., Bombay, 1911), p. 37, Stanza 37. See also the *Sūktimuktāvalī*.

and achievements must have sufficed to win him royal recognition and favour.[1]

But Harṣa was not a mere detached patron of letters. He himself appears to have wielded the pen with no less dexterity and effect than the sword. There are three plays, viz., the *Ratnāvalī*, the *Priyadarśikā*, and the *Nāgānanda*, which are said to have been composed by a king named Harṣadeva. This royal author has been identified with Harṣa of Kanauj, since it is contended that no other sovereign of this name can meet the requirements of the case. Now, ancient Indian history knows of three kings, besides Śīlāditya of Kanauj, who bore the name Harṣa: (*a*) the tyrannical king of Kashmir, who flourished between 1089-1101 A. D., according to the *Rājataraṅgiṇī*.[2] (*b*) Harṣa, the grandfather of king Bhoja of Dhārā, (*circa* 947-972 A. D.). (*c*) Harṣa-Vikramāditya of Ujjain[3], identified with Yaśodharman of Malwa by Dr. Hoernle[4]. Of these, the first two can easily be ruled out owing to chronological difficulties presented by these works being mentioned and quoted by earlier writers. Dāmodaragupta, who lived under Jayāpīḍa of Kashmir (779-810 A. D.) mentions in his work, the *Kuṭṭanīmata* (vv. 856f), the story and performance of the *Ratnāvalī*, which he ascribes to a king. Dr. Keith further points out that the poet Māgha, who may be assigned... to about A. D. 700, knew the *Nāgānanda*, "to which a reference is made in his Kāvya (xx, 44)."[5] Regarding the claims of the third Harṣa mentioned above, we may say that according to Kalhaṇa, Harṣa was only his secondary name, and Vikramāditya was his title. It

[1] Dr. Keith notes that some poems of this author are preserved (*Classical Sanskrit Literature*, p. 120).

[2] Stein, *Rājat.*, Bk. VII, p. 333 f.

[3] *Ibid.*, Bk. III, verse 125, p. 83.

[4] *J. R. A. S.*, 1909, p. 446 f.

[5] *Classical Sanskrit Literature*, pp. 54-55.

appears, therefore, improbable that if this Harṣa had been the author of these plays, he would have omitted to mention the prized title of Vikramāditya in the *prastāvanā*. Besides, he was not a Buddhist, and so he could not be associated with an almost Buddhistic play as the *Nāgānanda*. Thus applying the method of elimination, the only Harṣa left to hold the field is the Kanauj sovereign of that name.[1] Moreover, it is thought that the internal evidence of these plays also supports Harṣa's claims to their authorship. In the first place, they appear to bear the stamp of a common authorship, as they not only exhibit innumerable parallelisms of thought, style, structure, and diction, but sometimes contain even identical phrases and stanzas.[2] All the three dramas, again, are considered to betray here and there some of the actual incidents in the life of Harṣa, as also his ideals and achievements.[3] We must, however, urge caution against any undue reliance on conclusions based on such arguments only. That they are the work of one pen may probably be conceded by all critics; but it may as well be said—and such a charge has undoubtedly been made, as we shall presently see—that they were the productions of some literary protégé of Harṣa, who was thoroughly conversant with the religious tendencies and the chief events in his patron's life and career. Perhaps they were written to provide entertainment for the Kanauj audience and for dedication to the king, but the poet in his gratitude for the munificent gifts received and to honour Harṣa, who appears to have been singularly ambitious, went a step further and as-

[1] See also Dr. Keith's *Sanskrit Drama* (1924), pp. 170-81.

[2] See for similarities in all the three plays : *Priyadarśikā*, edited by Nariman, Jackson, and Ogden (Columbia University Series, 1923) Introduction, Part VI, pp. lxxvii-lxxxvii, to which I owe some references given here.

[3] See Dr. R. K. Mookerji, *Harṣa*, pp. 153-56.

cribed the composition of the plays themselves to him.

But our extraneous evidence for Harṣa's literary attainments seems to be more definite and conclusive. Thus Bāṇa states eulogising Harṣa: "In poetical contests he poured out a nectar of his own which he had not received from any foreign source;"[1] and again "his poetical skill finds words fail."[2] We must, however, note that Bāṇa's testimony is always to be taken with a certain amount of reserve owing to his tendency to lavish all sorts of praise on his hero. Next, Soḍḍhala, who wrote in the 11th century A. D. mentions Harṣa in his *Udaya-sundarī-kathā* along with other literary monarchs, as an instance of a poet-king and patron of literature (cf. "kavīndraiśca Vikramāditya-Śrī Harṣa-Muñja-Bhojadevādi-bhūpālaiḥ"—p. 150). And in another passage he punningly refers to him as the illustrious Harṣa, whose joy was in diction (gīr-harṣa). It runs thus:

"Śrī-Harṣa ityavanivartiṣu pārthiveṣu
Nāmnaiva kevalamajāyata vastutastu,
Gīr-harṣa yeṣa nijasaṁsadi yena rājñā
Saṁpūjitaḥ kanaka-koṭi-śatena Bāṇaḥ,"[3]

i.e., "There arose among the princes dwelling upon earth
(One who was) Śrī-Harṣa merely by name; but, in reality,
That one was speech-joy (or rejoicing in diction) in his own assembly—
A king by whom Bāṇa was honoured with (a gift of) a hundred crores of gold."

[1] *Hc. C. T.*, p. 58. Cf. "Kāvyakathāsva-pītamamritamudvamantaṁ." (Hc., Cal. ed., pp. 161-62).

[2] *Ibid.*, p. 65. Cf. "Api cāsya... kavitvasya vācaḥ ... na paryāpto viṣayaḥ" (*Ibid.*, p. 182).

[3] C. D. Dalal and Krishnamacharya's edition, p. 2 (Gaekwaḍ's Oriental Series, No. 11; Baroda, 1920).

The famous author Jayadeva, who flourished about the 12th century A. D., mentions Harṣa's name in the following stanza of the *Prasannarāghava* along with the earlier Bhāsa and Kālidāsa, as well as his own literary favourites Bāṇa and Mayūra, and also the later Cora, as well-known authors :

"Yasyāś-Coraścikuranikaraḥ karṇapūro Mayūro,
Bhāso hāsaḥ kavikulaguruḥ Kālidāso vilāsaḥ.
Harṣo harṣo hridayavasatiḥ pañcabāṇaśca Bāṇaḥ,
Keṣāṁ naiṣā kathaya kavitā kāminī kautukāya."[1]

i.e., "Oh, say, to whom would not poetry as a mistress be an object of admiration,

Since she has Cora (Bilhaṇa) as her mass of hair, Mayūra as her earrings,

Bhāsa as her laughter, Kālidāsa, guru of the race of poets, as her grace,

Harṣa as the joy dwelling in her heart, and Bāṇa as her god of love."

The *Subhāṣitaratna-Bhāṇḍāgāra*[2] also includes Harṣa's name in a list of well-known writers, who "gladden this universe by their compositions." To quote the passage:

"Māghaś-Coro Mayūro Muraripuraparo Bhāraviḥ sāravidyaḥ,
Śrī-Harṣaḥ Kālidāsaḥ kaviratha Bhavabhūtyāhvayo Bhojarājaḥ.
Śrī-Daṇḍi ḍiṇḍimākhyaḥ śrutimukuṭa gurur Bhallaṭo Bhaṭṭa-Bāṇaḥ
Khyātaścānye Subandhvādaya iha kritabhir-visvamālhādayanti."

i.e., "Māgha, Cora, Mayūra, the second Muraripu (i.e., Murāri), Bhāravi whose knowledge is renowned;

[1] *Prasannarāghava*, Act I, Stanza 22, p. 10, ed. Paranjpye and Panse (Poona, 1894).

[2] See Parab. 5th ed., Stanza 68, p. 38, (Bombay, 1911). The stanza is given here anonymously.

The illustrious Harṣa, Kālidāsa and also the poet named Bhavabhūti, Bhojarāja;
The illustrious Daṇḍin, called 'the drum,' Bhallaṭa, weighty with the diadem of fame, Bhaṭṭa-Bāṇa;
And other celebrities, chief of whom is Subandhu, gladden the Universe here by (their) compositions."

Bühler further informs us that the *Bhāvabodhinī* of Madhusūdana (17th century A. D.) contains the following passage: "Two eastern poets, called Bāṇa and Mayūra, lived at the court of Mahārāja Śrī-Harṣa, the chief of poets, the composer of the *nāṭikā* called the *Ratnāvalī* who was lord of Malwa, and whose capital was Ujjain."[1] Madhusūdana's account "learnt from the mouth of illustrious ancients" and written down a thousand years after Harṣa's time, is no doubt a mere literary anecdote, wrongly associating Harṣa with Malwa and Ujjain, but the contemporaneity and literary gifts of Bāṇa, Mayūra, and Harṣa certainly seem to be the substratum of truth in this erroneous statement.

Lastly, we are told on the authority of I-tsing that "king Śīlāditya versified the story of Bodhisattva Jimūtavāhana, who surrendered himself in place of a Nāga. This version was set to music. He had it performed by a band accompanied by dancing and acting, and thus popularised it in his time."[2] The record of I-tsing, who came to India just a quarter of a century after the death of Harṣa, seems to me by far the most important and reliable testimony regarding Harṣa's literary attempts and attainments.[3]

[1] *Ind. Ant.*, Vol. II (1873), pp. 127-28. Compare "Mālavarājasyojjayinī rājadhānīkasya kavijanamūrdhanyasya Ratnāvalyākhyanāṭikā kartur Mahārāja Śrī-Harṣasya."

[2] I-tsing, *A Record of the Buddhist Religion in India and the Malay Archipelago*, translated by J. Takakusu, pp. 163-64 (Oxford, 1896).

[3] Harṣa is also said to have composed the *Suprabhātastotra*, which mentions his name in the colophon (*J. R. A. S.*, 1903,

In spite of these corroborative allusions occurring in later and contemporary literature, Sanskrit authors seem to have entertained doubts regarding the authorship of these plays from quite early times. The first to express such scepticism was Mammaṭa, a Kashmiri writer of the 11th century A. D., who speaks in his *Kāvyaprakāśa* of gains accruing from the art of writing poetry. It is claimed that poetry "redounds to fame and makes for wealth" (kāvyaṁ yaśase arthakrite), and the author himself illustrates this statement by saying: "Fame—in case of Kālidāsa and others; wealth—as to Dhāvaka and other poets, from Śrī-Harṣa and other kings" (Kālidāsādīnāmiva yaśaḥ Śrī-Harṣāder Dhāvakādīnāmiva dhanaṁ).[1] It was presumably due to the composition of the above three dramatic works that Dhāvaka received handsome rewards from Harṣa. On the other hand, Bühler points out that some manuscripts of the *Kāvyaprakāśa*, found in Kashmir, read Bāṇa instead of Dhāvaka. This is no doubt confirmed by Soḍḍhala, who, as noted above, alludes to the fact that Harṣa honoured Bāṇa with a gift of a hundred crores of gold. Bāṇa's authorship of these dramas, however, seems out of the question. His style, as is

pp. 703-22). Dr. F. W. Thomas, however, ascribes it to king Harṣa of Kashmir (*Ibid.*, p. 704). Some lines in the Madhuban inscription as well probably bear the stamp of our Harṣa's authorship (Bühler, *Ep. Ind.*, Vol. I, p. 71). Besides, Yuan Chwang attributes the *Aṣṭamahāśrīcaitya-saṁskrita-stotra* to an Indian king called "Sun of virtue," which is equivalent to Śilāditya, the title given to Harṣa (see also Dr. Keith's *History of Sanskrit Literature* (1928), p. 215). It may not be out of place to add here that he was also a skilled calligraphist, as seems clear from his signature in the Banskhera charter (Cf. "Sva hasto mama Mahārājādhirājasya Śrī-Harṣasya").

[1] See *Kāvyaprakāśa*, B. V. Jhalkīkara's edition, pp. 6-7 (Bombay, 1921); Gangānātha Jhā's English Translation (1925), pp. 1-2.

evident from the *Harṣacarita* and the *Kādambarī*, was most extravagant and complicated, while the language of the plays is simple and unfettered by any artificiality and ornamentation. The plays are in no sense productions of a high order, and appear quite unworthy of a writer like Bāṇa.

This doubt was shared by several scholiasts of the 17th century A. D., who affirm that the plays were composed by Dhāvaka in the name of Harṣa. Thus says Nāgoji in his *Kāvyapradīpoddyota*: "Dhāvaka was a poet, and having composed the *Ratnāvalī* in Śrī Harṣa's name obtained much wealth, such is the report" (Dhāvakaḥ kaviḥ sa hi Śrī-Harṣa-nāmnā Ratnāvalīm kritvā bahu dhanaṁ labdhavān, iti prasiddhaṁ).[1]

Another scholiast, Paramānanda, repeats a similar story that "a poet by name Dhāvaka having sold his own work, a play called *Ratnāvalī*, obtained much wealth from the king named Śrī-Harṣa, so it happened of old" (Dhāvaka-nāmā kaviḥ svakritiṁ Ratnāvalīṁ nāmanāṭikāṁ vikrīya Śrī-Harṣa-nāmno rājñaḥ sakāsād bahudhanamavāpeti purāvrittaṁ).[2]

Now the question naturally arises: Are these assertions mere fictions lacking foundation, or are they based on truth? In the absence of any other definite confirmatory evidence it would be presumptuous to give a certain answer, but we may indicate a few difficulties in the way of implicit reliance on these passages. In the first place, Dhāvaka as a poet is unknown to Sanskrit literature, and none of his verses have been quoted in the *Subhāṣitāvalī*. Secondly, almost all the later doubting authors belong to the 16th or 17th century A. D., and this distance in time from Harṣa considerably

[1] *Ibid.*, D. Chandorkar's edition, p. 5, (Poona, 1898).

[2] Bhandarkar's *Report* for 1882 on Sanskrit Manuscripts, No. 208; Nariman, Jackson, and Ogden, *Priyadarśikā*, p. xlvii. See also Maheśvara's *Prakāśādarśa*.

lessens the weight of their authority. Thirdly, it is not clear from Mammaṭa—probably the original source of the later authors—whether the money received by the poets of Harṣa's court was an act of pure royal patronage, or was of the nature of a price for selling their authorship. The truth of the whole matter is that although we cannot be oversanguine about Harṣa's authorship of these plays, there is nothing intrinsically improbable in such a view. Instances of royal literati are not wanting in history, and we may cite the names of Bhoja Paramāra of Dhārā, the Pallava king Mahendravikramavarman,[1] Vigraharāja Cāhamāna of Sākambharī,[2] Babar and Jahangir in this connection. But this does not exclude the possibility that some literary protégé of Harṣa may have lent an obliging hand in polishing his patron's dramas, for as the proverb has it, royal authors are only half-authors.

[1] Dr. L. D. Barnett, *Bulletin of the School of Oriental Studies*, 1920, pp. 37-38.

[2] See the *Harakeli-Nāṭaka*, *Ind. Ant.*, XX (1891), pp. 211-12, lines 32, 35, 37, 40.

PART III

CHAPTER IX

SECTION A

KANAUJ AFTER HARṢA'S DEATH TO THE PRATĪHĀRA CONQUEST

Effects of Harṣa's death

After a momentous reign lasting for well-nigh half a century, Harṣa passed away in the year 647 or 648 A. D.[1] The withdrawal of his strong arm let loose all the pent-up forces of anarchy, and the result was that the mighty fabric of the empire reared by the genius of Harṣa soon collapsed like a house of cards. The outlying provinces fell off one by one, and Kanauj itself became the scene of a violent upheaval. Although all our indigenous sources of information are cut off at this period, it is fortunate that the Chinese writer Ma-twan-lin (13th century) affords us some ray of light on this tale of confusion.

We are told that in 648 A. D. the Emperor of China with whom, as already noted, Harṣa had cultivated diplomatic friendship, sent a superior officer named Wang-

[1] According to the *Life* (p. 156) Śīlādityarāja died "towards the end of the Yung Hwei period" (i.e., about 654-55 A. D.). Watters, on the other hand, states that "the date 648, or rather 647, is perhaps the correct one." It was in the early part of the year 648 A. D. that the Emperor of China sent an ambassador to Harṣa, who was, however, dead before his arrival (*J. A. S. B.*, VI (1837), pp. 69-70).

heuen-tse as head of a new mission "in order that the principles of humanity and justice which had been diffused in that country should have a protector and representative there."[1] But before he arrived, She-lo-ye-to or king Śīlāditya had died, and the country was in the throes of a revolution.[2] One of the ministers named Na-fo-ti-a-la-na-shun, or O-la-na-shun (i.e., Aruṇāśva or Arjuna) usurped the deceased monarch's throne and sent soldiers to oppose the entry of Wang-heuen-tse, who, however, took with him some tens of cavalry and directed a counter attack against the forces of the usurper. The small armed escort of the mission was massacred in cold blood, and the tributes received on the way were seized, but Wang-heuen-tse in the dead of night was lucky enough to make his way to the western frontiers of Too-fan or Tibet. This triumph of the usurper stimulated his ambitions, and he further "used violence to make other kingdoms pay him tribute."[3] But the Chinese envoy resolved to avenge his humiliation, and called upon the neighbouring kingdoms to render him assistance. The king of Tibet, the famous Srong-btsan-Gampo, who was married to the Chinese princess Weng Chang, sent him a contingent of one thousand armed men, and Nepal supplied 7,000 cavalry. Having organised this small force, Wang-heuen-tse descended into the plains to give battle, and took the city of Too-po-ho-lo[4] by assault in three days. Three

[1] *J. A. S. B.*, VI (1837), p. 69.

[2] The *Life* (p. 155) also represents Yuan Chwang as being told in a dream by a golden figure : "You should return soon, for after ten years Śīlādityarāja will be dead, and India be laid waste and in rebellion, wicked men will slaughter one another; remember these words of mine."

[3] *Ind. Ant.*, IX, p. 20.

[4] Substituting *Ca* (*cha*) for *Too* (the first character), the name is regarded as equivalent to Camparan or Chapra (*J. A. S. B.*, VI,

thousand men were beheaded, and ten thousand more were drowned in the river identified by Smith with the Bagmati. O-lo-na-shun or Arjuna escaped into another kingdom, and rallying his dispersed hosts attempted a fresh encounter. But he again met with a disastrous rout, being taken prisoner along with a large body of men, who were promptly beheaded. In a subsequent action the Chinese general captured 12,000 men and women, besides animals of all kinds amounting to 20,000. He also subdued 580 towns, and his power grew so strong that even She-keaou-mo or Śrīkumāra, who had been a firm ally of Harṣa, sent a large number of oxen, horses, weapons, and provisions for the victorious army. Wang-heuen-tse brought Arjuna to China to present him to the Emperor as a vanquished foe and received ample recognition of his services by being promoted to the rank of *Chao-san-ta-fu* (a sort of aulic councillor).[1] The authority of the usurper was thus subverted, and with it the last vestiges of Harṣa's power also disappeared.

What followed next was only a general scramble to feast on the carcase of the empire. Bhāskaravarman of Kāmarūpa (Assam), after breaking off friendly relations with Kanauj, appears to have annexed Karṇasuvarṇa and the adjacent territories, which were formerly

p. 69, note). But Smith identifies it with Tirhut (*Early. Hist. of India.*, 4th ed., p. 367).

[1] This account is mainly based on the translations of Ma-twan-lin (See *J. A. S. B.*, VI, pp. 69-70; *Early Hist. of India*, 4th ed., pp. 366-67; *J. R. A. S.*, 1869-70 (N. S. IV), pp. 85-86; *Ind. Ant.*, IX, p. 20; *Asiatic Journal and Monthly Register for British and Foreign India, China and Australia*, 1836, pp. 220-21). C. V. Vaidya, however, disbelieves this story (*H. M. H. I.*, Vol. I, pp. 334-35; See also N. Ray, *Ind. Hist. Quart.*, Dec. 1927, p. 792). The figures cited above must be taken with some reserve as they savour of Chinese vanity.

included within his great ally's dominions.[1] This is evident from the Nidhanpur plate issued from his camp there, and the learned editor of the inscription may even be right in asserting that it was in commemoration of his triumphant entry into the capital of Karṇa-suvarṇa that the king of Assam made this grant of land to a Brahman of the locality.[2]

In Magadha Ādityasena, the son of Mādhavagupta who was a feudatory of Harṣa, gave a good account of himself by reviving to some extent the lost glory of the Guptas. According to the Shahpur inscription he was ruling in the year 66 of the Harṣa era i.e., 672; and in the Mandar inscription he is given the imperial titles of Mahārājādhirāja and Paramabhaṭṭāraka.[3] In one inscription he is described as "the ruler of the (whole) earth upto the shores of the oceans; the performer of the Aśvamedha and other great sacrifices."[4] Another Nepalese record calls him "Great Ādityasena, the illustrious lord of Magadha."[5] It is thus indubitably clear from these facts that soon after the sceptre dropped from the hand of Harṣa, Ādityasena raised himself to a paramount position and brought under his domination lands formerly subject to Kanauj. In the west and north-west those powers that had lived in dread of Harṣa asserted themselves with greater vigour. Among them were the Gurjaras of Rajputana and the Punjab and the Karkoṭakas of Kashmir, who during the course of the next century became a formidable factor in the politics of Northern India.

[1] See *ante*.

[2] *Ep. Ind.*, XII, p. 66.

[3] *C. I. I.*, III, p. 212.

[4] *Ibid.*, p. 213, note.

[5] *Ind. Ant.*, IX, p. 181.

Blank in History

The period from the fall of the usurper to the rise of Yaśovarman, nearly three-quarters of a century later, is one of the darkest in the whole range of the history of Kanauj, and every event of that time is hidden from view by a thick veil of oblivion. Cunningham partially tried to unravel this mystery. He thought that Ranmul was ruling over Kanauj in A. D. 700, and invaded the distant Sindh.[1] Cunningham also asserted on the testimony of Abul-Fazl that Harcand, the contemporary of Mohammed-ibn-Kasim, ascended the throne of Kanauj in 715 A. D., which, if true, would make him almost the immediate predecessor of Yaśovarman.[2] But the distinguished archæologist's opinion is not substantiated by any other evidence, and so it is difficult to put any reliance on it. Besides, we do not know to what dynasty they belonged, and how they came to power. We must, therefore, refrain from vague speculations, and travel down the stream of time till we come to an anchorage of historical fact.

SECTION B

YAŚOVARMAN

Sources

After Harṣa's death the earliest monarch, whose name has been recorded in literature and also perhaps in an inscription,[3] is Yaśovarman. He was apparently

[1] *J. A. S. B.*, X, Part I, p. 188.

[2] *Āyīn-i-Akbarī*, II, p. 219; Elliot, *Cach-Nāma*, I, p. 208.

[3] Cf. the Nalanda stone inscription of Yaśovarmadeva. Dr. Hīrānanda Śāstrī, the editor of the inscription, however, identifies him with Yaśodharman of the Mandasor inscriptions (*Ep. Ind.*, Vol. XX (January, 1929), pp. 39-40). See *Infra* for this controversy.

a king of some note, and his exploits form the subject of a contemporary Prakrit document called the *Gauḍavaho*, which, though planned on an enormous scale (viyaḍa = vikaṭa), on the whole, as remarked by Dr. Keith, contains "as little history as possible."[1] Some welcome light on his career is also thrown by Kalhaṇa's *Rājataraṅgiṇī* and the Jain works like the *Prabhāvakacarita*, the *Prabandha-Koṣa*, and the *Bappabhaṭṭasūricarita*, and we shall appraise the value of their testimony later on.

His lineage

The first question that arises is whether Yaśovarman was a mere upstart adventurer who shot up like a brilliant meteor and soon vanished into nothingness, or had he any ancestral claims to the throne of Kanauj? Vākpati, the author of the *Gauḍavaho*, praises him as "an ornament to the lunar race of kings, to which he belonged,"[2] and we may, therefore, assume that he came of some celebrated Kṣatriya family. Cunningham thought that he was a descendant of the Maukharis, and the common termination—*varman*—of their names even lends some colour to this view.[3] Besides, they had ruled over Kanauj before the epoch of Harṣa, and it is possible that after the suppression of the usurper the kingdom was restored to some unrecorded member of this house, from whom it devolved on Yaśovarman. There is indeed a mention of a Bhogavarman, "the crest-jewel of the illustrious *varmans* of the valorous Maukhari race," who was contemporary with Ādityasena of Magadha and Śivadeva II of Nepal—being the

[1] *A History of Sanskrit Literature* (1928), p. 150.

[2] *Gauḍavaho* (S. P. Pandit's ed.) verses 1064-65. See also Introduction, p. xxxix.

[3] *Arch. Surv. Ind. Rep.*, XV, p. 164. See also N. Ray, *Cal. Rev.*, Feb., 1928, p. 216; E. A. Pires, *The Maukharis*, pp. 136-137.

son-in-law of the former and father-in-law of the latter—, in one of the Nepalese inscriptions,[1] but unfortunately it does not make it clear whether he had any connection with Kanauj. The late Jain work *Bappabhaṭṭasūricarita*, on the other hand, represents Yaśovarman as "the illustrious ruler of Kānyakubja, who was the head-jewel of the famous dynasty of Candragupta, by whom was made illustrious the already illustrious family of the Mauryas."[2] It is interesting to add that the *Prabhāvaka-carita* (13th or 14th century A. D.) also describes Yaśovarman as having descended from, and been a bright ornament in the family of Candragupta.[3] But the kings of the Maurya dynasty did not take names ending in—*varman*, and we have no other evidence to corroborate the Jain statement. Even the Nalanda stone inscription, which most probably belongs to the time of our Kanauj monarch, does not afford us any clue on this point. Thus in the absence of any positive proofs it is better not to credit Yaśovarman with any well-known ancestry, and for the present to let him stand isolated and unconnected.

Approximate date

Chronology being the weakest spot in Hindu history, it is obviously difficult to fix the limits of Yaśovarman's reign with any amount of accuracy. Smith was of opinion that he ruled from *circa* 728 to 745 A. D.,[4] and Sankara Pāṇḍuranga Pandit in his learned introduction of the *Gauḍavaho* comes to the conclusion that "Yaśovarman must have reigned in the latter part of the

[1] *Ind. Ant.*, IX, pp. 171, 181, verse 13.

[2] *J. B. B. R. A. S.*, Vol. III, May, 1928, pp. 103, 314.

[3] See H. M. Śarmā's ed. (Bombay, 1909), XI, verses 46-47, p. 131.

[4] *J. R. A. S.*, 1908, p. 784.

seventh and the first part of the eighth century A. D."[1] We may, however, first determine the period of Yaśovarman with reference to the chronological setting of his contemporary and rival, Lalitāditya of Kashmir, and then try to arrive at a closer approximation. The date of Lalitāditya can be worked out either by counting the years of all successive kings of the valley till he came to the throne, or by calculating back from the completion of Kalhaṇa's *Rājataraṅgiṇī* to his accession. But as the dates and reigns of kings back from Jayasiṁha, the contemporary of Kalhaṇa, rest on a far more sure basis than those of the distant predecessors of Lalitāditya, we shall follow the latter method here.

Kalhaṇa mentions the year 25 of the Laukika or Saptarṣi era as the time of the finishing of his great work, which he began in 24 Laukika era corresponding to 1070 Śaka according to the method of turning a Laukika into a Śaka year given in Sir R. G. Bhandarkar's *Report on Manuscripts* (1883-84, p. 84). The sum of the duration of reigns from Jayasiṁha, who had at this date ruled for twenty-two years, to Lalitāditya has been given by Śankara P. Pandit on the basis of his computation as 455 years, 7 months and 11 days.[2] If we, therefore, subtract these years from 1071 Śaka i.e., the year 25 of the Laukika era, we get *circa* Śaka 615 or 693 A. D., as the date of Lalitāditya's accession to the throne. He is recorded to have reigned for 36 years, 7 months and 11 days, and thus, according to Kalhaṇa, Lalitāditya's reign may be fixed between 693 and 730 A. D. A comparison with Chinese chronology, however, throws doubt on the correctness of these dates. The

[1] *Gauḍavaho*, Introduction, pp. xcv-vi.

[2] *Gauḍavaho*, Introduction, pp. lxxxvi-xcii. The total of the durations includes the reign-period of Saṃgrāmāpīḍa, which is 7 years. Some *Mss*. read "*vāsarān*" (days) for "*vatsarān*," which, however, is incorrect (See *Ibid*., p. lxxxvi note).

Chinese Annals of the Tang dynasty represent Tchen-t'o-lo-pi-li or Candrāpīḍa, the second predecessor of Muktāpīḍa, as having sent an embassy to the Chinese court in the year 713 A. D. to seek its aid against the Arabs, and as receiving investiture as king from the Emperor of China in 720 A. D., whereas according to Kalhaṇa's chronology Candrāpīḍa was already dead in 689 A. D. As the Chinese have been more precise in their system of chronology, evidently there must be a mistake of at least 31 years in Kalhaṇa's calculation, supposing Candrāpīḍa to have died the very year he received the title from China. Hence if we apply the correction of 31 years, Lalitāditya's date will fall between 724 and 760 A. D., and being his contemporary Yaśovarman must also be assigned to the same period.

Having arrived at this rough indication, we may now try to ascertain more definite limits of his reign. The Chinese authorities mention that a "king of Central India," of the name of I-cha-fon-mo, sent his minister Seng-po-ta to China in 731 A. D., and the former has, I suppose, been correctly identified with Yaśovarman of Kanauj.[1] Probably he despatched this embassy in order to enlist the support of the Emperor of China, who was by far the most powerful Asiatic potentate of those times, soon after his accession, which we may, therefore, approximately date in the year 725 A. D. With regard to the last limit of his reign, the Jain writers seem to give us a fairly correct clue. Most of them state that he was ruling in V. E. 800 or 743 A. D., and Rājaśekhara, the author of the *Prabandhakoṣa*, leads us a step further. He informs us that a Jain saint named Bappabhaṭṭi, who was initiated as a monk in V. E. 807, converted to Jainism Āmarāja, the son and successor of Yaśovarman. Bappabhaṭṭi was next raised to the

[1] Stein, *Rājat.*, Introd. p. 89; Bk. IV, verse 134, note.

dignity of Sūri in V. E. 811 after his royal disciple had ascended the throne. It is thus evident that Yaśovarman must have died sometime between the years 807 V. E. and 811 V. E., corresponding to 750 and 754 A. D., i.e., about the year 752 A. D. These dates (725-752 A. D.) fit in very well with the dates of Lalitāditya, and we may be sure that they leave little margin for error.[1]

Conquering expeditions

The author of the *Gauḍavaho* credits Yaśovarman with having carried on expeditions of conquest (Vijaya-yātrā) in the manner of the mythical "world-conquerors." These exploits read more like fiction than sober history, but before offering any destructive criticism let us pause to present the story as narrated by Vākpati. Yaśovarman is represented as having first turned his energies in a south-easterly direction, and the only indication given of the line of his advance is that he halted on the way to pay homage to the celebrated non-Aryan deity, the Vindhya-vāsinī-Devī, whose shrine now stands near the modern city of Mirzapur in the United Provinces. It is interesting to note in passing that human sacrifices were made to this goddess, and at this distance in time one may well shudder at the idea of kings subscribing to such a blood-thirsty and barbarous cult. The details of the march, however, are not recorded, but the road to this temple from Kanauj would ordinarily lie through the present districts of Cawnpore, Fatehpur and Prayāga or Allahabad. We may, therefore, assume that Yaśovarman followed that route. His adversary, who is simply described as "Magahanāha" or "Magadha-nātha" i.e., lord of Magadha, at first tried to avoid his

[1] See also the "*Collected works of Sir* R. G. *Bhandarkar*, Vol. II, pp. 429-33.

steel, but mustering courage returned to fight after some time. A tough battle ensued, and it resulted in the defeat and death of the ruler of Magadha, who was most probably identical with Jīvitagupta II.[1] As Vākpati has given the title of "*Gauḍavaho*" to his work, it may reasonably be supposed that the vanquished monarch held sway over parts—perhaps Western—of Bengal also. Yaśovarman is next said to have subjugated the king of the Vangas or eastern Bengal, who was "powerful in the possession of a large number of warlike elephants." Although we cannot be sure about the identity of the latter, Dr. R. G. Basak conjectures that he may have been Rājarājabhaṭṭa of the Khaḍga dynasty.[2] Yaśovarman then went by the road across the Malaya mountain (the southern Sahyādri), accepting the submission of an unnamed king of the Deccan. His arms are even represented to have penetrated as far as the seashore "where Vāli, taking under his armpit the mighty Rāvaṇa, roamed about at sea." It is difficult to make out what part of the country the poet speaks of, but probably the author takes his hero as far as the sea only to complete the conventional area of "world conquest." The next enemies whom he conquered in a hard-fought battle were the Pārasikas, who are a riddle to many. Bühler identified them with the Persians,[3] but beyond the superficial similarity in sound there is nothing to commend this view. They are placed among the countries of the south, and as Vākpati follows some sort of geographical order, we must look for

[1] See also R. D. Banerji, *Mem. As. Soc. Beng.*, Vol. V, No. 3, p. 43. For a different identification with king Harṣa of Assam, "in whose territory was included Bengal," see Krişṇasvāmī Aiyangar's article "Forgotten episodes in Mediæval India" in *Journal of Indian History*, Vol. V, pt. III, p. 327.

[2] *The History of North-Eastern India*, p. 208.

[3] *Ind. Ant.*, XLII (1913), p. 249.

them in the south. Curiously enough, a Cālukya inscription[1] gives us a clue to them, since among the southern conquests of the Cālukya Vinayāditya it includes the Pārasikas along with the Kāmeras or Kāveras, and the Coḷas. Levying tributes in regions made inaccessible by the western mountains, i.e., the Ghats, Yaśovarman followed the route across the Nerbudda and the Marudeśa or Marwar, and arrived in the land of Śrīkaṇṭha or Thanesvar made famous in history by the Vardhana dynasty. He is then alleged to have marched to the site of Ayodhyā, the city of Hariścandra,[2] and received the submission of the people living on the Mandāra mountains. These regions of the north, known in connection with the lord of the Yakṣas[3], are said to be "perfumed with the gum exuding from fissures in the Devadarus," which clearly indicates that we have an allusion to some Himalayan country. "Having thus conquered the world," Yaśovarman returned to the capital, and dismissed the numerous kings who had been compelled to accompany him after their subjugation.

Criticism of this campaign

Commenting on the story of Yaśovarman's expedition Smith says : "I see no reason to doubt the substantial truth of this contemporary testimony. There is

[1] *Ibid.*, IX, p. 129; see also Fleet, *Dynasties of the Kanarese Districts*, p. 368.

[2] Smith thinks that the reference to Ayodhyā cannot be to the well-known city of Rāma in Southern Oudh, but must mean some place much farther north to which the legend of Hariścandra's aerial city was attached (*J. R. A. S.*, 1908, p. 779).

[3] Dr. Hoernle thinks that this last move sounds very much as if it described the king's going to *svarga* i.e., his demise after his conquest (*J. R. A. S.*, 1909, p. 106). But this view is not tenable, as Yaśovarman is recorded to have come into conflict with Lalitāditya of Kashmir subsequently.

nothing incredible in the assertion that a powerful king, occupying at Kanauj a good central position, should have carried his arms eastwards across Bengal, southwards to the Narmada, and northwards to the foot of the mountains."[1] It is true that in ancient India such hostile operations with or without provocation were quite common, and each aspiring Kṣatriya king considered it his highest duty to wage successful wars and perform the Aśvamedha sacrifice as a mark of power and widespread suzerainty. But with all deference to the opinion of the late historian, I venture to say that the nature of Vākpati's poem itself does not allow us to give it any substantial measure of credence. Its non-completion shows that the poet conceived the *digvijaya* as a probable event and not an actual fact, while it may not even be unreasonable to suppose that he took the conquests of the mythical Raghu as a model for singing the alleged achievements of his hero. Moreover, no vanquished king is mentioned by name, and this introduces no small element of doubt into the whole story, which is obnoxiously full of vile flattery and vain exaggerations. Probably the central theme of the poem—the killing of the king of the Gauḍas and Magadha—was an historical reality, for, as we have seen above, this region had been controlled by Kanauj during the time of Harṣa and the Maukharis also. Yaśovarman, who appears to have been an ambitious monarch, perhaps attempted to regain control of the lower course of the Ganges, and it may be that the complete success of his campaign induced his panegyrist to invest him with the halo of a "world-conqueror."

Foundation of a town

Yaśovarman is credited with having founded a town

[1] *J. R. A. S.*, 1908, p. 779.

in his name in Magadha,[1] and this, I suppose, he did either to commemorate his victory over the "lord of Magadha and Gauḍa," or to mark the site of the battle. Such a practice was not uncommon in ancient times, and we may recall that Alexander similarly marked his victory by the foundation of two towns, one named Nikaia situated on the battlefield; and the other called Boukephala, located at a point whence Alexander started to cross the Hydaspes.[2] Yaśovarman's town has been identified by Cunningham with the present town of Bihar,[3] but Kielhorn was of opinion that preferably Ghosrawa was its modern representative[4]. We get a glimpse of its importance during the Pāla period also, for it was to the *Vihāra* of Yaśovarmapura that Vīradeva went after visiting the diamond throne at Mahābodhi (Bodh Gayā), and stayed there for a long time enjoying king Devapāla's patronage.[5]

War with Kashmir

Kalhaṇa represents Lalitāditya Muktāpīḍa as a mighty monarch, who, "being eager for conquests," passed most of his time in expeditions abroad, "moving round the earth like the sun."[6] His ambitions naturally brought him into conflict with the rising power of Yaśovarman, and in the struggle which followed his attack the "thoughtful ruler of Kānyakubja" is said to have, like a wise man, first "showed his back to the fiercely shining Lalitāditya, and (then) made his submission."[7] A treaty was drawn up, and the document

[1] *Arch. Surv. Ind. Rep.*, III, pp. 135-36; XV, 164.
[2] *Early Hist. of India*, 4th ed. pp. 74-75.
[3] *Arch. Surv. Ind. Rep.*, III, pp. 120, 135-36; VIII, p. 76.
[4] *Ind. Ant.*, XVII (1888), pp. 309, 311, note 30.
[5] *Ibid.*
[6] *Rājat.*, Bk. IV, verse 131, (Stein, p. 131).
[7] *Ibid.*, verse 135, (Stein, p. 132). Cf. "Matimān Kanyakubjen-

was called "the treaty of Yaśovarman and Lalitāditya," but Mitraśarman, the Kashmiri minister of Foreign Affairs (Sāndhivigrahika) refused to ratify it on the ground that it meant a slight to his victorious master, if the name of the defeated Kanauj sovereign were allowed to precede. Thereupon negotiations broke off, and Lalitāditya highly esteeming his minister's insistence on the proper form, bestowed upon him the five great offices distinguished by the term "great" (pañcamahā-śabda)[1]. This led to a resumption of hostilities, though his generals, "who were dissatisfied with the long duration of the war, blamed it."[2]

Its results

The consequences of the renewed military activities were of course disastrous to the arms of Yaśovarman, but we seem to have no certain information as to what happened to his throne and person. The *Rājataraṅgiṇī* in one place claims that "the land of Kanyakubja from the bank of the Jumna to that of the Kālikā was as much in his (Lalitāditya's) power as the courtyard of his palace,"[3]

draḥ pratyabhāt Krityavedināṁ, Dīptaṁ yat Lalitādityaṁ priṣṭaṁ datvā nyaṣevat."

[1] *Ibid.*, verse 140, (Stein, p. 133). According to Fleet also the above is the special significance of the term "pañca-mahāśabda" in the *Rājataraṅgiṇī*. But it usually denoted "the sounds of five great musical instruments (pañca-mahāvādya), the use of which was allowed, as a special mark of distinction to persons of high rank and authority (*Ep. Ind.*, XII, pp. 254-55). See also *Ind. Ant.*, I, p. 81; IV, pp. 106, 180, 204; XIII, p. 134, etc. Sometimes, however, the epithet was applied to paramount kings (*Ep. Ind.*, VI, p. 106; *C. I. I*, III, p. 296, n. 9).

[2] *Rājat.*, Bk. IV, verse 139, (Stein, p. 133).

[3] Bk. IV, verse 145, (Stein, p. 134). Cf. "Kimanyat Kanyakubjorvī yamunā pāratosya sā, Abhūdā Kālikātīraṁ gṛiha-prāṅganavadvaśe." The Kālikā may be identified with the present Kālīnadī, which joins the Ganges at a short distance below Kanauj.

and that Yaśovarman was "uprooted entirely" (samūlaṁ udapāṭayat).[1] Further, we are told that "swelled with pride the king (Lalitāditya) granted the land of Kanyakubja with its villages to the (shrine of) Āditya, (which he erected) at that town of Lalitapura" (Latpor).[2] It thus indicates that Kanauj was annexed to the dominions of Kashmir, and its king perhaps put to death during the course of the conflict.[3] But elsewhere Kalhaṇa affirms that Yaśovarman, "who had been served by Vākpatirāja, the illustrious Bhavabhūti, and other poets, (himself) became by his defeat a panegyrist of his (Lalitāditya's) virtues."[4] In the face of this dubious testimony, we would, therefore, suggest that although Yaśovarman was worsted in the fight, the stubborn resistance of the Kanaujias, as is evident from the reference to the "long duration" of the struggle, deterred Lalitāditya from proceeding to extremities, and he suffered his adversary after a nominal acknowledgement of supremacy to remain on the throne. Confirmation of this view may further be had from the *Travels* of Ou-Kông, according to which Mung-ti (Muktāpīḍa) was in alliance with the ruler of Central India (Yaśovarman) and together they blocked "the five passes" leading from Tibet. Here we may also refer to a hoard of Lalitāditya's coins discovered in the Banda district of the United Provinces.[5] This find, it has been urged, lends support to the theory that the kingdom of Kanauj passed under the jurisdiction of Lalitāditya and his coins became current there. Such a conclusion, however, does not appear to be quite warranted. The

[1] *Ibid.*, verse 140, (Stein, p. 133).
[2] *Ibid.*, verse 187, (Stein, p. 139).
[3] See *J. R. A. S.*, 1908, p. 777.
[4] *Rājat.*, Bk. IV, verse 144, (Stein, p. 134).
[5] *J. A. S. B.*, Numismatic Supplement, XLI (1928), pp. N. 7-8.

hoard may only represent part of the treasures Lalitāditya carried for the maintenance of his forces, which, to quote the evidence of the *Rājataraṅgiṇī*, progressed triumphantly eastwards to Gauḍa and other regions. The army perhaps encamped near Banda for sometime, and thus left its mark in the form of these coins.

Date of the defeat

From the account of Lalitāditya's embassy to China Dr. Stein thinks that he must have subdued Yaśovarman after the date of the embassy i.e., long after A. D. 736.[1] Smith, on the other hand, definitively places the event in 745 A. D.;[2] but in our humble opinion the catastrophe occurred earlier in his reign. In stanzas 827-31 of S. P. Pandit's edition of the *Gauḍavaho* we have mention of some portentous happenings, which took place on the occasion "when the corner of Yaśovarman's eye became twisted in consequence of a momentary shaking of his (kingly) position." This has been taken by Professor Jacobi to be a reference to Lalitāditya's invasion; and he seems to be right considering that his (Yaśovarman's) defeat did not entail death or dethronement. Among other portentous occurrences was the assumption by the disc of the sun when it was pierced through by the Ketu, of the form of an anklet as it were of the Lakṣmī (fortune) of the three worlds dislocated from her foot when she thrust it forth violently in anger (stanza 829). Evidently this passage alludes to an eclipse of the sun, which, according to astronomical

[1] *Rājat.*, Trans. Introd., Vol. I, p. 89. The claim of the Kashmiri ambassador that the king of Central India, identified with Yaśovarman, was his master's ally, would further confirm our contention that the two monarchs became friends after a trial of strength.

[2] *J. R. A. S.*, 1908-9, p. 761. The date has been fixed as A. D. 740 in *Early History of India*, 4th ed., p. 392.

calculations made by Prof. Jacobi, occurred and was visible at Kanauj on the 14th day of August, 733 A. D.[1] Hence this year also represents the date of the attack on Kanauj.

Nalanda stone inscription of Yaśovarmmadeva

This interesting inscription in high-flown Sanskrit was discovered a few years ago at Nalanda.[2] It is a Buddhist document, and its object is to record that Mālada, the son of Yaśovarmmadeva's minister, who is called *Mārgapati*, as well as *Udīcīpati* and *Pratīta-Tikiṇa*, made certain gifts to the community of Bhikṣus and to the temple erected by king Bālāditya at Nalanda in honour of the "son of Suddhodana" i.e., the Buddha. It extols Yaśovarman in hyperbolic terms as the *lokapāla* (guardian of the world), who "has risen after placing his foot on the heads of all the kings and has completely removed the terrific darkness in the form of all his foes by the diffusion of the rays of his sword."[3] Now the problem arises: Who was this great monarch? Unfortunately, the epigraph is not dated, and it does not also mention his ancestry or any of his successors. This has, therefore, been the source of some controversy with regard to his identity.[4] Dr. Hīrānanda Śāstrī thinks that he is identical with Yaśodharman of the Mandasor inscriptions, and further corrects the latter's name into Yaśovarman.[5] He relies mainly on the ground that the inscription "was written when Bālāditya was ruling, and when king Yaśovarmmadeva was holding

[1] *Gottingische Gelehrte Anzeigen*, 1888, vol. II, pp. 67-68.

[2] *Ep. Ind.*, Vol. XX (January, 1929), pp. 37-46.

[3] *Ibid.*, pp. 43, 45, verse 2.

[4] See for this controversy *Ind. Hist. Quart.*, VII (1931), p. 664; VIII (March, 1932), pp. 228-30; VIII (June, 1932), pp. 371-73; VIII (Septr., 1932), pp. 615-17.

[5] *Ep. Ind.*, XX, p. 40.

the reins of sovereignty."[1] Since this Bālāditya is, in Dr. Śāstrī's opinion, the same as "the homonymous chief whom Yuan Chwang eulogises as the subduer of Mihirakula and the founder of the grand temple at Nalanda," he finds it reasonable to identify Yaśovarmmadeva with Yaśodharmadeva, who was a contemporary of the Hūṇa chief, and hence also of Bālāditya. But, as pointed out by Dr. R. C. Majumdar, there is no warrant for the above assumption. The inscription merely alludes to a temple built by Bālāditya, and nowhere does it seem to imply that he was alive and ruling at the time it was set up. Besides, palæographical considerations indicate that the document probably belongs to a date much later than that of Yaśodharman. Dr. Śāstrī himself admits that the letters in which it is written present "a very marked development in contrast with those of the contemporary or even somewhat later inscriptions, and they largely resemble the characters of the Aphsad inscription of Ādityasena,"[2] whose known date from the Shahpur record is 66 = 672 A. D. He further notes that "the alphabet used in the inscription is, to a large extent, identical with the Devanāgarī or the Nāgarī."[3] And yet, strange to say, the similarity with the script of the Horiuzi (Japan) palm-leaf manuscript of the *Uṣṇīśavijayadhāraṇī* of uncertain date has lead Dr. Śāstrī to assign the epigraph to a ruler flourishing in 533-34 A. D. according to the Mandasor inscription. Lastly, the suggested correction of the name Yaśodharman into Yaśovarman has hardly any justification, and there can be absolutely no doubt from the facsimile that the latter name is the correct reading. We may add here that even Fleet, who considered the form of the name

[1] *Ibid.*
[2] *Ep. Ind.*, XX, p. 38.
[3] *Ibid.*

while editing the Mandasor inscription refrained from adopting any change in the termination.[1] It would thus appear from the above discussion that the present inscription most probably belongs to the reign of Yaśovarman of Kanauj, who, as we know from the *Gauḍavaho*, had brought Magadha under his subjection.

Consideration of coins

There have been discovered some crude coins of the Indo-Scythian type bearing the name of Yaśovarma,[2] which are more barbarous than those of Durlabhaka Pratāpāditya II (*circa* 700 A. D.), but not quite so degraded as the issues of Jayāpīḍa Vinayāditya (779 A. D.). Their proper place is thus between the coinage of these two kings from the numismatic point of view, and they have accordingly been ascribed to Yaśovarman on the ground that he is the only prince with this name recorded to have been ruling at this period, and that the Kashmir list knows of no such monarch.[3] The *Rājataraṅgiṇī*[4], of course, refers to a Yaśovarman, who was related to the royal family of Kashmir, but he never sat on the throne, and his date, *circa* 850 A. D., also appears to be very late. We cannot, however, be quite definite about their attribution, since the above view is open to certain objections. First, these coins have all been found in the Panjab, Kashmir and in the distant Manikyāla stūpa, none of

[1] *C. I. I.*, Vol. III, p. 145, note 2.

[2] Obverse—"Scarcely recognisable copy of the Kushan standing king; *Ki* below left arm."

Reverse—"Headless seated goddess, even more barbarous than on the Pratāpa coins. Brāhmī legend on the right "Śrī Yaśov (arma)." (Smith, *Cat. Coi. Ind. Mus.*, Vol. I, p. 268; Cunningham, *Coins of Med. India*, p. 44, note 20).

[3] *J. A. S. B.*, XXIII, p. 700; *J. R. A. S.*, 1908, pp. 783-84.

[4] *Rājat.*, Vol. I, Bk. IV, verse 706, (Stein, p. 184).

the specimens coming from the Kanauj territory. Secondly, their fabric and general appearance betray a Kashmiri or Panjabi origin, while there is nothing whatever, even in the exaggerated accounts of Vākpati, to show that Yaśovarman's arms ever penetrated so far northwards, much less that he was in possession of these regions. Thus it seems more probable from the provenance and deteriorated style of these coins that they were struck by an otherwise unknown minor king of the Panjab or Kashmir during the sixth or seventh century, rather than by Yaśovarman of Kanauj.[1]

Literary activity at Yaśovarman's court

Like many well-known kings of ancient India Yaśovarman was both a poet and a patron of letters, and the *Rājataraṅgiṇī* alludes to this in the following passage :

"Kavir-Vākpatirāja-Śrī-Bhavabhūty-ādi sevitaḥ,
Jito yayau Yaśovarmā tadguṇa-stutivanditāṁ."

i.e., "the poet Yaśovarman, who had been served by Vākpatirāja, the illustrious Bhavabhūti, and other poets, (himself) became by his defeat (at the hands of Lalitāditya) a panegyrist of his (Lalitāditya's) virtues."[2] Unfortunately, there is no extant work which we can attribute to him with certainty, although the play entitled *Rāmābhyudaya*[3] and some poems cited in Vallabhadeva's *Subhāṣitāvalī* are said to have been the compositions of one Yaśovarman, identified with his Kanauj namesake. The stanza also gives us the names of two literary geniuses—Vākpatirāja and Bhavabhūti[4]

[1] Dr. Hoernle assigns these coins to Yaśodharman of the Mandasor inscriptions (*J. R. A. S.*, 1903, p. 551; 1909, pp. 105-08; *Proc. As. Soc. Beng.*, 1888, pp. 181-82).

[2] Bk. IV, verse 144, (Stein, p. 134).

[3] *Ind. Ant.*, XLI (1912), p. 141.

[4] Prof. Max-Müller in interpreting the above verse made Rājyaśrī a separate poet (*India, What can it teach us?*, p. 334). But

—who adorned his court, and, as we shall see below, Kalhaṇa's testimony is amply confirmed by the literary tradition of the Jains and by Vākpati himself. Of the two, Bhavabhūti was the more gifted poet and Vākpati frankly acknowledges his debt to him saying : "even now in his rugged compositions excellences are sparkling like drops of the *amrita* liquid of poetry, which have come out of the ocean (called) Bhavabhūti." He is the author of the three well-known Sanskrit plays, *Mālatīmādhava*, *Mahāvīracarita* and *Uttararāmacarita*. Hertel is of opinion that "all of them must have been composed in Kanauj" in order to be performed "before an audience of pilgrims in the temple of Kālapriyanātha, who evidently was Yaśovarman's family deity."[1] It is, however, usually assumed that the Lord Kālapriya is the same as the Mahākāleśvara, whose famous shrine at Ujjain in Malwa is mentioned by Kālidāsa (*Raghuvaṁśa*, VI, 34), and Bāṇa (*Kādambarī*, p. 53, ed. Peterson) etc. But this identification seems inadmissible inasmuch as Bhavabhūti tells us in the *Mālatīmādhava* that his ancestral home in Padmapura, corresponding with modern Padmāvatī or Narvar in the Gwalior state,[2] is "on the road to the south" with reference to the shrine of the Lord Kālapriya. We have, therefore, to look for some place to the north of Padmāvatī, and it is quite likely that Yaśovarman, who was perhaps a Śaiva or a Śākta (witness his visit to the goddess Vindhyavāsinī) had a temple of this description in the capital also.[3] The

Sanskrit literature knows of no poet with this name. The word *rāja* here is to be connected with Vākpati, and Śrī is only an honorific prefixed to the name of Bhavabhūti. It is significant that in the *Gauḍavaho* Vākpati speaks of himself as Vappaïrāya or Vākpati-rāja.

[1] *Asia Major*, Vol. I, pp. 12-13.

[2] *Arch. Surv. Ind. Rep.*, 1862-65, Vol. II, pp. 307-08.

[3] Some scholars, however, think that the temple of Kālapriya was in Kalpi (U. P.).

genius of Bhavabhūti has received its full meed of appreciation from Sanskrit authors. Rājaśekhara calls him "an incarnation of Vālmīki" in his *Bāla-Rāmāyaṇa*[1] and some critics even declare that Bhavabhūti excels Kālidāsa in the *Uttararāmacarita*.[2] The other literary luminary of Yaśovarman's court was Vappaîrāya or Vākpati, described in the *Bappabhaṭṭacarita* as "the head-jewel of the Kṣatriyas and born of the Paramāra clan." He appears to have enjoyed royal favour to a greater extent than his senior Bhavabhūti. Vākpati calls himself the king's "paṇayī lavo" (literally a particle of a favourite friend), and claims that he was at the head of the poets (Kaî-rāya i.e., Kavirāja).[3] He wrote in Prakrit, and according to the Jain legends he was at first in the service of the king of Gauḍa at Lakṣamaṇāvatī, and thence passed to the court of the victorious Yaśovarman. It is alleged that in the latter part of his life he became a convert to Jainism, and after undergoing severe penances in Mathura voluntarily starved himself to death (*anaśana*) in accordance with the Jain rule for men desirous of making a good end. Before writing the *Gauḍavaho* Vākpati composed a poem entitled *Mahu-Maha-Viyaya* (Madhu-Matha-Vijaya). He considered it to be his best work;[4] but its text has not been discovered, and nothing can be said of it except that it probably dealt with the death of the demon Madhu at the hands of Viṣṇu. At present Vākpati's only extant work is the *Gauḍavaho* comprising 1209

[1] I, 16; see also *Bālabhārata*, I, 12.

[2] Cf. "Uttare Rāma-carite Bhavabhūtir viśiṣyate."

[3] Kalhaṇa's way of mentioning also supports this conclusion, as according to Vārttika 4 to Pāṇini II. 2. 34 that which is more "*abhyarhita*" or respected should come first. But we may at the same time urge that no undue emphasis should be laid on such a subtle point of grammar.

[4] *Gauḍavaho*, stanza 69.

couplets, which, as conjectured by Dr. Keith, was probably "left unfinished owing to Yaśovarman's death;" or it may be a "series of excerpts dealing with those topics which the Pandits liked, omitting tedious historical details."[1]

Yaśovarman's successors

We are left to grope in the dark after Yaśovarman except for the uncertain light thrown by Jain sources, which allege that he was succeeded by his son Āma, born of Yaśodevī during her temporary exile due to the machinations of a co-wife. The *Bappabhaṭṭacarita* and the *Prabandhakoṣa* indicate that Āma held his court at Gopagiri (Gwalior), but according to the *Prabhāvakacarita* he, like his father Yaśovarman, reigned at Kanauj and not altogether at Gopagiri. Whatever be the truth, the importance of the tradition probably lies in showing that the region of Gwalior formed part of the dominions of Kanauj at this time. It seems that Jainism occupied the supreme position in Āma's heart, and he regarded Bappabhaṭṭa as his spiritual *guru*. He is also represented as going to Jain holy places like Cambay (Stambatīrtha) Vimalagiri (Palitana), Raivatādri (Girnar), and Prabhāsa (Patan) etc. Further, he is said to have been in constant rivalry with one Dharma, king of Lakṣamaṇāvatī, but the details are wrapped in utter confusion. Āma was succeeded by his son, the immoral Dunduka, who, according to the *Prabhāvakacarita* (XI, 759), was murdered by his son Bhoja. After this event we have no information whatsoever. We cannot give much credence to these tales based on tradition and more concerned with religious edification than with the narration of sober facts of history with some respect for chronology. But as there is nothing to contradict

[1] Keith, *A History of Sanskrit Literature* (1928), p. 150.

them, we may with S. P. Pandit say for the present that "all the credit that the Jaina stories have a right to claim is that king Āma was perhaps the son of Yaśovarman, that Dunduka was Āma's son, and that Bhoja was the son of Dunduka."[1] None of them achieved anything of note, and one was even prematurely murdered. We may, therefore, well believe that, if they really had historical existence, the length of their combined reigns must have been of extremely short duration—say between 15 and 20 years.

SECTION C

THE ĀYUDHAS

Vajrāyudha

Another shadowy figure occurring in this obscure period of our history is Vajrāyudha, whose actual existence is borne out solely by an incidental reference made by Rājaśekhara, the dramatist, who flourished at the Pratīhāra court in the first half of the tenth century A. D. Thus he writes in the *Karpūramañjarī*[2] : "to the capital of Vajrāyudha, the king of Pāñcāla, to Kanauj," in connection with the itinerary of a merchant named Sāgaradatta, who had gone to the royal city on business. It is significant that Rājaśekhara uses the name Pāñcāla for the country of which Kanauj was the capital, although from its omission by the Chinese pilgrim we may infer that it was not the popular designation of this kingdom at that time.[3] Vajrāyudha must have ascended

[1] *Gauḍavaho*, Introduction, p. clix. See however, *J. B. B. R. A. S.*, Vol. III, N. S. 1927, pp. 101-33, where Dr. Kriṣṇasvāmī Aiyangar stoutly maintains the credibility of the *Bappabhaṭṭacarita* and equates Āmarāja with Nāgāvaloka.

[2] III, 5[2], pp. 74, 266 (Konow and Lanman's edition).

[3] The term Pāñcāla at first denoted the whole stretch of country

the throne sometime about A. D. 770, since, as we shall see below, the Jain *Harivaṁśa* informs us that a king named Indrāyudha was ruling in Kanauj in the year 783-84 A. D., while we also know from other sources that he was succeeded by Cakrāyudha. The form of these names suggests that all the three monarchs belonged to the same line. If so, they must have ruled over Kanauj one after the other, for it is difficult to find a vacant place for Vajrāyudha elsewhere except before Indrāyudha. We further learn on the authority of Kalhaṇa that Jayāpīḍa Vinayāditya (779-810 A. D.), who tried to emulate the exploits of his grandfather Lalitāditya in distant lands, "after defeating the king of Kanyakubja in battle, carried off his throne the ensign of royal power."[1] Evidently we have here an allusion to the defeat and dethronement of a king of Kanauj, and he is perhaps to be identified with Vajrāyudha, assuming that the attack on Kanauj took place soon after Jayāpīḍa became king of Kashmir. But if it occurred later in his career, the vanquished Kanauj monarch must have been Indrāyudha.

Indrāyudha

Vajrāyudha appears to have been succeeded by Indrāyudha or Indrarāja, but it is not clear what relationship they bore to each other. According to the passage

from the Chambal to the Himalayas, which was afterwards divided into North and South Pāñcāla. The Ganges formed the boundary between the two, and they had their capitals at Ahicchatra and Kāmpilya respectively. Varāhamihira (6th century A. D.) includes the Pāñcālas among the peoples of the *Madhyadeśa*, and reckons their country as one of the nine great kingdoms (*Brihatsaṁhitā*, XIV, 32; *Ind. Ant.*, XXII, p. 186). Presumably this list refers to much earlier times. Alberuni, who wrote in 1030 A. D., also mentions these nine divisions, but adds that the names were not then commonly used (Sachau, Trans., Vol. I, p. 298).

[1] *Rājat.*, Vol. I, Bk. IV, verse 471, (Stein, p. 163).

in the Jain *Harivaṁśa*,[1] Indrāyudha was ruling in Śaka year 705 or 783-84 A. D., being known as king of the north. Hence we may conclude from this description that, even when its glory had departed, Kanauj continued to enjoy pre-eminence among the kingdoms of the North. It was probably during Indrāyudha's reign that Dhruva Rāṣṭrakūta (*circa* 779-794 A. D.) invaded the territories of the Doab, and "added the emblem of the Ganges and the Jumna to his imperial insignia." For, a verse in the Baroda plates informs us that he "taking from his enemies the Gangā and the Yamunā, charming with their waves, acquired at the same time that supreme position of lordship (which was indicated) by (those rivers in) the form of a visible sign."[2] During this raid the Kanauj sovereign appears to have invoked the aid of his Gauḍa contemporary, who was, however, compelled to submit to the invader. This is evident if we take the above verse in conjunction with another occurring in the Sanjan plates, where we are told that Dhruva "seized the white umbrellas, the sporting lotuses of *Lakṣmī* (goddess of sovereignty), of the Gauḍa king, as he was fleeing between the Ganges and the Jumnā."[3] The monarch ruling in Gauḍa at this time must have been either Gopāla or Dharmapāla, but as the former is not known from the inscriptions of the Pāla dynasty to have wielded any considerable power, it is better to regard the latter as the adversary of Dhruva.

[1] The following seems relevant here:

"Śākeṣv-abdaśateṣu saptasu diśāṁ pañcottareṣūttarāṁ." The full verse will be discussed later on.

[2] Dr. Fleet took this line as referring to Govinda III (*Ind. Ant.*, XII, pp. 159, 163), but Dr. Majumdar has rightly pointed out that "the reference is not to Govindarāja but to his father Dhruva." (*Jour. Dept. of Letters*, Vol. X, p. 35; see also Dr. D. R. Bhandarkar, *Ep. Ind.*, XVIII, p. 239, note 4).

[3] *Ep. Ind.*, XVIII, line 14, pp. 244, 252.

Cakrāyudha

Indrāyudha's reign must have terminated about the close of the 8th century, for we are informed in two epigraphic documents that he was attacked and defeated by Dharmapāla of Bengal, who, undeterred by earlier reverses, had now launched his ambitious schemes of conquest. The Bhagalpur plate of Nārāyaṇapāla[1] records the result of this conflict as follows : "Jitv-endrarāja-prabhritīn arātin upārjjitā yena Mahodaya-Śrīḥ dattā punaḥ sā valin-ārthayitre Cakrāyudhay-ānati Vāmanāya," i.e., "This mighty one (balin) again gave the sovereignty, which he had acquired by defeating Indrarāja and other enemies, to the begging Cakrāyudha, who resembled a dwarf in bowing, just as formerly Bali had given the sovereignty (of the three worlds), which he had acquired by defeating Indra and his other enemies (the gods), to the begging Cakrāyudha (Viṣṇu), who had descended to earth as a dwarf." We have in this passage a distinct statement that king Dharmapāla conquered Indrarāja and other enemies, but returned the sovereignty of Mahodaya[2], which he had thus gained for himself, to one Cakrayudha—perhaps a brother or son of the vanquished monarch. And in making this arrangement Dharmapāla was only acting in consonance with the policy advocated by Kauṭilya[3] and Manu,[4] and sometimes followed by Indian Imperialists, that it is more prudent

[1] Edited in *Ind. Ant.*, XV, pp. 305, 307; mentioned *Ibid.*, XX, p. 187, etc. Also see *J. A. S. B.*, Vol. XLVII (1878), pt. I, p. 384 f.

[2] This is evident if we remember that the term "Mahodaya-śrīḥ," like the rest of the verse, has a double meaning, and that with reference to Dharmapāla it can only be interpreted as "the sovereignty over Mahodaya or Kanauj."

[3] *Arthaśāstra* (Shamasastry's Trans. 3rd ed., 1929), Bk. VII, ch. 16, p. 339.

[4] Cf. *Manusmriti* :

to raise a protégé in a distant conquest than to resort to direct annexation. The story of this dethronement is supplemented by the Khalimpur plate,[1] which details the subsequent transactions. We are told that the glorious Dharmapāla, who had humbled the great conceit of all rulers, "installed the illustrious king of Kānyakubja, who readily was accepted by Bhoja, Matsya, Madra, Kuru, Yadu, Yavana, Avanti, Gandhāra and Kīra kings, bowing down respectfully with their diadems trembling, and for whom his own golden-coronation-jar was lifted up by the delighted elders of Pāñcāla."[2] Although this contemporary record does not name the king of Kanauj, it is obvious that the event described is the installation of Cakrāyudha in succession to Indrarāja or Indrāyudha, as specifically mentioned in the late Bhagalpur grant. The gathering of distant sovereigns like those of Gandhāra and Avanti to give "respectfully" their stamp of recognition to the settlement made by the Gauḍa monarch not only shows the importance of Kanauj and the keen interest bestowed on its affairs by the contemporary states of northern India, but also indicates the power and position of Dharmapāla, who seems to have attained in his day the rank of the premier king of the North. We should, however, guard against making any such deductions, as was done by Mr. R. D. Banerji, that Dharmapāla "conquered or overran eastern Panjab and Sindh (Kuru and Yadu), W. Panjab and N.-W. Frontier Provinces (Yavana and Gandhāra), Kangra (Kīra), Malwa (Avanti) and North-Eastern Rajputana (Bhoja and Matsya)."[3] Similarly,

"Sarveṣāṁ tu viditvaiṣāṁ samāsena cikīrṣitaṁ, Sthāpayet-tatra tad vaṁśyaṁ Kuryācca samaya-kriyāṁ" (VII, 202).

[1] *Ep. Ind.*, IV, pp. 243-54; first faulty edition in *J.A.S.B.*, Vol. LXIII (1894), pt. I, pp. 39-62.

[2] *Ep. Ind.*, IV, pp. 248, 252.

[3] *Mem. As. Soc. Beng.*, Vol. V, No. 3, p. 51.

there is nothing in support of Mr. C. V. Vaidya's view that the enumeration of the nine kings shows that "the empire or suzerainty of Kanauj was acknowledged even in its decline over a very large extent of territory."[1] As already observed, the passage in question only gives us a list of the principal kingdoms that had dealings with Kanauj, and the assumption that they were subject to it seems altogether fantastic and wide the mark.

Perhaps a few words on the territories of these attendant powers will not be out of place here. The Bhojas were a people of antiquity, whose kingdom, known as the Bhojakaṭa according to the Cammak copper plate inscription of Pravarasena II, almost coincided with modern Berar.[2] When the installation took place the Vākāṭakas had long ceased to rule over this part, and it is likely that the people, who preserved the tribal name at this time, lived in a comparatively circumscribed area near the Nerbudda.

The Matsyas were settled to the south or south-west of Indraprastha, and their territory roughly corresponded to the modern Alwar State with portions of Jaipur and Bharatpur.[3]

The country of the Madras lay between the Ravi and the Chenab in the central parts of the Panjab, and had its capital at Sākala or modern Sialkot.[4]

The Kurus seem to have occupied the Cis-Sutlej districts, and may be associated with the Kurukṣetra or

[1] *H. M. H. I.*, Vol. I, p. 341.

[2] Fleet, *C. I. I.*, Vol. III, p. 236; *J. R. A. S.*, 1914, p. 321; see also Mark Collins, *Geographical Data of the Raghuvaṁśa and the Daśakumāracarita* (Leipzig, 1907), p. 28, for a discussion on the Bhoja kingdom.

[3] *Arch. Surv. Ind. Rep.*, XX, p. 2. *Cambridge History of India*, Vol. I, p. 84.

[4] For a fuller account of the Madradeśa, see *J. A. S. B.*, N. S., XVIII, pp. 257-268.

Thanesvar. In the *Brihatsaṁhitā*[1] they are classed among the Matsyas and the Pāñcālas as belonging to the Middle Country.

The Yadus or Yādavas were according to the Lakkha Mandal *praśasti*[2] long ruling in part of the Punjab, but the reference in this passage may be to the people of the Mathura territory. Of the Yavanas it is difficult to say with any confidence as the name was often used in a loose way to designate various races of foreign origin. Probably the word is used here simply in the sense of Mleccha, and is put in next to the word Yadu rather for "the sake of poetical ornamentation than with the object of conveying any very definite meaning."[3]

Avanti, of course, denoted Malava or the country round Ujjain; and Gandhāra presumably designates the Peshawar district with certain adjoining regions along the Kabul river and Rawalpindi in the northern Panjab. The Kīras occupied territory in the Kangra valley, where their name is preserved in Kīragrāma, the village in which the famous temple of Vaidyanātha stood[4].

Thus amidst a distinguished assemblage of kings from far and near the installation ceremony of Cakrāyudha was carried out with great solemnity under the protection of Dharmapāla. But his rule was not destined to run its full course, for it was suddenly cut short by the attack of the Pratīhāra Nāgabhaṭa II on Kanauj.

[1] *Ind. Ant.*, XXII, pp. 182-83; see also *Cambridge History of India.*, Vol. I, pp. 47, 116, etc.

[2] *Ep. Ind.*, I, p. 10 f; *J. R. A. S.*, (first series) XX, p. 452 f.

[3] Kielhorn, *Ep. Ind.*, IV, p. 246.

[4] *Śiva Purāṇa*, cited in *Arch. Surv. Ind. Rep.*, V, pp. 178-80. For an account of the kingdom of Kīra, see R. C. Majumdar, *Ind. Hist. Quart.*, IX (March, 1933), pp. 11-17.

PART III

CHAPTER X

THE IMPERIAL PRATĪHĀRAS

Section A

Circumstances of Nāgabhaṭa II's conquest

The exact circumstances which led Nāgabhaṭa II to attack Kanauj are more or less shrouded in mystery, but it seems the elevation of Cakrāyudha under the patronage of Dharmapāla was followed by troublous times. The Rāṣṭrakūṭas, who had now begun to intervene in the affairs of the north, as is evident from the raids of Dhruva (*circa* 779-794 A. D.),[1] could not long tolerate the Bengal king's assumption of supreme status in Northern India, and a trial of strength between the two rising powers became inevitable.[2] Govinda III (*circa* 794-814 A. D.), the son and successor of Dhruva, threw out a challenge to Dharmapāla's imperial pretensions, and the result of this conflict is preserved in the Sanjan plates of Amoghavarṣa I : "The water of the springs of the Himālaya mountains was drunk by Govinda III's horses and plunged into by his elephants, the thunder was redoubled in (its) caverns by the *tūrya* musical instruments of (his) ablutions, (and) to whom, the great one,

[1] See *Ante*; the Baroda grant of Karkarāja (*Ind. Ant.*, XII, pp. 159, 163), and the Sanjan plates (*Ep. Ind.*, XVIII, pp. 244, 252).

[2] It is significant that the Khalimpur record of Dharmapāla makes no mention of the Rāṣṭrakūṭas, when it enumerates the different powers that gave their assent to his political arrangement in Kanauj.

those (kings) Dharma and Cakrāyudha surrendered of themselves. He thus bore resemblance to the fame of Himālaya, and was consequently Kīrti-Nārāyaṇa."[1] Dharma and Cakrāyudha in this passage undoubtedly refer to the king of Kanauj and his liege-lord, whose combined strength even could not successfully resist the northward triumphant march of the Rāṣṭrakūṭa army. We may, therefore, be sure that this foreign invasion coming close on the heels of other depredations in the Doab, must have considerably harassed the populace and introduced anarchy and misrule. Such an unsettled state of affairs was bound to invite aggressions from ambitious quarters, and the Gwalior inscription of Bhoja thus informs us how Nāgabhaṭa II availed himself of this opportunity : "Who, desirous of the great growth of virtuous acts enjoined in the Vedas, performed a series of religious ceremonies according to the custom of Kṣatriya families; and after having defeated Cakrāyudha, whose lowly demeanour was manifest from his dependence on others, he became eminent, although he was humble through modesty."[2] After achieving this victory there are indications that Nāgabhaṭa boldly annexed Kanauj, but before taking up the thread of the history of the Pratīhāras, we must make a slight digression to trace their origin and briefly survey their antecedent position.

Who were the Pratīhāras?

There is a late legend in Cand's *Rāso*, which groups the Parihāras or Pratīhāras[3] along with three other

[1] *Ep. Ind.*, XVIII, pp. 245, 253, verse 23; see also the Nīlgund inscription in which Govinda III is said to have fettered the people of Gauḍa etc. (*Ibid.*, VI, pp. 102, 105).

[2] *Ann. Rep. Arch. Surv. Ind.*, 1903-04, pp. 281, 284; *Ep. Ind.*, XVIII, pp. 108, 112, verse 9.

[3] It is obvious that the two forms are variants of each other,

Rajput clans—the Cauhan (Cāhamāna), Powār (Paramāra), and Solanki (Caulukya)—as "Agnikula," deriving their origin from a sacrificial fire-pit (agnikuṇḍa) at Mount Abu. The myth is apparently absurd, but it may well represent, as observed by Crooke, "a rite of purgation by fire, the scene of which was in Southern Rajputana, whereby the impurity of the foreigners was removed and they became fitted to enter the Hindu caste system."[1] According to this view, therefore, the Pratīhāras were of foreign extraction, and we have further reason to hold that they were a branch of the famous Gurjaras—one of those nomadic Central Asian tribes that poured down into India along with or soon after the Hūṇas through the north-western passes during the period of political ferment following the disruption of the great Gupta Empire.[2] This seems evident from the Rajor (Rājyapura) stone inscription, dated V. E. 1016 or 959 A. D. in the reign of Mathanadeva, a feudatory of Vijayapāladeva of Kanauj.[3] The former is therein explicitly described as belonging to the Gurjara Pratīhāra lineage, since the phrase "Gurjara-Pratīhārānvayaḥ" occurring in it must be interpreted to mean "Pratīhāra clan of the Gurjaras."[4] Some scholars, on the other hand, think that the word Gurjara in this expression does not denote the tribe or people of that name but 'the Gurjara country (Gurjjaratrā-bhūmi).[5]

although by mistake one list of the traditional 36 clans gives a place both to Parihār and Pratīhāra (Forbes, *Rāsamālā*, II, pp. 235-36).

[1] *Journal Royal Anthropological Institute*, 1911, p. 42.

[2] See *Bom. Gaz.*, IX, pt. I, pp. 471-478; *Ind. Ant.*, XL, pp. 21-24; *J. R. A. S.*, 1904, p. 640; *Ibid.*, 1909, p. 54, etc.

[3] *Ep. Ind.*, III, pp. 263-267.

[4] *Ep. Ind.*, III, p. 266; see also *Ind. Ant.*, XL, p. 22.

[5] C. V. Vaidya, *H. M. H. I.*, Vol. II, pp. 31, 32, note; *Ind. Hist. Quart.*, June, 1934, pp. 337-38.

This view, however, will not bear scrutiny, as a close perusal of the Rajor inscription would show. In line 12 there occur the words "... Tathaitat pratyāsanna Śrī Gurjjara vāhita samasta-kṣetra sametaḥ ...," which has rightly been translated by "together with all the neighbouring fields cultivated by the Gurjaras." Here the cultivators themselves are clearly called Gurjaras, and it may, therefore, be reasonable to presume that in the earlier part of the grant, in line four too, the term bears a racial signification. That the Pratīhāras belonged to the Gurjara stock is also confirmed by the Rāṣṭrakūṭa records, and the Arab writers like Abu Zaid and Al Ma'sūdi who allude to their fights with the Juzr or Gujaras of the north[1]. These references are undoubtedly to be held as applying to the Pratīhāras of Kanauj, for at this period they were the only power to contend against the Rāṣṭrakūṭas, with whom sometimes the Arabs even co-operated against Kanauj. Besides, we have the important testimony of the Kanarese poet Pampa, who expressly calls Mahīpāla "Ghūrjararāja."[2] This epithet could hardly be applied to him, if the term "Ghūrjara" bore a geographical sense denoting what after all was only a small portion of Mahīpāla's vast territories. Lastly, support for the foreign or Gurjara origin of the Pratīhāras may further be found in certain outlandish personal names of the earlier Pratīhāra rulers of Mandor (Māṇḍavyapura, near Jodhpur), from whom, as remarked by Dr. R. C. Majumdar, "it is not impossible that the imperial Pratīhāras of Kanauj also branched off." Thus the Jodhpur inscription of Bāuka informs us that Haricandra was surnamed Rohillāddhi, and Narabhaṭṭa had another name Pellāpelli on account of his prowess.[3] Surely these do not sound Aryan names,

[1] *J. B. B. R. A. S.*, XXI, pp. 422-24.
[2] See *Infra.*
[3] *Ep. Ind.*, XVIII, pp. 97-98.

and what is more notable is that they were assumed when the Pratīhāras of Rajputana had wholly become merged into the Hindu Society.[1]

The inscriptions of the dynasty, however, suggest a different line of enquiry. The Gwalior inscription of Bhoja says:

"Slāghyas—tasyānujosau maghava-madamuṣo Meghanādasya saṁkhye,
Saumittris tīvra-daṇḍaḥ Pratiharaṇavidher yaḥ Pratīhāra āsīt."[2]

i.e., "Saumitri, his honourable younger brother of staff severe, was the door-keeper (Pratīhāra), since he repelled (the enemies) in the battle with Meghanāda, the destroyer of Indra's pride."

According to it, the forebear of this family was Lakṣamaṇa, the brother of Rāma, and he came to be known as Pratīhāra owing to his act of repelling (pratiharaṇa-videḥ) displayed against his enemies, like Meghanāda, in battle. Again, the Jodhpur inscription of Bāuka belonging to the Pratīhāra house of Rajputana tells us:

"Svabhrāttrā Rāmabhadrasya Prātīhāryaṁ kritaṁ yataḥ,
Srī-prattihāra-vaṁśo yaṁ atas—c—onnatiṁ-āpnuyāt."

i.e., "Inasmuch as the very brother of Rāmabhadra performed the duty of door-keeper (pratīhāra), this illustrious clan came to be known as Pratīhāra."[3] Thus in both the records although the name Pratīhāra is derived from different memorable events in the life of Lakṣamaṇa, the point common to both is that the clan is said to be descended from the same epic hero, and thereby held as

[1] See also *Ind. Hist. Quart.*, IV (1928), p. 746.

[2] *Ann. Rep. Arch. Surv. Ind.*, 1903-04, pp. 280, 283, verse 3; *Ep. Ind.*, XVIII, pp. 107, 110.

[3] *J. R. A. S.*, 1894, p. 4, verse 4; *Ep. Ind.*, XVIII, pp. 95, 97; *Prog. Rep. Arch. Surv. W. circle*, 1906-07, p. 30.

a genuine indigenous one. It may be added that in the Gwalior *praśasti* Vatsarāja, father of Nāgabhaṭa, is definitely represented as "foremost among the most distinguished Kṣatriyas" and as one who "stamped the noble race of Ikṣvāku with his own name by virtue of his blameless conduct."[1] This proud claim is further strengthened by Rājaśekhara, the dramatist at the Pratīhāra court, who calls his patron Mahendrapāla "Raghukulatilaka" i.e., ornament of the race of Raghu in the *Viddhasālabhañjikā*,[2] and "Raghugrāmaṇī" or leader of Raghu's family in the *Bālabhārata*.[3] Similarly the poet uses the expression "Raghuvaṁśamuktāmaṇi" or pearl-jewel of Raghu's line for Mahīpāla in the last named work.[4] But we need not attach any special significance to the above traditions, for such legendary origins are often ascribed to ruling families to give them a noble and well-known pedigree. The alleged connection with Lakṣamaṇa is clearly mythical; and it was perhaps fabricated by *praśastikāras* when the barbarian hordes had gained power and were thoroughly Hinduised, adopting Sanskritic names and Brahmanical forms of worship, and stood in dire need of carrying back their genealogy to find a respectable place in Hindu social polity.[5]

[1] *Ep. Ind.*, XVIII, pp. 108, 111, verse 7.

[2] Cf. "Raghukulatilako Mahendraḥ" (canto I, stanza 6, ed. Ārte).

[3] Cf. "Devo Mahendrapālanṛipatiḥ śiṣyo Raghugrāmaṇiḥ" (canto I, stanza 11).

[4] I, 7. See also R. R. Haldar, *Ind. Ant.*, Oct. 1928, pp. 181-184, for the view that the Pratīhāras belonged to the solar (Raghu's) race.

[5] See, however, Dr. D. C. Ganguly, *Ind. Hist. Quart.*, June, 1934, pp. 337-343, where he has tried to show that the Pratīhāras were originally Brahmans and then became Kṣatriyas, and that they were so called because the founder of the family occupied the office of Pratīhāra or door-keeper. For a criticism of the same, see *Indian Culture*, January, 1935, pp. 510-512.

Their original territories

There is a remarkable passage (stanza 51) in the colophon to the Jain *Harivaṁśa*, which gives us valuable information regarding the place where the Pratīhāras of Kanauj were settled prior to their northern conquest. It runs as follows :

"Śākesv-abdaśateṣu saptasu diśāṁ pañcottareṣū-ttarāṁ,
Pāti-Indrāyudha-nāmni Kriṣṇanripaje Śrīvallabhe dakṣiṇāṁ.
Pūrvāṁ Śrīmad-Avanti-bhūbhriti nripe Vatsā-dirāje-parāṁ,
Sauryāṇāṁ-adhimaṇḍale Jayayute vīre varāhe-vati[1].

Commenting on this stanza Dr. Fleet observed that the "work was finished in Śaka-*saṁvat* 705 (expired) = A. D. 783-84, when there were reigning—in various directions determined with reference to a town named Vardhamāna-pura, which is to be identified with the modern Waḍhwan in the Jhalavad divison of Kāṭhiāwāḍ—in the north, Indrāyudha; in the south, Śrīvallabha; in the east Vatsarāja, king of Avanti (Ujjain); and in the west Varāha or Jayavarāha, in the territory of the Sauryas[2]. This interpretation was later on called in question by Dr. D. R. Bhandarkar,[3] but, as in view of the new light thrown by the Sanjan plates, the learned professor himself has "no doubt now as to the correctness of Dr.

[1] *Bom. Gaz.*, 1896, Vol. I, pt. II, p. 197, fn. 2; *Ind. Ant.*, XV, pp. 141-42.

[2] *Fleet, Ep. Ind.*, VI, pp. 195-96; see also Dr. Hoernle, *J. R. A. S.*, 1904, p. 644; Dr. R. C. Majumdar, *Jour. Dept. Lett.*, (Calcutta University), Vol. X, pp. 23-25.

[3] *J. B. B. R. A. S.*, XXI, p. 421, fn. 4; this rendering was also endorsed by Smith in *J. R. A. S.*, 1909, p. 253; Sten Konow, *Ep. Ind.*, XII, p. 200; R. D. Banerji, *Mem. As. Soc. Beng.*, Vol. V, pt. III, p. 50.

Fleet's translation,"[1] we omit to discuss his rendering here.[2] Now the chief point to be noticed in Dr. Fleet's translation is that it gives the king's personal name in each case, and equates Vatsarāja with the ruler of Avanti (Ujjain). This Vatsarāja has been accepted on all hands to be identical with the monarch of the same name mentioned in the Kanauj Pratīhāra inscriptions as predecessor of Nāgabhaṭa II and grand-nephew of Nāgabhaṭa I, the founder of the line. We may, therefore, safely draw the inference that the predecessors of the Pratīhāra conqueror of Kanauj had their seat of power at Ujjain and not Śrīmāla or Bhinmal in Southern Rajputana, as was at one time asserted by Smith and other scholars.[3] Support for this view may further be found in a verse occurring in the Sanjan plates of Amoghavarṣa I, dated in the Śaka year 793 or 871 A. D.[4] It says:

"Hiraṇyagarbhaṁ rājanyaiḥ Ujjayinyāṁ yadāsitam,
Pratīhārīḥ kritaṁ yena Gurjjareś-ādi rājakaṁ,"

i.e., "By whom kings such as the Gurjara lord and others were made door-keepers when in Ujjayini the (great gift called) Hiraṇyagarbha was completed by the Kṣatriyas."[5] We thus learn from this passage that Dantidurga Rāṣṭrakūṭa reduced to subordinate rank a Gurjara ruler, and made him publicly attend on him as a

[1] *Ep. Ind.*, XVIII, p. 239.

[2] Dr. R. C. Majumdar has examined this point at some length; see *Jour. Dep. Lett.*, Vol. X, pp. 23-26.

[3] *J. R. A. S.*, 1909, p. 57; *Early Hist. of India*, 4th ed., p. 393; Sten Konow, *Ep. Ind.*, XII, p. 201.

[4] *Ep. Ind.*, XVIII, pp. 235-57.

[5] *Ibid.*, pp. 243, 252, verse 9. The Ellora Daśāvatāra cave temple inscription also informs us that Mahārāja Sarva, apparently another name of Dantidurga, conquered Mālava and instituted a *Mahādāna* ceremony, in which he freely distributed large sums of money and other precious objects among supplicants (*Arch. Surv. Ind. W. Circle*, V, p. 88).

pratīhāra or door-keeper at a grand ceremony at Ujjain. Now, if the Gurjara was not king of Ujjain, this act would not have much point, for it was evidently meant to create an impression. Besides, the special mention of the Gurjara among the princes compelled to do homage and the play on the word *pratīhāra*, suggests that he was the chief then ruling over the territories of Ujjain.

Their power prior to the transfer of the capital

The inscriptions give us some glimpses of the doings of the Pratīhāras in their homelands, which brought them into prominence and ultimately enabled Nāgabhaṭa II to subjugate the kingdom of Kanauj. The family began well under Nāgabhaṭa, who is credited in the Gwalior inscription with "having crushed the large armies of the powerful *Mleccha* king, the destroyer of virtue."[1] Evidently we have here a reference to his successful stand against the vanguards of Islam that were at this time sweeping down the western borders of India. This conclusion is also in accordance with the information supplied by Al Bilādūri, who after mentioning the different regions overrun by the Arabs in India says : "They made incursions against Uzain and they attacked Baharīmad and burnt its suburbs. Junaid conquered Al Bailaman and Jurz."[2] It is thus clear that the Arabs could not make any headway against Ujjain, for whereas Junaid, who was governor of Sind under Khalif Hishām (724-743 A. D.) subdued other places, he is represented to have simply carried on raids in the direction of Ujjain. During the time of his weak and incompetent successor, Tamim, the Arabs

[1] *Ep. Ind.*, XVIII, pp. 107, 110-111.
Cf. "Yen āsau sukṛita pramāthi va (ba) lavān Mlecchādhip—ākṣauhiṇīḥ."

[2] Elliot, *History of India*, Vol. I, p. 126.

even "retired from several parts of India and left some of their positions,"[1] and this decline in their power may have in no small measure been due to the vigorous drive of Indian rulers like that of Ujjain. Perhaps it was in the course of these fights that Nāgabhaṭa carried his arms as far as Bhrigukaccha or Broach, where the Cāhamāna feudatory Bhartrivaddha II is recorded in V. E. 813 = 756 A. D. to have made a grant of the village Arjunadevīgrāma situate in the Akrūreśvara *viṣaya* (Anklesvar Taluka) to the Brahman Bhaṭṭabhūṭa "in the reign of increasing victory of the illustrious Nāgāvaloka,"[2] who is in all likelihood no other than the founder of the Pratīhāra line.[3]

The second king, Kakustha, was the son of an unnamed brother of Nāgabhaṭa; he was also called Kakkuka on account of his habit of saying welcome things in an inverted manner, but beyond this curious fact we know nothing about him.

The third king, Devaśakti or Devarāja, younger brother of Kakkuka, seems to have maintained the dignity of the house in tact, although the reference in the Gwalior inscription to the curbing of the movements (gati) of a "multitude of kings" (bhūbhrit) and their powerful allies" (pakṣāḥ) indicates that sometime during his reign the Pratīhāra authority was threatened by external danger. His son and successor Vatsarāja, born of Bhūyikādevī and known to have been ruling in the year 783-84 A. D., was certainly more than a mere name. The Gwalior inscription asserts that "with strong bows as his companion he forcibly wrested (haṭhād-agrahīt) the empire (sāṁrājyaṁ), in battle from the famous Bhaṇḍi clan, hard to be overcome

[1] *Ibid.*

[2] Hansot grant, *Ep. Ind.*, XII, pp. 203, 204.

[3] Sten Konow, *Ibid.*, p. 200; Dr. Bhandarkar, *Ind. Ant.*, 1911, p. 240.

by reason of the rampart made of infuriated elephants."[1] It is difficult to identify this Bhaṇḍi clan, as history does not record any other Bhaṇḍi except the prince mentioned in the *Harṣacarita*, but we do not know what happened to him and where he established his authority. A conjecture may, however, be hazarded that the name stands for the Bhaṭṭi clan, whose political importance may best be inferred from the fact mentioned in the Jodhpur inscription that Padminī, the mother of Pratīhāra Bāuka, belonged to it.[2] We may, therefore, take the passage as an allusion to Vatsarāja's attainment of the supreme status in Gurjaratrā or Central Rajputana, which is to some extent confirmed by the Osia and Daulatpura inscriptions. The former is engraved in the porch of a Jain temple and speaks of it as existing in the time of Vatsarāja,[3] and according to the latter charter he granted the village of Sivā in the Ḍeṇḍavānaka *viṣaya* (modern Didwāna) of the Gurjaratrā *bhūmi* to the Bhaṭṭavāsudeva.[4]

But the most noteworthy tribute to his achievements is paid by the inscriptions of his victorious rivals, the Rāṣṭrakūṭas themselves. We are, for example, told in the Wani-Dindori[5] and Radhanpur grants[6] that Vatsarāja had become "intoxicated with the goddess of the sovereignty (of the country of) Gauḍa that he had acquired with ease," and that his fame "had reached to the extremities of the regions." Again, the Baroda plates of 812 A. D. inform us that the lord of Gurjaras became "evilly inflamed by conquering the lord of

[1] *Ep. Ind.*, XVIII, pp. 108, 111, verse 7.
[2] *Ibid.*, pp. 96, 98, verse 26.
[3] *J. R. A. S.*, 1907, p. 1010.
[4] *Ep. Ind.*, V, pp. 211, 213.
[5] *Ind. Ant.*, XI, p. 161.
[6] *Ep. Ind.*, VI, pp. 243, 248, verse 8.

Gauḍa and the lord of Vanga."[1] It is, however, not necessary to suppose that Vatsarāja's armies overran Bengal, for he may have come into conflict with the Gauḍa monarch, identified with Dharmapāla, far away during the latter's foreign expeditions. Perhaps after this trial of strength their relations became more happy. This would be evident if we remember that the Khalimpur plates depose that the ruler of Avanti approved of the installation of Cakrāyudha at Kanauj under the ægis of Dharmapāla. Presumably Vatsarāja made this diplomatic gesture on account of the Rāṣṭrakūṭa danger then looming large on the political horizon. But nothing availed him, and the storm soon burst in all its destructive fury. For, the Wani and Radhanpur grants attest that Dhruva caused Vatsarāja "to enter upon the path of misfortune in the centre of (the deserts of) Maru," which expression probably means that the Rāṣṭrakūṭa monarch met his rival in a successful encounter and compelled him to take shelter in the inhospitable tracts of Rajputana, where, as shown above, the Pratīhāras of Ujjain had already established their supremacy.

SECTION B

Nāgabhaṭa II

According to the list of kings given in inscriptions, which are our chief sources of information for the Pratīhāra dynasty,[2] Vatsarāja's successor was his son Nāgabhaṭa by the queen Sundarī-Devī. His earliest known date is (Vikrama) *Saṁvat* 872 or 815 A.D. (Buckalā inscription), and although we have no evi-

[1] *Ibid.*, XII, p. 164. The overlordship of Gauḍa and Vanga explains the expression "Gauḍa's two umbrellas of state," which, according to the Radhanpur grant, Dhruva took away from Vatsarāja.

[2] See Appendix.

dence to fix the year of his accession, it may tentatively be assumed to have taken place about 805 A. D. It appears that in the beginning he tried to retrieve the fortunes of his family and to avenge the crushing defeat of his father at the hands of the Rāṣṭrakūṭas, but the stars were as unfavourable to him as to his predecessor. For the Sanjan plates of Amoghavarṣa I, dated Śaka 793 = 871 A. D., credit Govinda III with "carrying away in battles the fair and unshakable fame of kings Nāgabhata and Candragupta,"[1] and there can scarcely be any doubt that the former represents the son of Vatsarāja.[2] That the result of the struggle was decisively against Nāgabhaṭa is clear from other records also. The Pathari pillar inscription, for instance, tells us that Karkarāja "caused Nāgāvaloka quickly to turn back,"[3] and the vanquished opponent has rightly been identified by Dr. D. R. Bhandarkar with Nāgabhaṭa II. The inscription is dated in V. E. 917 = 861 A. D. in the reign of Parabala,[4] and assuming that he had a long reign, we may reasonably conclude that his father Karkarāja was a contemporary of Govinda III and possibly also his feudatory, in which capacity he must have helped the latter against Nāgabhaṭa. Again, the Radhanpur inscription says that "the Gurjara in fear (of Govinda III) vanished nobody knew whither, so that even in a dream he might not see battle."[5] As the Wani grant of Govinda III does not give us this additional information regarding the defeat of the Gurjara

[1] *Ep. Ind.*, XVIII, pp. 245, 253, verse 22.

[2] *Ibid.*, p. 240.

[3] *Ibid.*, IX, p. 255, verse 14.

[4] The identity of this chief has been the subject of controversy. See Kielhorn, *Ibid.*, IX, p. 51; Fleet, *Dynasties of the Kanarese Districts*, p. 198.

[5] *Ep. Ind.*, VI, pp. 244, 250, verse 15. Cf. "Gūrjaro naṣṭaḥ kvāpi bhayāt tathā na samaraṁ svapnepi paśyet yathā."

king, we may reasonably place the event between 806-07 A. D., the date of the above grant, and 808 A. D., the year of the Radhanpur record. Govinda III, however, continued to apprehend trouble, as Mālava was now almost the bone of contention between his house and the Pratīhāras, and so according to the Baroda plates of Karkarāja, he "for the purpose of protecting Mālava...... caused his (Karkarāja's) arm to become an excellent door-bar of the country of the lord of the Gurjaras."[1]

Nāgabhaṭa's preliminary attempts thus proved abortive, but success in another direction was not long to come. His Rāṣṭrakūta adversary, Govinda III, who had also overrun the north upto the Himālayas, and to whom Cakrāyudha of Kanauj and his liege-lord Dharmapāla had submitted of their own accord[2], got engrossed towards the close of his reign with internal affairs in order to secure the succession of his son, Amoghavarṣa. And when Govinda III died early in 814 A. D., his young successor was unable to stem the rising tide of serious domestic seditions with the result that the kingdom was soon plunged in anarchy and confusion.[3] This freedom of reprisals from the Rāṣṭrakūṭas probably gave to Nāgabhaṭa the opportunity to wage war, as we have seen above, against Cakrāyudha "whose lowly demeanour was manifest from his dependence on others." The defeat was evidently followed by the annexation of the kingdom, and the transfer of the Pratīhāra capital to Kanauj, since Cakrāyudha disappears about this time from the stage of

[1] *Ind. Ant.*, XII, pp. 160, 164.

[2] *Ep. Ind.*, XVIII., pp. 245, 253, verse 23.

Cf. "... Svayaṁ eva upanatau ca yasya mahataḥ tau Dharma-Cakrāyudhau ..."

[3] *Bom. Gaz.*, Vol. I, pt. II, pp. 402, 409; *Rāṣṭrakūṭas and their Times* (Poona, 1934), pp. 69, 73.

history, and Nāgabhaṭa's successors for several generations are definitely known to have held their court there. The conquest of Kanauj at once gave to the Pratīhāras the supreme power in the north, and Nāgabhaṭa felt himself justified in assuming the full imperial titles—Paramabhaṭṭāraka, Mahārājādhirāja, and Parameśvara—in the Buckalā inscription issued in the year 815 A. D.[1]

But though Nāgabhaṭa was now immune from the Rāṣṭrakūta danger on account of their internal dissensions and rivalries, Dharmapāla of Bengal, who had raised Cakrāyudha to the throne, took the field against him to avenge his vassal's deposition. A reminiscence of this struggle is preserved in the Gwalior inscription of Bhoja in terms suggestive of its importance and arduous character. We are told that "having vanquished his enemy, the lord of Vanga, who appeared like a mass of dark, dense cloud in consequence of the crowd of mighty elephants, horses and chariots, Nāgabhaṭa who alone gladdens (the heart of) the three worlds, revealed himself, even as the rising sun, the sole source of manifestation of the three worlds, reveals himself by vanquishing dense and terrible darkness".[2] The battle was probably fought at Monghyr, since the Jodhpur inscription of Bāuka, dated in the (Vikrama) year 894 or 837 A. D., informs us that his father Kakka "gained renown by fighting with the Gauḍas at Mudgagiri."[3] From the date of the record it is evident that Kakka must have been a contemporary of Nāgabhaṭa; and as the house of the latter had already risen to ascendancy in Rajputana, we may assume that Kakka proceeded as far as Monghyr only to help his suzerain in a conflict that was to decide the fortunes of the Pratīhāras in Kanauj. Perhaps another feudatory chief, who fought

[1] *Ep. Ind.*, IX. p. 199 f.
[2] *Ibid.*, XVIII, pp. 108, 112, verse 10.
[3] *Ibid.*, pp. 96, 98, verse 24.

30

against the ruler of Bengal on behalf of Nāgabhaṭa, was Saṁkaragaṇa. The Cātsū inscription of Bālāditya[1] says that he "defeated the king of Gauḍa, a great warrior (bhaṭa), and made the whole world, gained by warfare, subservient to his overlord."[2] As well pointed out by Dr. R. C. Majumdar, this Saṁkaragaṇa must have been a contemporary of Nāgabhaṭa about the commencement of the 9th century, since the former was the great-grandson of Dhanika, who is known to have been ruling in 725 A. D.[3] Thus having dispersed the dense clouds in the form of the mighty hosts of Dharmapāla the sun of Nāgabhaṭa's glory shone in the political horizon, and soon its brilliant rays began to permeate and radiate all round. For the Gwalior inscription, which details his subsequent achievements, tells us that the kings of Andhra, Sindhu, Vidarbha and Kalinga succumbed to his youthful energy as moths do unto fire."[4] The Andhra country lay between the Godāvarī and the Kriṣṇā; Sindhu denotes the lower course of the Indus; Vidarbha and Kalinga were the ancient designations of the modern provinces of Berar and Orissa. And if these alleged conquests were really in accordance with facts, Nāgabhaṭa's sphere of suzerainty must have covered all the regions from the east to the west, and from the Himālayas to the Nerbuda, excluding, of course the north-western parts and the Pāla dominions. But there is little reason to accept any such conclusion, for the simile itself used by the poet is significant. We are told that just as moths cannot resist rushing headlong towards the fire, similarly the kings of the countries

[1] *Ep. Ind.*, XII, p. 10 f.

[2] *Ibid.*, pp. 14-15, vs. 14-16. See, however, Dr. D. R. Bhandarkar's remarks (*Ibid.*, p. 12).

[3] *Jour. Dep. Lett.*, X, pp. 40-41, Note. I have followed Dr. R. C. Majumdar's interpretation.

[4] *Ep. Ind.*, XVIII, pp. 108, 112, verse 8.

named were attracted of their own accord towards Nāgabhaṭa—or in other words they sought his powerful aid or alliance against their respective enemies who may be identified with the incoming Moslems in the west, the Rāṣṭrakūṭas in the south, and the Pālas in the east.

Verse eleven in the same record, however, makes more specific mention of his victories, which comprised the "forcible seizure" (haṭhāpahāraḥ) of the hill-forts of Ānartta or northern Kāṭhiāwāḍ; Mālava or Central India; the Matsyas or eastern Rajputana; the Kirātas, who were perhaps the wild tribes of the Himālayan region;[1] the Turuṣkas, probably designating the earliest Moslem settlements in Western India; and the Vatsas in the territory of Kausambi (Kosam). It is difficult to see how far they represent actual annexations, but making due allowance for any exaggeration we may roughly define the kingdom of Kanauj under Nāgabhaṭa as comprising parts of Rajputana, a large portion of the modern United Provinces and Central India, perhaps northern Kāṭhiāwāḍ, with Kosambi and adjacent territories for its south-eastern limit. That Nāgabhaṭa was a powerful king exercising sway over a number of petty chiefs is also clear from the Harṣa stone inscription of Vigraharāja, dated the Vikrama year 1030 or 973 A. D.,[2] wherein one of his predecessors, the Cāhamāna Gūvaka I, is described as having obtained honour at the court of Nāgāvaloka, which evidently seems a polite way of expressing a feudatory rank. The relevant passage runs as follows:

"Ādyaḥ Śrī-Gūvakākhyā-prathita-narapatis
Cāhamānānvayo bhūt,

[1] For Kirātas see *Indian Culture*, January 1935, pp. 381-82.

[2] *Ep. Ind.*, II, pp. 121, 126 and notes; see also *Ind. Ant.*, 1911, pp. 239-40 for the identification of Nāgāvaloka with Nāgabhaṭa II.

Śrīman-Nāgāvaloka-pravara-nṛipasabhā-labdha vīrapratiṣṭhaḥ."

The *Prithvīrājavijaya*[1] also throws interesting side-light on the relations between the two families, for it says that with a view to cementing them further Gūvaka's sister, Kalāvatī, married the lord of Kanauj in preference to other suitors.

Rāmabhadra

Nāgabhaṭa ceased to rule in the Vikrama year 890 or 833 A. D. according to the Jain *Prabhāvakacarita*[2] and was succeeded by Rāmabhadra, sometimes also called Rāma or Rāmadeva, his son by queen Iṣṭādevī. Rāmabhadra's reign seems to have been marked by some crisis, for we are told in the Gwalior inscription that he had "the haughty and cruel commanders of armies forcibly bound down by (his subordinate) kings who had the best cavalry under their charge"[3] It is difficult to detect precisely who these enemies were. Dr. R. C. Majumdar identifies them with the Pālas of Bengal,[4] who, as we shall see below, claim to have made some depredations in Northern India about this time, and he may be right considering that the Rāṣṭrakūṭa monarch, Amoghavarṣa I, was then far too occupied with domestic troubles to think of emulating the exploits of Dhruva and Govinda III. Although the record, as usual, speaks of the destruction of "evil-doers," the disturbances caused by them must have been sufficiently serious, since Rāmabhadra, being unable to cope with

[1] V, verses 30-31, p. 137 (Belvalkar's edition).

[2] Verses 720-22, p. 177 (ed. H. M. Śarmā, Bombay, 1909); *Ep. Ind.*, XIV, p. 179, note 3.

[3] *Ibid.*, XVIII, pp. 108, 112, verse 12. Cf. "... pravara-harivala nyasta bhūbhṛit-pravandhair-āvadhnan vāhinīnāṁ prasabhaṁ adhipatīn uddhata-krūra-satvān ..."

[4] *Jour. Dept. Lett.*, X, p. 46.

the danger single-handed, is here recorded to have invoked the good offices of his feudatory chiefs.

The fact that two grants—one in the Kālañjaramaṇḍala first made by his predecessor,[1] and the other in the Gurjaratrā-bhūmi originally made by Vatsarāja and confirmed by Nāgabhaṭa[2]—fell into abeyance during Rāmabhadra's reign doubtless points to the same conclusion that he occupied the throne during a period of stress and storm. We have no definite evidence how far he maintained the kingdom intact, but it is certain that his authority continued to be recognised as far distant as Gwalior, where Vaillabhaṭṭa, son of Nāgarabhaṭṭa of the Varjara family, was acting for him in the capacity of the chief of the boundaries.[3]

Mihira-Bhoja (*circa* 836-885 A. D.)

After a very short reign lasting for about three years, Rāmabhadra was succeeded by his son Bhoja I, whose mother was queen Appādevī. It was believed that he came to the throne about 840 A. D.[4] until the recently discovered copper plate at Barah furnished the Vikrama year 893 or 836 A. D. as his earliest date;[5] and so his accession must be carried back at least four years. He is designated in the inscriptions by various names and titles, the most common being Bhoja. The Gwalior record calls him by the personal name (abhidhāna) Mihira, which is also used, as we shall see below, in one of the Rāṣṭrakūṭa inscriptions. In the Daulat-

[1] Barah copper plate, *Ep. Ind.*, XIX, pp. 18, 19.

[2] Daulatpura inscription, *Ibid.*, V, p. 213. The charter and consent remained in abeyance during the earlier years of Bhoja's reign until he renewed it in 843 A. D. (see *Infra*).

[3] *Ibid.*, I, pp. 156, 157, verse 7.

[4] Smith, *J. R. A. S.*, 1909, p. 262; Dr. R. C. Majumdar, *Jour. Dept. Lett.*, X, p. 47.

[5] *Ep. Ind.*, XIX, pp. 15-19.

pura inscription, however, he is given the title of Prabhāśa,[1] which means splendour, and perhaps refers to the name Mihira (the sun). Another title assumed by him in the Gwalior Caturbhuj epigraph and in certain coins of base silver was that of "Ādivarāha," showing that he posed to identify himself with the boar-incarnation of Viṣṇu, although we are otherwise told that his predilections were towards the worship of the goddess Bhagavatī.

At the beginning of his career Bhoja appears to have attempted the consolidation of the Pratīhāra power, which had received a shock during his father's feeble government. First, he re-established the supremacy of his family in Bundelkhand soon after coming to the throne, for the Barah copper plate, dated in (Vikrama) year 893 or 836 A. D., records his renewal on the old terms of the grant of Valākāgrahāra, lying in the Udumbara-*viṣaya* of the Kālañjara *maṇḍala*, which was first sanctioned by Nāgabhaṭa, but had been disturbed in the reign of Rāmabhadra. That Bundelkhand was at this time included in the kingdom of Kanauj is also affirmed by local traditions, which, though confused and discrepant, nevertheless yield this much of historical information that before the rise of the Candellas the country was in the possession of the Pratīhāras.[2] It may further be noted here that until the former became a strong power under Yaśovarman they continued to acknowledge the suzerainty of the latter. Indeed, the Candella inscriptions themselves appear to support this conclusion, as they call the first few princes simply *nripa*, *mahīpati*, or *Kṣitipa*, and bestow on them only vague conventional praises. Next Bhoja revived a grant in the year 843 A. D. in Gurjaratrā-bhūmi (Jodhpur or

[1] *Ibid.*, V, pp. 212, 213, line 15.
[2] *J. A. S. B.*, 1881, pt. I. p. 3 f; LXXI (1902), pt. I, p. 102.

Marwar) originally made by Vatsarāja and confirmed by Nāgabhaṭa, but which had fallen into desuetude probably during the time of Rāmabhadra, and remained as such in the earlier years of Bhoja's reign even. This shows that sometime before the year 843 A. D., he succeeded in restoring his authority over his ancestral desert territories. It is possible that this disturbance was caused by the feudatory Pratīhāra family of Mandor, and the Jodhpur inscription dated 837 A. D.[1], which credits Bāuka with certain military achievements in spite of the odds arrayed against him, even lends some colour to this view.

In the north Bhoja's suzerainty was certainly acknowledged upto the foot of the Himālayas. This is evident from the Kahla plates of the Vikrama year 1134 or 1077 A. D., discovered in *pargana* Dhuriapur of the Gorakhpur district,[2] wherein we are told that Guṇāṁbodhideva, a chief of the Kālacuri family, obtained some land from Bhojadeva (Bhojadevāpta-bhūmiḥ), whom Dr. Kielhorn has, I suppose, rightly identified with Bhojadeva I of Kanauj.[3] For the grant is dated in the year 1077 A. D., and Soḍhadeva, the donor, formed the ninth generation of Guṇāṁbodhideva. This fact at the usual rate of 26 years for a generation[4] will naturally place Guṇāṁbodhideva at about 843 A. D. i.e., the time when Bhoja I flourished. A reminiscence of his struggles is also preserved in the Cāṭsū inscription of Bālāditya, which affirms that Harṣarāja Guhila conquered kings in the north, and presented horses to Bhoja.[5]

[1] *Ep. Ind.*, XVIII, pp. 96, 99.

[2] *Ibid.*, VII, pp. 85-93.

[3] *Ibid.*, p. 86, note 4.

[4] *Ind. Ant.*, XIII, p. 417.

[5] *Ep. Ind.*, XII, p. 15, verse 19. Cf. "Jitvā yaḥ sakalān-udicya-nṛipatīn Bhojaya bhaktyā ca ādau saṁktā-sekata-sindhu laghanavi Śrīvaṁśajān Vājinaḥ."

(*Read* śaktān saikata-sindhu-laṅghana-vidhau.)

This Bhoja is in all probability identical with his great Pratīhāra namesake, and as a minor chief like Harṣarāja could not have overrun the north on his own account, it is reasonable to assume that he undertook these northerly campaigns only to render assistance to his Kanauj overlord in his ambitious schemes of conquest and consolidation.

Having thus made himself the dominant power in the *Madhyadeśa*, Bhoja turned to measure swords with the Pālas of Bengal, who under the vigorous rule of king Devapāla had once again launched upon their Imperial schemes, and are even poetically described in the Badal pillar inscription as having, on account of the sagacious policy of the first minister Darbhapāṇi, "made tributary the earth as far as Reva's parent (the Vindhya hills), whose piles of rocks are moist with the rutting juice of elephants, as far as Gaurī's father (i.e., the Himālayas), the mountain which is whitened by the rays of Īśvara's moon, and as far as the two oceans whose waters are red with the rising and setting of the sun."[1] Similarly, verse 15 of the Monghyr grant avers that Devapāla enjoyed the whole region bounded on the north by the Himālayas, in the south by Rāma's bridge, and by the abodes of Varuṇa and Lakṣmī (i.e., oceans) on the east and west.[2] Now all these hyperbolic descriptions are no doubt mere bombast, but one thing they certainly indicate that Devapāla did lead some successful military incursions, and thus the presence of two vigorous and masterful personalities in the politics of northern India made a clash inevitable. Soon the war-drum was sounded, and the legions began to move. At first Bhoja appears to have gained some ground, probably on the western frontiers of the Pāla kingdom, with the

[1] *Ep. Ind.*, II, pp. 162, 165, verse 5.
[2] *Ibid.*, XVIII, p. 305.

assistance of his feudatory Guṇāṁbodhideva, who, as alleged in the Kahla plates, by a warlike expedition took away the fortune of Gauḍa.[1] Again, verse 18 of the Gwalior inscription, which speaks of Lakṣmī becoming his consort, seems to indicate that Bhoja achieved some victories over Dharma's (Dharmapāla's) son.[2] The former then tried to shatter his rival's power finally, but Bhoja's further efforts in this direction met with some reverses, as we are informed in the Badal pillar inscription that king Devapāla "brought low the arrogance of the lord of the Gurjaras" (Kharvīkrita Gurjaranātha darpaṁ).[3] This exploit is attributed to the good advice of his minister Kedāra Miśra, the grandson of his first minister Darbhapāṇi, which shows that the event must have occurred late in his reign. Now, Devapāla is known to have ruled for a long time, from about 815 to *circa* 855 A. D.,[4] and it is therefore fair to presume that the "lord of the Gurjaras" referred to in the above inscription is no other than Bhoja I Pratīhāra of Kanauj.

Undaunted by this effective check to his advance eastward, Bhoja next directed his energies towards the south, from which side the Rāṣṭrakūṭas had so often emerged to despoil the smiling fields of Kanauj. The Partabgarh inscription of Mahendrapāla II, discovered in southern Rajputana,[5] probably contains an allusion to his expeditions in the south-western regions, since we are told therein that a Cāhamāna family of kings was "a source of great pleasure to king Bhojadeva,"[6] who

[1] *Ep. Ind.*, VII, pp. 86, 89, verse 9.
Cf. "Asi-prakaṭa-prithu-pathenāhṛitā Gauḍalakṣmīḥ."

[2] *Ibid.* XVIII, pp. 109, 113, verse 18.

[3] *Ibid.*, II, pp. 163, 165, verse 13.

[4] The Nalanda plate of the year 39 (*Ep. Ind.*, XVIII, pp. 310-27) furnishes his last known regnal year.

[5] *Ibid.*, XIV, pp. 176-88.

[6] *Ibid.*, pp. 180, 184.

clearly appears from the context of the passage to be identical with our Bhoja I. Thus with the help of this local Cāhamāna dynasty Bhoja must have overrun southern Rajputana and the tracts round Ujjayinī upto the Narmada river, which had many a time in the past been the field of Rāṣṭrakūṭa operations. Perhaps it was during his time that these parts were definitely assimilated in the Kanauj empire, and, as we shall see later on, they continued to be under Mahendrapāla II even, who had stationed one Mādhava as "the great feudatory lord and governor," at Ujjayini, and another officer Śrīśarman was carrying on the affairs of state at Maṇḍapikā or Maṇḍū.

These distant campaigns, which may have been a sort of reconnaissance, brought Bhoja close to the Rāṣṭrakūṭa monarchy, and he therefore resolved to try his strength against the avowed enemies of his house. Fortune was, however, no more favourable to him than to any of his predecessors, for the Bagumra plates inform us that alone Dhruva II, who belonged to the collateral but not independent branch of the Rāṣṭrakūṭas of Mānyakheta (Malkhed), "easily put to flight the very strong army of the Gurjaras that was eager (for the fray) and reinforced by his kinsmen."[1] Who was this vanquished Gurjara lord is then specifically revealed in the following line : "Though Mihira was united to fortune and surrounded by crowds of noble kinsmen, though owing to his courage he conquered all the regions of the world, he nevertheless disappeared, his face being covered by the darkness of defeat, after he had looked upon the eminence of Dhārāvarṣa that was greater than his own."[2] This disaster, which reads like a repetition

[1] *Ind. Ant.*, XII, pp. 184,1 89, verse 38. Cf. "Gūrjara-balaṁ-iti balavat samudyataṁ vriṁhitaṁ ca kulyena, Ekākinaiva vihitam parāñmukhaṁ līlayā yena.

[2] *Ibid.*

of Harṣa's rout at the hands of Pulakeśi II, probably did not occur much earlier than the Śaka year 789 or 867 A. D., the date of the Bagumra grant, for none of the earlier Rāṣṭrakūṭa inscriptions mentions it; and moreover Bhoja must have spent a fairly long time after his accession about 836 A. D. in campaigns in other directions so as to deserve the proverbial credit of "having conquered all the regions of the world" in a record of the rival dynasty. What was the cause of this unexpected blow to Bhoja's arms? Did Dhruva II receive any help from his Mānyakheta kinsman and overlord in this conflict? To these questions, of course, no answer can be given in our present state of knowledge. But certain it is that this repulse must have rankled in the mind of Bhoja, and he is therefore represented even in a late inscription of the year 875 A. D. as "wishing to conquer the three worlds."[1] Indeed, towards the close of his reign he appears to have paid off old scores by compelling Kriṣṇarāja, identified with Kriṣṇa II Rāṣṭrakūṭa (875-911 A. D.), to retreat hastily to his own country. Unfortunately, however, the extant portion of this inscription is so fragmentary that it is difficult to draw further any definite conclusions from its evidence.[2] The Rāṣṭrakūṭa records, on the other hand, indicate otherwise. The Bagumra plates of Indra III dated Śaka *Saṁvat* 836 or 915 A. D., for example, refer to the vivid descriptions, which old men gave, of the courage and heroism of Kriṣṇa II in his sanguinary wars with the "roaring Gurjara."[3] Another Bagumra inscription of Kriṣṇa of the feudatory Gujarat family even speaks of his victories gained sometime before Śaka 810 or 888 A. D., the date of the epigraph in Ujjayinī, the veritable

[1] Cf. "Śrīmad-ādivarāhena trailokyaṁ vijigīṣunā."

[2] Barton Museum (Bhavanagar) fragmentary Pratīhāra inscription, *Ep. Ind.*, XIX, pp. 174-177.

[3] *Ind. Ant.*, XIII, p. 66.

cockpit of those times.[1] In the face of these conflicting versions what no doubt seems probable is that the hereditary enemies unsheathed their swords, but their wars were inconclusive and did not prove advantageous to either party.

Sometime during the course of his long reign Bhoja directed his imperialistic gaze towards the north-west also, and is definitely known to have annexed some territories on the eastern side of the river Satlej according to an inscription of the year 882 A. D., discovered at Prithūdaka or Pehoa in the Karnal district of the Panjab, which records the transaction of business at the local horse-fair by certain horse-dealers "in the auspicious and victorious reign of Bhojadeva."[2] We have even indications that Bhoja's arms penetrated farther into the Panjab, for a verse in the *Rājataraṅgiṇī*[3] contains the following statement:

"Hṛitaṁ Bhojādhirājena sa sāṁrājyaṁ adāpayat,
Pratīhāratayā bhrityībhūte Thakkiyakānvaye,"

i.e., "He (Śaṁkaravarman) caused to be restored the dominion which had been taken away by the Adhirāja Bhoja, when the Thakkiya family was reduced to the condition of servants by being put to the duty of door-keepers."[4] The passage is a little obscure, but one thing is surely clear that at this period the name Bhoja with the title of "Adhirāja" can have reference only to the supreme lord of Kanauj, and that it testifies to the seizure of certain territories from the Thakkiyakas, who must

[1] *Ep. Ind.*, IX, p. 24.

[2] *Ep. Ind.*, I, pp. 186, 188.

[3] Vol. I, Bk. V, verse 151, (Stein, p. 206).

[4] Fleet, *Ind. Ant.*, XV, p. 110, note 31. The verse has been the subject of considerable discussion and different interpretation. See Bühler, *Ep. Ind.*, I, p. 186; Cunningham, *Arch. Surv. Ind. Rep.*, Vol. II (1862-65), p. 225; X, p. 101; Hoernle, *J. R. A. S.*, 1904, p. 649; Hultzsch, *Ep. Ind.*, I, p. 155.

have been settled somewhere in the eastern part of the Panjab.

Further, Dr. H. C. Raychaudhuri has brought to light a piece of evidence, which tends to show that Bhoja's authority was recognised in Saurāṣṭra or Kāthiāwāḍ.[1] According to the Vastrāpatha Māhātmya, a section in the Prabhāsa Khaṇḍa of the Skanda Purāṇa dealing with the sacred sites of Girnar (Vastrāpatha), there lived in ancient times a righteous king named Bhoja who ruled over Kānyakubja.[2] Once a Warden of the forests (Vanapāla) reported to him as follows: "Sire! I have seen a woman with the face of a doe roaming with a herd of deer in the forests at Raivataka." The king felt curious, and collecting his forces he advanced towards Raivataka and encircled the hill with a net. The *Balādhyakṣa* ultimately succeeded in capturing the deer-maiden, and brought her to Kānyakubja. She then related the story of her previous births, and also dilated upon the sanctity of the waters of the Suvarṇarekhā. The king was so much impressed with what he learnt about Saurāṣṭra that he made up his mind to abdicate in favour of his son and go on a pilgrimage to its holy sites. Much of the story is no doubt absolutely unworthy of credence, but the connection of Bhoja of Kanauj with Saurāṣṭra, as evidenced by the appointment of a Vanapāla (VI, 22 f.) and sending of an army (*Ib.*, 25 f.), appears to be the substratum of truth. Dr. Raychaudhuri even accepts the story of Bhoja's abdication, and finds confirmation for it in the Ahar stone inscription, whch gives the dates 864-65, 865-66, 867-68, 886, 886-87, 888-89, 902-03, 904-05, although purporting

[1] *Ind. Hist. Quart.*, V (1929), pp. 129-133.

[2] Cf. "Kānyakubje Mahākṣetre rājā Bhojeti viśrutaḥ, Purā Puṇyayuge Dharmyaḥ prajādharmeṇa śāsati," (VI, 20). It is worth noting that the past tense is used here, and the *Purāṇa* does not say in the form of a prophecy.

to belong to the reign of Bhoja. But I venture to differ from the views of the learned Professor on this point, since the earliest known date for Mahendrapāla is 893 A. D., and the anomaly presented by the Ahar record can satisfactorily be explained by supposing with Mr. C. D. Chatterjee that "a portion of this inscription was engraved in 259 Harṣa *Saṁvat* = 865-66 A. D. during the administration of Bhoja I and other portions were added later on," or that "there was a transfer to stone of a copy of all the deeds made on less durable materials, later than 298 H. E. = 904-05 A. D."[1] Thus under Bhoja the kingdom of Kanauj grew to enormous dimensions, and it may be roughly defined as limited by the Satlej in the north-west; the foot of the Himālayas in the north; the western boundaries of the Pāla dominions in the east; Bundelkhand and the Vatsa territories in the south and south-east; possibly the lower course of the Narmadā and Saurāṣṭra on the south-west, and including the major portion of Rajputana on the west.

Sulaiman's account

Unfortunately no Bāṇa or Yuan Chwang has left a detailed record of how Bhoja organised the defence and internal administration of so vast a country in order to prevent any of its component parts flying asunder, but we have some faint echoes coming from the writings of the Arab traveller Sulaiman, who thus alludes in 851 A. D. to the king of Juzr (Gurjara), identified by scholars with the great Pratīhāra ruler of Kanauj: "This king maintains numerous forces, and no other Indian prince has so fine a cavalry. He is unfriendly to the Arabs, still he acknowledges that the king of the Arabs is the greatest of kings. Among the princes of

[1] *Journal of the U. P. Historical Society*, Vol. III, pt. 2, (Sept., 1926), p. 101.

India there is no greater foe of the Muhammadan faith than he. His territories form a tongue of land. He has got riches, and his camels and horses are numerous. Exchanges are carried on in his states with silver (and gold) in dust, and there are said to be mines (of these metals) in the country. There is no country in India more safe from robbers."[1] This brief notice is all that we possess about Bhoja's government, but it suffices to prove that the country was rich in resources and strong in political power. The king stood forth as the champion of indigenous culture, and maintained large armies so as to ensure the safety of the citizens against both external and internal dangers. The last remark is specially noteworthy, and speaks highly of Bhoja's administration, since we might recall here that even during the palmy days of Harṣa's rule, the kingdom continued to be infested by brigands and Yuan Chwang was stripped by them more than once.

Coins of Bhoja

Certain specimens of rude coins, better known to numismatists as the Ādivarāha type, have usually been ascribed to Bhojadeva of Kanauj.[2] They are minted in alloyed silver, which indicates a period of financial stringency, probably as a result of Bhoja's numerous wars. The obverse contains the Brāhmī legend "Śrīmad ā di varāha," and below it there are indistinct marks indicative of the Sassanian fire-altar. The reverse exhibits a man with a boar's head, signifying the boar-incarnation of Viṣṇu, with a solar wheel in front of him. The Siyadoni record mentions them as "Śrīmad Ādivarāha dramma," thus furnishing an additional proof

[1] Elliot, *History of India*, Vol. I, p. 4.

[2] Smith, *Cat. Coi. Ind. Mus.* (Calcutta), Vol. I, pp. 232, 233, 241, 242; Cunningham, *Coins of Med. Ind.*, pp. 49-50, plate VI, Nos. 20, 21.

of their descent from the greek *drachma* through Sassanian types.

Mahendrapāla I

The last known date of Bhoja I's long reign, according to the Pehoa inscription, is 882 A. D., and we may therefore assume that he died two or three years later—say about 885 A. D. He was succeeded by Mahendrapāla, his son by queen Candrabhaṭṭārikādevī. This form of name is used in the majority of inscriptions, but the variants are Mahīndrapāla,[1] Mahendrāyudha,[2] Mahiṣapāladeva,[3] and also Nirbhayarāja and Nirbhayanarendra in the plays of Rājaśekhara.

Like previous rulers of Kanauj, Mahendrapāla attempted the conquest of Magadha and Bengal, which, as we have repeated so often, were vital to the economic prosperity of Kanauj owing to their control of the lower course of the Ganges; and as we learn from the findspots of certain inscriptions, his enterprise met with some success. One of them dated year 8 of Mahīndrapāla's coronation was discovered at Rāmgayā, opposite the Gadādhar temple at Gaya, and records the gift of Riṣi Saudi's son Sahadeva on the pedestal of the figures of Viṣṇu incarnations.[4] Another of the 9th year was found at Guneriya in the southern part of the Gaya district. It is engraved on the pedestal of an image of the Buddha, which was the pious gift of Śrīpāla, the son of the merchant Haridatta.[5] A third

[1] *Mem. As. Soc. Beng.*, V, pt. III, p. 64.

[2] *Ep. Ind.*, IX, pp. 2, 5.

[3] *Ind. Ant.*, XVI, p. 174.

[4] *Mem. As. Soc. Beng.*, V, pt. III, pp. 64-65.

[5] *Ind. Ant.*, 1918, p. 110. Smith thought that this Mahendrapāla was a Pāla king (*Ibid.*, XXXVIII, p. 246). Mr. R. D. Banerji, on the other hand, rightly asserted that "a comparison with the Asni inscription of Mahīpāla confirmed him in the opinion

votive inscription has been unearthed at Itkhori in the Hazaribagh district of Bihar[1]. Here we have got the name of Parameśvara Mahendrapāla incised on the pedestal of an image of Tārā, and there is hardly any doubt that it refers to the Pratīhāra king. A fourth votive inscription on an image of the Buddha taming the elephant Nalagiri comes from Bihar and yields the year 4 of the same ruler.[2] Lastly a stone pillar, dedicated in the fifth year of king Mahendrapāla to the Buddha by Sthavira Jayagarbha, was discovered by Mr. R. D. Banerji in 1926 in a Buddhist temple at Paharpur in the northern part of the Rajshahi district of Bengal[3], which shows that the greater part of Magadha upto even northern Bengal had come under the suzerainty of the Pratīhāra monarch.

This view also agrees with what we know of the Pāla kingdom about this time. Thus the Viṣṇupāda (Gaya) stone inscription of the 7th year, the Bihar (now Indian Museum) stone record of the 9th, and the Bhagalpur plate of the 17th year of Nārāyaṇapāla—issued from Mudgagiri and granting the village of Mukuṭikā in the Kakṣaviṣaya in Tīrabhukti (modern Tirhut)—prove that in the earlier half of his reign Magadha continued to remain under the Pālas, but after this until the close of Nārāyaṇapāla's long rule of about 54 years no Pāla inscriptions have been discovered in this region. Hence the Pratīhāras must have occupied Magadha and

that no other person than the great Pratīhāra monarch was being referred to." (*Mem. As. Soc. Beng.*, V, p. 64).

[1] *Ann. Prog. Rep. Arch. Surv. Ind.* Central Circle, 1920-21, p. 5.

[2] *Ann. Rep. Arch. Surv. Ind.*, 1923-24, pp. 101-02. Two more records of Mahendrapāla dated year 6 and 2 (?) respectively are preserved in the British Museum, and according to Mr. R. D. Banerji they were also discovered in Bihar.

[3] *Ann. Rep. Arch. Surv. Ind.*, 1925-26, p. 141; see also *J. B. O. R. S.*, Dec., 1928, p. 505.

northern Bengal sometime during this interval, and as no inscription gives the credit for this achievement to Bhoja, nor any of his records has been found outside the eastern limits of the United Provinces, it is reasonable to conclude that the event probably took place soon after Mahendrapāla's accession.[1] Perhaps the Cāṭsū inscription also contains a reference to it, since we learn that Guhila with excellent horses from the sea-coast vanquished the king of Gauḍa and levied tribute from princes in the east.[2] Now, Guhila was the son of Harṣarāja, the feudatory of Bhoja I, and as such a minor chief of Rajputana is not expected to invade the distant eastern regions on his own account, we may well suppose that he accompanied his Pratīhāra suzerain in his expedition against Magadha and Bengal, and shared victories with him.

In the west Mahendrapāla was certainly successful in maintaining and perhaps even in extending his hold over the peninsula of Saurāṣṭra, which gave him access to the sea. This seems clear from two grants found at Unā, a town in the southernmost part of Kāthiāwāḍ in the Jūnāgaḍh state;[3] the one is dated in the (Valabhi) year 574 or 893 A. D., and the other in the (Vikrama) year 956 corresponding to 899 A. D. They record grants of the villages of Jayapura and Amvulaka in the Nakṣipur group of 84 in the Saurāṣṭra *maṇḍala* to the temple of the sun (Taruṇāditya-deva) by the Cālukya Balavarman and his son Avanivarman II Yoga respec-

[1] As regards the extent of the Pāla territories Mr. R. D. Banerji rightly says: "With eastern Bengal in the hands of the Candras, and eastern Magadha and northern Bengal in the hands of the Gurjara Pratīhāras, the Pāla dominions were limited to the northern parts of the Gangetic delta and Western Bengal" (*J. B-O. R S.*, Dec., 1928, p. 508).

[2] *Ep. Ind.*, XII, p. 15, verse 23.

[3] *Ibid.*, IX, pp. 1-10.

tively, who are described as feudatories (or, as the inscription expresses it, "had obtained the five Mahāśabdas") of the Paramabhaṭṭāraka, Mahārājādhirāja, Parameśvara Mahendrāyudhadeva. This suzerain is evidently the same as the Pratīhāra king of Kanauj, for not only does the first record correctly represent him as meditating on the feet of Bhojadeva, but the second one even gives the standard form of his name, Mahendrapāla. Incidentally it is interesting to note that Balavarman is said to have "freed the earth from the Hūṇa race" by slaying Jajjapa and other kings. This shows that the south-western frontiers of Mahendrapāla's dominions were not free from disturbances, which were, however, effectively suppressed by the vigilance of his local feudatory.

But the glory of Mahendrapāla's reign is partially dimmed by the diminution that his kingdom suffered in the north-west, for the verse of the *Rājataraṅgiṇī* quoted above informs us that the territories which were seized by the superior lord Bhoja were afterwards restored to the Thakkiya family during the course of Śaṁkaravarman's expeditions abroad. This transaction has sometimes been assigned to the reign of Bhoja himself, but without adequate reason, as the context of the passage indicates that the Kashmiri monarch could not have "put forth great efforts to conquer the world" till long after his accession in *c.* 883 A. D. In the beginning he had to face a civil war "during which the kingdom was as if placed in a swing," and his position was so weakened that his commands were "disregarded in the purlieus of his own capital." If we, therefore, assume that he took some years—say about four years—to quell these disturbances, which, we are told, he did "with difficulty," and to make his throne secure, the date of his foreign undertakings would fall about 887-88 A. D. This would bring us very near the date of

Mahendrapāla's campaigns in the eastern regions—the earliest known date of the Pratīhāra occupation of Magadha being the regnal year 2(?) and that of Northern Bengal the year 5 or *circa* 590 A. D. according to the Paharpur inscription[1]—and we may not even be wrong in supposing that it was his rival's preoccupation in the east which gave the opportunity to Śaṁkaravarman to carry out the transfer of the territories annexed earlier by Bhoja.

Whatever possessions Mahendrapāla might have thus lost in the Panjab it is certain from another Pehoa inscription that the district of Karnal continued to remain under Kanauj as it had been in the reign of his predecessor.[2] In the north his authority certainly extended upto the foot of the Himālayas, for the Dighwa-Dubauli plate issued by him from Kanauj records the grant of the village of Pānīyakagrāma, which lay so far distant as the Vālayikā Viṣaya of the Srāvasti-Maṇḍala in the present Nepalese Tarai, to the Bhaṭṭa Padmasara.[3] The extent of Mahendrapāla's kingdom in other directions is no doubt difficult to determine but it may well be presumed that he retained his jurisdiction over the territories, which were transmitted to him by his father Bhoja. Thus, the Siyadoni inscription, mentioning Mahendrapāla as the ruling sovereign in 903 and 907 A. D., makes it clear that the Gwalior region continued to be included within the Pratīhāra realm. In passing we may add that there are certain indications of sporadic fights and unrest in this part, since the chieftain Uṇḍabhaṭa, who is recorded as a donor in this epigraph, is known from another inscription discovered at Terahi[4] to have fought against the

[1] See *ante*.

[2] *Ep. Ind.*, I, pp. 245, 248.

[3] *Ind. Ant.*, XV, pp. 107, 112-13.

[4] *Ibid.*, XVII, pp. 201-02.

forces of a rival chief Guṇarāja, in which Caṇḍiyana, an adherent of the latter, was killed.

Rājaśekhara

Mahendrapāla was not only a worthy ruler; he was also a liberal patron of polite letters. The greatest literary ornament of his court was Rājaśekhara, who has left a number of works of varying merit. He represents himself as the *Guru* or *Upādhyāya* (spiritual teacher) of king Mahendrapāla or Nirbhayarāja in all the extant plays,[1] and proudly traces his poetic descent from Vālmīki through one Bhartṛimeṇṭha and the well-known Bhavabhūti.[2] He continued his residence during the reign of his royal disciple's son Mahīpāla,[3] but we do not know how long he maintained his connection with the latter's court. Of Rājaśekhara's literary productions we know of the following :—

(*a*) *Karpūramañjarī*, produced at the request of his wife, Avanti-Sundarī, who was born of a Cāhamāna family.

(*b*) *Bāla-Rāmāyaṇa*, relating the story of Rāma from Sītā's *Svayaṁvara* to the death of Rāvaṇa, and the return to Ayodhyā after Sītā's fire-ordeal.

(*c*) *Viddha-sālabhañjikā*, represented at the request of Yuvarājadeva. The occasion may have been his installation in the joint administration of the government.

(*d*) *Bālabhārata*, sometimes called Pracaṇḍa-Pāṇḍava, staged at Mahodaya before Mahīpāla, the "paramount sovereign of Āryāvarta."

(*e*) *Kāvyamīmāṅsā*.[4]

[1] See e.g. *Karpūramañjarī*, I, 5, 9; *Viddha-sālabhañjikā*, I, 6.

[2] *Bāla-Rāmāyaṇa*, I, 16; *Bāla-bhārata*, I, 12.

[3] See e.g., *Ibid.*, pp. 2, 16 (Cappeller's edition).

[4] See Dr. L. D. Barnett, *Bulletin of the School of Oriental Studies*, for a short criticism of the work.

(*f*) *Bhuvana Koṣa*, to which he alludes in the 17th chapter of the last work.[1]

(*g*) *Hara-vilāsa*, referred to by Hemacandra as an example of a poem bearing the name of its author.[2]

Unfortunately Rājaśekhara has not, like Bāṇa, left any account of his patron's career, but here and there in his writings we get faint traces of the position and importance of Kanauj. He describes the imperial city as a very sacred place, whose people were "elegant like new compositions," and from which the directions were to be measured[3]. The poet also speaks of the dress of the ladies of Mahodaya as "adorable,"[4] and their ornamentation, braiding and speech as being studied by females of other countries.[5] From these brief references it is evident that Kanauj had revived the pre-eminence it once enjoyed under Harṣa, and was again considered the centre of politics, fashion and culture.

[1] See *Kāvyamīmāṅsā*, (Gaekwaḍ's Oriental Series, 1924), ch. XVII, p. 98.

[2] Cf. "Svanāmāṅkitā yathā Rājaśekharasya Haravilāse" (*Kāvyānuśāsana-viveka*, p. 335).

[3] *Kāvya-mīmāṅsā*, ch. XVII, p. 94.

[4] Cf. "Uttarīyaṁ veṣaṁ namasyata Mahodaya-sundarīṇāṁ" (*Ibid.*, ch. III, p. 8).

[5] *Bāla-Rāmāyaṇa*, Act X, p. 306, verses 88, 90 (Benares edition, 1869).

PART III

CHAPTER XI

THE IMPERIAL PRATĪHĀRAS (*Continued*)

Bhoja II

It is difficult to fix the exact date of Mahendrapāla's death, but as his last known date is 907-08 A. D., we may tentatively accept the year 910 A. D. as a close approximation to the event. According to the so-called Asiatic Society's plate of Vināyakapāla, he was succeeded by his son Bhoja, usually designated Bhoja II, whose mother was queen Dehanāgā-Devī. The Asni inscription on the other hand makes no mention of him, and represents his half-brother Mahīpāla, born of Mahīdevī,[1] as having come after Mahendrapāla. This omission may therefore be explained either by the extreme shortness of Bhoja's reign, or by the assumption that there was a war of succession and at first the victorious claimant did not think it prudent to recall on stone the existence of one whom he had overthrown. But when with the lapse of time his memory had faded away, he felt no scruples in mentioning the name of his rival in the genealogical list. Probably the latter hypothesis finds some support from the following passage in the Bilhari inscription : "Having conquered the whole earth, he (Kokalladeva I) set up two unprecedented columns of his fame,—in the quarter of the pitcher-born (Agastya) (i.e., in the south) that well-known

[1] Mahādevī according to the Partabgarh inscription, *Ep. Ind.*, XIV, pp. 178, 183.

Krişṇarāja, and in the quarter of Kuvera (i.e., in the north) Bhojadeva, a store of fortune."[1] This statement is further corroborated in the Benares grant of Karṇa-deva, dated (Cedi) year 973 or 1042 A. D., which says that Kokalla "granted freedom from fear to Bhoja and others."[2] The Bhoja referred to in these inscriptions must be identified with Bhoja II, as it seems out of the question that Bhoja I, who was a mighty monarch holding wide sway, could have owed or retained his position owing to the protecting hand of Kokalla I. It appears therefore that in his attempt to gain the throne Bhoja II invoked the aid of Kokalla, possibly on the strength of some matrimonial relations with the Kalacuri family, and succeeded in ousting his rival brother. Mahīpāla, however, did not despair at this initial defeat, and as we shall see below, the tide soon turned in his favour.[3]

Mahīpāla

The enthronement of his step-brother Bhoja II was naturally unacceptable to Mahīpāla; he therefore sought the support of the Candella king Harṣadeva as a counterpoise to the alliance between his rival and the Cedi ruler Kokalla I. The Candella chief, who probably still recognised the supremacy of Kanauj, at once took up his cause, and according to the Khajuraho inscription No. I signalised his intervention in imperial affairs

[1] *Ibid.*, I, pp. 256, 264, verse 17.

[2] Cf. "Yasya asīt abhayadaḥ pāṇiḥ" (*Ep. Ind.*, II, p. 306, verse 7).

[3] Mr. Niharranjan Ray tries to identify Bhoja II with Mahīpāla on the ground that, like the earlier Vikramāditya, Bhoja was the title adopted by the Pratīhāra rulers (*Ind. Ant.*, Oct., 1928, p. 232). It is, however, difficult to appreciate the force of this identification, as there is no justification to regard this epithet as a common feature of the Pratīhāra names.

by placing Kṣitipāla on the throne, which thus increased the power and prestige of his own house.[1] This Kṣitipāla has been identified on all hands with Mahīpāla, and the fact that the two terms *Kṣiti* and *Mahī* are synonymous no doubt goes far to confirm this identification. But it appears from a comparison of the Siyadoni and Khajuraho inscriptions that Mahīpāla was known by other names as well. In the former Kṣitipāla is said to have had a son named Devapāla, who was ruling in 948-49 A. D., while in the latter we are told that the Candella Yaśovarman received an image of Vaikuṇṭha from one Devapāla, son of Heraṁbapāla. As Yaśovarman's reign closed about the year 954 A.D., it is reasonable to hold that the two Devapālas were identical, and consequently in all likelihood the names of their fathers Kṣitipāla and Heraṁbapāla also refer to one and the same person.[2] Mahāmahopādhyāya Pandit Gaurishankar Ojha, on the other hand, does not accept the identity of the two Devapālas, as in the Khajuraho inscription Devapāla is given the epithet of *Hayapati*, and it was "never the accepted title of the Pratīhāra kings of Mahodaya, and is not met with in their ins-

[1] Cf. "Punar yena Śrī-Kṣitipāla-devanṛipatiḥ siṁhāsane sthātsāditārātiśakti-kīrti-vibhūṣaṇaḥ" (*Ep. Ind.*, I, p. 122, line 10). The word "punaḥ" has so far been taken by scholars in the sense of "again;" and they think that it alludes to Mahīpāla's "replacement" after a temporary loss of kingly dignity. In my opinion, however, "punaḥ" here means "further," "besides," or "now" (cf. Monier Williams' *Sanskrit Dictionary*, p. 581), and is used simply to introduce further details about the achievements of the Candella king who has been identified by Hoernle with Yaśovarman (J. R. A. S., 1904, p. 654). But it seems more correct to identify him with Harṣadeva Candella, for according to the Khajuraho inscription No. II, Yaśovarman was a contemporary of Mahīpāla's son, Devapāla (*Ep. Ind.*, I, pp. 129, 134, verse 43), and the above incident relates to the beginning of the career of Mahīpāla.

[2] *Ep. Ind.*, I, pp. 134, 171.

criptions."[1] This need not, however, be an insuperable objection in view of the fact that the Pratīhāras of Kanauj were then widely noted for their cavalry. Thus, Sulaiman, the Arab traveller, referring to Bhoja says that "no other prince has so fine a cavalry".[2] Again, according to the Cāṭsū inscription Harṣarāja presented horses to Bhoja, perhaps because of the latter's fondness for them. Similarly the Gwalior epigraph speaks of the "best cavalry" in charge of the feudatories of Rāmabhadra. The occurrence of the term *Hayapati* in an inscription of another dynasty, therefore, probably indicates that the Pratīhāras continued to enjoy among their contemporaries a reputation for maintaining an excellent cavalry, and as such were regarded "lords of horses" *par excellence*, although they did not, like the Gāhaḍavālas who used the epithet Aśvapati, adopt it as an official title in their records. Another name of Mahīpāla seems to have been Vināyakapāla, which is used in the Bengal Asiatic Society's plate.[3] The identity of the two is probable on the ground that the two terms Vināyaka and Heraṁba are synonymous, both being names of Gaṇapati,[4] and also because the record describes Vināyakapāla as "begotten on Mahīdevī and who meditated on the feet of his father Mahendrapāla and his brother Bhojadeva." If, however, we assume that the names Vināyakapāla and Mahīpāla represent two distinct persons, there is nothing in the absence of any evidence regarding a fratricidal war to explain the circumstance why the plate mentions one brother and omits all reference to another. Further, it need not militate against the above identification that in the

[1] *Ibid.*, XIV, p. 180.
[2] Elliot, *History of India*, Vol. I, p. 4.
[3] *Ind. Ant.*, XV, p. 140.
[4] *J. B. B. R. A. S.*, XXI, pp. 406-07.

earlier inscriptions and in the writings of Rājaśekhara the name Mahīpāla is uniformly given, whereas Vināyakapāla occurs for the first time in a late inscription of the year 931 A. D. There is no such overlapping even in the known dates of Mahīpāla and Kṣitipāla, but this does not prevent scholars from accepting that the two names denoted the same person. Thus Mahīpāla may be regarded as having borne at least three other names—Kṣitipāla, Vināyakapāla, and Heraṁbapāla;[1] this multiplicity of nomenclature was obviously due to the Hindu love for synonyms, which, as well remarked by Colonel Tod, "in the east is very destructive to history."[2]

We do not know when Mahīpāla effected his *Coup d'etat*, but as the Haddala grant of his feudatory Dharaṇivarāha[3] mentions him as ruling in Śaka *saṁvat* 836 or 914 A. D., his accession may be approximately fixed in the year 912 A. D. At the very beginning of his career Mahīpāla was seriously menaced by the war-fever of the Rāṣṭrakūṭas, the hereditary enemies of his house; and the effects of their renewed activity seem to have been for the time disastrous to the prosperity of Kanauj, for we are told in the Cambay plates of Govinda IV that Indra III "completely devastated (nirmmūlaṁ unmūlitaṁ) that hostile city of Mahodaya, which is even today greatly renowned among men by the name of Kuśasthala."[4] A close perusal of the record further reveals that the invader's line of march lay through Ujjain where "the courtyard (of the temple of the god) Kālapriya (became) uneven by the strokes of the tusks of his rutting elephants," and across the valley of the "unfathom-

[1] See also *Jour. Dep. Lett.*, X, pp. 59-62; *Dy. Hist. North. Ind.*, vol. I, pp. 572-75.

[2] *Rājasthāna* (Crooke's edition) Vol. I, p. 50.

[3] *Ind. Ant.* XII, p. 195.

[4] *Ep. Ind.*, VII, pp. 38, 43, verse 19.

able Jumnā which rivals the sea."[1] Thus if the region of Ujjain continued to remain under Kanauj during the disturbed reign of Bhoja II—and there is nothing to prove that it did not—this campaign must have caused its loss, although, as we shall see below, it was only temporary. In his expedition against Kanauj, Indra III was probably accompanied by his feudatory chief Narasiṁha Cālukya, who, according to the *Vikramārjunavijaya* or *Pampabhārata* written by the Kanarese poet Pampa under the patronage of Arikeśarin Cālukya, is said to have "plucked from the Ghūrjararāja's arms the goddess of victory, whom, though desirous of keeping he had held too loosely. Mahīpāla fled as if struck by thunder-bolts, staying neither to eat, nor rest, nor pick himself up; while Narasiṁha pursuing bathed his horses at the junction of the Ganges."[2] The reference to the confluence of the Ganges shows that the army overran the greater part of modern United Provinces, and advanced as far east as Prayāga. Some scholars on the other hand take the junction of the Ganges to be with the sea and not with the Jumnā, but this view is obviously wrong, for Mahīpāla's dominions did not extend upto the seashore, and there is no evidence that Indra III's expedition brought him into conflict with his Pāla contemporary, Rājyapāla. Was its success, therefore, due to the unsettled state of Kanauj, as a result of the troubles which had culminated in Mahīpāla's accession? At any rate the date of the raid raises a strong presumption in favour of this hypothesis. The Nausari grant specifies 915 A. D. as the year of Indra III's coronation,[3]

[1] *Ibid.* The god Kālapṟiya in the above passage refers to the temple of Mahākāla in Ujjayinī.

[2] Ed. Lewis Rice (Bangalore, 1898), pp. 3-4; *Karṇāṭaka Śabdānuśasana*, p. 26; *J. R. A. S.*, N. S., Vol. XIV (1882), p. 20; *Bom. Gaz.*, Vol. I, pt. II, p. 380.

[3] Fleet, *Dynasties of the Kanarese Districts*, p. 415.

and his successor is known from the Daṇḍapur (Dhārwāḍ district) inscription to have been ruling in 918 A. D.[1] Hence we may feel certain that the Rāṣṭrakūta attack must have taken place sometime between the years 916 and 917 A. D. i.e., just a few years after the civil turmoil in Kanauj. As regards the results of the conflict, Dr. R. C. Majumdar is of opinion that "Mahīpāla fled from his capital, hotly pursued by his enemies," and that later on Harṣadeva Candella assisted the Imperial ruler "to re-establish his authority over the shattered kingdom."[2] For the latter part of the statement, however, I am unable to find any evidence, since the passage in the Khajuraho inscription discussed above, on which the learned Professor evidently bases his conclusion, does not refer to Mahīpāla's restoration, but merely to his accession to the throne with the help of the Candella prince. Besides, we even know from the Asni inscription that Mahīpāla was ruling in (Vikrama) year 974 = 917 A. D., and his authority was recognised so far from the capital as the modern district of Fatehpur.[3]

But in the east the Pālas, who had already re-occupied Uddaṇḍapura or Bihar probably in the confusion following the fratricidal struggle for the throne,[4]

[1] *Ibid.*, p. 417; *Ind. Ant.*, XII, pp. 222-23; *Ep. Ind.*, VI, pp. 176, 177.

[2] *Jour. Dept. Lett.*, X, pp. 66, 68. The effects of this invasion have been greatly exaggerated. Thus says Dr. R. C. Majumdar: "But the prestige of the Pratīhāras suffered a severe blow from which they never completely recovered" (*Ibid*, p. 68). At another place, however, he affirms contrariwise: "It may be safely laid down that the Pratīhāra empire remained intact and probably its boundaries were extended in Mahīpāla's time" (*Ibid.*, p. 64).

[3] *Ind. Ant.*, XVI, p. 174.

[4] Cf. the Bihar image inscription of Nārāyaṇapāla's reign, dated year 54, recording the dedication of Thāruka, son of Rānaka Ucha (Utsa). *Ind. Ant.*, XLVII (1918), p. 110.

seem to have taken advantage of this temporary shock to the fortunes of the Pratīhāra family, and they recovered some of their ancestral possessions upto the eastern banks of the river Son. This is evident from the Baragaon (Patna district) pillar inscription of the 24th year of Rājyapāla[1], and two other Pāla inscriptions that refer to the time of Gopāla II, and are incised on pedestals of images. One of them was discovered in the ruins of Nalanda in the Patna district, and records that an individual did honour to the image of the goddess Vāgīśvarī by covering it with gold leaf in the first year of Gopāla II's reign[2]. The other was discovered in the ruins of Mahābodhi temple at Bodhgaya; it is undated and commemorates the installation of an image of the Buddha by Dharmabhīma[3]. These inscriptions no doubt belong to a period about two decades after the invasion of Indra III, but the re-assertion of Pāla power in Magadha cannot be far removed from this event, as the subsequent career of Mahīpāla appears to have been a glorious one.

Thus although there were some secessions in the outlying parts of the kingdom, in the home provinces themselves Indra III's campaign meant in effect no more than a successful raid, and it left no traces behind save the horrid marks of sanguinary war. Kanauj soon revived, and we have even indications that Mahīpāla resumed his predecessors' schemes of conquest. For the court-poet Rājaśekhara, who must have lived in the early part of Mahīpāla's reign, not only speaks of him as the "pearl-jewel of the race of Raghu," and the "Mahārājādhirāja of Āryāvarta," but also in a magniloquent verse in the introduction to the *Pracaṇḍa Pāṇḍava*

[1] *Ibid.*, p. 111.
[2] *Arch. Surv. Ind. Rep.*, Vol. I (1862-65), p. 36.
[3] *Ind. Ant.*, XXXVIII, p. 237.

or *Bāla-Bhārata* attributes to him the following victories in distant lands : "And in that (lineage of Raghu) there was born the glorious Mahīpāladeva who has bowed down the locks of hair on the tops of the heads of the Muralas; who has caused the Mekhalas to suppurate; who has driven the Kalingas before him in war; who has spoilt the pastime of (the king who is) the moon of the Keralas; who has conquered the Kulūtas; who is a very axe to the Kuntalas; and who by violence has appropriated the fortunes of the Ramaṭhas"[1]. It is difficult to identify Murala in this passage; possibly it stands for the Narbada and the Muralas were consequently those who inhabited its banks. Some scholars on the other hand take it to signify the country watered by the river Muralā in or around the Kerala country (*Raghuvaṁśa*, IV, 55). Mekhala is another name for the Amarkanṭak hills, where the Narbada rises, and so the Mekhalas may be the people living in that region. The Kalingas were certainly the natives of the coast of Orissa, perhaps extending as far south as the Ganjam district. The Keralas or Ceras are the well-known kingdom in the south between the Western Ghats and the sea-coast. The Kulūtas, of course, were a people who dwelt in the Kangra district of the Panjab on the banks of the Bias river[2]. The name Kulūta is probably represented by the modern Kullu. The Kuntalas lived in the western part of the Deccan. Indeed, Kuntala denoted more or less the old Cālukya kingdom in the highlands of the Western Ghats.[3] The Ramaṭhas

[1] See I, 7. Carl Cappeller's edition (1885), p. 2.
Cf. "Namita-Murala-mauliḥ pākalo Mekalānāṁ,
Raṇa-kalita-Kalingaḥ keli taṭa Keral-endoḥ,
Ajani jita Kulūtaḥ Kuntalānāṁ kuṭhāraḥ,
Haṭha-hrita-Ramaṭha-śrīḥ śrī-Mahīpāladevah."

[2] *Ann. Rep. Arch. Surv. Ind.*, 1907-08, p. 260.

[3] See also *Arch. Surv. W. Ind.*, Vol. IV, pp. 126, 127; *Ind. Ant.*, XXII p. 182.

were, according to the *Kāvyamīmāṁsā* (ch. XVII, p. 94) of Rājaśekhara, a people who dwelt beyond the Prithūdaka in the north, and are mentioned with the Kulūtas and Kīras etc. Taking the passage literally, it would appear that Mahīpāla's arms penetrated remote regions extending from the upper course of the river Bias in the north-west to Kalinga or Orissa in the south-east; and from the Himālayas to the Kerala or Cera country in the far south.[1] But as we have no epigraphic evidence to corroborate these claims of victories, it is more reasonable to hold that by attributing to him this conventional area of "world-conquest" the poet primarily intended to show in a general way that his patron was a mighty monarch, who undertook many warlike expeditions in Āryāvarta or Northern India, and struck terror into the hearts of his contemporary rulers. That Mahīpāla must have overrun the territories as far as the lower course of the Narbada seems also evident from the Partabgarh inscription, which informs us that in the year 946 A. D. Ujjain was being ruled by a governor of his son Mahendrapāla II. Now the latter is nowhere credited with any achievements, and we have seen above that Ujjain was occupied by the Rāṣṭrakūṭas during the northern campaigns of Indra III. There can therefore be no doubt that the recovery of the Ujjain region was the work of Mahīpāla himself. Support for this conclusion is also lent by the Kahla plate, according to which Bhāmāna is said to have gained fame by conquering Dhārā.[2] This Bhāmāna must have been a contemporary and vassal of Mahīpāla, being the successor of Ullabha, who was preceded by Guṇāṁbodhideva. the feudatory of Mahī-

[1] *Jour. Dept. Lett.*, X, p. 64; Wilson, *Theatre of the Hindus*, II, p. 361.

[2] *Ep. Ind.*, VII, pp. 89-90, verse 13.
Cf. "...... nija vijayi pa (do) ddhāra Dhārāvanīśa (hrisya) t-senajaya-śrī-haṭha-haraṇa-kalā-dhāma Bhāmāna-devaḥ."

pāla's grandfather Bhoja I. As it is unlikely that a minor prince like Bhāmāna would by himself lead an expedition from Gorakhpur District, where this Kalacuri family was settled, to distant Ujjain, we may reasonably suppose that he accompanied his suzerain Mahīpāla in his southern campaigns and helped him in his victories. Another chief who rendered him similar assistance was perhaps his Guhila contemporary, Bhaṭṭa, who is represented in the Cāṭsū inscription as having defeated the armies of the kings of the south at the behest of his overlord.[1] Presumably the progress of Mahīpāla's arms was facilitated by the then moribund condition of the Rāṣṭrakūṭa monarchy, for we are told in the Karhad plates that Indra III's successor, Govinda IV, instead of looking to the affairs of the state, had taken to "vicious courses" and had thus "with his intelligence caught in the noose of the eyes of women displeased all beings."[2] The weakness of Govinda IV's rule is also apparent from the fact that according to the *Vikramārjunavijaya* of the Kanarese poet Pampa he was defeated by one of his feudatories, Arikeśarin II of Puligere.[3] This event must have occurred soon after Śaka 851 or 930 A. D., the date of the Kalas inscription, which bestows conventional praises on Govinda IV.[4]

As regards the Ramaṭhas and the Kulūtas of the Panjab of whom Rājaśekhara expressly states that they were "conquered" and their "fortunes appropriated by violence," there is nothing improbable in the view that

[1] *Ep. Ind.*, XII, pp. 12, 16, verse 26.

[2] *Ibid.*, IV, pp. 283, 288, verse 20.

[3] *Ibid.*, XIII, pp. 328-329.

[4] *Ibid.* The fact that in some records Govinda IV is described as being served by the Gaṅgā and the Yamunā in his palace need not be taken to mean that he retained possession of the Doab. As shown above, Indra III's invasion did not produce any lasting results, and Govinda IV was far too busy with sensual pleasures to think of foreign affairs.

they were actually compelled to accept the suzerainty of Mahīpāla. This conclusion is further reinforced by the fact that the district of Karnal was included within the Pratīhāra kingdom since the days of Bhoja I, and Mas'udī records that "the Mihran of Sindh comes from well-known sources in the highlands of Sindh, from the country belonging to Kanauj in the kingdom of Baüüra and from Kashmir......,"[1] which clearly shows that parts of the Panjab continued to be under Kanauj. The south-western limit of Mahīpāla's jurisdiction is of course fixed by the Haddala plates dated Śaka 836 or 914 A. D., from which we learn that at the beginning of his reign eastern Saurāṣṭra was being governed by his feudatory (Mahā-sāmantādhipati) Dharaṇīvarāha, who granted to Maheśvarācārya on the day of the winter solstice the village named Viṁkala.[2] Bühler on the other hand identified the Mahīpāla of the Haddala grant with one of the Cūḍāsamas of Girnar-Junāgaḍh,[3] but considering the fact that the Unā grant mentions Avanivarman II Yoga, the feudatory of Mahendrapāla, as an opponent of a Dharaṇīvarāha, identified with the Mahāsāmantādhipati of the Haddala record, it seems more reasonable to suppose that the latter eventually came under the Pratīhāra yoke and that the name Mahīpāla refers to his Kanauj suzerain. It has sometimes been assumed that Saurāṣṭra, which had been connected with the Pratīhāras since the reign of Nāgabhaṭa II, must have slipped away from their hands after the raid of Indra III, but there is no evidence of any such rupture until the rise of Mūlarāja Cālukya. A powerful monarch like Mahīpāla must certainly have made his authority felt there, and even after him we

[1] Elliot, *History of India*, I, p. 21.
[2] *Ind. Ant.*, XVIII, pp. 90-91; *Ep. Ind.*, IX, p. 4.
[3] *Ind. Ant.*, XII, p. 192.

may well believe that for a time the local chiefs of Kāthiāwāḍ continued to make a show of submission, as the Nawabs of Oudh found it profitable to do during the declining days of the Great Moghul at Delhi. Towards the east, however, after the Pālas had recovered some of their lost territories, the Pratīhāra kingdom does not seem to have extended much beyond the western borders of Bihar. The Bengal Asiatic Society's plate, issued from Mahodaya, which records the grant in V. E. 988 or 931 A. D. to Bhaṭṭa Bhullāka of a village named Tikkarigrāma in the Vārāṇasī-*viṣaya* of the Pratisthāna-*bhukti*, at any rate shows that the Benares region was still under Kanauj[1].

There are indications that the closing years of Mahīpāla were again disturbed by a renewal of the Rāṣṭrakūṭa attacks on northern India. For the Deoli and Karhad plates of Kriṣṇa III, while eulogising his achievements in the usual style of inflated panegyric specifically inform us that "on hearing of the conquest of all the strongholds in the southern regions simply by means of his angry glance, the hope about Kālañjara and Citrakūṭa vanished from the heart of the Gurjara."[2] A critical study of the Deoli plates shows that Kriṣṇa III undertook these expeditions sometime before Śaka 862 or 940 A. D., the date of the inscription, and while he was still a mere crown-prince or *Kumāra*. Accordingly we can be certain that the term Gurjara in this passage signifies Mahīpāla. It has been suggested that Kriṣṇa III was successful in occupying Kālañjara and Citrakūṭa. This may perhaps be true, although all we learn from our Rāṣṭrakūṭa version of the incursion is that hearing of the

[1] *Ind. Ant.*, XV, pp. 140, 141.

[2] *Ep. Ind.*, IV, pp. 284, 289, v. 30; V, p. 194, verse 25.
Cf. "Dakṣiṇadig-durga vijayaṁ-ākarṇya,
Galitā Gūrjara-hṛidayāt Kālañjara-Citrakūṭa-āśā."

triumphant progress of Krisna III's arms, the Gurjara ruler became so panic-stricken as to lose all hopes of the defence and safety of two of his most strategic strongholds. That Krisna III's claims of conquests in northern India are not a mere vaunt is no doubt clear from the discovery of a Kanarese *praśasti* inscribed on a stone slab at Jura in the Maihar state of the Baghelkhand Agency.[1] But it is significant that he assumes the full imperial titles of Paramabhaṭṭāraka, Mahārājādhirāja, and Parameśvara in this record, and the suspicion cannot, therefore, be entirely avoided that the credit for actual occupation of any territory in the north belongs to the subsequent career of Krisna III, who, as king, may have led a second expedition when the power of the Pratīhāras was distinctly on the wane.

Arab testimony

The Arab traveller Al Mas'ūdī,[2] who visited the valley of the Indus in *Hijri* 303-04 or 915-16 A. D. at the beginning of Mahīpāla's reign and wrote an account of his travels in 332 H = 943-44 A. D.,[3] bears eloquent testimony to the power and prestige of the king of Kanauj. He informs us in his *Murūj-ul-Zahāb* that "one of the neighbouring kings of India who is far from the sea, is the Baüüra, who is lord of the city of Kanauj. This title is given to all the sovereigns of that kingdom." Evidently the term Baüüra is an Arabic corruption of the term Pratīhāra or its Prakrit equivalent Paḍihāra, and the description of being "far from the sea" also answers well to the position of Kanauj. The Arab chronicler then testifies to the Rāṣṭrakūṭa-Pratīhāra struggle that was the characteristic feature of this epoch.

1 *Ibid.*, XIX, pp. 287-90.
2 Elliot, *History of India*, Vol. I, pp. 21-23.
3 *Ibid.*, p. 454.

He says : "This Baüüra who is the king of Kanauj is an enemy of the Balhara, the king of India." Further he gives a rough indication of the dimensions of the kingdom of Kanauj, which according to him extended about one hundred and twenty square *parasangas* of Sindh, each *parasang* being equal to eight miles of this country. We are also told that the king of Kanauj maintained a large army both for aggression and defence. "He has large armies in garrisons on the north and on the south; on the east and on the west, for he is surrounded on all sides by warlike kings." In another passage Mas'ūdī gives the huge numbers of the army: "The king has four armies according to the four quarters of the wind. Each of them numbers 700,000 or 900,000 men." Lastly, the traveller indicates the political disposition of the times, and mentions some of the powers that had relations with Kanauj. "The army of the north wars against the prince of Multan, and with the Musulmans, his subjects, on the frontier. The army of the south fights against the Balhara, king of Mankir. The other two armies march to meet enemies in every direction." From these brief references it is clear that to an observant foreigner Kanauj appeared as the leading state of northern India, whose western limits extended upto Sindh, and whose ruler kept other kingdoms in awe and subjection by his vigilant forces.[1]

Mahendrapāla II

The name of this shadowy monarch was brought

[1] See *J. A. S. B.*, N. S. XVI (1920), p. 84, also pl. XII, No. 1, for certain gold coins which have been attributed by Mr. R. D. Banerji to Mahīpāla Pratīhāra. On the obverse the king's name appears in three lines and on the reverse there is the seated goddess of the Gupta type. The form of *ha* no doubt shows that the coins are earlier than the 12th century A. D., but their ascription is rather doubtful.

to light a few years ago by the discovery of a long inscription at Partabgarh, the capital of a state of the same name in southern Rajputana.[1] He is therein described as the son of Vināyakapāla (Mahīpāla) by queen Prasādhanādevī of the Devathāddhi family, and must have come to the throne shortly before the year 1003 or 946 A. D., when this inscription was issued from Mahodaya. It says that at the request of one Dhanasūra Mahendrapāla II bestowed the village of Kharparapadraka, in the holding of Talavargika Hariṣaḍa, and situated in the vicinity of Ghontā-varṣikā in the western *pathaka* of Dasapura (Mandasor), upon the goddess Vaṭa-Yakṣiṇī Devī, whose shrine was connected with the *maṭha* of Hari Riśīśvara. The chief point to be noticed is that even during Mahendrapāla II's reign the kingdom of Kanauj extended so far south as Ujjain, where Mādhava, son of Dāmodara, was acting as the "great feudatory, great governor, and *charge d' affaires* (Tantrapāla, Mahāsāmanta, Mahādaṇḍanāyaka), and his Commander-in-chief (Balādhikrita), Śrī-Śarman, was carrying on the affairs of state at Maṇḍapikā or Māṇḍū. The record adds that on the *Mīna Saṁkrānti* day Mādhava, having bathed and paid devotions at the sanctuary of Mahākāla, granted at the request of the Cāhamāna feudatory, Mahāsāmanta Indrarāja, the village of Dhārāpadraka for the worship of the idol, and repairs of the temple, of Taruṇāditya-deva. In my opinion this important document alone is sufficient to shatter the current theories that date the downfall of the Pratīhāra empire from the time of the Rāṣṭrakūṭa Indra III's invasion of Kanauj.[2] And luckily we have got epigraphic evidence to prove the continued inclusion of the intervening regions of Gwalior also, for the Rakhetra

[1] *Ep. Ind.*, XIV, pp. 176-186.
[2] See e.g., R. D. Banerji, *J. B. O. R. S.*, Dec., 1928, p. 486.

stone inscription,[1] discovered in the village of that name, near Canderi in Gwalior, says that Vināyakapāla constructed certain water-works there at an immense cost in the year (Vikrama) 999-1000 or 942-43 A. D. i.e., just one or two years before Mahendrapāla II ascended the throne.

Devapāla

Mahendrapāla II's reign must have terminated sometime before the (Vikrama) year 1005 or 948 A. D., when according to the Siyadoni inscription another son of Kṣitipāla *alias* Mahīpāla named Devapāla was ruling in Kanauj[2]. This record describes him as the immediate successor of his father, and we may therefore explain the omission of Mahendrapāla II's name by the extreme shortness of his reign, or by the assumption that their relations were unfriendly. The reign of Devapāla appears to have been marked by the rise of the Candellas to virtual independent power, for we are told in a Khajurāho inscription that Yaśovarman Candella was "a scorching fire to the Gurjaras," and that he "easily conquered the fort of Kālañjara"[3], which, as we have seen above from the Barah copper plate, was subject to the authority of Kanauj. But if we admit that it was taken by Krisṇa III from the Pratīhāras before the Deoli plates were issued in 940 A. D.[4], then evidently Yaśovarman must have reconquered Kālañjara from the Rāṣṭrakūtas, although it is significant they are not mentioned in the Khajurāho inscription among the peoples defeated by the Candella ruler. Whatever be the fact regarding the capture of this important stronghold, it was probably because of his growing

[1] *Ann. Rep. Arch. Surv. Ind.*, 1924-25, p. 168.
[2] *Ep. Ind.*, I, p. 170 f.
[3] *Ibid.*, p. 132, verse 23; p. 133, verse 31.
[4] See *Ante.*

strength and independence that Yaśovarman compelled Devapāla to surrender to him a celebrated image of Vaikuṇṭha, which was subsequently set up in a temple built by the former himself. It is interesting to note that Devapāla had obtained this image for a force of elephants and horses from Śāhī, the king of Kīra,[1] who in his turn had received it as a token of friendship from the lord of Bhoṭa,[2] and the latter again is said to have acquired it in the Kailāśa mountains.[3] Such a transaction by a quondam feudatory was doubtless a great blow to the prestige of the Pratīhāras, and from this time onward the decline sets in, and the empire reared by the genius of Bhoja I and Mahendrapāla I begins to crumble to pieces.

Vijayapāla

Like his predecessors, Devapāla also appears to have enjoyed a very short reign, for we learn from the Rajor inscription that a king named Vijayapāla was in power in Kanauj early in the year 959 A. D. This epigraph represents him as meditating on the feet of Kṣitipāladeva—a phrase commonly used in inscriptions to signify the relation of father and son[4]—and consequently the inference may safely be drawn that Vijayapāla was a brother or half-brother of Devapāla. It has, however, been a matter of some controversy among scholars whether Vijayapāla was the immediate successor of Devapāla or there were other intervening kings. Recently the

[1] The Kīras have been identified with the Kashmiras by some, but it seems more plausible to locate them in the Kangra valley of the Panjab. For an account of the Kīra kingdom, see *Ind. Hist. Quart.*, IX (March, 1933), pp. 11-17.

[2] Lassen identifies Bhoṭa with modern Tibet (*Ep. Ind.*, I, p. 124).

[3] *Ibid.*, p. 134, verse 43.

[4] It may also sometimes denote the relation of brother.

latter view has been advocated by Mr. Niharranjan Ray, who thinks that between Devapāla and Vijayapāla two more kings ruled viz., Vināyakapāla II, son of Mahendrapāla II (?) and Mahīpāla II, son of Devapāla (?).[1] Vināyakapāla II is introduced in the Pratīhāra genealogy on the strength of the Khajuraho inscription dated V. E. 1011 = 954 A. D., the last line of which runs as follows : "While the illustrious Vināyaka (?) pāladeva is protecting the earth, the earth is not taken possession of by the enemies, who have been annihilated."[2] Now, the identification of this Vināyakapāla has been a puzzle to scholars. Kielhorn, the editor of the inscription, was unable to offer any conjecture, and he felt even some doubts about the correctness of his reading.[3] But the above description in terms suggestive of his suzerain power, and the form of the name, which is quite clear in the facsimile, make it almost certain that he can be no other than a Pratīhāra monarch. Are we, therefore, to identify him with Vināyakapāla *alias* Mahīpāla, or take him as a separate ruler? Chronological considerations go against the first alternative, as the Khajurāho inscription is dated in 954 A. D., and we know it definitely that Vināyakapāla's successor was already on the throne in the year 946 A. D. It has, no doubt, been sometimes supposed that the name of Vināyakapāla occurred in the original record of Yaśovarman, and after the latter's death it was set up in 954 A. D. during the reign of his successor Dhanga with the addition of some verses at the end describing his martial exploits.[4] This assumption, however, does not appear to be cogent, for why should the name of a monarch, who was dead and gone, be retained in the

[1] *Ind. Ant.*, Oct. 1928, pp. 230-34.
[2] *Ep. Ind.*, I, p. 135.
[3] *Ibid.*, p. 124.
[4] *Jour. Dep. Lett.*, X, p. 61.

"subsequent modification" of an official document made in the time of Dhanga, when Vināyakapāla was no longer "protecting the earth"? Thus we are driven to recognise the existence of a second Vināyakapāla after Devapāla's reign. As regards his connection with the Pratīhāra line, Mr. N. Ray may be right in thinking that he was the son of Mahendrapāla II, for among Indian Royalty it is not unoften the practice to give to the grandson the same name as that of the grandfather.[1] But there is just one point which seems to militate against the view that Vināyakapāla II followed Devapāla. We have already noted that Yaśovarman is represented in the same Khajurāho inscription as a "scorching fire to the Gurjaras," and is even credited with the easy conquest of Kālañjara. If, therefore, Yaśovarman had practically wrested the independence of the Candellas, how could his successor Dhanga continue to invoke the name of the Pratīhāra king as his overlord. Perhaps the explanation to this apparent anomaly is that like the Nizam of the Deccan and the Nawabs of Oudh, who were virtually independent and yet nominally acknowledged the suzerainty of the Great Moghul at Delhi, the Candel ruler also did not all at once break off formal relations with the effete imperial power at Kanauj, but for some time maintained an outward show of submission. Now, if Vināyakapāla II was an historical reality, as appears quite likely from the foregoing discussion, who was his successor? With regard to Mahīpāla II, we are rather on uncertain ground. He has been mentioned in a stone inscription, discovered at Bayana in the Bharatpur state, which records the erection of a temple of Viṣṇu by Citralekhā,[2] and the reasons

[1] *Ind. Ant.*, Oct., 1928, p. 233.

[2] *Ann. Prog. Rep. Arch. Surv. Ind.*, Western circle, 1919, pp. 43-44; *Ep. Ind.*, XXII (July, 1933), pp. 120–27.

of his identification as a Pratīhāra monarch are twofold. First, he is given the imperial title of Mahārājādhirāja; and secondly, the Bayana region must have been included within the kingdom of Kanauj, since it is known with certainty that Rajor, lying further to its northwest, continued to acknowledge the authority of Kanauj till afterwards. That Bayana formed part of the kingdom of Kanauj in Vikrama year 1012 = 955 A. D., the date of the epigraph, nobody would probably deny, but the question is how far are we justified in regarding Mahīpāla as a Pratīhāra from the mere title of Mahārājādhirāja? The document does not mention any of the predecessors of Mahīpāla, which is almost an uncommon feature in the records of the dynasty. Besides, it is highly improbable, although by no means impossible, that within the short space of about a decade—948 to 959 A. D.—three kings viz., Devapāla, Vināyakapāla II, Mahīpāla II, ruled in close succession, and the fourth, Vijayapāla, also began his career. Presumably Mahīpāla was a vassal chief, and this supposition is doubtless to some extent strengthened by the evidence of the Rajor inscription, which shows that even the feudatories had then begun to adopt the so-called imperial titles of Parameśvara and Mahārājādhirāja on account of the decadent condition of the imperial government at Kanauj.[1] Similarly, we cannot include Vatsarāja into the dynastic list merely on the strength of a fragmentary stone inscription of the Vikrama year 1013 = 956 A. D., discovered at Osia in the Jodhpur state.[2] It is indeed noteworthy that this record calls him a Pratīhāra, but he may have been only a scion of some local branch of the family, or a gubernatorial representative over

[1] See *Infra*.

[2] *Ann. Prog. Rep. Arch. Surv. Ind.*, Western circle, 1907, p. 15. This record should not be confused with that of Nāgabhaṭa II's father.

whom the control of Kanauj had become very loose[1]. The truth of the whole matter is that although the historicity of a second Vināyakapāla may be accepted, there is nothing definite in our present state of knowledge to support the insertion of Mahīpāla II or Vatsarāja II into the Imperial line.

To turn to Vijayapāla, it is difficult to ascertain the exact limits of his reign, but we know that he must have come to the throne about 959 A. D., and ceased to rule long before 1019 A. D., when his successor Rājyapāla was killed in battle. Thus the period between 959 and 1019 A. D. covers two reigns; and if we, therefore, assign thirty years to each—leaving a slight margin for error—the date of Vijayapāla's death would fall sometime about the year 988-89 A. D. The gradual process of decline, which began in the time of Devapāla with the rise of the Candellas, continued steadily under Vijayapāla's rule, so that when the sceptre dropped from his hand, the mighty kingdom of the Pratīhāras had become a ghost of its former self, and on its ruins new states had appeared. Among the earliest defections was that of the south-western province of Saurāṣṭra (Kāthiāwāḍ), which along with Gujarat came under the Solanki or Caulukya dynasty founded by Mūlarāja at Anhilwāḍa (Anhilla-pāṭaka) about the middle of the tenth century A. D.[2] The Kādi plates[3] and the Gujarat chronicles describe him as a son of Mahārājādhirāja Rāji, and we may, therefore, suppose that Mūlarāja was

[1] This suggestion perhaps receives some confirmation from the Rajor inscription, which represents another feudatory, Mathanadeva, as belonging to the Gurjara-Pratīhāra family.

[2] According to Merutunga's *Vicāraśreṇī*, Mūlarāja ascended the throne in V. E. 1017 = A. D. 961 (*Bom. Gaz.*, vol. I, pt. I, p. 156). But the Sambhar inscription gives the Vikrama date 998 or 941 A. D. for the event (*Ind. Ant.*, 1929, pp. 235, 236, verse 8).

[3] *Ind. Ant.*, VI, pp. 191, 192.

not a mere upstart adventurer, but belonged to some notable family.[1] The Kādi inscription also states that he acquired the Sāraswata-*maṇḍala* by the prowess of his arms.[2] The Vaḍnagar *praśasti*[3] further informs us that Mūlarāja "made the fortune of the kingdom of the Cāpotkaṭa princes, whom he took captive at will, an object of enjoyment for the multitude of the learned, of his relatives" etc., which shows that he must have aggrandised himself in southern Rajputana—the homelands of the opponents named. In northern Rajputana also the authority of the Pratīhāras must have been only nominal, for Mathanadeva, son of Sāvaṭa of the Gurjara-Pratīhāra lineage (Gurjara-Pratīhārānvayaḥ), adopts the imperial titles of Mahārājādhirāja and Parameśvara in the Rajor inscription discovered among the ruins of Parnagar in the Alwar state, while in the same breath he represents himself as a feudatory of Vijayapāla.[4]

The kingdom of Jejākabhukti rapidly grew in power and saw its palmy days under Dhanga (circa 950-1000 A. D.), who is alleged in the Mhow inscription to have attained to "supreme lordship after inflicting a defeat over the king of Kānyakubja."[5] The success of the Candellas against the Pratīhāras is further confirmed by a Khajurāho inscription, wherein we are told that Dhanga ruled the earth "playfully acquired by the action of his long and strong arms, as far as Kālañjara, and as far as Bhāsvat situated (?) on the banks of the river Mālava; from here to the banks of the river Kālindī (Jumnā), and from here also to the frontiers of the Cedi country, and even as far as that mountain called Gopa

[1] *Ibid.*, p. 181 f; *Bom. Gaz.*, Vol. I, pt. I, p. 156 f.
[2] *Ind. Ant.*, VI, p. 191, line 7.
[3] *Ep. Ind.*, I, pp. 296, 301, verse 5; *Ibid.*, X, p. 77.
[4] *Ep. Ind.*, III, p. 266.
[5] *Ibid.*, I, pp. 197, 203, verse 3. Cf. "yaḥ Kānyakubjaṁ narendraṁ samara bhuvi vijitya prāpa sāṁrājyaṁ-uccaiḥ."

(Gopādri), which is the unique abode of marvel."[1] The Sāsbahū inscription, however, attributes the conquest of Gwalior to the Kacchapaghāta prince Vajradāman, who is said to have "put down the rising valour of the ruler of Gādhinagara, and his proclamation drum ... resounded in the fort of Gopādri."[2] As his only known date 977 A. D.[3] falls within the limits of Dhanga's reign, we may assume that Vajradāman was a local feudatory chief of the Candella ruler, whom he assisted in the conquest of Gwalior. The loss of this ancient possession must have dealt a severe blow to the strength of the Pratīhāras, as thereby the Candellas got hold of a strategic position, which they could well use as a base for further encroachments. Indeed, it is likely that towards the close of his reign Dhanga carried his arms as far as Benares, since a copper plate of (Vikrama) year 1055 = 998 A. D. records that he made a grant of the village of Yulli (?) situated in the Uṣāravāha to the Bhaṭṭa Yaśodhara at Kāśikā or Benares.[4]

Next, the Cedis, who occupied the country between the Candellas and the Cālukya territories, appear to have given some trouble to the decadent power at Kanauj, for the Goharwa plates of the year 1047 A. D. affirm that the Cedi king, Lakṣamaṇarājadeva, who must have flourished sometime in the latter half of the tenth century being three generations anterior to the issuer of the grant, defeated the kings of Vangāla, Kasmīra, and Gurjara etc.[5] The Cedis had also intervened in Imperial affairs previously, when Kokalla I espoused the cause of Bhoja II, and so we may be sure that Gurjara here refers to the Pratīhāra monarch.

[1] *Ibid.*, I, pp. 124, 134, verse 45.
[2] *Ind. Ant.*, XV, pp. 36, 41.
[3] *J. A. S. B.*, XXXI, p. 393.
[4] *Ind. Ant.*, XVI, pp. 203, 206.
[5] *Ep. Ind.*, XI, p. 142, v. 8.

As regards Malwa, it was governed between the years V. E. 1005 = A. D. 949 and V. E. 1029 = A. D. 973 by Sīyaka-Harṣa of the Paramāra dynasty,[1] who, according to the Udepur inscription, "took away in battle the wealth of Khoṭṭiga,"[2] rightly identified by Bühler with his Rāṣṭrakuṭa namesake (*circa* 955-970), successor of Kriṣṇa III (*c.* 940-955 A. D.). Sīyaka-Harṣa was followed by another powerful ruler named Muñja *alias* Vākpati whose kown dates range from 974 to 994 A. D. He is credited in the same Udepur *praśasti* with many notable victories over the Karṇāṭas, Lāṭas, Keralas, Colas and Cedis[3]; we may, therefore, safely assume that he was, like his predecessor, free from any foreign control. Malwa must have overthrown the Pratīhāra authority and declared its independence soon after the death of Mahendrapāla II, for we know from the Indore plates that even as early as V. E. 1031 = 974 A. D. the three immediate predecessors of Muñja[4] are given the usual titles of Paramabhaṭṭāraka, Mahārājādhirāja, and Parameśvara generally signifying sovereign status.

The Cāhamānas of Sākambhari or Sambhar, originally feudatories of the Pratīhāras[5], also took advantage of the prevailing confusion and made themselves supreme

[1] See the Harasola grant (*Ep. Ind.*, XIX, p. 226 f.) for the former date and Dhanapāla's *Pāiya-lacchi*, v. 198, for the latter.

[2] *Ep. Ind.*, I, pp. 235, 237, v. 12.

[3] *Ibid.*, v. 14.

[4] *Ind. Ant.*, VI, p. 51. The Udepur *praśasti* gives a longer genealogy by duplicating names, but Dr. Hoernle remarks it is mythical (*J. R. A. S.*, 1904, p. 657, note 1; see also C. V. Vaidya, *H.M.H.I.*, Vol. II, pp. 118, 123; D. B. Diskalkar, *Proc. & Trans. 3rd Or. Conf.* (Madras, 1924), p. 303 f. See, however, D. C. Ganguly, *History of the Paramāra Dynasty* (Dacca, 1933), pp. 29-30 and note; Dr. H. C. Ray, *Dy. Hist. North. Ind.*, II, p. 844 f. for the contrary view).

[5] See *ante* under Nāgabhaṭa II.

in Central Rajputana. This is evident from the Harṣa stone inscription, which gives us the Vikrama year 1030 = 973 A. D. for Vigraharāja II,[1] and represents him as having "rescued both the fortune of his family and the fortune of victory from the distress which had befallen them."[2] Indeed, if the "universal sovereign of the earth in Ragu's race" (Raghukula-bhu-cakravarti) mentioned in verse 19 of the above record, is identical with one of the later Pratīhāra monarchs, as supposed by Dr. D. R. Bhandarkar[3] on the authority of Rājaśekhara, the power and prestige of the Cāhamānas must have grown considerably even during the time of Vigraharājaś predecessor, Siṁharāja, for otherwise how are we to explain the unique circumstance of the suzerain personally visiting his feudatory in order to secure the release of the princes captured by the latter in his war against the Tomara chief Salavaṇa.

Perhaps the Guhilas (Guhilots) also broke off all relations with the Pratīhāras not long after the Vikrama year 1003 or 946 A. D., the date of the Partabgarh inscription, for we learn from the Atpur inscription that Mahārājādhirāja Bhatṛipaṭṭa II, who is recorded in the former epigraph to have made a perpetual land grant to the deity Indrarājāditya-deva of Ghoṇṭāvarṣikā in V. E. 999 = 943 A. D., married a Rāṣṭrakūṭa princess[4], which clearly indicates that he had formed an alliance with their traditional rivals. Lastly, the kingdom

[1] *Ep. Ind.*, II, pp. 124, 129.

[2] *Ibid.*, pp. 122, 127, verse 20; *Ind. Ant.*, XLII (1913), p. 62, v. 20.

[3] *Ind. Ant.*, XLII (1913), pp. 59, 62; see also Dr. H. C. Ray, *Dy. Hist. North. Ind.*, Vol. II, p. 1064. Kielhorn, however, thinks that the reference is to Rāma or Viṣṇu and the taking away of Simharāja to heaven (*Ep. Ind.*, II, p. 127 and note).

[4] *Ind. Ant.* 1910, p. 191, verse 4.

of Bhatinda[1] came into prominence in the Panjab, and gradually extended "in length from Sirhind to Lumghan and in breadth from the kingdom of Kashmir to Mooltan."[2] Thus within the course of half a century the disintegration of the Pratīhāra empire was almost complete, and once more Northern India presented its normal aspect of a group of independent and mutually warring states.

Rājyapāla

When Rājyapāla came to the throne, he was in no position to make any attempt to retrieve the fallen fortunes of his family, for not only were the frontiers of his attenuated kingdom hemmed in on all sides by powerful principalities, but the political situation had become further complicated by the aggressions of the Moslems of Ghazni, who now directed all their "thoughts to the conquest of the infidels." We must, therefore, turn to trace the course of their progress eastward in order to understand the circumstances of the ultimate overthrow of the Pratīhāra power in Kanauj. The rumblings of the coming storm were naturally first heard in the north-west, when Jayapāla, the ruler of Udabhāṇḍapur, driven to desperation by the gradual diminution of his ancestral kingdom, determined to retaliate and check the further advance of the Moslems by organising a counter-invasion of their territory. But the effete Hindu soldiers were no match for the hardy hosts of Sultan Sabuktigin, and Jayapāla was soon compelled to retreat after concluding a humiliating

[1] At first the Śāhīs had their capital at Uda-bhāṇḍapur or Waihind, but probably owing to the pressure of the advancing Moslems it was shifted to Bhatinda.

[2] Briggs, Firishta (*History of the Rise of the Mohamedan Power*), Vol. I, p. 15.

agreement.[1] In the safety of his capital, however, he repudiated the terms of the compact and imprisoned the Amir's officers, which provoked the latter to such an extent that he at once marched like a "foaming torrent" to punish Jayapāla for his treachery. The latter, despairing of success, invited the prominent Hindu states to help him in resisting the alien invader, to which the "neighbouring kings, particularly those of Delhi, Ajmer, Kālañjara, and Kanauj" readily responded with men and money[2]. Jayapāla advanced to meet his adversary on the confines of Lamghan,[3] but the ponderous forces consisting of 100,000 cavalry, "many elephants" (Nizam-uddin), and "an innumerable host of foot" (Firishta), at his command soon gave way before the masterly manœuvres of Sabuktigin's army with the result that the conqueror obtained immense booty, besides 200 elephants of war, and "the best things in Jayapāla's most distant provinces." The king of Kanauj whose contingent shared in this defeat was probably Rājyapāla, although we have no evidence that he himself took any active part in the battle. The next attack was made by Sultan Mahmud, the son and successor of Sabuktigin, in the year 392 *Hijri* or 1001 A. D. Here again the issues were decidedly against Jayapāla, who, being unable to bear the ignominy of another defeat, handed

[1] Elliot, *History of India*, II, p. 21; Briggs, Firishta, I, p. 17.

[2] Briggs, Firishta, I, p. 18; see also *Cambridge History of India*, III, pp. 15-16. Mahmud's contemporary, Al Utbi, however, makes no mention of any such confederacy in the *Ta'rīkh-i-Yamīnī* (Elliot, II, p. 23). The mention of Delhi indeed throws an element of doubt upon Firishta's late account, for at this period it was a comparatively obscure town. It is significant that Utbi omits Delhi in the campaigns of Mahmud of Ghazni and Alberuni is also silent about it.

[3] Briggs, I, p. 18. Raverty on the other hand thinks that the battle took place in the Kurram valley (Darrah) or nearby (see *Notes on Afghanistan*, p. 321).

over the cares of the kingdom to his son, Ānandapāla, and then immolated himself by fire.[1] But Mahmud's insatiable thirst for harrying the "idolaters" would not allow Ānandapāla to have a peaceful reign, and in the spring of the year 399 or 1008 A. D. the Sultan again formed plans to punish him for having lent his aid to Da'ud of Multan in his treasonable designs. Hearing this, Ānandapāla despatched ambassadors to all parts of Hindustan appealing for assistance from other rulers, who "now considered the expulsion of the Muhammadans from India as a sacred duty."[2] The king of Kanauj, who had helped his father on an earlier occasion, promptly answered the call of his campatriot by sending a huge contingent, his example being followed by the Rājās of Ujjain, Gwalior, Kālañjara, Delhi, and Ajmer.[3] The confederate army, "the greatest that had yet taken the field", encamped on the confines of the province of Peshawar, where it remained for forty days without going into action. A wave of sullen enthusiasm seems to have swept over Hindustan; the women "sold their jewels and melted down their golden ornaments to furnish resources for the war", and even the Khokhars (Gukkurs) and other warlike tribes rose up to defend the gates of India. But nothing availed the Hindus. Their forces were signally routed just when victory seemed in sight, and Mahmud was suffering heavy losses by their furious charges. All of a sudden Ānandapāla's elephant became unruly from the effects of naphtha balls and fled. This circumstance

[1] According to Firishta, there was a custom among the Hindus that "whatever Rājā was twice overpowered by strangers, became disqualified to reign" (Briggs, I, p. 38). See also Elliot, II, p. 27, for a slightly different explanation given by Utbi.

[2] Briggs, Firishta, I, p. 46.

[3] *Ibid.* There is no mention of this second confederacy also either in Utbi's *Ta'rīkh-i-Yamīnī*, or in Ibn Asir's *Kamil-ut-Tawārīkh*.

caused a panic among the Hindus who thought that their commander had deserted them, and the battle ended in a victory for Mahmud amid scenes of awful carnage and confusion.

This was the last united effort of the states of Northern India to check the progress of the Moslems, and henceforth each one of them had to bear singly the brunt of Mahmud's ever-recurring aggressions. The turn of Kanauj came after several years, but unfortunately we have no information as to what happened there during the interval. On the 13th *Junaidi* of 409 *Hijri* = 27th September, 1018 A. D., the Sultan at last "bade farewell to sleep and ease", and departed along with his valiant warriors (11,000 regulars and 20,000 volunteers) for Kanauj, over which the shadow of the imperial power still hovered. Crossing the Jun or Jumnā on the 20th dəy of *Rajab*, 409 *Hijri*, or 2nd December, 1018, he arrived at the citadel of Barba (Baran) identified with Bulandshahr;[1] the local Rājā, Haradatta, became terror-stricken and purchased his life and kingdom by conversion to Islam with 10,000 of his followers. The next chief against whom Mahmud directed his attention on his way, was Kulacandar (Kulacandra) of Mahāban (Muttra district), "one of the leaders of the accursed satans, who employed his whole life in infidelity, and was confident in the strength of his own dominions."[2] The battle resulted in a victory for the Moslems, and Kulacandra slew his wife and himself with a dagger instead of submitting to forcible conversion. Then having sacked and desecrated the magnificent temples of Mathura, the cradle-land of Kriṣṇa, Mahmud proceeded towards Kanauj, appearing before its gates on the 8th day of *Shában* or 20th Decem-

[1] Elliot, II, p. 42, note 3.
[2] *Ibid.*, p. 43.

ber, 1018,[1] with a "small body of troops, leaving the greater part of his army behind".[2] He there saw "a city which raised its head to the skies, and which in strength and beauty might boast of being unrivalled".[3] He also found that the city held a very strategic position on the right bank of the Ganges, and its fortifications consisted of seven distinct forts. It was reputed, moreover, to contain 10,000 temples of high antiquity. But on hearing of Mahmud's sudden approach Rājyapāla (Utbi has corrupted the name into Rai Jaipāl or Rājā pāl),[4] who had perhaps already shared in the defeat of the confederate armies on two occasions previously, became panic-stricken and fled across the Ganges to Bari; and the Sultan thus meeting with little or no opposition took all the seven forts in one day. He then gave free license to his soldiers to plunder the city, raze the temples to the ground, and massacre the unfortunate "infidels"; and he eventually returned to Ghazni laden with immense booty.

This pusillanimous submission of Rājyapāla, however, enraged the native chiefs and soon after the invader's departure Ganda, the Candella chief,[5] formed

[1] This date has been fixed from Wüstenfeld's "*Vergleichungs-Tabellen der Muhammedanischen und Christlichen Zeitrechnung.*"

[2] The *Tabakāt-i-Akbarī* of Nizamuddin and the *Ta'rīkh-i-Firishta* have reversed the order of Mahmud's march against Kanauj. They represent him as proceeding direct to Kanauj, then back to Baran, from there to Mahawan, and lastly to Mathura (see Elliot, II, p. 460; Briggs, I, pp. 57-58). The correct order, however, is given in the *Ta'rīkh-i-Yamīnī* of Utbi, *Rauzat-us-Safā* of Mīr-Khond, and the *Habīb-us-Siyar* of Khond Mīr, which has been adopted in the text (See also Elliot, II, pp. 458-59).

[3] Briggs, I, p. 57.

[4] Similarly, other authorities have also wrongly given the name. Thus Mīrkhond writes Jaipāl Rai and Khond Mīr makes it simply Jaipāl. Nizamuddin calls him Kora, and following him Firishta gives the form Koowur-Ray.

[5] Elliot, II, p. 463 and note 1; Briggs, I, p. 63. The Persian

a confederacy with the neighbouring princes to punish the cowardly ruler of Kanauj. The command was entrusted to the Candella crown-prince named Vidyādhara[1], and a fierce battle ensued in which, as we are told in the Dubkuṇḍ inscription of the Kacchapaghāta Vikramasiṁha, Arjuna "being anxious to serve the illustrious Vidyādharadeva", slew Rājyapāla "with many showers of arrows that pierced his neckbone"[2]. The same event is probably referred to in the Mahoba inscription, which represents Vidyādhara as having "caused the destruction of the king of Kanyākubja".[3] In the *Kamil-ut-Tawārīkh* Ibn-ul-Asir also deposes that Bīdā[4] the accursed, who was the greatest of the rulers of India in territory and had the largest armies, and whose kingdom was called Kajurāha, sent messengers to the Ray of Kanauj named Rājaypāl rebuking him for his flight and the surrender of his dominions to the Musulmans. Hostilities then broke out between them with the result that Rājaypāl was killed in the fight and most of his soldiers also perished".[5] When Mahmud received

texts call him Nanda, which appears to be a mistake, due to the omission of a stroke, for the form Ganda found in inscriptions (see e. g., *Ep. Ind.*, I, p. 295, etc.).

[1] That Vidyādhara was at this time a crown-prince, seems evident from the fact of Ganda being alive when Mahmud undertook the punitive expedition after the murder of Rājyapāla (Elliot, II, p. 464; see also *J. R. A. S.*, 1909, p. 280 note).

[2] *Ep. Ind.*, II, pp. 233, 237, line 12. Cf. "Śrī-Vidyādharadeva kārya-nirataḥ Śrī-Rājyapālaṁ haṭhāt, Kaṇṭhāsthi-cchīdaneka bāṇanivahairhatvā mahatyāhave."

[3] *Ibid.*, I, pp. 219, 222, verse 22. Cf. "... vihita-Kanyākubja-bhūpālabhaṅgaṁ."

[4] This is obviously a corrupted form of Vidyā (or Vidyādhara).

[5] *Kamil-ut-Tawārīkh*, ed. Bulak (1874) Vol. IX, p. 115 f. Ibn-ul-Asir is here wrong in representing Bīdā as king, for we know from other Moslem writers that Nanda or Ganda was alive during this expedition of Mahmud. Dr. H. C. Ray, to whom I owe this reference, on the other hand makes the novel suggestion that

advices that a Rājā named Nanda (Ganda) had slain the "Rai of Kanauj" for "placing himself in subjection to him he was furious and forthwith determined to chastise the miscreant Hindu rulers for their audacity. He accordingly marched from Ghazni in the autumn of 410 *Hijri* i.e., October, 1019 A. D.,[1] and first advanced against Tarū Jaibāl or Tarū Jaypāl (Trilocanapāla), the son of the dead king,[2] who had ascended the throne probably as a protégé of Ganda. Unlike his father, Trilocanapāla tried to offer resistance,[3] but a surprise attack by a selected body of the Sultan's troops, who had crossed the river Rahib or Rāmgangā[4] unnoticed, threw his army into utter confusion; and Bari, which had become a sort of capital after Rājyapāla's retirement thither,[5] fell an easy prey to the cruel sword of the invader. This city lay to the east of the Ganges at a distance of three to four days' journey from Kanauj,[6]

Nandā is a mistake not for Ganda but for Bīdā (*Dy. Hist. North. Ind.*, Vol. I, p. 606).

[1] Ibn Asir, however, wrongly gives the date as 409 *Hijri*.

[2] Other variant readings for this name are Pur Jaipal, or Parū, Narū, or Barū Jaypāl. Some scholars doubt if all the forms refer to the same person. There are no doubt certain difficulties in accepting this, but we must not forget to make allowance for the author's as well as the copyists' errors, and the peculiarities of the Persian or Arabic script (see *Dy. Hist. North. Ind.*, Vol I, pp. 600-08 for a detailed discussion).

[3] Nizamuddin's statement that Pur Jaypāl or Tarū Jaibal had often fled before Mahmud's troops, appears to be substantially correct, because the son must have, as well observed by Smith, shared his father's flight in the year preceding (see *J. R. A. S.*, 1909, p. 280 note).

[4] According to Utbi the scene of the battle was the Rahib, but Nizamuddin erroneously places it on the Jumnā.

[5] The transfer of the capital to Bari is attested by Nizamuddin and Abu Rihān Alberuni. (See Elliot, I, p. 54; II, p. 464; Sachau, I, p. 199).

[6] *Ibid.*

most of which, as testified by Alberuni, was then "in ruins and desolate" owing to the transfer of the capital. Mahmud next dealt with Ganda, who came forward to oppose him with a stupendous force, but just at the psychological moment he also became alarmed at the intrepidity and strength of the Moslem hosts, whereupon under cover of the night he "fled with some of his personal attendants leaving all his baggage and equipments".[1] Thus the Pratīhāra power, which was long tottering to its fall, received the final blow from the ever-victorious arms of Mahmud, and although Trilocanapāla escaped death, history has not condescended to record anything of note about him or his successors, if any.

Trilocanapāla and his successors

We do not know whether after this raid of Mahmud, Trilocanapāla abandoned Bari also for some safer corner of the kingdom, but it is certain that he survived the disaster, and continued to exercise a loose authority over the surrounding region.[2] This is evident from an inscription, discovered at Jhusi in Allahabad, which records that on the 26th June, 1027 A. D., he was in residence somewhere on the bank of the Ganges near Prayāga, and was in a position to make a grant of the village Labhundaka in the Asurabhaka *viṣaya* to the Brahmans of Praṭiṣṭhāna.[3] It is significant that he is therein honoured with the full imperial titles of P. M. P., but as the Pratīhāra empire had now vanished as if into dreamland, it can only be interpreted as signifying that he wielded sovereign rights within his

[1] Elliot, II, p. 464.

[2] Ibn Asir, however, wrongly states that Barū-Jaypāl was killed by the Hindus themselves in the course of his struggle with Mahmud.

[3] *Ind. Ant.*, XVIII, pp. 33-35.

territory, and was free from external control. It is not recorded when Trilocanapāla ceased to rule, nor is there any definite information regarding his successor, but it appears likely that the Mahārājādhirāja Yaśaḥpāla, whose Karā (Allahabad district) inscription mentions the grant of a village named Payalāsa *grāma* in the Kausambi *Maṇḍala* in the (Vikrama) *saṁvat* 1093 or 1036, A. D., ascended the throne of Kanauj after him.[1]

The names of the monarchs, who followed Yaśaḥpāla, are still more open to doubt. A stone inscription from Saheṭ-Maheṭh, dated in the Vikrama year 1176 or 1118 A. D.,[2] however, mentions a king of Gādhipura (Gādhipurādhipa) named Gopāla. It belongs to the time of Madana, and records that his minister Vidyādhara established a monastery or *Vihāra* for Buddhist monks. Unfortunately the epigraph does not explicitly indicate the relation between Gopāla and Madana, but it appears from the manner of description and from the fact that Vidyādhara's father, Janaka, was Gopāla's minister that they belonged to the same line and the one was succeeded by the other. We may, therefore, suppose that Gopāla ruled over Kanauj just before its conquest by Candradeva Gāhaḍavāla about the last decade of the eleventh century A. D. That Madana is content with the general epithet of "Kṣitipati" or lord of the land, and does not call himself the sovereign of Kanauj, also shows that after Gopāla the family was reduced to vassalage, the real power having passed into other hands. Now, the question is : Who were these rulers? The form of the name with the suffix *pāla*, which is found in almost all the names of the later

[1] *J. R. A. S.*, October 1927, pp. 694-95; Colebrooke's *Essays*, II, p. 246; *J. A. S. B.*, V. (1836), p. 731, etc.

[2] Kielhorn, *Ind. Ant.*, XVII, pp. 61-64; *Ibid.*, XXIV, p. 176; *J. A. S. B.*, LXI, pt. I, extra No. 1, p. 60 f.

Pratīhāra sovereigns, no doubt lends some colour to the view that they were Pratīhāras. But the Badaun inscription[1] gives us a different clue to the solution of the problem. Curiously, it mentions one Madana and also his father Gopāla in a list of Rāṣṭrakūṭa princes ruling over ancient Voḍāmayuta. This region was not far from Kanauj, and, as we shall see in the next chapter, Madana must have flourished in the beginning of the 12th century A. D. as a feudatory of Govinda-candra. Hence we may with Mr. N. B. Sanyal[2] identify Gopāla and Madana of the Saheṭ Maheṭh inscription with their namesakes of the Badaun record, and thus it appears that a branch of the Rāṣṭrakūṭas ruled over Kanauj for a short time before the rise of the Gāhaḍavālas.

Note A

Religion of the Pratīhāra kings

The eclectic tendencies of the times were remarkably reflected in the religious ideals of the royal family, for although the Pratīhāra kings were all officially Brahmanical Hindus, they did not confine their spiritual allegiance to one and the same deity. Nāgabhaṭa, the founder of the Kanauj dynasty, along with Mihira Bhoja and Mahendrapāla I, are described in inscriptions as "devotees of Bhagavatī", whereas Rāmabhadra and Mahīpāla are said to have been "devotees of the sun-god". Bhoja II and Mahendrapāla II, on the other hand, are respectively represented as "Vaiṣṇava" and "Māheśvara". Of these, Bhoja I appears to have been devoted to a special manifestation of Viṣṇu also, as is clear from his Ādivarāha type of coins, and Mahīpāla had predilections

[1] *Ep. Ind.*, I, p. 61 f.

[2] See N. B. Sanyal, "The Predecessors of the Gāhaḍavālas," *J. A. S. B.*, (1925), Vol. XXI, No. 1, pp. 103-06.

for the worship of Bhagavatī as well as of the sun, the image of the former occurring on his seal. Thus three facts reveal themselves clearly; firstly, Buddhism had now distinctly declined in the *Madhyadeśa*, and the veneration of the Brahmanical gods was firmly re-established. This is further confirmed by land-grants, which are invariably in favour of Brahmans. Secondly, the worship of Bhagavatī is prominent. Thirdly, this frank divergence in beliefs must have engendered a great spirit of toleration. We must not, however, mistake it for its modern conception, as between these rival sects there was no such gulf as yawns between Hinduism, Christianity and Islam, and their votaries hardly differed from one another in actual life and practice. The Brahmans on the whole allowed people to select the object of their faith from among the gods and goddesses of their extensive pantheon, but this latitude was not extended beyond the pale of Brahmanism; and as an instance of Brahmanical bigotry we may cite the notorious declaration of Puṣyamitra setting a price of one hundred gold pieces on the head of every Buddhist monk (Yo me Śramaṇaśiro dāsyati tasyāhaṁ dīnāraśataṁ dāsyāmi)[1].

[1] *Divyāvadāna*, ed. Cowell and Neil, pp. 433-34; see also *J. B. O. R. S.*, 1918, p. 263. Further details of the religious, social and administrative conditions will be noticed below together with such facts gleaned from the Gāhaḍavāla inscriptions.

PART III

CHAPTER XII

THE GĀHAḌAVĀLAS

SECTION A

Chaotic conditions

We have seen above that the successors of Trilocanapāla were mere nonentities shorn of all dignity and power, and under their weak rule the kingdom of Kanauj seems to have suffered much from the rapacity of a succession of invaders. The Moslems, who had now become a permanent feature of the political situation in the north, repeated their cruelties in the Doab, for we are told in the *Tārīkh-us-Subuktigin* of Baihaki that in the summer of 424 *Hijri* or 1033 A. D. Ahmad Nialtigin, the governor of the Panjab, led an expedition against Benares in order to further his schemes of independence from Ghazni by getting hold of the accumulated riches of its myriad temples[1]. Marching down the Ganges he suddenly arrived in Benares, which was then in possession of 'Gang', and which no Moslem army is said to have reached before. The city was plundered of its gold, silver, perfumes and jewels from "morning to mid-day prayer," and overrunning the intervening territories Nialtigin soon returned to Lahore by way of Indar-dar-bandi[2] (Indar-bedi) or Antarvedi, which appears from Kalhaṇa to signify the land between

[1] Elliot, *History of India*, Vol. II, pp. 123-24.
[2] *Ibid.*, p. 124.

the Ganges and the Jumna with Gādhipur or Kānyakubja as its chief town.[1]

Another important item of information obtained from the testimony of the Moslem historian is that the eastern portions of the former kingdom of Kanauj were at this time under the domination of Gang, who must be identical with Gāngeyadeva Cedi, known to have been ruling in A. D. 1019,[2] 1030,[3] 1037,[4] and 1041.[5] The latter's connection with the north may further be supported by the discovery of his coins on the site of Kanauj[6]—although this is a very weak argument—and also by the fact that according to the Jabalpur copperplate he "found salvation" i.e. died at Prayāga along with his hundred wives.[7] Besides, Gāngeyadeva is called Vikramāditya,[8] and is even styled as "conqueror of the universe" in a Candella inscription found at Mahoba,[9] which doubtless indicates that he must have extended the bounds of the Cedi realm. His power was, however, eclipsed by the rise of Bhoja who, according to the Kalvan plates,[10] Udepur inscription,[11] and the *Pārijāta-mañjarī*,[12] defeated Gāngeya. The Paramāra ruler then carried his arms to distant regions, and in the Udepur *praśasti* he even claims to have "possessed the earth upto the Kailāśa mountains."[13] This may not be

[1] Stein's *Rājataraṅgiṇī*, Vol. I, Bk. IV, verses 132-133.
[2] *J. A. S. B.*, 1903, p. 18.
[3] Sachau, *Alberuni's India*, Vol. I, p. 202.
[4] See Kielhorn's list, *Ep. Ind.*, V, No. 406; *Arch. Surv. Ind. Rep.*, XXI, p. 113.
[5] *Ep. Ind.*, VIII, p. 146.
[6] *Ind. Ant.*, XIV, p. 99.
[7] *Ep. Ind.*, II, pp. 4, 6, verse 12.
[8] *Ibid.*, p. 3.
[9] *Ibid.*, I, pp. 219, 222, line 14.
[10] *Ibid.*, XIX, pp. 71, 74.
[11] *Ibid.*, I, pp. 235, 239, v. 19.
[12] *Ibid.*, VIII, pp. 98, 101.
[13] *Ep. Ind.*, I, pp. 237-38.

true literally, but that it contains some grains of historical information is clear from the following verse of the Basahi plate :

"Yāte Śrī-Bhoja-bhūpe vivu (bu) dha-vara vadhū-
netra sīmātithitvaṁ,
Śrī-Karṇṇe kīrtti-śeṣaṁ gatavati ca nripe kṣmāt-
yaye jāyamāne.
Bharttāraṁ yaṁ dharitrī tri-diva-vibhu-nibhaṁ
prīti-yogād upetā,
Trātā viśvāsa-pūrvaṁ samabhavad iha sa kṣmā
-patis' Candradevaḥ,"

i.e. When king Bhoja became a guest of the eyes of the celestial damsels, and when Karṇa existed only in renown and the earth was sorely troubled, the husband whom she (earth) chose from love and took with confidence as the protector was Candradeva.[1]

The Bhoja mentioned in the above passage is to be identified with Bhoja Paramāra (*circa* 1000-1050 A. D.)[2], although he has sometimes been equated with Bhoja Pratīhāra without sufficient justification[3], as the latter had died in *circa* 885 A. D., and the context also does not suggest that the reference is to a king who lived about two centuries earlier. Now, it is important to note that Bhoja's name occurs in an inscription of the Gāhaḍavāla dynasty, and this would not have much point if he had not made some incursions in the north and for a time established his hegemony over Kanauj. Support for this view may further be found in Merutunga's *Prabandhacintāmaṇi*;[4] which states that when Bhoja went out for conquests "the king of Kānyakubja is here bent double".

[1] *Ind. Ant.*, XIV, p. 103, line 3.
[2] See also *H. M. H. I.*, Vol. III, p. 166.
[3] See *Ind. Hist. Quart.*, V (1929), pp. 89-90.
[4] See II, 72 (ed. Jinavijaya Muni, p. 31).

Next, Gāngeyadeva's son, Karṇa, who ruled from *circa* 1041 to 1072 A. D., aggrandised himself in northern India. He was a great monarch, and he even defeated Bhoja with the help of Bhīma of Gujarat (1022-1064 A. D.). Indeed, the Kalacuri monarch's military achievements were of such a high order as have won for him the proud epithet of "Hindu Napolean."[1] According to the Jabalpur copper plate he erected a lofty temple at Benares called Karṇa's Meru,[2] and in the Karanbel inscription of Jayasiṁhadeva we are informed of the progress of his arms as far north-west as the Kīra country or the Kangra valley.[3] This shows that Karṇa must have made some depredations in the Kanauj territory and asserted his influence there, and it is no doubt significant that the Basahi plate mentions him along with Bhoja in connection with the "earth's distress" before the rise of the Gāhaḍavālas. But Karṇa's power was not long after shattered by Kīrtivarman Candella and the Cālukya Someśvara I Āhavamalla (*circa* 1042-1068 A. D.), while there are even reasons for believing that the latter also turned his attention towards Kanauj, since the Yewur tablet tells us that afraid of his might "the king of Kānyakubja, who was uncontrolled from the beginning, quickly experiences an abode among the caves."[4] When the "earth" was thus badly disturbed by political upheavals and destructive raids, a bold adventurer of the Gāhaḍavāla sept named Candradeva arose, and, as the dynastic inscriptions say, by his "noble prowess" put an end to "all distress of the people".[5]

[1] *J. B. O. R. S.*, IX, p. 300.
[2] *Ep. Ind.*, II, pp. 4, 6, verse 13.
[3] *Ind. Ant.*, XVIII, p. 217, line 11.
[4] *Ibid.*, VIII, p. 19.
[5] *Ibid.*, XVIII, pp. 16, 18, line 4.
Cf. "Yenodāratara pratāpa śamitāśeṣa prajopadrava."

Meagre sources

The materials regarding the Gāhaḍavālas are even more scanty than those for preceding dynasties. The inscriptions of other contemporary families are almost totally silent about them, nor are they alluded to in the whole range of literature except in some Moslem and Sanskrit works and the unauthentic *Prithvīrāja-Rāso.* A large number of copper plates issued by these kings have no doubt been discovered,[1] but, as we shall see below, they do not furnish much historical information.

Who were the Gāhaḍavālas?

The Gāhaḍavālas emerge into the light of history so suddenly that it is difficult to clear away the obscurity hanging over their origin. None of their numerous charters connects them with any of the well-known lines of the Sun and the Moon,[2] although it is worthy of note that they expressly mention the name of the family or clan and call them Kṣatriyas.[3] Their modern representatives are the Gaharwars of the United Provinces, and the family bards of the head of the sept—the Rājā of Kantit in the Mirzapur district—narrate a fanciful legend to explain this designation.[4] We are told that in the line of Yayāti's youngest son, in whose favour the father had abdicated, there was born after many generations one named Devadāsa, who ruled over

[1] See Appendix.

[2] The splendour of these monarchs is, of course, poetically likened to both luminaries (see *Ind. Ant.*, XV, pp. 7-8, 10; XVIII, pp. 11, 12-13, 18, etc.).

[3] Cf. "Jagati Gahaḍavāle Kṣatravaṁśe prasiddhe" (*Ep. Ind.*, IX, pp. 324, 327, verse 14). Also see *Ind. Ant.*, XIV, p. 103, line 2. These references indicate that the forms Gahaḍavāla and Gāhaḍavāla were used indiscriminately.

[4] Crooke's *Tribes and Castes of N. W. P. and Oudh.*, Vol. II, pp. 371-72; *Mirzapur Gazetteer*, p. 204.

the Benares region. He incurred the wrath of the malignant deity Śani or Saturn by his virtuous deeds, so much so that the deity tried to mislead him. But the king resisted all evil influences, thus gaining the title "Grahavara" or 'Overcomer of the Planet," which afterwards became corrupted into Gaharwar or Gahaḍavāla.[1] It is significant that this tradition traces the Gahaḍavālas back to an obscure descendant of Yayāti, and refrains from linking them up with any hero of popular mythology. Does it, therefore, hint that the Gahaḍavālas were originally an unimportant autochthonous tribe, who came into prominence as Kṣatriyas only after seizing political power and championing the cause of Brahmanism? The Paurāṇik texts, at any rate, refer to a people called "Gahvara or Girigahvara", who are described as dwellers in jungles and caves,[2] and since "Gahvara" might conceivably correspond in meaning to the Prakrit "Gāhaḍa" (both words being derived from the same root), it may indeed be tempting to conjecture that the term "Gāhaḍavāla" is equivalent to "Gahvaravāsī." Pandit Bisheswar Nath Reu has, however, another theory to offer. He thinks that Gāhaḍavāla is used in the sense of "*balavān*" and that they were so called because they conquered the most important kingdom of the times.[3] Mr. C. V. Vaidya, on the other hand, derives it, like Agarwāla, from some place Gāhaḍa in the Deccan.[4]

[1] The variants are explicable if we remember that in Sanskrit *ra*, *la*, and *ḍa* are often interchangeable. See *Cawnpore Settlement Report*, p. 22, for another fanciful derivation.

[2] Wilson's *Viṣṇu Purāṇa*, p. 196.

[3] *History of India* (Hindi), Vol. III, p. 462.

[4] *H. M. H. I.*, Vol. III, p. 217 f. Dr. R. C. Majumdar throws out a suggestion that the Gāhaḍavālas were perhaps of Karṇāṭaka origin like the Senas of Bengal and Nānyadeva of Mithila. He traces the name Gāhaḍavāla to Gawarmād mentioned in a Kanarese inscription of Śaka 994 (See *Ind. Hist. Quart.*, VII (1931), p. 634, note 1).

But some scholars[1] affirm that the Gāhaḍavālas were a branch of the famous Rāṣṭrakūṭas or Rathors, and their arguments may be thus summed up :

Legend avers that the Rathors of Marwar are descended from one Sīhāji, the son or grandson or grandnephew of Jayacandra, who escaped the wreck of the latter's kingdom. It is contended that the descendants of Sīhāji would not be called Rathors unless we assume the inclusion of the Gāhaḍavālas within the larger body of the Rathors. Secondly, support for this view is found in the list of 36 Rajput clans as mentioned in Cand Bardāi's *Prithvīrāja Rāso*, which omits to give a separate place to the Gāhaḍavālas. Thirdly, it is generally believed that Jayacandra belonged to the Rathor stock, and the great Hindi bard also applies the epithets Kamadhaja and Rathor to him. Lastly, there are indications that the Rāṣṭrakūṭas were settled in the United Provinces prior to the rise of the Gāhaḍavālas. A passage in the Surat grant of Trilocanapāla dated 1151 A. D. bears testimony to their earliest connexion with Kanauj, when it says: "O thou Caulukya, king of kings, marrying the princess of the Rāṣṭrakūṭas in Kanyākubja, bless thou (the world) with offspring obtained from her".[2] But even if the verse be differently interpreted, as has been done by Dr. Hoernle[3], the evidence of the Badaun stone inscription of Lakhanapāla, in conjunction with that of the Saheṭ-Maheṭh record, has been taken to

[1] Pt. Ramkaran, *Sir Āśutosh Mookerjee Silver Jubilee Volume*, Orientalia, Part II, pp. 259-61; Pt. B. N. Reu, *J. R. A. S.*, January, 1930, pp. 111-21; C. V. Vaidya, *H. M. H. I.*, Vol. III, pp. 217-221, etc.

[2] *Ind. Ant.*, XII, pp. 201, 203, verse 6. Cf. "Kanyākubje Mahārāja Rāṣṭrakūṭasya kanyakāṁ, Labdhvā sukhāya tasyāṁ tvaṁ Caulukyāpnuhi saṁtatiṁ."

[3] *J. R. A. S.*, 1905, p. 10. Dr. Hoernle considers the verse as of no historical value.

prove definitely that "princes born in the Rāṣṭrakūṭa lineage" were ruling over Kanauj about the third quarter of the 11th century A. D. Indeed, Pandits Rāmakaran and Bisheswar Nath Reu go so far as to assert that Candra of the former epigraph is identical with Gāhaḍavāla Candra, the conqueror of Kanauj according to the copper plates.[1]

The theory doubtless has some apparent cogency, but it is far from conclusive, for the Gāhaḍavālas never call themselves Rathors (Rāṣṭrakūṭas) in any of their grants; and we also know that the two clans intermarry and they differ from one another in their *gotras*, being Kāśyapa and Gotama respectively. Secondly, the tradition of Sīhāji is perhaps vitiated by an inscription at Bithu on a memorial tablet which gives for his death the Vikrama date 1330 or 1273 A. D. thereby making him rather removed in time from Jayacandra[2]. Besides, the Hathauṇḍi (Hastikuṇḍi) inscription, dated in the vikrama year 1053 = 997 A. D.,[3] testifies to the fact that Rāṣṭrakūṭa princes ruled over tracts of Marwar long before the supposed migration of the Gāhaḍavālas from Kanauj. It appears probable that the legend was concocted only to establish some connection with a distinguished Kṣatriya family that was once the master of the principal kingdom of Northern India. Thirdly, Cand Bardāi's omission of the Gāhaḍavālas in the traditional list of 36 clans is at best an *argumentum ex silentio*, although they are elsewhere mentioned by him in a way which shows that he was aware of their separate entity. In the *Ālhā-Prastāva*, for example, we read "Sajji Gaharwar Gohila aneka", i.e., "there were many

[1] *A. S. M. Jubilee Volume*, Pt. II, p. 259; *J. R. A. S.*, January, 1930, p. 116.

[2] *Ind. Ant.*, XL, p. 181.

[3] *Ep. Ind.*, X, pp. 17-24; *Imp. Gaz. of India*, VI, p. 247.

Gaharwars and Gohils arrayed".[1] Lastly, the presence of Rāṣṭrakūṭa ruling families in Kanauj and adjacent regions during the latter half of the 11th century A. D. would hardly prove anything regarding their collateralness with the Gāhaḍavālas. And chronological considerations distinctly go against identifying the Rāṣṭrakūṭa king Candra of the Badaun inscription with the Gāhaḍavāla Candra. As shown below, Madanapala, who represented the fifth generation from Candra, the founder of this Rāṣṭrakūṭa line, lived about the beginning of the 12th century, and so the latter must have flourished about the first quarter of the 11th century A. D., i.e., at least half a century before the Gāhaḍavāla Candra.

Section B

Candradeva

According to the testimony of inscriptions, the Gāhaḍavāla dynasty was founded by one Yaśovigraha "after the lines of the protectors of the earth born in the solar race had gone to heaven",[2] but it is not clear where he and his successor Mahīcandra (also called Mahiala and Mahītala) ruled at first. In fact, the absence of royal titles in case of both has sometimes been taken to indicate that they were not even royal personages, although in the records the former is called "a noble (personage)......... (who) by his plentiful splendour (was) as it were the sun incarnate",[3] and the latter is represented

[1] Elliot's *Races of N. W. P. and Oudh*, Vol. I, p. 122 and Note.

[2] *Ep. Ind.*, XIII, p. 218; IX, p. 304, etc.,
Cf. "Āsīdaśītadyutivaṁśa – jāta – kṣmāpāla-mālāsu divaṁ gatāsu".

[3] *Ind. Ant.*, XV, p. 7, verse 2.
Cf. "Sākṣāt vivasvān iva bhūridhāmnā nāmnā Yaśovigraha iti Udāraḥ".

as having "defeated the host of his enemies, (and) by entrusting to whose arm the whole burden of the earth, Śeṣa enjoyed permanent comfort."[1] The family was thus brought into prominence by Mahītala or Mahīcandra, who appears to have been a chief with some military power. His son, Candradeva, was also an enterprising character, and he availed himself of the anarchy rampant in the Gangetic Doab, for we learn that he "by the valour of his arm acquired the matchless sovereignty over the glorious Kānyakubja or Gādhipura".[2] None of the epigraphs mentions the name of the vanquished monarch, but a conjecture may be hazarded that it was probably Gopāla of the Badaun inscription, who, as shown elsewhere, was perhaps identical with the "Gādhipurādhipa" Gopāla of the Saheṭ-Maheṭh inscription. Whosoever he may be, Candradeva inflicted a crushing defeat upon him and his allies somewhere on the banks of the Jumnā, since we are told in the Sarnath inscription that "by the streams of the tears of the wives of the kings who could not resist him (Candradeva), the water of the Yamunā forsooth became darker".[3] This conquest, which is evidently referred to in the copper plates as his greatest exploit, raised Candradeva to imperial dignity—he being the first in the family to be honoured with the so-called imperial formula of Parama-Bhaṭṭāraka, Mahārājādhirāja, and Parameśvara[4]—and inaugurated in Kanauj another era of peace and stable government until the kingdom received its death-blow from the victorious arms of Islam. We have unfortu-

[1] *Ibid.*, XVIII, pp. 15, 17.

[2] *Ibid.*, p. 18. Cf. "Nija-bhujopārjita-Kānyakubjādhipatya Śrī-Candradevaḥ."

[3] *Ep. Ind.*, IX, pp. 324, 327, verse 14.
Cf. "Yadsahananṛipā-ṇāṁ kāminī-vāspa-vāhaiḥ Śitataramidamāsīd Yāmunāṁ nūnamaṁbhaḥ".

[4] *Ibid.*, XIV, pp. 193-94.

nately no definite data whereby to fix the date of this momentous event, but as it followed the inroads of Karṇa Cedi (died *circa* 1072 A. D.) and other invaders and the earliest known date of Candradeva is 1090 A. D.,[1] we may assume in round numbers that it took place between the years 1080 and 1085 A. D. Nor is our information regarding the extent of his suzerainty less obscure, for the only reference to it is contained in the proud claim that Candradeva was "the protector of the holy places of Kasi, Kuśika, Uttarakosala, and the city of Indra after he had obtained them".[2] Kasi is beyond doubt the modern city of Benares, and Kuśika signifies Kanauj itself[3], while Uttarakosala was the old denomination for the vicinity of Ayodhyā (Fyzabad district),[4] Indrasthāna being perhaps Indraprastha or ancient Delhi.[5] It will thus be seen that Candradeva's jurisdiction comprised almost the whole length of the present United Provinces. The Candravati plates further describe him as having made his power felt by Narapati, Gajapati, Triśankupati, and Giripati[6]. The true import of these terms has not been determined so far. The first two, besides Aśvapati, appear generally as epithets of the kings of this period, e.g., they are used in the Bakerganj grant of Keśavasena,[7] or the Goharwa plates of Karṇa-

[1] See the Candravati plates, *Ep. Ind.*, IX, pp. 302-05.

[2] *Ind. Ant.*, XV, pp. 7, 8; XVIII, pp. 16, 18.
Cf. "Tīrthāni Kāsi-Kuśikottara-Kośalendrasthānīyakāni paripālayatādhigamya."

[3] See *Ante*, Introduction.

[4] See also Wilson's *Viṣṇu Purāṇa*, p. 190, fn. 79.

[5] That there was a village (*mauzā*) of the name of Indarpat near Delhi about this time is also clear from the *Tāj-ul-Maāsir* (Elliot, *History of India*, Vol. II, p. 216). In some later inscriptions, however, Delhi is called Yoginīpura, e.g., Mangalana stone inscription (*Ind. Ant.*, 1912, pp. 85-88) and Batihagarh stone inscription (*Ep. Ind.*, XII, pp. 44-47).

[6] *Ep. Ind.*, XIV, p. 193, lines 11-12.

[7] *J. A. S. B.*, 1838, p. 49.

deva.[1] Some scholars think that Narapati was the title borne by kings of Telingānā and Karṇāṭa and Gajapati by those of Orissa,[2] but it is not at all likely that these rulers ever paid allegiance to Candradeva. We should therefore seek for an explanation elsewhere, and perhaps it would not be unreasonable to suggest that these expressions denoted so many feudatories or classes of feudatories, who had accepted Candradeva as the paramount power in this Gangetic kingdom.[3]

In the east, Candradeva seems to have taken part in repressing the aggressive activities of Vijayasena, who, according to the Deopara inscription, had attacked the king of Gauḍa, defeated and imprisoned Nānyadeva of Mithila; and whose fleet was once sailing "in its playful conquest of the western regions up the whole course of the Ganges".[4] The monarch, with whom Candradeva allied himself, must have been Madanapāla of the Pāla dynasty,[5] and it is perhaps in allusion to this help that the *Rāmacarita* of Sandhyākara Nāndi speaks of him so eulogistically in the following verses :

"Siṁhīsutavikrāntenārjunadhāmnā bhuvaḥ pradīpena,
Kamalāvikāśabheṣaja-bhiṣajā Candreṇa bandhunopetaṁ,
Caṇḍīcaraṇasaroj-prasāda-saṁpannavigraha-śrīkaṁ,

[1] *Ep. Ind.*, XI, pp. 141, 144.

[2] *J. A. S. B.*, XLII, pt. I, (1873), p. 327, Note.

[3] But according to the *Si-yu-ki*, when there is no paramount monarch, the Southern, Western, Northern and Eastern parts of Jambūdvīpa are respectively supposed to be ruled over by four sovereigns called Gajapati, Chattrapati, Aśvapati and Narapati (Beal, I, p. 13 and Note).

[4] *Ep. Ind.*, I, pp. 309-10, 314.

[5] MM. H. P. Śāstrī, *Mem. As. Soc. Beng.*, III, No. I, p. 16; R. D. Banerji, *Ibid.*, V, p. 103.

Na Khalu Madanaṁ sāngeśamīśamagād jagadvijayalakṣmīḥ."[1]

Besides, the Naihati grant of Ballālasena informs us that Vijayasena "outshone Sāhasāṅka by his deceitless prowess".[2] Now, we know from Maheśvara's *Viśvaprakāśa*[3] that there was a sovereign of Gādhipura named Sāhasāṅka, in whose court the author's grandfather, Śrīkriṣṇa, lived as a physician. The date when the work was compiled is given as Śaka 1033 or 1111 A. D.,[4] and since it is usual among native rulers to have old physicians, we may not unreasonably assume that Śrīkriṣṇa lived upto a very advanced age, and that his patron was no other than Candradeva. Although it may seem fanciful, I venture to suggest that Candradeva asssumed the name or epithet Sāhasāṅka, compounded as it is of *Sāhasa* (valour) and *aṅka* (mark of distinction), in allusion to his proud boast that he "acquired the kingdom of Kānyakubja by the valour of his arm." Thus if this identification be correct,[5] we get an epigraphic corroboration that there was some conflict between the Gahaḍavāla king and Vijayasena.[6]

[1] *Ibid.*, III, p. 52, verses 20-21. Dr. R. G. Basak identifies this Candra not with Candradeva Gahaḍavāla, but with Candra of Anga, son of Suvarṇadeva and grandson of Mahana (*Ind. Hist. Quart.*, V (1929), p. 46).

[2] *Ep. Ind.*, XIV, pp. 159, 162, verse 7. Cf. "Nirvyājavikramatiraskrita Sāhasāṅka".

[3] *Viśvaprakāśa* (Caukhambā Sanskrit Series, Bombay, 1911), verses 5-6, and 10-12.

[4] Keith, *A History of Sanskrit Literature*, (1928), p. 414.

[5] Mr. R. D. Banerji, however, identifies this Sāhasāṅka with Prince Sālivāhana of the Chamba grant of his son Somavarmadeva (*Ep. Ind.*, XIV, pp. 157-58). But this identification seems doubtful, as that prince must have lived in the first quarter of the eleventh century A. D. (*Ind. Ant.*, XVII, p. 9).

[6] It is worth noting that the expression used does not indicate any defeat.

Lastly, Candradeva is described in the copper plates as an ardent and philanthropic Brahmanist, who made numerous land-grants and *Tulādānas* to Brahmans[1] and divinities. The latter, which is a characteristically Indian ceremony, consists of gifts of gold and other articles equal in weight to that of one's own body. History preserves instances showing how this ceremony has persisted in India throughout the ages.[2]

Madanapāla

The Candravati plates[3] furnish us with the Vikrama year 1156 or 1099 A. D. as the last date for Candradeva's reign, and we learn from the Basahi plate of Mahārāja-putra Govindacandra[4] that his father Madanapāla was on the throne in Vikrama *saṁvat* 1161 = 1104 A. D. Hence we may safely assume that Candradeva died and his son Madanapāla[5] succeeded him sometime between the years 1100 and 1104 A. D. The Sarnath inscription of Kumāradevī describes the latter as "a crest-jewel among impetuous kings........., the lord who brought the circle of the earth under one sceptre, the splendour of the fire of his valour being great and mighty, and who even lowered the glory of Maghavan by his glory".[6] Similarly, other charters bestow high praise on Madanapāla,[7] but much of it is simply conventional and vague

[1] In one case 500 Brahmans were the grantees (*Ep. Ind.*, XIV, p. 192).

[2] See *Dānakhaṇḍa* of Hemādri for a full description. It is recorded in the *Tuzuk-i-Jahangir* that Jahangir also followed the same practice.

[3] *Ep. Ind.*, XIV, p. 192 f.

[4] *Ind. Ant.*, XIV, pp. 101-04.

[5] Sometimes called Madanadeva (*Ibid.*, XVIII, pp. 12, 14) or Madanacandra (*Ep. Ind.*, IX, pp. 324, 327, v. 15).

[6] *Ibid.*, IX, pp. 324, 327, verse 15.

[7] See e.g., *Ind. Ant.*, XVIII, pp. 16, 18.

bombast, which is of no value to the historian. In fact, he does not even seem to have taken any active part in the state affairs, for except confirming the gift of the village of Ahuāma in the Dhanesaramaua *Pattalā* made by his father to the Brahman Vāmanaśvāmīdeva,[1] no grants by Madanapāla are known, and those that refer to his reign were executed on his behalf by the crown-prince (Mahārājaputra) Govindacandra and his two queens Rālha-Devī (Rālhaṇa-Devī) and Prithvī-Śrīkā. Was this circumstance due to Madanapāla's wars, which mostly kept him busy far away from the capital? Or, does it show that he was an invalid? If the latter alternative be true, he may have studied the science of medicine during his illness, and the *Madana-Vinoda-Nighaṇṭu* ascribed to a king Madana, lord of Kasi,[2] may be his compilation. It may, however, be added that no undue weight should be attached to this suggestion.

Coins

Some specimens of billon (copper) and base silver coins (containing on the obverse a horseman with the indistinct legend Madana or Madanapāladeva, or sometimes simply Mada or Śrī Ma, and on the reverse the figure of a recumbent humped bull with the legend Mādhava Śrī Sāmanta or Mādhava Śrī Sām, or sometimes Sāmanta or Mādha) have been discovered, and they have usually been attributed to Madanapāla of Kanauj.[3] The point to be noted is that these coins confirm by their bull-emblem the testimony of inscriptions, which

[1] *Ibid.*, XVIII, pp. 10-11, 13.

[2] See verse 4, p. 1.

[3] See Rapson, *Indian Coins*, p. 31; Smith *Cat. Co. Ind. Mus.*, Calcutta, pp. 257, 260; Cunningham, *Mediæval Coins*, p. 87; Bidyāvinod, *Coins in the Indian Museum, Calcutta*, Vol. I, (Non-Moslem-Series), p. 65.

describe the Gāhaḍavāla kings as "Parama-māheśvara" or devotees of Śiva.

Govindacandra

Madanapāla was succeeded by his son Govindacandra[1] at some date between the years V. E. 1166= 1109 A.D., when the former is known to have been alive,[2] and 1114 A. D., when the latter first issued a charter in his own name as the ruling sovereign.[3] His mother's name was probably Rālhadevī or Rālhaṇadevī, who gave her consent to a grant made by him in 1105 A. D. during his father's lifetime.[4] Besides executing deeds, Govindacandra seems to have wielded substantial power in the state while he was only a "yuvarāja" or crown-prince. He defeated the invading bands of Moslems sometime before 1109 A. D., for the Rahan plate records that he "again and again by the play of his matchless fighting" compelled the Haṁmīra (i.e., Amir) to "lay aside his enmity."[5] The immunity from the Moslem danger that Govindacandra thus secured for the kingdom was apparently so effective that according to the Sarnath inscription of his queen Kumāradevī he gained fame as the incarnation of Hari "who had been commissioned by Hara in order to protect Bārāṇasī from the wicked

[1] Called Govindapāla in the Sarnath inscription (*Ep. Ind.*, IX, pp. 324 327, v. 16).

[2] *Ind. Ant.*, XVIII, pp. 16, 17.

[3] *Ep. Ind.*, IV, p. 102. Vincent Smith, however, fixes 1100 A. D. (*Oxford History of India*, 2nd ed., p. 195) or 1104 A. D. (*Early Hist. of India.*, 4th ed., p. 400) as the earliest limit of Govindacandra's reign. Evidently this misapprehension is due to a confusion of the grants that he made as crown-prince.

[4] *Ep. Ind.*, II, pp. 359, 361.

[5] *Ind. Ant.*, pp. 16, 18, line 9. (*Add* XVIII.)

Cf. "Haṁmīraṁ nyasta-vairaṁ muhurasama-raṇa-krīḍayā yo vidhatte."

Turuṣka warrior, as the only one who was able to protect the earth."[1]

It is very likely that the inscriptions refer to the expedition reported in the *Dīwān* of Salman, which was sent by the Ghaznavide king Masud III (492 to 509 *Hijri*[2] or 1098 to 1115 A.D.)[3] against Kanauj, "the capital of Hind......, the Kaāba of the Shamans and the Kibla of the infidels," where "the treasures of Hind were collected just as all rivers flow into the sea."[4] At first its king Malhī or Malhīrā, which is perhaps a corrupted form of the name Madanacandra or Madanapāla, suffered serious reverses, for we are told that he was even "compelled to ransom his person by a large sum of money,"[5] but it appears Govindacandra soon retrieved the situation and hurled back the Moslem advance. The *Tabaqāt-i-Nāsirī* further testifies that during the reign of Masud III, the Hajib Tughatigin "crossed the river Gang (Ganges ?) in order to carry on holy war in Hindustan, and penetrated to a place where except Sultan Mahmud no one had reached so far with an army before".[6] Now, we know that Mahmud did not proceed further east than Kanauj or Asi;[7] and we may therefore be sure from the date and the description given above that it was this inroad against which Govindacandra

[1] *Ep. Ind.*, IX, pp. 324, 327, verse 16.
Cf. "Bārāṇasīṁ bhuvana-rakṣaṇa dakṣa eko duṣṭāt Turuṣka-
Subhaṭā-davituṁ Hareṇa.
Ukto Hariḥ sa punaratra babhūva
Tasmād Govindacandra iti prathitābhidhānaḥ."

[2] *Tabaqāt-i-Nāsirī* (Raverty's Eng. Trans.), Vol. I, p. 107.

[3] Woollaston's *English-Persian Dictionary*, p. 454.

[4] Elliot, *History of India*, Vol. IV, p. 526.

[5] *Dy. Hist. North. Ind.*, Vol. I, p. 514; see, however, Elliot, *History of India*, IV, p. 526 for a different interpretation.

[6] Raverty, Eng. Trans., Vol. I, p. 107; see also Briggs, *Firishta*, Vol. I, p. 143.

[7] Elliot, *History of India*, Vol. II, (*Tarīkh-i-Yamīnī*) p. 46.

had to contend. In his fight with the Moslem raiders Govindacandra was probably assisted by the Rāṣṭrakūṭa Madanapāla in the capacity of a vassal, for the Badaun inscription informs us that "in consequence of his distinguished prowess there never was any talk of Haṁbīra's coming to the banks of the river of the gods."[1] Kielhorn has assigned this undated epigraph on palæographic grounds to the 12th century or more possibly to the 13th century A. D.,[2] but as Badaun was conquered by Qutb-ud-dīn Aibak in 1202 A. D. (*Hijri* 599),[3] and conferred as a fief upon Altamash,[4] its date must not be brought down later than the 12th century A. D. We also know that it was engraved in the reign of Lakhanapāla, whose great-grandfather Devapāla ruled after, and was the younger brother of Madanapāla. Hence the latter may be considered to have flourished about the beginning of the 12th century; and as he was obviously a minor prince, and the Gahaḍavāla suzerainty had extended to the confines of Indraprastha even during the time of Candradeva, Madanapāla must have helped the paramount power in its wars against the Moslems.

The Rahan plate further describes Govindacandra as "terrific in cleaving the frontal globes of arrays of irresistible mighty large elephants from Gauḍa,"[5] which shows that he must have made some encroachments in Magadha. This was probably due to the decadent state of the Pāla monarchy, whose power had been considerably weakened at this time by the aggressions of Vijayasena of the Sena dynasty. Availing himself

[1] *Ep. Ind.*, I, pp. 62, 64, line 4.
Cf. "Yat pauruṣāt pravarataḥ surasindhu-tīra-Haṁbīra saṁgama-kathā na kadācid āsīt."

[2] *Ibid.*, I, p. 61; *Ibid.*, V, Appendix, Kielhorn's list, No. 605.

[3] Elliot, *History of India*, Vol. II, p. 232.

[4] Raverty, *Tabaqāt-i-Nāsirī*, (Eng. Trans.), Vol. I, p. 530.

[5] *Ind. Ant.*, XVIII, pp. 16, 18, line 9.

of this favourable opportunity, evidently according to certain Michiavellian precepts of some Indian manuals on state-craft,[1] Govindacandra annexed portions of Magadha, where in the Vikrama *saṁvat* 1183 or 1126 A. D. he is definitely known to have made a grant of the village Padali, situated in the Maniyara (Maner) *pattalā* in the western part of the Patna district, to a Brahman named Ganeśvaraśarman.[2] At a later date, however, Govindacandra pushed his conquest further towards the east, for we learn from the Lar plates of 1202 V. E. or 1146 A. D. that when in residence at Mudgagiri (Monghyr) after bathing in the Ganges on the occasion of the Akṣaya-tritīyā festival he granted the village of Potacavada in the Paṇḍala *pattalā* to the Ṭhakkura Śrīdhara.[3] This inscription, therefore, proves that Mudgagiri passed into the hands of the Gahaḍavālas, but we do not know for certain whether the Pālas maintained their independent existence in some safer corner of the kingdom or were reduced to subordination. At any rate, two rulers who must have belonged to this line seem to have come after Madanapāla. One of them, Palapāla, dedicated an image in the 35th year of his reign according to the Jayanagar inscription;[4] and another Govindapāla is known from the Gadādhar Gaya inscription, which states that the Vikrama year 1232 was "Śrī-Govindapāladeva gatarājye caturdaśasaṁ-

[1] Compare for example Kauṭilya's *Arthaśāstra* : "Whoever is superior in power shall wage war" (Bk. VII, ch. I, p. 293; see also Bk. VI, ch. 2, p. 290, etc.).

[2] *J. B. O. R. S.*, (1916), Vol. II, Pt. IV, pp. 441-47. Maner must have been an important place then, for Bakhtyar Khilji directed his operations against it before proceeding eastwards (Raverty, *Tabaqāt-i-Nāsirī*, Vol. I, p. 550 and note 6).

[3] *Ep. Ind.*, VII, pp. 98, 99.

[4] R. D. Banerji, *J. B. O. R. S.*, December, 1928, pp. 490, 496; Cunningham, *Arch. Surv. Ind. Rep.*, Vol. III, plate XLV, No. 33,

vatsare".[1]

Next, a copper plate of Vikrama *saṁvat* 1177 or 1120 A. D. mentions that Govindacandra sanctioned the transfer of the village of Karanda and the *talla* of Karanda in the *pattalā* of Antarāla, which was originally granted by Yaśaḥkarṇa, from the possession of Bhaṭṭāraka Rudraśiva, a royal chaplain, into that of the Ṭhakkura Vasiṣṭha.[2] Unfortunately it is impossible to identify the localities mentioned, but the name of Yaśaḥkarṇa is enough to show that Govindacandra must have aggrandised himself at the cost of the Cedis. In the earlier stages of his rule, however, he was on quite friendly terms with them. This is evident from the Ratnapur inscription of Jājalladeva, who belonged to a line founded by one of the eighteen sons of Kokalla of Tripurī. It informs us that "on account of his prowess he (Jājalladeva) was like a friend honoured with fortune" by the king of Kānyakubja, who must be identified with Govindacandra, considering that the grant is dated in the *Cedi* year 866 or 1114 A. D.[3]

The *Rambhāmañjarī* of Nayacandra even testifies that Govindacandra achieved a victory against Daśārṇa on the day of his grandson Jayacandra's birth[4]. According to the *Meghadūta* of Kālidāsa,[5] Daśārṇa denoted eastern Malwa, of which Vidisā or modern Bhilsa was the capital, but it is rather doubtful if this region actually submitted to the yoke of Kanauj.

[1] *Ibid.*, p. 125; *J. B. O. R. S.*, December, 1928, p. 534.

[2] *J. A. S. B.*, XXXI, p. 124.

[3] *Ep. Ind.*, I, pp. 35, 38, verse 21.

[4] See Bom. ed. (1899), p. 4.

[5] Cf. "Teṣāṁ (Daśarṇānāṁ) prathita Vidisā-lakṣaṇāṁ rājadhānīṁ," Ed. Hultzsch (London, 1911) verse 24. See also R. G. Bhandarkar's *Early History of the Deccan*, Sec. III, p. 18. In the *Viṣṇu Purāṇa* (p. 186, note 17), however, Wilson is of opinion that the modern Chattisgarh district might represent the site of ancient Daśārṇa. See also *J. A. S. B.*, 1905, N. S., p. 7.

Govindacandra also seems to have come into touch with the Candellas, for the Mau inscription records some transactions of Sallakṣaṇavarman (*circa* 1100-1115 A. D.) in the country of Antarvedi;[1] unfortunately the inscription is so hopelessly mutilated that it is beyond the range of possibility to recover the historical allusion contained therein. In fine, Govindacandra made himself a considerable power, and under him the glories of Kanauj revived, so that the Gagaha plate[2] could represent him as having captured the elephants of the "nine kings," an expression which probably signifies that he placed himself in the position of almost the leading monarch in Jambūdvīpa.

Foreign relations

Govindacandra also extended the sphere of his influence by forming alliances with contemporary kings like Jayasiṁha (1128-49 A. D.), who, as the *Rājataraṅgiṇī* puts it, "made the rulers in Kānyakubja and elsewhere who were powerful owing to the possession of excellent territories, proud by his friendship."[3] Moreover, we are told in the *SrīKaṇṭhacarita* of Mankha or Mankhaka that Govindacandra deputed one Suhala to attend the assembly of Kashmirian scholars and officials, convoked at the instance of Alaṁkāra, the minister of king Jayasiṁha.[4] This mission was no doubt non-political, but it must have materially contributed to cementing good relations between Kanauj and Kashmir. Perhaps

[1] *Ep. Ind.*, I, pp. 201, 206, verse 38.

[2] *Ibid.*, XIII, p. 218, line 8. The *Navakhaṇḍas* or *Navarājyas* are the traditional nine divisions of Jambūdvīpa according to Hindu Geography.

[3] *Rājataraṅgiṇī*, Vol. II, Bk. VIII, verse 2453, (Stein, p. 191).

[4] *Śrīkaṇṭhacarita*, canto 25, verse 102.

Cf. "Anyaḥ sa Suhalas tena tato'vandyata paṇḍitaḥ,
Dūto Govindacandrasya Kānyakubjasya bhūbhujaḥ."

Govindacandra had diplomatic intercourse with another monarch named Siddharāja Jayasiṁha, who, according to the *Prabandha-Cintāmaṇi*, sent a messenger to the lord of Kaśi.[1] This must surely have happened during the time of Govindacandra (*circa* 1112-1155 A. D.), and not Jayacandra, as stated in the *Prabhandha-Cintāmaṇi*, for the latter's reign-period being 1170-94 A. D. he was never a contemporary of Jayasiṁha Cālukya, who ruled from *circa* 1095 to 1143 A. D. We may further refer here to an inscription, found as far south as Gangai-Koṇḍa-Colapuraṁ, the ancient Cola capital in the Trichinopoly district of the Madras Presidency, which forms part of a document of the 41st regnal year of Kulottuṅga I, equivalent to 1110-11 A. D., and thus belongs to the interval between the earliest known date of Govindacandra and the last of Madanapāla. The record is in a very damaged condition, but Mr. Venkayya assures us that "what is actually found on the stone may be taken to show that some sort of relationship or connection existed between the Gāhaḍavālas of Kanauj and the Colas of Tanjore."[2] Does it allude to a friendly visit paid by a Gāhaḍavāla prince to the distant south and his benefactions to local Brahmans and temples?

Literary activity

Govindacandra's reign was marked by the literary efforts of his minister for peace and war (Sāndhivigrahika) named Lakṣmīdhara. He seems to have produced a crop of works on law and procedure, of which the most important is the *Kritya-Kalpataru* or *Kalpadruma*. Among its chief *khaṇḍas* are:

(*a*) *Vyavahāra-Kalpataru*.

[1] III, 121, p. 74 (ed. Jinavijaya Muni); see also *Dy. Hist. North Ind.*, II, p. 972.

[2] *Ann. Rep. Arch. Surv. Ind.*, 1907-08, p. 228.

(*b*) *Vivāda Kalpataru*, quoted by Raghunandana.
(*c*) *Dāna-Kalpataru.*
(*d*) *Rājadharma-Kalpataru.*

Perhaps there were many other authors of repute in the court of Govindacandra, who is himself described in the grants as "vividhavidyā-vicāra-vācaspati," but their works having disappeared it is impossible to rescue their names from the oblivion of time.

Coins

Some copper and gold coins of Govindacandra have been discovered in northern India. Of these the latter are more abundant, for in 1887 Nanpara in the Bahraich district of U. P. alone yielded a hoard of 800 gold *Drammas*. They have a large percentage of alloy, and their fabric is also very rude, which apparently indicates a period of financial stringency. On the reverse they have a seated goddess with four arms as on those of Gāṅgeyadeva Cedi; on the obverse, the legend "Śrīmad Govindacandra" (in some "deva" is added), followed by the representation of a *Triśūl.*[1] The fact that they are copied from the coins of Gāṅgeya-Deva-Cedi is important, since it confirms the Cedi connections with the north during the period of anarchy.

Family relations

The inscriptions give us to understand that Govindacandra had at least four wives, viz.,

(*a*) Nayanakelidevī, entitled Paṭṭamahādevī and Mahārājñī.[2]

(*b*) Gosaladevī. This wife was also called Paṭṭamahādevī Mahārājñī, which shows that she

[1] Smith, *Cat. Co. Ind. Mus.*, Calcutta, pp. 257, 260-61; Bidyavinod, *Non-Moslem Series*, Vol. I, p. 65; Cunningham, *Coins of Mediæval India*, pp. 80, 87.

[2] *Ep. Ind.*, IV, pp. 107, 109.

was raised to this dignity after the death of the first wife.[1]

(*c*) Kumāradevī, daughter of Devarakṣita, king of Pīṭhī or Pīṭhikā of the Cikkora clan, who had married Śankaradevī, daughter of the Anga ruler Mahana of the Rāṣṭrakūṭa family. The Sarnath inscription records that Kumāradevī restored the "Lord of the Turning of the Wheel" (Dharmacakra-Jina) in accordance with the form in which it existed in the time of Dharmāśoka, the ruler of men[2]. The marriage of Kumāradevī, a Buddhist, with an orthodox Hindu like Govindacandra proves that matrimonial alliances between Buddhists and Brahmanists were possible at this time, although such instances must have been rare.

(*d*) Vasantadevī : She is mentioned in a colophon of a manuscript of the *Aṣṭasāhaśrikā* in the Nepal durbar library (No. 381 of the third collection), which runs thus :

"Śrīmad Govindacandradevasya pratāpa-vasataḥ Rājñī Śrīpravara-Mahāyāna-yāyinyāḥ paramopāsikā Rājñī Vasantadevyā Deya dharmo 'yaṁ."[3]

Some scholars, however, identify the last two on the ground that both were Buddhists, and one of the meanings of Vasanta is youth=Kumāra. But as some eastern potentates used to keep notoriously big harems it is better to regard them as two different persons.

Regarding Govindacandra's sons, the plates give us the names of three :

(*a*) Mahārājaputra Āsphoṭacandradeva, who being endowed with all royal prerogatives (Samas-

[1] *Ibid.*, V, pp. 116-18; *Arch. Surv. Ind. Rep.*, Vol. I, (1871), p. 96.

[2] *Ep. Ind.*, IX, pp. 325, 328.

[3] *Ibid.*, IX, p. 321.

tarājaprakriyopeta) and anointed as Heir—Apparent (Yauvarājyābhiṣikta), made a grant in the year 1134 A. D. with the consent of the king[1].

(*b*) Rājyapāladeva, who granted a village by the "consent of the lotus-feet" of Govindacandra in the Vikrama year 1199 or 1142 A. D.[2] A plate also mentions a town named Rājyapālapura, which was probably called after him.[3]

(*c*) Vijayacandra, the successor of Govindacandra. It appears, therefore, probable that the other two must have died quite young, or else were beaten in the race for the throne.

[1] *Ep. Ind.*, VIII, p. 155.
[2] *Ibid.*, XIII, pp. 217, 219; *Ind. Ant.*, XVIII, p. 21.
[3] *Ep. Ind.*, VIII, pp. 157, 158.

PART III

CHAPTER XIII

GĀHAḌAVĀLAS (*Continued*)

Vijayacandra

Govindacandra must have ceased to reign shortly after 1154 A. D., which is his last known date.[1] He was succeeded by his son Vijayacandra, also sometimes called Vijayapāla[2] or Malladeva.[3] The *Prithvīrāja-Rāso*[4] credits him with victories against the Somavaṁśī king Mukundadeva of Kaṭak, Anangapāla of Delhi, Bholābhīm of Paṭṭanapura (Anhilvāḍ), and with having carried his arms to the regions of Tailanga, Karṇāṭa, and Konkan etc. These bardic accounts may be summarily rejected, for none of the monarchs named can be regarded to have been a contemporary of Vijayacandra. Orissa was perhaps then ruled by the Gangā Rāghava (*circa* 1156-1170 A. D.), and besides sober history does not know of any Somavaṁśī Mukundadeva. Again, as we shall presently see, it was the Cāhamāna Vigraharāja Vīsaladeva, to whom Vijayacandra lost Delhi, and there can therefore be no question of the latter's fight with Anangapāla. Similarly, if Bholābhīm is identical with Bhīmadeva II Cālukya (*circa* 1179-1240), he came to the throne several years after the time of the Gāhaḍavāla

[1] *Ep. Ind.*, IV, p. 16.

[2] *Prithvīrāja-Rāso*, p. 123f, verses 617f. (Shyamsundar Das' edition).

[3] *Rambhāmañjarī*, (Bom. ed., 1899), p. 4.

[4] See canto XLV, pp. 1255-58; *J. B. B. R. A. S.*, 1928, p. 166.

ruler. How could they then ever have come into conflict with each other? On the other hand, the *Kumārapālacarita-Prakrit-Dvyāśraya-Mahākāvya* of Hemacandra represents Kumārapāla as having devastated Kānyakubja and terrified its sovereign in the course of his glorious career.[1] Now, Kumārapāla is known to have ruled from *circa* 1144 to 1172 A. D., and so if there be any truth in the above statement, which is, of course, doubtful, surely he must have triumphed against Vijayacandra, for it appears rather improbable that Kumārapāla's earlier Gāhaḍavāla contemporary, Govindacandra —a powerful potentate—could have ever suffered a reverse at his hands. Thus though we cannot rely upon Cand-Bardāi, one thing appears certain that Vijayacandra maintained his authority over a portion of Magadha. This is evident from an inscription of Vikrama *saṁvat* 1225 = 1169 A. D., discovered at Tārācaṇḍi in the vicinity of Sahasram in South Bihar,[2] in which the local ruler of Japila,[3] Pratāpadhavala of the Khayaravala *vaṁśa* according to the Phulawariya (Rohtasgaḍh) inscription,[4] makes a curious proclamation. He announces that a certain copperplate grant of the villages of Kalahandi and Badapila has been fraudulently procured by several Brahmans, on giving a bribe of goodly staves and ploughs, from one Deu, "a slave of the lord of Kānyakubja, the fortunate king Vijayacandra." He concludes by exhorting his successors not to place dependence on it, but to continue the collection of the "proprietor's share of produce and the like" as usual. Thus whatever resentment Pratāpadhavala might have

[1] Canto VI, v. 79, p. 209, ed. S. P. Pandit (Bombay, 1900).

[2] *Jour. Am. Or. Soc.*, VI, pp. 547-49.

[3] According to Colebrooke, Japila is a portion of Ramgarh in South Bihar (*Ibid.*, p. 549, Note).

[4] *Ep. Ind.*, IV, p. 311.

felt,[1] the fact that in the year 1169 A. D. Vijayacandra was in a position to grant villages situated in the former's territory, proves beyond doubt that he was under the suzerainty of Kanauj.

Like his father, Vijayacandra also stood as a bulwark against the Moslems. It is recorded in a copper plate that he "swept away the affliction of the globe by streams (of water flowing as) from clouds from the eyes of the wives of Haṁmīra, the abode of wanton destruction to the earth."[2] Unfortunately we have no information regarding any Moslem incursion in the Doab at this time, but it would appear probable that Vijayacandra came into conflict with the forces of Amir Khusrau or his son Khusrau Malik who were in occupation of Lahore after having been driven out of Ghazni by Ala-ud-Dīn Ghorī. The defeat of the Moslem marauders was probably due to the waxing strength of the Ghoris, which must have arrested the Amir's attention more towards the west. Khusrau, however, died in 555 *Hijri* or 1160 A. D. without recovering Ghazni, and during the reign of his son Malik, Sihab-ud-Dīn Ghorī threatened the Panjab itself and "overran the provinces of Peshawar, Mooltan and the Indus."[3]

Lastly, there are indications that the ambitions of the Cāhamāna king Vigraharāja Vīsaladeva of Sākambharī brought him into conflict with Vijayacandra. An inscription dated in Vikrama *saṁvat* 1220 or A. D. 1164, which is engraved on the Delhi-Siwalik pillar or Firoz-Koṭla's Lāṭ, boastfully records that Vigraharāja "made tributary the land between the Himālaya and

[1] This was probably because he had retained semi-independence.

[2] *Ind. Ant.*, XV, pp. 7, 9, verse 9.
Cf. "Bhuvana-dalana-helā-harmya-Haṁmīra-nārī-nayana jaladadhārā-dhauta-bhūlokatāpaḥ."

[3] Briggs, Frishta, Vol. I, p. 157.

Vindhya,"[1] while another found at Bijolia (Mewar) specifically credits him with the conquest of Delhi.[2] Similarly, the Delhi Museum inscription mentions that Delhi was for some time "the residence of the Cāhamānas until it was conquered by the Mleccha Sahābadīn" (Sihab-ud-Din).[3] If, therefore, the Gāhaḍavāla suzerainty had extended upto Delhi in the time of Candradeva, as we have surmised above, we may be sure that during the course of these expeditions Vijayacandra must have suffered defeat at the hands of Vigraharāja.

Jayacandra

Vijayacandra was succeeded by his son Jayacandra,[4] whose mother was Queen Candra-lekhā according to the *Raṁbhāmañjarī* of Nayacandra.[5] It is alleged that he was given this name on account of his grandfather having achieved a victory against the Daśārṇa country on the very day of his birth.[6] We learn the

[1] *Ind. Ant.*, XIX, p. 219.

[2] Faulty edition in *J. A. S. B.*, LV, pt. I, (1886), p. 42, verse 22. Cf. "Pratolyāṁ Valabhyāṁ ca yena viśrāmitaṁ yaśaḥ, Ḍhillikāgrahaṇa śrāntamāśikā lābha laṁbhitaḥ."

[3] *Ep. Ind.*, I, pp. 93, 94, verse 4.

[4] The name occurs as Jayacandra in copperplates. But Rājaśekhara (the author of the *Prabandhakoṣa*) and Nayacandra call him respectively Jayantacandra (See Śivadatta's *Introd. to the Naiṣadhīya*, p. 3, etc.) and Jaitracandra (*Raṁbhāmañjarī*, Bom. ed. 1889, p. 4). Merutunga on the other hand uses the normal form Jayacandra (*Prabandhacintāmaṇi*, v. 210, ed. Jinavijaya Muni, p. 113).

[5] See *Raṁbhāmañjarī*, Introd., p. 4; see also Act I, p. 6. Cf. "...... Candralekhāyās tanujanmā Jaitracandro." According to Cand Bardāi, however, Jayacandra was born of Anangapāla's eldest daughter Sundarī Devī (*Rāso*, verses 681-82, p. 134; S. S. Das's edition).

[6] See Act I, p. 23. Cf. "Pitāmahena tajjanmadine Daśārṇadeśeṣu prāptaṁ prabalaṁ yavanasainyaṁ jitaṁ ata eva tannāma Jaitra-Candraḥ."

actual date of his installation as crown-prince from an inscription which informs us that Jayacandra was "installed in the dignity of *yuvarāja* and endowed with all royal prerogatives" on the 10th *tithi* of the bright half of the month of Āṣāḍha of the Vikrama year 1224, corresponding exactly to Sunday, 16th June, 1168 A. D. It was on the same occasion that he was initiated as a worshipper of the god Kriṣṇa after bathing in the Ganges at Benares, and he granted the village of Haripura in the Jiavai *pattalā* to the preceptor of the performance of the Vaiṣṇava worship, the Mahāpurohita Prahārāja Śarman.[1] We are further told definitely in another epigraph, recording the grant of the village of Osia in the Brihadgrihakamisvara *pattalā* to the Mahāpurohita Prahlāda Śarman, that Jayacandra came to the throne on the 6th *tithi* of the bright half of the month of Āṣāḍha of the Vikrama year 1226, corresponding to Sunday, 21st June, 1170 A. D.[2]

Not many details of Jayacandra's career are known, for the copper plates contain little historical information beyond recording the usual gifts to the Brahmans, while Hindu works like the *Prithvīrāja-Rāso*[3] stultify themselves by their bardic character, exaggerations and anachronisms. They tell us that Jayacandra bore the epithet of "Pangu" or "Dal Pangula" from the circumstance that he maintained a stupendous force,[4] of which Cand-

[1] *Ep. Ind.*, IV, pp. 118, 119.

[2] *Ibid.*, IV, pp. 120-21.

[3] Commenting on the *Rāso*, Bühler was even of opinion that it "had better be left unprinted." (*Proc. As. Soc. Beng.*, 1893, p. 95). See also *J. B. B. R. A. S.*, May, 1928, pp. 203-11 for "Some Reflections on the *Rāso*" *J. A. S. B.*, LV, pt. I (1886), pp. 5-27, for Kavirāj Syāmal Das' views on the authenticity of the same.

[4] Cf. "Sainyātiśayāt Pangubirud dhārakaḥ." Introduction to the *Rambhāmañjarī*, p. 4; also Act I, p. 6; *Prabandhacintāmaṇi*, v, 210 (ed. Jinavijaya Muni, p. 113).

Bardāi observes that in the march "the van had reached their ground ere the rear had moved off."[1] According to the *Sūraj-Prakāś* it consisted of 80,000 men in armour 30,000 horse covered with Pakhar or quilted mail; 300,000 Paiks or infantry; 200,000 bowmen and battle-axes; besides a host of elephants bearing warriors.[2] We are asked to believe that with the help of these incredibly huge numbers Jayacandra embarked upon a career of conquest and subjugated the earth as far as 700 *yojanas*,[3] one *yojana* being roughly equal to eight English miles. Cand-Bardāi further informs us that Jayacandra attacked the Yādavarāja of Devagiri, but had to withdraw when Prithvīrāja sent his feudatory Cāmuṇḍarāya to the help of the besieged capital. Besides this, Jayacandra is credited with having overcome the king of Ghor before his final engagement with him.[4]

The *Puruṣaparīkṣā* of Vidyāpati and the *Raṁbhāmañjarī* lend support to this claim, for in the former "Yavaneśvara Sahāvadīn" (Sihābuddin) is said to have fled several times after sustaining defeat,[5] and the latter calls Jayacandra "Nikhila-yavana-kṣayakaraḥ" i.e., "the destroyer of all the Yavanas."[6] The Cauhan chronicles also testify to his greatness, affirming that Jayacandra "overcame the king of the North, making eight tributary kings prisoners; twice defeated Siddharāja, king of Anhilwāḍ, and extended his dominions south of the

[1] Tod's *Annals and Antiquities of Rājasthan* (Crooke), Vol. II, p. 936.

[2] *Ibid.*, Vol. II, p. 936.

[3] Cf. "yojanaśatamānāṁ prithvīm asādhayat."

[4] *Rāso-Sāra*, pp. 95-98.

[5] Vidyāpati's *Puruṣaparīkṣā*, Eng. Trans., Nerurkar's ed., (Bombay, 1914), ch., IV, 11th tale (Ghasmara-Kathā), pp. 146-47.
Cf. "Vāraṁ vāraṁ ca Yavaneśvaraḥ (Sahāvadīnaḥ) parājayī palāyate."

[6] *Raṁbhāmañjarī*, Act I, p. 5.

Nerbudda."[1] Whatever little grains of truth these statements may contain, it is certain that Jayacandra was the last great monarch of Kanauj, whose power and extensive jurisdiction struck even the Moslem historians. Referring to him Ibn Asir says in the *Kāmil ut-Tawārīkh* that "the king of Benares was the greatest king in India, and possessed the largest territory, extending lengthwise from the borders of China to the province of Malwa, and in breadth from the sea to within ten days' journey to Lahore."[2] We have unfortunately no means of ascertaining the exact bounds of his kingdom, but that it must have been comparatively limited in extent is evident from the contemporaneous existence of several strong principalities. In the first place, there were the Cauhans, who, starting from their territories in Ajmer, had annexed Delhi and were at this time bidding for supremacy in the north under the vigorous rule of Prithvīrāja III or Rai Pithaura of the Moslem historians. Towards the south, there were the Candellas, whose power was at its height during the reign of Madanavarman (*circa* 1125-1165 A. D.). He defeated Siddharāja Jayasiṁha of Gujarat,[3] and in the Mau inscription he even claims to have forced "the king of Kasi," who is probably identical with Vijayacandra, to pass his time "in friendly behaviour."[4] The *Raṁbhāmañjarī*, on the other hand, affirms that Jayacandra's "arms were like pillars to tie down the elephant-like goddess of Madanavarman's royal fortune,"[5] which proves that he must

[1] Tod's *Annals and Antiquities of Rājasthan* (Crooke), Vol. II, p. 936.

[2] Elliot, *History of India*, Vol. II, p. 251.

[3] *J. A. S. B.*, XVII, pt. I, pp. 317-20.

[4] *Ep. Ind.*, I, pp. 198, 204, verse 15.
Cf. "Kālaṁ sauhārddavrittyā gamayati satatam trāsataḥ Kāśirājaḥ."

[5] *Raṁbhāmañjarī*, Introd. p. 4; Act I, pp. 5-6.

have defeated the Candella king sometime as a prince. Such conflicting claims—by no means rare in ancient Indian History—show how necessary it is to exercise the utmost caution and critical judgment before accepting any statement. Whichever version may be true, this much is certain from the Madanapur inscription that during the time of Madanavarman's successor Paramardi or Parmāl (1165-1203), Prithvīrāja, and not Jayacandra, occupied Mahoba and other fortresses in Bundelkhand.[1] As to the north, the phrase "borders of China" may be presumed to denote that the kingdom extended upto the foot of the Himalayas; while in the east it must have comprised the Gaya region, where an inscription presumably belonging to Jayacandra's reign records that a hermit named Śrīmitra served as spiritual guide to the king of Benares (Kāśīśa), who was attended by a hundred chieftains (nripa-śata-krita-sevaḥ)."[2] It is also definitely known from inscriptions that Allahabad, Benares, and the surrounding tracts were included within Jayacandra's kingdom. The Gāhaḍavāla connection with Benares was more intimate, and perhaps because of the habitual residence of the kings there, or owing to its religious importance and advantageous situation "in the centre of the country of Hind,"[3] it became a sort of second capital almost from the beginning of their rule. Indeed, the Moslem historians significantly style Jayacandra "Rai

Cf. "Abhinavarāmāvatāra – Śrīman – Madanavarma-medinī dayita – sāṁrājya-lakṣmī – kareṇuK – ālāna-stambhāyamāna-bāhu-daṇḍasya..."

[1] *Prog. Rep. Arch. Surv. Ind.*, 1903-04, p. 55.

[2] *Proc. As. Soc. Beng.*, 1880, pp. 76-80; *Ind. Hist. Quart.*, V (1929), pp. 14-30. The date is not quite clear as the fourth digit has been erased. The first three are of course 124, and taking the fourth to be any number from 1 to 9, it is obvious that the record must belong to the "last decade of the 12th century A. D."

[3] Elliot, *History of India*, II, p. 223.

of Benares,"[1] and so also do several other authorities cited above, and Merutunga in his *Prabandhacintāmaṇi.*[2] The Bakerganj inscription of Keśavasena[3] and the Madhianagar grant,[4] on the other hand, claim that Lakṣamaṇasena, who has been identified with the Rai Lakhmaniyā of the Moslem writers, and who was thus the Sena contemporary of Jayacandra, erected many "pillars of victories" in Benares and Allahabad. But in view of the position of Benares in the Gāhaḍavāla realm, and Lakṣamaṇasena's craven flight without offering any resistance to the small force led by Bakhtyar Khilji, we may unhesitatingly say that "the monuments of his greatness never existed elsewhere than in the poet's imagination."

Celebration of an Imperial ceremony

The *Rāso* alleges that after the conclusion of his conquests Jayacandra prepared to celebrate the *rājasūya-yajña* as a mark of universal supremacy, which was to culminate in the *svayaṁvara* (self-selection of the bride-groom) of his daughter Saṁyogitā.[5] Invitations were sent to all the princes to attend the ceremony, but Prith-vīrāja Cauhan and Samarasiṁha of Mewar refused to come. Jayacandra caused effigies of them to be made of gold, and in order to humiliate them placed these representations in a position that indicated low rank. Prithvīrāja took the insult to heart; he suddenly attacked

[1] *Ibid.*, pp. 222, 223, 300, etc. Firishta calls Jayacandra "the prince of Kanauj and Benares" (Briggs, I, p. 178).

[2] *Prabandhacintāmaṇi*, v, 210, (ed. Jinavijaya Muni, p. 113); also see III, 121, p. 74. Cf. "Atha Kāśī nagaryāṁ Jayacandra iti nripaḥ."

[3] *J. A. S. B.* VII, pt. I, (1838), pp. 42, 48. Re-edited by R. D. Banerji, *Ibid.*, N. S. X, (1914), pp. 97-104.

[4] *Ibid.*, N. S. V, (1909), pp. 473, 476, verse 11.

[5] *Rāso-sāra*, p. 167f.

Kanauj and carried away the not-unwilling princess, who appears to have cherished love for him. Cand holds that this friction between Jayacandra and Prithvīrāja was the cause that led to Sihābuddin Ghori's invasion resulting in the fall of both. It is, however, difficult to accept this romantic story as a historical fact, for at this time *svayaṁvaras* and *rājasūyayajñas* had become obsolete, and if they had been performed they must have found mention in inscriptions. Moreover, even the *Raṁbhāmañjarī*, of which Jayacandra is the hero, is silent about these ceremonies. Lastly, the available evidence does not indicate that his conquests were so extensive as to justify him in holding a celebration indicative of paramount rank.

Moslem conquest of Kanauj

The kingdom of Kanauj was swept away by the whirlwind of Moslem invasion, and so in order to understand the full circumstances of its destruction we now proceed to trace how step by step the arms of Islam penetrated into the heart of Hindustan. The Ghori chieftains, having established themselves in Ghazni, gradually turned their attention towards the alluring Moslem territories in the Panjab. Multan was wrested from the sway of the Ismailian sect of heretics in 1175 A. D., and a stratagem soon led to the capture of Uccha also.[1] Peshawar followed in 1179 A. D., and during the course of a series of expeditions conducted in the years 1180, 1184 and 1186 A. D., Sihābuddin eventually took Khusrau Malik prisoner. He also annexed Lahore, where he stationed Ali Kirmani, Governor of Multan, to manage the affairs of government.[2] Thus getting hold of the last remnants of the

[1] Briggs (Firishta), Vol. I, pp. 169-70.
[2] *Ibid.*, pp. 170-71.

Ghaznavide empire, Sihābuddin Ghori, who aimed at founding a permanent dominion, began to devote himself systematically to the conquest of Hindustan. In the year 1190-91 A. D. he advanced against the strategic fortress of Bhatinda, which was probably within the territories of Prithvīrāja, and after its reduction he left there a garrison of over a thousand chosen horse and some foot under Malik Ziauddin Toozuky[1].

When Sihābuddin was about to return to Ghazni, the Cauhan king, assisted by other Rajput princes, marched against him with a mighty army consisting of 200,000 horse and 3,000 elephants.[2] Sihābuddin turned to meet him on the historic field of Narain or Tarain (Taroari) near Thanesvar, where a deadly encounter took place. The Moslems were completely overwhelmed by the huge Hindu hosts, and the Sultan himself would have met death on the battle-field, but for the courage and alacrity of a Khilji retainer who rescued him from the furious charges of the Cauhans. This great debacle constantly troubled the Ghori, and the very next year, in 1192 A. D., he again proceeded towards Hindustan with a reorganised force of 12,000 horse to avenge it. War was the very element of Prithvīrāja, and he "wrote for succours to all the neighbouring princes" to repeat, as it were, the anniversary of his victory. The Rajput chiefs to the number of one hundred and fifty enthusiastically responded to his appeal "having sworn by the water of the Ganges that they would conquer their enemies, or die martyrs to their faith."[3] Thus a formidable army of 300,000 horse, besides above 3,000 elephants and a body of infantry, encamped on the former field of battle with the breadth

[1] *Ibid.*, p. 172.
[2] Briggs (Firishta), Vol. I, p. 172.
[3] *Ibid.*, p. 175.

of the river Sarsuti (Sarasvati) dividing the opposing hosts. But Jayacandra, the king of Kanauj, kept himself in proud isolation thinking probably that the defeat of Prithvīrāja, who was his rival for supremacy in the north, would clear the way for him and enable him to attain that distinction. Indeed, Major Raverty, following Cand-Bardāi, asserts that Jayacandra was even in secret communication with Sihābuddin to ensure the humiliation of Prithvīrāja.[1] This does not, however, appear to be true, as the contemporary Moslem historians are totally silent about any such invitation having been made by the Gahaḍavāla monarch. In the battle that ensued fortune frowned on the Hindus, and the Moslems "carried death and destruction" so desperately that by sunset there was complete confusion in the Hindu ranks. Prithvīrāja fled from the field for dear life, but was captured near the Sarsuti (Sarasvati) and "sent to hell."[2] The forts of Sarsuti, Samana, Kahram, Hansi, and Ajmer surrendered soon after, and Sihābuddin became master of northern India almost to the gates of Delhi. On his return homewards the command was entrusted to Qutbuddin, who conquered Meerut the same year, thus establishing a Moslem outpost to the east of the Jumna. Delhi fell in *Hijri* 589 or 1193 A.D., as also did the fortress of Kol in the Aligarh district. These victories of the Moslems prepared the way for their attack on Kanauj, the overthrow of which city had now become necessary, if they were to obtain a firm control over Hindustan.[3] In 590 *Hijri* or 1194

[1] Raverty, *Tabaqāt-i-Nāsirī* (Eng. Trans.), Vol. I, p. 466, Note 1; and p. 467. See also Tod's *Annals and Antiquities of Rajasthan* (Crooke), Vol. I, p. 300.

[2] Elliot, *History of India*, II, p. 297; Briggs (Firishta), Vol. I, p. 177.

[3] The *Prabandhakoṣa* and the *Prabandhacintāmaṇi*, V, 210-12, (ed. Jinavijaya Muni, pp. 113-14), however, depose that feeling

A. D., therefore, Sihābuddin marched against Jayacandra with a huge force of "50,000 mounted men clad in armour and coats of mail" according to the *Tāj-ul-Maāsir*.[1] He was met on the way by his trusted general Qutbuddin, whom he ordered to proceed with the vanguard of 1,000 cavalry. The latter made an incursion into the territories of the "enemies of religion," but withdrew after having taken many prisoners and immense booty.[2] When Jayacandra, "the chief of idolatry and perdition," was informed of this inroad, he advanced to oppose the alien aggressors with an army "countless as the particles of sand," his force consisting of 700 elephants, besides about one million men.[3] The contending parties met on the plain between Candawar and Etawah, and in the contest that followed Jayacandra sustained a signal defeat at the hands of the Moslems.[4] The slaughter was appalling, for "none were spared except women and children; and the carnage of men went on until the earth was weary." The "Rai of Benares," who "prided himself on the number of his forces and war elephants," seated on a lofty *howdah* received a deadly wound from an arrow discharged by Qutbuddin,[5] and "fell from his exalted seat to the earth." His head was carried on the point of a spear to the commander, and "his body was thrown to the dust of contempt."[6] We are further told in the

mortified at the non-recognition of her son's claims for the throne, Suhavādevī, whom Jayacandra had kept as a concubine, invited the Moslems to attack Kanauj.

[1] Elliot, *History of India*, Vol. II, p. 222.

[2] *Ibid.*, p. 223; also see p. 250.

[3] *Ibid.*, p. 251 (*Kāmil-ut-Tawārīkh*).

[4] *Ibid.*, p. 251; Briggs (Firishta), I, p. 178.

[5] Briggs (Firishta), I, p. 192.

[6] The *Rāso* testifies that the battle continued for seven days, when Jayacandra lost his life fighting (*Rāsosāra*, p. 455). According

Kāmil-ut-Tawārīkh that no one would have recognised Jayacandra's dead body "but for the fact of his teeth, which were weak at their roots, being fastened in with golden wire."[1] As a result of this victory, the Moslem historians naively assure us that "the impurities of idolatry were purged by the water of the sword from that land, and the country of Hind was freed from vice and superstition."[2] Immense booty was obtained "such as the eye of the beholder would be weary to look at," including one (according to Firishta) three hundred elephants.

Next, Sihābuddin marched to the fort of Asni, where Jayacandra had deposited his treasure; there much precious spoil of all kinds fell into the hands of the victors.[3] He then proceeded to the other important town of the kingdom,viz., Benares, "which is the centre of the country of Hind;" here the invaders destroyed over one thousand temples, and "raised mosques on their foundations."[4] Sihābuddin bestowed the government of the conquered territories upon Qutbuddin, "the most celebrated and exalted servant of the State," in

to Vidyāpati's *Puruṣaparīkṣā*, Jayacandra was killed in war with Sihābuddin by the treachery of his queen Śubhadevī (See Nerurkar's Eng. Trans., Bom. 1914), ch. IV, 11th tale (Ghasmarakathā), pp. 146-153; Darbhanga ed., 41st tale, pp. 225-233). No stress, however, need be laid on such tales.

[1] Elliot, *History of India*, II, p. 251; Briggs (Firishta), Vol. I, p. 192. Another version says that Jayacandra was not killed in battle, but in order to avoid the disgrace and dishonour of defeat he met a "death congenial to the Hindu by drowning himself in the sacred Ganges" (See Forbes, *Rāsamālā*, I, p. 223).

[2] *Tāj-ul-Maāṣir* : Elliot, *History of India*, II, p. 223.

[3] Both Firishta and Hasan Nizami depose to the march on Asni (Briggs, I, pp. 178-79; Elliot, *History of India*, II, p. 223). Asni seems to have been an important stronghold of the kingdom of Kanauj from the time of the Pratīhāras. It was here that an inscription of Mahīpāla was discovered.

[4] Briggs (Firishta), I, p. 179; Elliot, *History of India*, II, p. 223.

order that he "might do justice and repress idolatry; and having thus settled affairs the former returned towards Ghazni with the captured elephants and 1400 camels bearing booty.[1] With a view to securing the full allegiance of the nobles of the Kanauj kingdom, Qutbuddin also planted his standards for some days on the fort of Asni. This halt soon had the desired effect; "the chiefs and elders all around hastened to his service with various kinds of rarities and presents, and his noble court became the scene where the princes and generals of the world came to bow their heads in reverence."[2]

Śrīharṣa

Jayacandra's name has been made memorable in the history of Sanskrit literature for the patronage that he extended to the poet Śrīharṣa, son of Hīra by Māmalladevī. Śrīharṣa's connection with the royal court is not only attested by the Jain Rājaśekhara in his *Prabandhakoṣa*,[3] but he himself states in the colophon to his chief work, the *Naiṣadhacarita*, that he was honoured by the king of Kānyakubja with a pair of betel-leaves,[4] it being customary with the Hindu Rājās to welcome men of eminence thus. A curious story is associated with this poet, and we therefore apologise for alluding to it in brief. He is believed to have been the nephew of Mammaṭa, to whom he showed the *Naiṣadhīya* after having composed it in one hundred cantos. The latter

[1] *Ibid.*, p. 224; Briggs (Firishta), 1, p. 179.

[2] *Tāj-ul-Maāṣir* : Elliot, *History of India*, II, p. 224; *Kāmil-ut-Tawārīkh* : Elliot, II, p. 251.

[3] Cf. Rājaśekharasya kathanaṁ ,"Śrīharṣaḥ Kānyakubjādhipati Jayacandrasya sabhāsanmahākavirāsīt ...."

[4] Cf. "Tāmbūladvayaṁ-āsanaṁ ca labhate yaḥ Kānyakubjeśvarāt." *Naiṣadhīyacarita*, ed. Śivadatta (Bombay, 1919), XXII, p. 528.

turning over its pages remarked : "What a pity! you did not show this to me before I wrote the seventh chapter of my *Kāvyaprakāśa*, where I have dealt with the defects of poetry. It would have saved me the trouble of hunting for examples of several defects."[1] Dejected by this severe criticism, the young poet threw away his manuscript into a river, whence his disciples rescued the portion that has come down to us in the shape of the twenty-two cantos. Historically Śrīharṣa's works are valueless, but he was doubtless a man of parts, and earned the praises of Govinda Ṭhakkura in his *Kāvyapradīpa* as "one who was superior to him in all good qualities and inferior only in age."

Among Śrīharṣa's other known works are :

(*a*) *Khaṇḍana-khaṇḍa-khādya*, "The most famous and important of those Vedānta treatises which emphasise the negative or sceptical side of the system."

(*b*) *Sthairya-vicāraṇa*, mentioned in the fourth canto of the *Naiṣadhacarita*.

(*c*) *Vijayapraśasti*, mentioned in the concluding stanza of the fifth canto.

(*d*) *Gauḍor-visa-kula-praśasti*, mentioned in the seventh canto.

(*e*) *Arṇava-varṇana*, mentioned in the ninth canto.

(*f*) *Chinda praśasti*, mentioned in the seventeenth canto.

(*g*) *Śiva-śakti-siddhi*, mentioned in the eighteenth canto.

(*h*) *Navasāhasāṅka-carita*, mentioned in the twenty-second canto, verse 151.

We may also add here that tradition affirms that Śrīharṣa was one of the five Brahmans of Kānyakubja, who were invited by king Ādiśūra of Bengal to re-

[1] *Indian Thought*, Vol. VII, No. I (1914), p. 75.

organise the caste-system and intoduce Kulinism there. The story is no doubt persistent, but it does not deserve much credence, as it is not confirmed by any inscriptions or authentic work.

Final disappearance of the kingdom of Kanauj

With the defeat and death of Jayacandra in 1194 A. D., the kingdom of Kanauj lay prostrate at the feet of the Moslems. They do not, however, appear to have resorted to immediate annexation or the destruction of the royal family. For a charter found at Machlisahr in the Jaunpur district of the United Provinces records that on the 15th *tithi* of the bright half of the month of *Pauṣa* in the Vikrama *saṁvat* 1253 or Sunday, the 6th January 1197 A. D., his successor, king Hariścandra, who is therein given the full sovereign titles of *Paramabhaṭṭāraka*, *Mahārājādhirāja*, *Parameśvara*, *Paramamāheśvara-Aśvapati*, *Gajapati*, *Narapati*, *Rajatrayādhipati*, *Vividha vidyā-vicāra-vācaspati*, after having bathed in the Ganges at the bathing-ghat named Cyavaneśvara, granted the village of Pamahi together with its outlying hamlets to one Rahīhiyaka.[1] The name of Hariścandra as son of Jayacandra is also known from two other copper plates. One of them, found at Kamauli, informs us that he was born on the 8th *tithi* of the dark half of *Bhādrapada* of the year 1232, equivalent to Sunday, the 10th of August, 1175 A. D., when his father gave the village of Vadesara in the Kangali *pattalā* to the Purohita Praharājaśarman in honour of his "*Jātakarma*" ceremony.[2] Another, which is now preserved in the Benares Sanskrit College library, records that on the 13th *tithi* of the dark half of the same month and year, corresponding to Sunday, the 31st of August, 1175 A. D., Hariś-

[1] *Ep. Ind.*, X, pp. 94, 98-99.
[2] *Ibid.*, IV, pp. 126, 127.

candra's "*Nāmakaraṇa*" (the ceremony of giving a name) was performed, on which occasion Jayacandra granted two villages to the Mahāpaṇḍita Hṛiṣīkeśa-Śarman.[1]

Thus we learn from the combined testimony of these inscriptions that Hariścandra was nineteen years old, when his father was killed in battle, and that he ruled for at least three years after that event. But what was the nature of his authority? It is unthinkable that this boy-king could have maintained his independence, even within a circumscribed area, when many a war-worn veteran had fallen, and the Moslem army had reduced the kingdom as far east as Benares. It would, therefore, appear reasonable to hold that as "on a promise of punctual payment of a large tribute he (Sihābuddin) had delivered over the country of Ajmer to Gola or Kola, a natural son of Prithvīrāja,"[2] similarly Hariścandra was allowed to reign in a portion of his ancestral dominions after he had acknowledged himself a tributary of the newly-established Moslem power at Delhi.[3] This hypothesis probably finds support from an inscription of Vikrama *saṁvat* 1253 or 1197 A. D., discovered at Belkhara (ancient Veḷaṣarā), a few miles to the south-east of Chunargarh (Chunar) in the Mirzapur district of United Provinces, which records the erection of a pillar when Rāṇaka Vijayakarṇa was the ruler of that region. The chief point to be noted, however, is that it does not mention the name of the king of Kanauj, but simply uses the phrase "Śrīmat Kānyakubja-vijayarā-

[1] *Ind. Ant.*, XVIII, pp. 129-34.

[2] Briggs (Firishta), Vol. I, pp. 177-78; see also *Tāj-ul-Maāsir*: Elliot, *History of India*, II, pp. 214, 215, 219.

[3] It has been stated that Zafarabad, four miles to the south-east of Jaunpur, was the site of a palace of the later rulers of Kanauj (Cunningham, *Arch. Surv. Ind. Rep.*, XI, p. 104; Smith, *J. R. A. S.*, 1908, p. 792; Führer, *Sharqi Architecture of Jaunpur*, p. 64.

jye."[1] This indicates that although Vijayakarṇa had not made himself independent of Kanauj, the Moslem supremacy over the kingdom was perplexing or abhorrent to him, and so he discreetly omitted any specific reference to Hariścandra or his Moslem overlord.

The royal family was probably spared from extermination owing to the political foresight of Sihābuddin, who must have thought that concentration of all power in the hands of his Viceroy at Delhi might tempt the latter to hatch the egg of independence; and moreover, the loyalty of these distant conquests would best remain assured under such feudatories as owed their position to the Sultan's protection and generosity. But the sudden assassination of Sihābuddin by a fanatic of the Mulhidah sect in 602 *Hijri* or 1205-06 A. D. gave Qutbuddin the opportunity of becoming king of Hindustan, which he was duly proclaimed by the Moslem generals and nobles at Delhi, and was also accepted by the unambitious brother of Sihābuddin. Henceforth Qutbuddin and his able lieutenant Altamash were free to reduce the whole of Northern India and to place Moslem rule on permanent foundations. We have no evidence as to how and when the last vestiges of Hindu authority in Kanauj were destroyed, but from a coin it is certain that during the reign of Altamash the land-revenue of Kanauj went to the Imperial coffers at Delhi.[2] Besides, the *Tabaqāt-i-Nāsirī* testifies that in *Hijri* 623 or 1226 A. D. the territory of Oudh was placed in charge of Malik Nāsir-uddin Mahmud, who overcame the "refractory infidels," and brought a "considerable number under obedience."[3] This shows that by this date the

[1] *Arch. Surv. Ind. Rep.*, XI, pp. 128-30; see also *J. A. S. B.*, 1911, N. S., pp. 757-70.

[2] *J. A. S. B.*, 1881, Pt. I, p. 66.

[3] Raverty. Eng. Trans. Vol. I, pp. 628-29.

Moslems were absolute masters of the Ganges-Jumna Doab, and their governors were ruling over the different provinces of the kingdom. Thus Kanauj, which had held pre-eminence in northern India for nearly six centuries and had been the centre of many a proud dynasty, ceased to exist as an independent Hindu state and soon sank into insignificance. Well may the hectic career of Kanauj remind one of the following stanza of Bhartrihari, the epitaph of its glories :

"Bhrātaḥ kaṣṭamaho mahān sa nripatiḥ sāmanta-cakraṁ ca
Tat-pārśve tasya ca sā api rāja-pariṣattāś candra-biṁbānanāḥ,
Udriktaḥ sa ca rājaputra nivahas te vandinas tāḥ kathāḥ,
Sarvaṁ yasya vasādagāt smritipadaṁ Kālāya tasmai namaḥ,"[1]

i.e., "Alas, brother, the mighty king, the train of barons, the witty court at his side, the damsels with faces like the moon's orb, the haughty troop of princes, the minstrels, the tales-homage to Time, by whose will all this hath passed into mere memories."

[1] *Vairāgyaśataka*, v. 36.

PART III

CHAPTER XIV

We have seen above how under the vigorous rule of the Pratīhāras and the Gāhaḍavālas the kingdom of Kanauj recalled the glories of Harṣa's epoch by absorbing within itself distant parts of northern India. We now pass on to deal with its administrative machinery and religious condition during their sway. Unfortunately, no mediæval Kauṭilya or Megasthenes has left to posterity any work throwing light on such topics, but a few facts may be gleaned from the records of both the dynasties; and although here and there they reveal differences of detail in some of the institutions of the Pratīhāras and the Gāhaḍavālas, it may reasonably be assumed that the general structure of government and religious traditions continued to be more or less the same.

Section A—Administration

At the head of the state was the king, whose office was hereditary. He exercised despotic powers, and except his immediate advisers the people in general had hardly any share in the determination of his policy in peace or war. The inscriptions usually apply to him the epithets *Paramabhaṭṭāraka*, *Mahārājādhirāja* and *Parameśvara*, which have been taken to imply Imperial status. But sometimes to the names of even mighty potentates like Mihira Bhoja are prefixed merely the honorific *Śrīmat*[1] or the unassuming title of Mahārāja.[2] In the Gahaḍa-

[1] *Ep. Ind.*, I, p. 156, line 6.
[2] *Ep. Ind.*, XIX, p. 18, line 6 (Barah copper plate).

vāla epigraphs the kings are also given the appellations of *Aśvapati*, *Gajapati*, *Narapati*, *Rājatrayādhipati*, *Vividha-vidyā-vicāra-vācaspati*; the exact connotation of the first three terms is no doubt obscure, but if our surmise, made elsewhere, be correct, they may be understood either to signify various classes of feudatories or to stand for the lordship over the three branches of the army[1]. Next to the sovereign were the chief queen (*Agra* or *Paṭṭamahiṣī*) and the crown-prince (*Yuvarāja* or *Mahārājaputra*), and from the Gāhaḍavāla plates they appear to have been quite important personages being invested with certain "royal prerogatives" of granting land.[2] Their grants had, however, to receive the consent of the ruling monarch before they could take effect. Thus, when the Yuvarāja Jayacandra[3] and the Mahārājñī Gosaladevī[4] make a grant, they do so with the approval of Vijayacandra and Govindacandra respectively. Sometimes the crown-prince was more closely associated with the government, as was Govindacandra during his father's lifetime.

The suzerain was the centre of a number of vassal chiefs, who helped him in military undertakings, and rendered him personal attendance when required. Such, for instance, were the chieftains named Uṇḍabhaṭa of Siyadoni,[5] Balavarman and Avanivarman II Yoga of Saurāṣṭra,[6] Mathanadeva of Rajorgarh[7]

[1] See *Ante*. In the Candravati plates we come across two more epithets of rulers vanquished by Candradeva, viz., *Giripati* and *Triśaṅkupati*, whose meaning is not quite clear (*Ep. Ind.*, XIV, p. 193).

[2] *Ind. Ant.*, XIV, p. 103; *Ep. Ind.*, II, pp. 359-60; *J. R. A. S.*, 1896, pp. 787-88.

[3] *Ep. Ind.*, IV, pp. 118, 120.

[4] *Ibid.*, V, pp. 117-18.

[5] *Ibid.*, I, pp. 169, 173.

[6] *Ibid.*, IX, pp. 1-10 (Unā copper plate inscription).

[7] *Ibid.*, III, pp. 263-67. (Rajor inscription).

during the Pratīhāra times; and Singara (Śringaroṭa) Kamalapāla and Vatsarāja under the Gāhaḍavālas.[1] These feudatories are described as having obtained from their overlord the "*Pañcamahāśabda*"[2] or the "*Rājapaṭṭi* i.e., the royal fillet or tiara.[3] The inscriptions bestow on them such subordinate titles as *Mahāsāmantādhipati*, *Samadhigataśeṣamahāśabda*, and *Mahāpratīhāra*;[4] but sometimes they even assumed the bombastic epithet of *Mahārājādhirāja*, as did Mathanadeva (Rajor inscription), Durbhaṭa and Niṣkalaṅka (Siyadoni inscription), which was probably due to varying degrees of dependence. The powers of these subordinate chiefs must have been considerably restricted, since we learn from certain inscriptions that even their grants were countersigned by provincial representatives of the suzerain. Thus, according to the Unā charter Dhīika, who was perhaps such an official under Mahendrapāla, gave his approval to a grant made by the Mahāsāmanta Avanivarman II Yoga.[5] Again, the Partabgarh inscription represents that it was to the provincial governor of Ujjain named Mādhava that Indrarāja, the Cāhamāna feudatory (Mahāsāmanta), after having built a temple to the sun-god (Indrādityadeva), applied to make an endowment for its upkeep. The record calls Mādhava a "*Tantrapāla*," and also gives him the titles of *Mahāsāmanta* and *Mahādaṇḍanāyaka*. These governors were assisted in the enforcement of their authority by the military, which were posted at strategic points in the outlying pro-

[1] *Ibid.*, IV, pp. 130-33. (Kamauli copper plate inscription dated V. E. 1191).

[2] *Ep. Ind.*, IX, p. 1 f. See also for an explanation, *Ind. Ant.*, V, pp. 251-52; XII, pp. 95-96; *Ep. Ind.*, XII, pp. 254-255; *C. I. I.*, III, p. 296, note 9, etc.

[3] *Ep. Ind.*, IV, p. 130.

[4] *Ibid.*, I, pp. 169, 173.

[5] *Ibid.*, IX, pp. 2, 6.

vinces. Thus, Maṇḍapikā (Māṇḍū), near Ujjain, was the military headquarters for the southern regions, as we are told that Mahendrapāla II stationed there one Śrīśarman as his commander-in-chief.[1] Besides, provincial defence was organised by building forts, which were placed in charge of officers called "*Koṭṭapāla*" (guardian of fort). Under Bhoja I one such official was Alla. But his father Vaillabhaṭṭa, who was in the service of Rāmadeva, is given the designation of *Maryādādhurya* or *Dhurodhikārī*, meaning chief of the boundaries. This shows that one of his functions was also to watch that the existing boundaries were not disturbed by foreign encroachments.[2] Another provincial officer whom we know from the Barah copper-plate was the "*Vyavahārin*" or controlling officer.[3] He supervised the grants that were made by kings with a view to avoiding their lapse into abeyance. These charters (śāsana) were conveyed by an officer called "*Dūtaka*," which literally means "messenger."[4] Regarding his duties, Fleet remarks that "the Dūtaka's office was to carry, not the actual charter itself, for delivery into the hands of the grantees, but the king's sanction and order to the local officials, whose duty it was then to have the charter drawn up and delivered."[5]

In connection with the village administration we

[1] *Ibid.*, XIV, pp. 180, 185-87.

[2] *Ep. Ind.*, I, pp. 156, 157, 159, 160.
Maryādā may also mean a constitution or regulation-system, especially of corporate bodies; and so *Maryādādhurya* may denote a person responsible for its maintenance. *Dhurodhikāra*, on the other hand, means only an officer in control, and Dr. L. D. Barnett is of opinion that it may not be a technical term.

[3] *Ibid.*, pp. 16, 18; Cf. also *Vyavaharaṇa* in *Ep. Ind.*, XI, p. 145, line 41.

[4] *Ibid.*, V, pp. 212, 213.

[5] *C. I. I.*, III, p. 100, note 3.

learn of officials designated as *Gāmagāmika*, *Mahattara*, and *Mahattama*.[1] The first term probably stands for headmen of the villages who were responsible to the government for the maintenance of peace and order within their boundaries. The other two terms have evidently the same political significance, although they have comparative and superlative inflexions. *Mahattara* literally means "one higher in rank;" *Mahattama*, "one highest in rank." It seems they were the two classes of elders of villages, who co-operated with the government officials in the management of rural affairs.

This list is further supplemented by the Gāhaḍavāla records, which it will be noticed, mix together court officials and strictly political functionaries, local or central:

(*a*) *Mantrin*, or minister. He advised the king on matters of moment, but the inscriptions do not give any idea if there was a separate minister for each department. In the Unā charter the term Amātya occurs in the sense of counsellor.

(*b*) *Purohita*, or chaplain. He ministered to the spiritual needs of royalty, whom he assisted in the maintenance of the Dharma. He was also the recipient of the royal gifts. The plates often mention the term *Mahāpurohita*, which shows that there was a high-priest in the kingdom.[2]

(*c*) *Pratīhāra*, or door-keeper. The office of the chamberlain has always been a prominent one in the states of ancient India. This official is also mentioned in the records of the Pratīhāra

[1] *Ep. Ind.*, III, p. 266.

[2] See Kauṭilya's *Arthaśāstra* (Eng. Trans.), p. 15, for his duties and qualifications.

kings,[1] and in the *Mahābhārata* and the *Artha-śāstra* of Kauṭilya he is called "Dvārapāla" and "Dauvārika" respectively.

(*d*) *Senādhipati*, or commander of troops.

(*e*) *Bhāṇḍāgārika*, or superintendent of stores. He had to see that all necessary articles were kept in readiness and that their distribution was in accordance with the king's orders.

(*f*) *Akṣapaṭalika*, or keeper of records. Considering the large number of Gahaḍavāla grants, his office must have been a very important one. Some inscriptions mention the superior officer called Mahākṣapaṭalika.[2]

(*g*) *Bhiṣak*, or the physician. He looked after the health of the king, and was perhaps the head of the public health department.

(*h*) *Naimittika*, or astrologer. He was responsible for forecasting the effects of particular conjunctions of the stars, portents, etc. : it was probably after his reading of the omens that undertakings were embarked upon.

(*i*) *Antaḥpurika*, or superintendent of the seraglio. As kings not unoften used to have several wives, a special officer was appointed to look after the needs of the harem.

(*j*) *Dūtas*, or envoys. These formed a diplomatic corps responsible for maintaining proper relations with foreign powers.

(*k*) *Karyā-adhikāra-puruṣas*, or officers in charge of elephants. They were probably charged with the management of elephants, wild or domesticated.

(*l*) *Turagādhikāra-puruṣas*, or officers in charge of

[1] *Ep. Ind.*, XVIII, pp. 107, 110; see also *Ibid.*, p. 97, etc.
[2] *Ind. Ant.*, XVIII, p. 136.

horses. These two sets of functionaries formed a very important part of the state machinery, as its defence and power largely depended upon the efficiency and organisation of the cavalry and elephant forces.

(*m*) *Pattanādhikāra-puruṣas*, or officers in charge of towns. These may be compared to the Drāngika of the Unā record and the "Nāgarika" of Kauṭilya's *Arthaśāstra*, being charged with the administration of cities. From the Siyadoni record it also appears that during Pratīhāra times some sort of municipal government was not unknown. For it tells us that the town affairs were managed by an assembly of five called "Pañcakula," and by a committee of two, appointed from time to time by the town.[1]

(*n*) *Ākarādhikāra-puruṣas*, or officers in charge of mines. They must have been very important officials, as the mines were one of the chief sources of revenue.

(*o*) *Sthānādhikāra-puruṣas*, or officers of police-stations. They corresponded to modern *Thānādārs*, and were responsible for policing and maintaining law and order. The Unā inscription uses the term Daṇḍapāśika, which literally means "one who holds the fetters or noose of punishment" i.e.—a policeman. Or, does it connote a hangman or executioner?

(*p*) *Gokulādhikāra-puruṣas*, or officers of cattle-stations. As agriculture was the main industry, it was necessary to have a separate officer for cattle in order to rear good breeds etc.

(*q*) *Kāyastha* or *Karaṇika*, i.e., the scribe. He was apparently the writer of the records or legal documents.

[1] *Ep. Ind.*, I, pp. 170, 177.

Besides these officers, the Unā charter mentions Rājasthānīya, Uparika, Cāṭa, Bhaṭa, Daṇḍoddharaṇika (either a judicial officer from *daṇḍa* in the sense of fine; or a police officer, from the same word in the sense of rod of chastisement), Āyuktaka, Niyuktaka (perhaps subordinate functionaries of the government); and the Sarnath inscription of Kumāradevī adds the term Pattalikā,[1] which according to Sten Konow is the feminine form of Pattalaka or head of a *pattalā*.[2]

The Lucknow Museum plate of Kīrtipāla, found in the Gorakhpur district of the United Provinces, further refers to Aṣṭavargika, Mahātthāśāsanika, Mahāsādhanika, Dharmādhikaraṇika, Daivāgārika, Daivajña, and Sankhadhārī[3] etc. The last four appear to be religious dignitaries, but it is difficult to determine exactly the functions of the other officials.

Territorial Divisions

For purposes of administration the kingdom was divided into numerous provinces. These provinces were usually called *bhukti*, as the Kānyakubjabhukti in the Barah copper plate;[4] or *bhūmi*, as the Gurjaratrābhūmi in the Daulatpura charter;[5] or *maṇḍala*, as the Saurāṣṭra maṇḍala in the Unā grant.[6] According to the Barah copper plate, however, *maṇḍala* was the next lower unit after *bhukti*, and was not a synonymous term. The provinces were further subdivided into *Viṣayas* or districts. Among examples of them we find mention

[1] *Ep. Ind.*, IX, pp. 325, 327, verse 22.

[2] *Ibid.*, p. 320, note 2; see also *Ibid.*, III, p. 44, line 33, for the term Pattalaka.

[3] *Ibid.*, VII, p. 97.

[4] *Ibid.*, XIX, pp. 18, 19.

[5] *Ibid.*, V, pp. 211, 213.

[6] *Ibid.*, IX, pp. 3, 9.

of Udumbara[1] and Dindavanaka.[2] The term *bhoga* also seems to have been used sometimes in the same sense, as we read of the Vaṁśapoṭakabhoga.[3] The headquarters of a district were called *Adhiṣṭhāna* or *Pattana*.

The next unit in the descending scale was the *Agrahāra* or a modern *Tahsil.* We thus read of the Valākāgrahāra in the Barah copper-plate. In the Gahaḍavāla records, however, the term *Pattalā* is used in the same sense.

Last came the *grāma* or village, which has been the most stable unit of administration in India from time immemorial. Furthermore, in some records the term *pāṭaka* appears; this, according to the lexicographer Hemacandra denoted one-half of a village.[4] It may be pertinent to note that Kielhorn also explains it as "grāmaikadeśa" i.e., "the outlying portion of a village or a kind of hamlet which had a name of its own, but really belonged to a larger village."[5]

Group-life

As some Pratīhāra inscriptions show, persons following the same occupation normally formed themselves into corporations for regulating their business. For example, the Gwalior (Vaillabhaṭṭasvāmin) epigraph[6] refers to the guild of oil-millers (tailikaśreṇī) and gardeners (Mālikaśreṇī), who in their corporate capacity made gifts to a temple. The members of these guilds had their chiefs called

[1] *Ibid.*, XIX, pp. 18, 19.
[2] *Ibid.*, V, pp. 211, 213.
[3] *Ibid.*, III, p. 266.
[4] Cf. "Pāṭakas-tu tadardhe syāt (see *Abhidhāna-Cintāmaṇi*, Boehtlingk's edition, p. 179).
[5] *Ind. Ant.*, XVIII, p. 135.
[6] *Ep. Ind.*, I, pp. 160, 161.

respectively *Tailikamahattaka* (lines 12, 13 and 14) and *Mālikamahar* (line 17). Similarly the Siyadoni record mentions such traders as potters, distillers of spirituous liquors, sugar-boilers, betel-sellers, oil-makers, stone-cutters,[1] and the Pehoa inscription adds to this list the horse-dealers,[2] whose organisation into guilds is proved by their joint action in matters of common concern, and by the fact that they had a foreman or *deśī*. We are told, for instance, that the distillers of liquors were required to give on every cask liquor worth half a *vigrahapāladramma* to the god Viṣṇu. Or, we may cite the joint agreement of the horse-dealers belonging to "various countries," whereby they imposed upon themselves and upon their customers certain taxes, the proceeds of which were distributed among the temples and the priests in specified proportions.

Such guilds must have been of benefit to the state, inasmuch as they certainly fostered a law-observing spirit in the interests of the community, and thus facilitated the task of government, besides rendering useful service in organising society and administering justice in internal affairs.[3]

Fiscal conditions

We may now set forth the evidence regarding the principal sources of revenue, on which depended the stability and strength of the state.[4] The Rajor inscription of the Pratīhāra feudatory Mathanadeva mentions numerous dues from a village[5] like the *Bhoga* and the

[1] *Ibid.*, pp. 167-68, 174-78.

[2] *Ibid.*, I, pp. 184-90.

[3] Cf. R. C. Majumdar, *Corporate Life in Ancient India*, (Calcutta, 1922).

[4] Cf. e.g. "Koṣamūlo hi rājeti pravādaḥ sārva-laukikaḥ" (*Kāmandakīya Nītisāra*, XXI, 33.

[5] *Ep. Ind.*, III, pp. 264, 266.

Mayūta income (probably the contributions of fruits, firewood, etc.), with all customary and not customary, fixed and not fixed receipts; the shares of all sorts of grain; the *Khalabhikṣā* (cess on threshing floors);[1] *Prasthaka*; *Skandhaka*; and *Mārgaṇaka*.[2] The meaning of these three terms is not quite clear. Dr. Ghoshal, however, thinks that *Mārgaṇaka* represented benevolences of a general character levied upon the villages, as distinguished from the special forms called *Prasthaka* (a cess on each *prastha* of grain over and above the usual grain-share) and *Skandhaka* (perhaps a cess at a certain rate per load).[3]

Fines for ten offences (*daśāparādhandaṇḍa*),[4] gifts, likewise *aputrikādāna* (literally the property of a person who in the absence of a son has not appointed his daughter to raise a male issue for him, or in other words, it signifies the crown's right to confiscate the property of one who dies sonless?) and *naṣṭibharata* (*naṣṭabharata*?) were other sources of revenue. Besides these, the state laid claim to treasure-trove and mineral products. The record also mentions the following taxes for purposes of worship : three vimśopakas on every sack of agricultural produce brought for sale to the market (haṭṭadāna); two pālikas on every ghaṭaka-kūpaka of clarified butter and oil; two vimśopakas per mensem on every shop; fifty leaves on every collika (of leaves) brought from outside the town. The Unā charters specify the usual dues—*bhāgabhoga*, *hiraṇyadāna*,

[1] Cf. also *Ibid.*, II, p. 179, verse 42. See *Ind. Ant.*, XVIII, p. 114, line 55, for Khalaka as a revenue term.

[2] See also *Ind. Ant.*, XVIII, p. 83, line 20. Compare *Mārgaṇaka* with the Hindi word "māṅganā."

[3] *Hindu Revenue System*, pp. 294, 296, 298, etc.

[4] Jolly's *Hindu Law and Custom* (B. K. Ghosh's Eng. Trans., 1928), pp. 268-70. Also consult Fleet, *C. I. I.*, Vol. III, p. 189, note 4; Hira Lal, *Ep. Ind.*, IX, p. 47, note 1, etc.

daśāparādhadaṇḍa—and add the *Udranga* (revenue imposed upon the permanent tenants?), *Uparikara* (tax on cultivators who have no proprietory rights in the soil), *Collaka*, and other minor imposts.[1]

Further, the Gāhaḍavāla plates mention the following sources of revenue :

(*a*) *Bhāga*, or share : this possibly represents a stipulated share exacted by the actual owner from the farmer who cultivated the land.

(*b*) *Bhoga*, or enjoyment : probably certain rights that the landlord enjoyed when the land was left fallow. Or, it might refer to the use of waste and taking of grass, etc., from the field when the cultivator's crops had been removed. Or, is "bhāga" partial and "bhoga" complete proprietorship?

(*c*) *Kara*, or rent proper, payable in cash or kind.

(*d*) *Hiraṇya*, or gold : probably a money-tax levied on profits of trade or manufacture. It is, however, possible that "*Kara*" represents dues in kind and "*hiraṇya*" dues commuted into cash.

(*e*) *Pravanikara* : a tax on turnpikes intended to preserve the peace of the village by discouraging the advent of large numbers of visitors. Or, is it a tax for the upkeep of roads? Sometimes it has also been taken to stand for a tax imposed upon certain classes of merchants.[2]

(*f*) *Turuṣka-daṇḍa* : a term that is most difficult to explain. It has been variously interpreted as a tax on aromatic reeds,[3] or tribute paid to Ghazni by the ruler of Kanauj,[4] or a tax levied

[1] *Ibid.*, IX, pp. 5, 10.
[2] Ghoshal, *Hindu Revenue System*, p. 296.
[3] *J. A. S. B.*, LVI, pt. I (1887), p. 113.
[4] C. V. Vaidya, *H. M. H. I.*, Vol. III, p. 211.

on the Hindus to ward off the Moslems.[1] But, as pointed out by Sten Konow, it might also mean a tax imposed on the Moslems,[2] who, according to the *Kāmil-ut-tawārīkh*, settled in the Kanauj kingdom in the time of Mahmud-bin-Sabuktigin, and "were faithful to the law of Islam and constant in prayer and good works."[3] Thus it would be a sort of Hindu counterpart of the Moslem *Jizya*.

(*g*) *Jalakara*, or tax on water. This must have been a fruitful source of income as the prosperity of the village largely depended upon irrigation.

(*h*) *Gokara* : probably a tax on the breeding of cattle just as in the south there was a tax of "the good bull." Or, was it charge covering grazing rights?

(*i*) *Viṣayadāna* : This must have been some kind of district tax.

(*j*) *Nidhi-nikṣepa*, i.e., treasure-trove.

(*k*) *Kumāragadyāṇaka* : an obscure term. It has sometimes been explained as a tax at the rate of so much per *gadyāṇaka* (= 32 guñja berries) on behalf of royal princes.[4] Presumably it was something like modern *nazar* offered to royal personages on ceremonial occasions.

(*l*) *Ākara* : a tax on mines.

In addition to the above the Gāhaḍavāla inscriptions mention the following taxes, but unfortunately their exact signification is unknown.

(*m*) *Yamali-Kambala*.

(*n*) *Kūṭaka* (e.g., *Ep. Ind.*, IV, p. 111).

[1] V. A. Smith, *Early Hist. of India*, 4th ed., p. 400, note 1.
[2] Sten Konow, *Ep. Ind.*, IX, p. 329.
[3] Elliot, *History of India*, Vol. II, p. 251.
[4] See *Hindu Revenue System*, p. 294.

(*o*) *Valadī* (*Ind. Ant.*, XVIII, p. 17).
(*p*) *Viṁśaticchavathā* (*Ibid.*).
(*q*) *Akṣapaṭalādāya* (*Ibid.*).

The last two are respectively called *Viśatiaṭhu* (*Viṁśatyaṭhū*) *prastha* and *Akṣapaṭalaprastha* in the Basahi plate (*Ind. Ant.*, XIV, p. 103), which refers to other imposts also like *Varavajjhe*, *Pratīhāraprastha*, and *Daśabaṁdha*, etc.

We also learn from inscriptions that there were regular customs-houses, called "*Mattadāva*" or "*Maṇḍapikā*," where perhaps taxes on sales and manufactures were levied and collected.

Regarding land settlement the details are meagre to the extreme. All the information that we get is that the village lands were measured by "*hastas*" and "*nālukas*" and they were well demarcated by boundaries.[1]

Further, we are told in the Gāhaḍavāla plates of the rights possessed by owners of villages, and granted to donees, viz., water (*Jala*); waste-land (*sthala*); iron-mines and salt-mines (*lohalavaṇakara*); fisheries (*matsyakara*); ravines (*garta*), saline soil (*Oṣara*); groves of *madhuka* and mango (*madhukāmravanavāṭikā*), grass and pasture land etc. (*triṇa-yutigocaraparyantaḥ*).

Lastly, we may make a few observations about the currency of the period. As already shown, copper and silver coins of Madanapāla, and gold and copper issues of Govindacandra, have been discovered. It would, therefore, not be unreasonable to suppose that the Gāhaḍavāla kings minted in all the three metals. The copper pieces were probably meant for small transactions, for which barter may also have been practised. The gold and silver coins vary in their types and values, and the percentage of alloy indirectly throws light on the financial condition of the kingdom

[1] *Ep. Ind.*, V, pp. 113, 114.

under their rule. For the Pratīhāra times our extant evidence consists of the silver *Drammas* of Mihira Bhoja and the doubtful gold issues of Mahīpāla. The former are derived from the Indo-Baktrian (Greek) *Drachmae* weighing 65 grains, and the Siyadoni inscription enumerates several distinct kinds of these *Drammas* in connection with donations:

Dramma; Pañcīyaka-dramma; Vigrahapālīya-dramma; Vigrahasatka dramma; Vigrahatungīya dramma; Ādivarāha; Ādivarāha dramma; Varāhakaya Viṁśopaka (?); Vigraha-dramma visovaka; Kapardaka; Kākinī; Varāṭaka.[1]

Judging from this comprehensive system of coinage and taxation, it would appear that the fiscal administration was fairly developed, and the government knew how to squeeze money out of people.

Section B

Religion

The Gahaḍavāla kings, like the Pratīhāras whose religion has already been stated, did not confine their devotions to one member only of the great Hindu pantheon. Thus, while they officially describe themselves as "*Paramamāheśvara*," i.e., "devout worshippers of the god Śiva," their records also invoke in the beginning the blessings of Śrī (Lakṣmī), the goddess of prosperity, and Dāmodara (Gaṇeśa), and on the seals attached to the copper-plates there are representations of the flying Garuḍa and conch-shell (Pāñcajanya conch?), which may indicate their predilections towards Vaiṣṇavism. Indeed, one of the Kamauli inscriptions even asserts that Jayacandra was initiated, with the consent

[1] *Ep. Ind.*, I, pp. 169, 173-79.

of his father, as a devotee of the god Krișṇa on the 10th *tithi* of the bright half of the month of *Āṣāḍha* of the Vikrama year 1224, corresponding to Sunday, the 16th of June, 1168 A. D.—the day of his installation to the dignity of *Yuvarāja*.[1] But so marked was the royal eclecticism that according to a Bodhgayā inscription in later life Jayacandra, out of reverence for a Buddhist monk named Śrīmitra, himself became his disciple "with a pleasing heart and an indescribable hankering."[2] Moreover, we are uniformly told in their documents that the Gāhaḍavāla monarchs made grants "after having worshipped the sun (sūrya), after having praised him (Śiva), after having performed adoration to Vāsudeva, and after having sacrificed to the fire an oblation of abundant milk, rice and sugar, and after having offered oblations to the manes."

Turning now to the matter of popular religion, the outstanding features during both the Pratīhāra and Gāhaḍavāla periods were the worship of idols and the variety of gods. Temples were built in large numbers, being known as "devagrihas"[3] or "caityas."[4] With their lofty spires, rich ornamental designs, and graceful sculptures, the construction of these elaborate structures must have entailed great engineering skill and workmanship. Sometimes, it is interesting to note, they were even hewn out of a single piece of rock.[5] But unfortunately almost all these noble monuments of the liberality and religious zeal of the princes and peasants alike have disappeared owing to the ravages

[1] *Ep. Ind.*, IV, pp. 118, 119.
[2] *Ind. Hist. Quart.*, V. (1929), p. 26, verse 10.
[3] *Ep. Ind.*, IX, p. 200, line 17.
[4] *Ind. Ant.*, XVI, p. 175. In the Pehoa inscription the word "Sthāna" occurs for a sanctuary (*Ep. Ind.*, I, pp. 186, 188).
[5] *Ibid.*, I, pp. 157, 159, verse 27.
Cf. "Ramyesmin-ekaśile Viṣṇuḥ bhaktyā pratiṣṭhito bhavane."

of time, or were razed to the ground by the iconoclastic fury of the victorious Moslems. For instance, the *Tāj-ul Maāsir*[1] and Firishta's account[2] testify that in Benares alone Sihābuddin Ghori destroyed more than one thousand temples, and raised mosques on their foundations.

Among the gods, Viṣṇu was the most highly venerated. The Siyadoni inscription gives several names for him such as Viṣṇubhaṭṭāraka, Nārāyaṇabhaṭṭāraka, Vāmanasvāmīdeva (also mentioned in the Ahar inscription), Cakrasvāmīdeva, Tribhuvanasvāmīdeva, and Murāri.[3] In the Gwalior inscription of Bhoja he is called Narakadviṣa,[4] and in the Buckala record the term Parameśvara occurs for his image.[5] The Pehoa inscription, however, simply describes him as the god riding on garuḍa (Viṣṇu garuḍāsana).[6] The Gāhaḍavāla copper plates often allude to the god Vāsudeva and the temple of Ādikeśava at the confluence of the Varuṇā and the Ganges. We may also add here that the Ahār epigraph (No. VII) refers in general terms to all the ten incarnations of Viṣṇu, but in other documents there is specific mention of only three manifestations of the deity, viz., Kriṣṇa or Hriṣīkeśa, Varāha, and Vāmana.

The inscriptions further mention such gods as :

(*a*) Sūrya, also called Taruṇādityadeva,[7] Indrarājādityadeva or Indrādityadeva,[8] or Gangāditya.[9] Another form of the sun was Lolārka,[10] whose

[1] Elliot, *History of India*, Vol. II, p. 223.
[2] Briggs, I, p. 179.
[3] *Ep. Ind.*, I, pp. 168, 173-79.
[4] *Ep. Ind.*, XVIII, pp. 107, 110, verse 1.
[5] *Ibid.*, IX, p. 200.
[6] *Ibid.*, I, pp. 187, 189.
[7] *Ibid.*, IX, pp. 1, 5.
[8] *Ibid.*, XIV, pp. 180-85.
[9] *Ibid.*, IV, pp. 121-23.
[10] *Ibid.*, V, pp. 116-18; IV, pp. 128-29.

festival is even now annually celebrated in Benares during the rainy season. In the Siyadoni inscription occurs the term Bhaillasvāmideva, which according to a Bhilsa record was a designation of the sun.[1]

(*b*) Śiva (Jhusi inscription), also called Umāmaheśvara (Siyadoni inscription) or simply Maheśvara (Gāhaḍavāla plates), Trilocana,[2] Lacchukeśvara Mahādeva, so named after Mathanadeva's mother (Rajor inscription), Yogasvāmin,[3] Paśupati,[4] and Śambhu (Haddala grant).

(*c*) Vināyaka[5] or Dāmodara (Gāhaḍavāla plates).

(*d*) Kumāra (Kārtikeya) with his host of Mātṛikas i.e., female companions who performed wonderful deeds.[6]

(*e*) Mahākāla (Partabgarh inscription) or Kālapriya (Cambay plates) in Ujjain.

Among other names and temples of gods we come across Nityapramuditadeva[7]; Aghoreśvara, Indramādhava, Lauḍeśvara, Pañcoṁkāra;[8] Krittivāsas[9] etc.

The inscriptions refer to names of goddesses also, such as Bhagavatī or Durgā (Partabgarh inscription) or Vaṭayakṣṇīdevī;[10] Sri Amba Lohīdevī (Siyadoni inscription);[11] Kanakadevī or Kāñcanadevī, Gandhadevī, Sarva-

[1] *J. A. S. B.*, XXXI, p. 112.
[2] *Ind. Ant.*, XVIII, pp. 11, 13.
[3] *Ibid.*, VI, pp. 174, 175 (Asni inscription).
[4] *Ep. Ind.*, VII, p. 95. (Lucknow Museum plate of Kīrtipāla dated 1111-12 A. D.).
[5] *Ep. Ind.*, IX, p. 279.
[6] *Ibid.*, VIII, pp. 109, 114, verse 22.
[7] *Ibid.*, III, p. 266.
[8] *Ibid.*, VIII, p. 153, lines 18-19.
[9] *Ibid.*, IV, p. 126, line 22.
[10] *Ibid.*, XIV, p. 188, line 33.
[11] *Ibid.*, I, p. 178, line 35.

mangaladevī (Ahar inscription); Śrī or Laksmī (Gāhaḍavāla inscriptions); Vasudhārā[1] etc.

Position of the Brahmans

The Brahmans had gained complete ascendancy, and it was considered meritorious by the other castes—Kṣatriyas, Vaiśyas and Śūdras—to make them gifts. Sometimes, however, the Gāhaḍavāla monarchs gave lands to a hereditary *Rāuta* or a Kṣatriya, as for example, Jayacandra made six grants in favour of the *Rāuta* Rājyadharavarman, who is expressly called a Kṣatriya.[2] This shows that non-Brahmans were not then altogether excluded from the bounty of donors. Further, there are some instances of Buddhists being objects of royal generosity. The Saheṭ-Maheṭh inscription records that Govindacandra, having been gratified by the Saugata Parivrājaka, the Mahāpaṇḍita Śākyarakṣita (a resident of the Utkala country) and his disciple the Saugata Parivrājaka, the Mahāpaṇḍita Vāgīśvararakṣita (a resident of the Coḍa country), bestowed the villages of Vihāra, Paṭṭanā, Upalaüṇḍa, Vavvahali, Meyī-sambaddha-Ghosāḍī, Pothivāra-sambaddha Payāsi upon "the most respectable community of Buddhist friars (Śākyabhikṣu), of which Buddharakṣita was the chief, residing in the holy convent of Jetavana."[3] Incidentally the above inscription proves that Buddhism was still lingering on, and that the Gāhaḍavāla kings were tolerant enough to extend their patronage to its votaries. This view is also supported by the Bodhgayā inscription, which describes Jayacandra as a disciple of the Buddhist saint Śrīmitra, and the Sarnath inscription of Kumāradevī, the Buddhist queen of Govindacandra, who repaired or res-

[1] *Ibid.*, IX, pp. 325, 327, verse 21.
[2] *Ind. Ant.*, XVIII, pp. 135-43.
[3] *Ep. Ind.*, XI, pp. 24-26.

tored the Dharmacakra Jina, originally set up by Dharmāśoka and placed it in a new *vihāra* at Sarnath. It was customary for donors to make grants by a libation of water after bathing in a sacred river such as the Ganges,[1] the Jumna,[2] confluences of rivers such as the Sarayū and the Ghargarā,[3] the Triveṇī at Allahabad,[4] or that of the Varuṇā and the Ganges at Benares.[5] The usual occasions for such gifts were the lunar[6] or solar eclipse,[7] the annual *Śrāddha* in honour of one's father,[8] the royal birthday (*Jātakarma*),[9] the name-giving (*Nāmakaraṇa*),[10] or the installation ceremonies,[11] the Uttarāyaṇa[12] and the Dakṣiṇāyana Saṁkrāntis,[13] the Akṣayatritīyā festival[14] and so on. The gifts were as a rule absolute, and were to hold good "as long as the sun and moon endure." Resumption was expressly forbidden with dire imprecations, it being laid down that whoever took back land once given, or obstructed its enjoyment, "cannot be purified by a hundred horse-sacrifices, but lives in hell until the destruction of all beings."

The Brahmans are distinguished by their *Gotras* and *Pravaras* in inscriptions, which mention among the former : Kāsyapa, Kātyāyana, Bhāradvāja, Bandhula, Gobhila, Vatsa, Vasiṣṭha, Pārāvasa, Śarkarākṣa, Sāṇḍilya,

[1] See e.g., *J. A. S. B.*, V, (1922), p. 83.
[2] " " *Ind. Ant.*, XIV, p. 103.
[3] " " *Ep. Ind.*, XIV, pp. 194, 196.
[4] " " *Ibid.*, XIII, p. 219.
[5] " " *Ibid.*, XIV, pp. 198, 199.
[6] " " *Ibid.*, IV, p. 101.
[7] " " *Ibid.*, IV, p. 108.
[8] " " *Ibid.*, IV, p. 105.
[9] " " *Ibid.*, IV, p. 127.
[10] " " *Ind. Ant.*, XIII, pp. 131, 134.
[11] " " *Ep. Ind.*, IV, p. 121.
[12] " " *Ibid.*, VIII, p. 159.
[13] " " *Ind. Ant.*, XVIII, p. 35.
[14] " " *Ep. Ind.*, VII, pp. 98, 99.

Gautama, Kriṣṇātreya, Sāṁkritya, Kauśika, Kapisthala, Kauṇḍinya, Upamanyu, Parāsara, Bhārgava, Jīvantyāyana, Garga, Gārgya, Dhaumya, Sausravasa, Sāvarṇa, Kūtsa, Gālava, Sārkara, Dakṣa, Candrātreya, Jātukarṇa, Gauṇya, Pippalāda, Maunya, Harīta, Maudgalya, Darbha, Kaṇva, Agasti, Ātreya, etc.[1]

The *Pravaras* are enumerated as : Bandhula, Aghamarṣaṇa, Visvāmitra, Gobhila, Āngirasa, Ambarīṣa, Bhārgava, Cyāvana, Apnavāna, Aurva, Jāmadagna, Maudgalya, Bharmyāsva, Kāsypa, Āvatsara, Naidhruva, Bhāradvāja, Bārhaspatya, Kāṅkāyana, Kauśika, Dhaumya, Audalya, Devarāta, Gautama, Aitatha, Avitatha, etc.[2]

In some records we also find mention of such Brahmanic surnames as Miśra[3], Dvivedī or Dvivedin,[4] Tripāṭhī or Tripāṭhin,[5] Dīkṣita[6], Śarman[7], Avasthī,[8] Caturvedin[9] or Caturvaidya[10], and the title Paṇḍita, which shows that terms in modern use had at this time begun to come into vogue. In some inscriptions even

[1] See *Ep. Ind.*, VII, p. 99;
Ibid., V, pp. 118, 212-13;
Ibid., XIX, pp. 18-19;
Ibid., IV, pp. 101, 132, 133;
Ibid., VIII, p. 154;
Ibid., XVIII, pp. 12, 222;
Ibid., XIV, pp. 202-09.

[2] *Ep. Ind.*, IV, p. 101; *Ibid.*, p. 112; *Ibid.*, pp. 130, 133; *Ibid.*, VII, pp. 99-100; *Ibid.*, XVIII, pp. 12, 13, 17, 19, 222, 224; *Ind. Ant.*, XIV, p, 103, etc.

[3] *Ibid.*, XIV, p. 207.

[4] *Ibid.*, p. 205.

[5] *Ibid.*, p. 208.

[6] *Ibid.*, IV, p. 98.

[7] *Ibid.*, XVIII, p. 123.

[8] *Ibid.*, p. 226.

[9] *Ibid.*, XIV, p. 204.

[10] *Ibid.*, XIX, p. 54.

the terms Ṭhakkura and Rāuta[1] are applied for Brahmans, whereas in another record the title Prāṇācārya with Bhaṭṭa occurs.[2]

The Brahmans are further described as practising Yoga[3] and pursuing the study of the Vedas, of which the inscriptions mention all the four, viz., the Rigveda, Yajurveda, Sāmaveda and the Atharvaveda. Among the vedic *Śākhas* they specially refer to the Āśvalāyana,[4] Vājasneya,[5] Chāndogya,[6] and the Sānkhyāyana-Bahvrica.[7] According to Alberuni, who wrote his *Tahkīk-i-Hind* in 1030 A. D., the Brahmans learnt the Vedas by heart, and many could recite them without difficulty, although their contents were understood by a few only.[8] The Brahmans also studied such works as the 18 Purāṇas, Smritis composed by "twenty sons of *Brahman*," philosophical treatises on the Sāṁkhya, Nyāya, Vaiśeṣika Mīmāṅsā etc., the Epics, and those dealing with the exact sciences like Grammar, metrics, Astronomy, Astrology, Mathematics, and medicine etc.[9] These texts were written down in the current alphabet of the times, about which Alberuni remarks : "The most generally known alphabet is called *Siddha Mātrikā*, used in Kashmir and Vārāṇasī. These are the high schools of Hindu sciences. The same writing is used in *Madhyadeśa*, the country all around Kanauj, also called Āryāvarta."[10] But in spite of the widespread knowledge of the art of writing, the Brahmans preferred to trust their trained

[1] *Ind. Ant.*, XV, pp. 8, 10, 12, 13, etc.
[2] *Ep. Ind.*, VIII, p. 154.
[3] *Ind. Ant.*, XVI, pp. 174, 175.
[4] *Ep. Ind.*, V, pp. 212, 213.
[5] *Ibid.*, XIX, pp. 18, 19.
[6] *Ind. Ant.*, XVIII, pp. 12, 13; *Ep. Ind.*, V, pp. 117-18.
[7] *Ind. Ant.*, XIV, p. 103; *Ep. Ind.*, VIII, p. 154.
[8] Sachau, *Alberuni's India*, Vol. I, p. 125.
[9] *Ibid.*, I, pp. 130-59.
[10] *Ibid.* I, p. 173.

memories for the preservation of the Veda, and Alberuni explains their attitude thus : "They do not allow the Veda to be committed to writing because it is recited according to certain modulations, and they therefore avoid the use of the pen, since it is liable to cause some error, and may occasion an addition or a defect in the written text."[1] Besides this, the Brahmans did not want any encroachment upon their monopoly by extending to the bulk of the population the privilege of knowing the "sacred word." This is evident from the following general observation of Alberuni : "The Brahmans teach the Veda to the Kṣatriyas. The latter learn it, but are not allowed to teach it, not even to a Brahman. The Vaiśya and Śūdra are not allowed to hear it, much less to pronounce and recite it. If such a thing can be proved against one of them, the Brahmans drag him before the magistrate, and he is punished by having his tongue cut off."[2] Such unmeaning laws must have engendered a spirit of tyranny and exclusiveness among the higher castes, and crushed the enthusiasm of the masses for the existing order of things. It is no wonder, therefore, that the hardy races of the north-west, fired as they were by a new message of equality and brotherhood, scored an easy triumph against a power that countenanced invidious distinctions between man and man.

[1] Sachau *Alberuni's India*, Vol. I, pp.125-26
[2] *Ibid.*, I, p. 125; see also Vol. II, p. 136.

APPENDIX A

List of the Pratīhāra inscriptions of Kanauj

Serial No.	Inscription	Date in Indian Era	A. D.	References
		Nāgabhaṭa II		
1	Buckalā (Bilar district, Jodhpur) stone inscription.	V. E. 872	815	*Ep. Ind.*, IX pp. 198-200; also noticed in *J. R. A. S.*, 1907, p. 1011.
		Bhojadeva I		
2	Barah copper plate inscription.	V. E. 893	836	*Ep. Ind.*, XIX, pp. 15-19.
3	Daulatpura (Jodhpur) copper plate inscription.	V. E. 900	843	*Ep. Ind.*, V, pp. 208-13; for controversy about the date see *J. B. B. R. A. S.*, XXI, p. 410f; *J. R. A. S.*, 1904, p. 641; *Ep. Ind.*, VIII. Appendix, p. 1.
4	Deogaḍh (Lalitpur, Jhansi) stone inscription.	V. E. 919	862	*Ep. Ind.*, IV, pp. 309-10; *Arch. Surv. Ind. Rep.*, X, p. 101.
5	Vaillabhaṭṭasvāmin (Gwalior) temple stone inscription.	V. E. 932	875	*Ep. Ind.*, I, pp. 154-162.

Serial No.	Inscription	Date in Indian Era	A. D.	References
6	Vaillabhaṭṭasvāmin (Gwalior) temple stone inscription.	V. E. 933	876	*Ep. Ind.*, I, 154-162.
7	Pehoa (Karnal district) stone inscription.	Harṣa Era, 276	882	*Ep. Ind.*, I, pp. 184-90.
8	Gwalior (Sāgar-Tal) stone inscription.			*Ep. Ind.*, XVIII, pp. 99-114; *Ann. Rep. Arch. Surv. Ind.*, 1903-04, pp. 277-85.
9	Ahar (Bulandshahr district) stone inscription.	H. E. 259 (It gives other dates also)	865	*Ep. Ind.*, XIX, pp. 52-62; *Journal of the U. P. Historical Society*, Vol. III, pt. II, (September, 1926), pp. 82-119; also noticed in *Ann. Rep. Arch. Surv. Ind.*, 1923-24, p. 97.
10	Pāṇḍava-kā-kilā (Delhi) stone inscription.			*Ann. Rep. Rajputana Museum*, 1923-24, p. 3.
11	Barton Museum (Bhavnagar) fragmentary stone inscription.			*Ep. Ind.*, XIX, pp. 174-77.
		Mahendrapāla I		
12	Unā (Junāgaḍh State, Kāthiāwāḍ) copper plate inscription, No. I.	Valabhi Era 574	893	*Ep. Ind.*, IX, pp. 1-6.

Serial No.	Inscription	Date in Indian Era	A. D.	References
		Mahendrapāla I		
13	Dighwā-Dubaulī (Saran district, Bihar) copper plate inscription.	V. E. 955	898	*Ind. Ant.*, XV, pp. 105-13; first mentioned in *J. A. S. B.*, XXXIII, p. 321 f.
14	Unā copper plate inscription No. II.	V. E. 956	899	*Ep Ind.*, IX, pp. 6-10.
15	Siyadoni (Gwalior) stone inscription.	V. E. 960	903	*Ep Ind.*, I, pp. 162. 179; first mentioned in *J. A. S. B.*, XXXI, pp. 6-7.
16	Siyadoni (Gwalior) stone inscription.	V. E. 964	907	*Ep. Ind.*, I, pp. 162-179.
17	Pehoa (Karnal district) stone inscription.			*Ep. Ind.*, I, pp. 242-50.
18	British Museum stone inscription.	Regnal year 2		Mentioned in Kielhorn's list, *Ep. Ind.*, V, Appendix, p. 47, note 5.
19	British Museum stone inscription.	Regnal year 6		Mentioned in Kielhorn's list, *Ep. Ind.*, V, Appendix, p. 47, note 5.
20	Paharpur (North Bengal) stone pillar inscription.	Regnal year 5		Noticed in *Ann. Rep. Arch. Surv. Ind.*, 1925-26, p. 141.

Serial No.	Inscription	Date in Indian Era	A. D.	References
21	Itkhori stone image inscription.			*Ann. Rep. Arch. Surv. Ind.*, 1920-21, p. 35.
22	Ramgayā stone inscription.	Regnal year 8		*Mem. As. Soc. Beng.*, Vol. V, No. 3, p. 64; referred to in *Arch. Surv. Ind. Rep.*, III, p. 123; XV, p. 154; *Ind. Ant.*, 1918, pp. 109-11.
23	Guneriya stone inscription.	Regnal year 9		*Arch. Surv. Ind. Rep.*, III, p. 124; *Mem. As. Soc. Beng.*, Vol. V, No. 3, p. 64; *Ind. Ant.*, 1918, p. 110.
		Mahīpāla		
24	Haddalā (eastern Kāthiāwāḍ) copper plate inscription.	Śaka Era 836	914	*Ind. Ant.*, XII, pp. 190-95; *Ind. Ant.*, XVIII, p. 90.
25	Asni (Fatehpur district, U. P.) stone inscription.	V. E. 974	917	*Ind. Ant.*, XVI, pp. 173-75.
26	Bengal Asiatic Society's copper plate.	V. E. 988	931	*Ind. Ant.*, XV, pp. 138-41; first noticed in *J. A. S. B.*, XVII (1848), p. 70f; see also *Ibid.*, XXXI (1862), p. 1f; *J. B. B. R. A. S.*, XXI, p. 405f.

Serial No.	Inscription	Date in Indian Era	A. D.	References
27	Rakhetra (Gwalior) stone inscription.	V. E. 999 and 1000	942 -43	*Ann. Rep. Arch. Surv. Ind.* 1924-25, p. 168.
		Mahendrapāla II		
28	Partabgarh (southern Rajputana) stone inscription.	V. E. 1003	946	*Ep. Ind.*, XIV, pp. 176-188.
		Devapāla		
29	Siyadoni (Gwalior) stone inscription.	V. E. 1005	948	*Ep. Ind.*, I, pp. 162-79.
		Vijayapāla		
30	Rajorgarh (Alwar State) stone inscription.	V. E. 1016	959	*Ep. Ind.*, III, pp. 263-67; first faulty edition in *Proc. As. Soc. Beng.*, 1879, p. 157f.
		Trilocanapāla		
31	Jhusi (ancient Pratiṣṭhāna, opposite Allahabad) copper plate inscription.	V. E. 1084	1027	*Ind. Ant.*, XVIII, pp. 33-35.
		Yaśaḥpāla		
32	Karā (Allahabad district) stone inscription.	V. E. 1093	1036	*J. R. A. S.*, 1927, pp. 692-95; noticed in *As. Res.*, IX, pp. 440-41; *Ann. Rep. Arch. Surv. Ind.*, 1923-24, pp. 122-24; Colebrooke, *Essays*, II, pp. 245-46.

Some inscriptions of other dynasties throwing light on the Pratīhāra history

Serial No.	Inscription and name of king	Date in Indian Era	A. D.	References
1	Khajurāho stone inscription No. 1 of Harṣadeva.			*Ep. Ind.*, I, pp. 121-22.
2	Khajurāho stone inscription No. II of Dhanga.	V. E. 1011	954	*Ep. Ind.*, I, pp. 122-35.
3	Sāsbahū temple inscription of Mahīpāla.	V. E. 1150	1093	*Ind. Ant.*, XV, pp. 33-46.
4	Dubkuṇḍ stone inscription of Kacchapaghāta Vikramasiṁha.	V. E. 1145	1088	*Ep. Ind.*, II, pp. 232-40.
5	Bilhari stone inscription of Yuvarājadeva.			*Ep. Ind.*, I, pp. 251-70.
6	Benares copper plate inscription of Karṇadeva.			*Ep. Ind.*, II, pp. 297-310.
7	Kahla copper plate inscription of Soḍhadeva.	V. E. 1134	1031	*Ep. Ind.*, VII, pp. 85-93.
8	Cāṭsū inscription of Bālāditya.			*Ep. Ind.*, XII, pp. 10-17.
9	Harṣa stone inscription of Vigraharāja.	V. E. 1030	973	*Ep. Ind.*, II, pp. 116-30.

Serial No.	Inscription and name of king	Date in Indian Era	A. D.	References
10	Khalimpur copper plate of Dharmapāla.	Regnal year 32		*Ep. Ind.*, IV, pp. 243-54.
11	Monghyr copper plate inscription of Devapāla.	Regnal year 33		*Ep. Ind.*, XVIII, pp. 304-07.
12	Bhagalpur copper plate inscription of Nārāyaṇapāla.	Regnal year 17		*Ind. Ant.*, XV, pp. 304-10.
13	Badal pillar inscription of Guravamiśra, minister of Nārāyaṇapāla.			*Ep. Ind.*, II, pp. 160-67; also see *As. Res.*, I, pp. 131-44; *J. A. S. B.*, XLIII, pt. I, pp. 356-63.
14	Baragaon pillar inscription of Rājyapāla.	Regnal year 24		*Ind. Ant.*, 1917, p. 111.
15	Baragaon or Nalanda stone-image inscription of Gopāla II.	Regnal year 1		*J. A. S. B.*, 1908, N. S. Vol. IV, pp. 105-06.
16	Bodhgayā inscription of Gopāla II.			*Ibid.*, pp. 102-05; *Ibid.*, Vol. V (1909), pp. 103-04.
17	Wani copper plate inscription of Govinda III.	Śaka Era 730	808	*Ind. Ant.*, XI, pp. 156-163.
18	Radhanpur copper plates of Govinda III.	Śaka Era 730	808	*Ep. Ind.*, VI, pp. 239-51.

Serial No.	Inscription and name of king	Date in Indian Era	A. D.	References
19	Pathari pillar inscription of Parabala.	V. E. 917	860	*Ep. Ind.*, IX, pp. 248-56; *Ind. Ant.*, 1911, pp. 239-40.
20	Baroda copper plate inscription of Karkarāja.	Śaka Era 734	812	*Ind. Ant.*, XII, pp. 156-65.
21	Bagumra copper plate inscription of Dhruvarāja.	Śaka 789	867	*Ind. Ant.*, XII, pp. 179-90.
22	Nilguṇḍ inscription of Amoghavarṣa.	„ 788	866	*Ep. Ind.* VI, pp. 98-108.
23	Sanjan copper plates of Amoghavarṣa	„ 793	871	*Ep. Ind.*, XVIII, pp, 235-57; *J. B. B. R. A. S.*, XXII, p. 116f.
24	Cambay copper plate inscription of Govinda IV.	„ 852	930	*Ep. Ind.*, VII, pp. 26-47.
25	Karhaḍ copper plates of Kriṣṇa III.	„ 880	959	*Ep. Ind.*, IV, p. 278f.
26	Ghatiyala stone inscription of Kakkuka.	V. E. 918	859	*J. R. A. S.*, 1895, pp. 513-21; *Prog. Rep. Arch. Surv. West Ind.*, 1906-07, p. 30, para 17; p. 34, para 29.
27	Jodhpur stone inscription of Bāuka.	V. E. 894	837	*J. R. A. S.*, 1894, pp. 1-9; *Ep. Ind.*, XVIII pp. 87-99.

APPENDIX B

Inscriptions of the Gāhaḍavāla dynasty

Serial No.	Inscription	Date in Vikrama Era	A. D.	References
		Candradeva		
1	Candravati—Benares district—(now Lucknow Museum) copper plate inscription.	1148	1090-91	*Ep. Ind.*, IX, pp. 302-05.
2	Candravati (now Lucknow Museum) copper plate inscription.	1150	1093	*Ep. Ind.*, XIV, pp. 193-96.
3	Bengal Asiatic Society's copper plate of Candradeva and Madanapāla.	1154	1097	*Ind. Ant.*, XVIII, pp. 9-14; *J. A. S. B.*, XXVII, pp. 220-41.
4	Candravati (now Lucknow Museum) copper plate inscription.	1156	1099	*Ep. Ind.*, XIV, pp. 197-209.
		Mandanapāla		
5	Basahi (Etawah district, U. P.) copper plate grant of Yuvarāja Govindacandra.	1161	1104	*Ind. Ant.*, XIV, pp. 101-04; *J. A. S. B.*, XLII, pp. 314-21.

Serial No.	Inscription	Date in Vikrama Era	A. D.	References
6	Kamauli—Benares district — (now Lucknow Museum) copper plate grant.	1162	1105	*Ep. Ind.*, II, pp. 358-61.
7	Copper plate grant of Madanapāla and his queen Prithvīśrīkā.	1164	1107	*J. R. A. S.*, 1896, pp. 787-88.
8	Rāhan (now Beng. As. Soc.) copper plate of Madanapāla and Govindacandra.	1166	1109	*Ind. Ant.*, XVIII, pp. 14-19; *Proc. As. Soc. Beng.*, Vol. XLV (1876), pt. I, pp. 131-35.
		Govindacandra		
9	Kamauli (now Luck. Mus.) C. P.	1171	1114	*Ep. Ind.*, IV, pp. 101-03.
10	Bhadaini Temple —Benares—(now Luck. Mus.) C. P.	,,	,,	Ep. Ind. VIII, pp. 152-53.
11	Pali—Gorakhpur district—(now Luck. Mus.) C. P.	,,	,,	Noticed in *Ep. Ind.*, V, p. 114, note 4; see also *Ibid.*, VII, pp. 98-99.
12	Kamauli (now Luck. Mus.) C. P.	1172	1115-16	*Ep. Ind.*, IV, pp. 103-04.
13	Basahi (now Luck. Mus.) C. P.	1174	1117	*Ind. Ant.*, XVIII, pp. 19-20; *J. A. S. B.*, XLII, pt. I, pp. 324-28.

Serial No.	Inscription	Date in Vikrama Era	A. D.	References
14	Kamauli (now Luck. Mus.) C. P.	,,	,,	*Ep. Ind.*, IV, pp. 104-06.
15	Kamauli (now Luck. Mus.) C. P.	1175	1118	*Ep. Ind.*, IV, pp. 106-07.
16	Kamauli copper plate inscription of Govindacandra and queen Nayanakelidevī.	1176	1119	*Ep. Ind.*, IV, pp. 107-09.
17	Kamauli copper plate inscription of Govindacandra.	,,	,,	*Ep. Ind.*, IV, p. 109.
18	Don Buzurg (Gorakhpur district) copper plates.	,,	,,	*Ep. Ind.*, XVIII, pp. 218-23.
19	Chattarpur (Cawnpore district) copper plates.	1177	1120	*Ep. Ind.*, XVIII, pp. 224-26.
20	Bengal Asiatic Society's copper plate grant sanctioning transfer of land previously given by Kālacuri Yaśaḥ-Karṇa.	,,	,,	*J. A. S. B.*, XXXI, pp. 123-24.
21	Lucknow Museum copper plate.	1177	1120	Unpublished. See *Ann. Rep. Arch. Surv. Ind.*, 1921-22, p. 115.

Serial No.	Inscription	Date in Vikrama Era	A. D.	References
22	Kamauli (now Luck. Mus.) C. P.	1178	1121-22	*Ep. Ind.*, IV, pp. 109-11.
23	Benares (now Luck. Mus.) C. P.	1181	1124	*J. A. S. B.*, LVI, pt. I, pp. 114-19.
24	Kamauli (now Luck. Mus.) C. P.	1182	1125-26	*Ep. Ind.*, IV, pp. 99-101.
25	Beng. As. Society's C. P.	"	"	*J. A. S. B.*, XXVII, 242-50.
26	Maner (Dinapore, Patna district) copper plate inscription	"	"	*J. B. O. R. S.*, 1916, pp. 41-47; *J. A. S. B.*, 1922, pp. 81-84.
27	Kamauli (now Luck. Mus.) C. P.	1184	1127	*Ep. Ind.*, IV, p. 111.
28	Bhadavana copper plate inscription.	1184	1127	*Ep. Ind.*, XIX, pp. 291-94.
29	Benares (now Beng. As. Soc.) C. P.	1185	1128-29	*J. A. S. B.*, LVI, pt. I, pp. 119-23.
30	Itaunja (now Luck. Mus.) C. P.	1186	1129	*Ep. Ind.*, XIII, pp. 295-97.
31	Saheṭ Maheṭh–Gonda district—(now Luck. Mus.) C. P.	1186	1129	*Ep. Ind.*, XI, pp. 20-26.
32	Benares (now Luck. Mus.) C. P.	1187	1130	*Ep. Ind.*, VIII, pp. 153-54.

Serial No.	Inscription	Date in Vikrama Era	A. D.	References
33	Raiwan—Sitapur district—(now Luck. Mus.) C. P.	1187	1130	*J. A. S. B.*, LVI, pt. I, pp. 106-13; see also *Ind. Ant.*, XVIII, p. 56f.
34	Ren—Fatehpur district—(now Luck. Mus.) C. P.	1188	1131	*Ind. Ant.*, XIX, pp. 249-52.
35	Pali (now Luck. Mus.) C. P.	1189	1132	*Ep. Ind.*, V, pp. 113-15.
36	Kamauli (now Luck. Mus.) C. P.	1190	1133	*Ep. Ind.*, IV, pp. 111-12.
37	Benares copper plate grant of Govindacandra and Yuvarāja Āṣphoṭacandra.	1190	1133	*Ep. Ind.*, VIII, pp. 155-56.
38	Kamauli (now Luck. Mus.) copper plate inscription of Singara Vatsarāja and Govindacandra.	1191	1134	*Ep. Ind.*, IV, pp. 130-33.
39	Kamauli (now Luck. Mus.) C. P.	1196	1139	*Ep. Ind.*, II, pp. 361-63.
40	,, ,, ,,	1197	1140	*Ep. Ind.*, IV, p. 114.
41	Kamauli (now Luck. Mus.) C. P.	1198	1141	*Ep. Ind.*, IV, pp. 113-14.

Serial No.	Inscription	Date in Vikrama Era	A. D.	References
42	Gagaha—Gorakhpur district—(now British Museum) copper plates.	1199	1142	*Ep. Ind.*, XIII, 216-20; *Ind. Ant.*, XVIII, pp. 20-21; *Arch. Surv. Ind. Rep.*, XXII, p. 59f.
43	Kamauli (now Luck. Mus.) copper plate inscription.	1200	1143	*Ep. Ind.*, IV, pp. 114-15.
44	Machlisahr—Jaunpur district—(now Luck. Mus.) copper plate inscription.	1201	1144	*Ep. Ind.*, V, pp. 115-16.
45	Lār—Gorakhpur district—(now Luck. Mus.) copper plates.	1202	1145	*Ep. Ind.*, VII, pp. 98-100.
46	Bhadaini temple—Benares—copper plate of Govindacandra and Mahārājaputra Rājyapāladeva.	1203	1146	*Ep. Ind.*, VIII, pp. 156-58.
47	Benares copper plate grant.	1207	1150-51	*Ep. Ind.*, VIII, pp. 158-59.
48	Hathiya—ḍah (midway between Azamgarh and Benares) pillar inscription.	1207	1150-51	*Arch. Surv. Ind. Rep.*, Vol. I, pp. 95-96; *Ind. Ant.*, XX, p. 131, n. 18.

Serial No.	Inscription	Date in Vikrama Era	A. D.	References
49	Bangavan (Bara-Banki district) copper plate inscription of Govinda-candra and Queen Gosalladevī.	1208	1151	*Ep. Ind.*, V, pp. 116-18.
50	Kamauli (now Luck. Mus.) copper plate inscription.	1211	1154	*Ep. Ind.*, IV, pp. 116-17.
51	Sarnath (Benares district) stone inscription of queen Kumāradevī.	Undated		*Ep. Ind.*, IX, pp. 319-28.
	Vijayacandra			
52	Kamauli (now Luck. Mus.) copper plate inscription of Vijayacandra and Yuvarāja Jayacandra.	1224	1167	*Ep. Ind.*, IV, pp. 117-20.
53	Jaunpur stone pillar inscription.	1225	1168-69	*Arch. Surv. Ind. Rep.*, XI, p. 123; see also *Ep. Ind.*, V, Appendix, p. 22, No. 150.
54	Royal Asiatic Society's copper plate inscription of Vijayacandra and Yuvarāja Jayacandra.	"	"	*Ind. Ant.*, XV, pp. 7-13.

Serial No.	Inscription	Date in Vikrama Era	A. D.	References
55	Tārācaṇḍī (Shahabad district, South Bihar) Rock inscription of Mahānāyaka Pratāpadhavala, mentioning Vijayacandra.	1225	1168-69	*Jour. Am. Or. Soc.*, VI, pp. 547-49; first noticed in *Miscellaneous Essays*, Vol. III (1873), p. 256; see also *Ep. Ind.*, V, Appendix p. 22, No. 153.
		Jayacandra		
56	Kamauli (now Luck. Mus.) C. P.	1226	1170	*Ep. Ind.*, IV, pp. 120-21.
57	Kamauli (now Luck. Mus.) C. P.	1228	1171	*Ep. Ind.*, IV, pp. 121-23.
58	Kamauli (now Luck. Mus.) C. P.	1230	1173	*Ep. Ind.*, IV, pp. 123-24.
59	Kamauli (now Luck. Mus.) C. P.	1231	1174	*Ep. Ind.*, IV, pp. 124-26.
		Post script		
		1235	1178	
60	Kamauli (now Luck. Mus.) C. P.	1232	1175	*Ep. Ind.*, IV, pp. 126-28.
61	Sihvar—Benares district—(now Luck. Mus.) copper plate inscription.	1232	1175	*Ind. Ant.*, XVIII, pp. 129-34.
62	Kamauli (now Luck. Mus.) C. P.	1233	1176	*Ep. Ind.*, IV, pp. 128-29.

Serial No.	Inscription	Date in Vikrama Era	A. D.	References
63	Benares (now Beng. As. Soc.) C. P.	1233	1276	*Ind. Ant.*, XVIII, pp. 134-36.
64	Benares (now Beng. As. Soc.) C. P.	,,	,,	*Ind. Ant.*, XVIII, pp. 134-36.
65	Benares (now Beng. As. Soc.) C. P.	1234	1177	*Ibid.*, pp. 137-39.
66	Benares (now Beng. As. Soc.) C. P.	1236	1179	*Ibid.*, pp. 139-40.
67	Benares (now Beng. As. Soc.) C. P.	,,	,,	*Ibid.*, pp. 140-42.
68	,, ,,	,,	,,	*Ibid.*, pp. 142-43.
69	Fyzabad (Oudh) C. P.	1243	1186	*Ind. Ant.*, XV, pp. 10-13; *J. A. S. B.*, X, pt. I (1841), pp. 98-104.
70	Meohād (Allahabad district) C. P.	1245	1189	*J. R. A. S.*, Oct. 1927, pp. 695-96; noticed in *Arch. Surv. Ind. Rep.*, 1921-22, p. 120.
71	Bodhgayā stone inscription.	124(?)		*Proc. Beng. As. Soc.*, 1880, pp. 76-80; *Ind. Hist. Quart.*, 1929, pp. 14-30; see also *Ep. Ind.*, V, Appendix, p. 26, No. 177.

Serial No.	Inscription	Date in Vikrama Era	A. D.	References
		Hariścandra		
72	Machlīsahr—Jaunpur district—(now Luck. Mus.) copper plate inscription.	1253	1196-97	*Ep. Ind.*, X, pp. 93-100; see also *J. A. S. B.*, 1911, p. 762.
73	Belkhara (Mirzapur district) stone inscription. (Name of the king is omitted).	1253	1196-97	*J. A. S. B.*, 1911, pp. 763-65; *Arch. Surv. Ind.*, *Rep.*, XI, pp. 128-30.

APPENDIX C

Table of Maukhari Genealogy

Serial No.	Name of King	Relation to Predecessor	Titles	Name of queen	Titles of queens	Remarks
1	Harivarman.	Founder of the line.	Mahārāja (Asirgadh seal), Jvālāmukha (Haraha Ins.), Avanibhuja (Ibid.)	Jayasvāminī	Bhaṭṭārikādevī.	Began to rule about the close of the fifth century A. D.
2	Ādityavarman.	Son of 1.	Mahārāja (Asirgadh seal), Nṛipati (Haraha Ins.)	Harṣaguptā	,,	Probably he was a contemporary of the Later Gupta king Harṣagupta.
3	Īśvaravarman.	Son of 2.	Mahārāja (Asirgadh seal), Nṛipati (Jaunpur Ins.), Kṣitipati (Haraha Ins.)	Upaguptā	,,	
4	Īśānavarman.	Son of 3.	Mahārājādhirāja (Asirgadh seal), Avanipati	Lakṣmīvatī	Bhaṭṭārikā Mahādevī.	Fought against the Later Gupta ruler Kumāragupta. Ac-

			(coins), Nṛipa.			cording to the Haraha Inscription one of the known dates of Īśānavarman is 554 A. D.
5	Sarvavarman.	Son of 4.	Mahārājādhirāja (Asirgadh seal), Parameśvara (Deo-Baranark Ins.)	...	...	Defeated the Later Gupta king Dāmodaragupta.
6	Avantivarman.	Relation uncertain. Presumably son of 5.	Parameśvara (Deo-Baranark Ins.), Avanipati (coins)	...	...	
7	Grahavarman.	Son of 6.	...	Rājyaśrī	...	Formed matrimonial alliance with the Vardhanas of Thanesvar. Subsequently he fell a victim to the machinations of Devagupta of Malwa and Śaśāṅka of Gauḍa.

APPENDIX D

GENEALOGY OF HARṢAVARDHANA

(*Note*—The predecessors of Harṣa had their capital in Thanesvar and not in Kanauj)

Serial No.	Name of king	Titles	Name of queen	Religion	Remarks
1	Puṣyabhūti or Puṣpabhūti			Śaiva	Remote ancestor of Harṣa according to Bāṇa's *Harṣacarita.*
2	Naravardhana	Mahārāja	Vajriṇīdevī		Kings upto No. 6 ruled in Thanesvar only.
3	Rājyavardhana (son of 2)	„	Apsarādevī	Paramādit-yabhakta	Called the first, as there was another king of the same name in the dynasty.
4	Ādityavardhana (son of 3)	„	Mahāsenaguptā-devī	„	His wife was perhaps a sister of the Later Gupta monarch Mahāsenagupta.

5	Prabhākaravardhana (son of 4)	Parama-bhaṭṭāraka, Mahārājādhirāja	Yaśovatī or Yaśomatī.	„	He was the first to bring the family into prominence.
6	Rājyavardhana II (eldest son of 5)	„		Parama Saugata	Sat on the throne for a very short time.
7	Harṣavardhana (son of 5 and younger brother of 6)	„	Durgā (?)	Paramamāheśvara; subsequently he inclined towards Buddhism with a curious coating of eclecticism	Transferred his capital from Thanesvar to Kanauj after the murder of his sister Rājyaśrī's Maukhari husband Grahavarman. Harṣa ruled from 606 to 647 A. D.

APPENDIX E

LINE OF YAŚOVARMAN

Yaśovarman
(*c.* 725—752 A. D.)
|
Āma
|
Dunduka
|
Bhoja

THE ĀYUDHAS

Vajrāyudha
(ascended the throne in *circa* 770 A.D.)
|
Indrāyudha
(according to the Jain *Harivaṁśa* he is known to have been ruling in the year 783—84 A. D.)
|
Cakrāyudha
(defeated and dethroned by Nāgabhaṭa Pratīhāra)

APPENDIX F

Pratīhāra kings of Kanauj

Serial No.	Name of King	Relationship	Titles	Name of queen	Religion	Known dates	Approximate date of accession
1	Nāgabhaṭa or Nāgāvaloka.	Son of Vatsarāja.	Mahārāja, Mahārājādhirāja, Paramabhaṭṭāraka, Parameśvara.	Iṣṭādevī.	Devotee of the goddess Bhagavatī.	815, 833 (*Prabhāvakacarita*)	805 A. D. conquered Kanauj about the year 810.
2	Rāma, Rāmabhadra or Rāmadeva.	Son of 1.	,,	Appādevi.	Devotee of the Sun-god.	...	A.D. 833
3	Mihira, Bhoja I, Prabhāśa, Ādivarāha.	Son of 2.	,,	Candrabhaṭṭārikādevī.	Devotee of the goddess Bhagavatī. The Ādivarāha type of coins show that he had Vaiṣṇava predilections also.	836, 843, 862, 864-65, 865-66, 867-68 (Ahar Ins.) 875, 876, 882 A. D.	836 A. D.

Serial No.	Name of King	Relationship	Titles	Name of queen	Religion	Known dates	Approximate date of accessions
4	Mahendrapāla I, Mahendrāyudha, Mahiṣapāla, Nirbhayarāja, Nirbhayanarendra	Son of 3.	,, also Bhāka.	(*a*) Dehanāgādevī. (*b*) Mahīdevīdevī.	,, ,,	893, 898, 899, 903, 904-05 (Ahar Ins.) 907	885 A. D.
5	Bhoja II	Son of 4 by Queen No. A.			Vaiṣṇava		910 A. D.
6	Mahīpāla, Kṣitipāla, Vināyakapāla I, Heraṁbapāla	Son of 4, and half-brother of 5.	,, Rājādhirāja (Haddalā grant)	Prasādhanādevī.	Devotee of the Sun-god	914, 917, 931, 942	912
7	Mahendrapāla II	Son of 6	,,		Devotee of the god Maheśa or Śiva	946	944

8	Devapāla.	Son of 6.	Hayapati (Khajurāho Ins.)		Perhaps a devotee of Viṣṇu	948	947
9	Vināyakapāla II.					954	953
10	Vijayapāla.		Parama-bhaṭṭāraka, Mahārājādhirāja, Parameśvara			959	957
11	Rājyapāla.	Son of 10.	"			1018,1019	988
12	Trilocanapāla.	Son of 11.	"			1019,1027	1019
13	Yaśaḥpāla.	Not known				1036	1035. After this date follows a period of confusion

APPENDIX G

Gāhaḍavāla kings of Kanauj

Serial No.	Name of king	Relation to predecessor	Titles	Name of queen	Religion	Known dates A. D.	Approximate date of accession	Remarks
1	Candra, Candradeva or Candrādityadeva.	First Gāhaḍavāla ruler of Kanauj.	Parama-bhaṭṭāraka, Mahārājādhirāja, Parameśvara.		Parama-māheśvara	1091, 1093, 1097, 1099.	c. 1085	His father and grandfather were respectively named Mahīcandra (Mahiala or Mahītala) and Yaśovigraha, but their seat of power is not definitely known.
2	Madanapāla, Madanacandra, Madanadeva.	Son of 1.	"	Prithvīśrīkā, Rālhadevī or	"	1104, 1105, 1107, 1109.	c. 1100	He does not appear to have taken an active part in the ad-

				Rālhaṇa-devī.				ministration, and the known grants of his time were made either by the crown-prince or by the queen.
3	Govinda-candra.	Son of 2.	Parama-bhaṭṭāraka, Mahārājādhirāja, Parameśvara, Aśvapati, Gajapati, Narapati, Rājatrayādhipati, Vividha-vidyā-vicāra-vācaspati.	Nayana-kelidevī, Gosala-devī, Kumāra-devī, Vasanta-devī.	,,	1114, 1115, 1117, 1118, 1120, 1122, 1124, 1125, 1126, 1127, 1128, 1129, 1130, 1131, 1132, 1133, 1134, 1139, 1140, 1141, 1142, 1143, 1144, 1145, 1146, 1150, 1151, 1154.	*c.* 1110	Besides Vijaya-candra, he had two other sons, viz., Yuvarāja Āsphoṭa-Candra and Rāja-putra Rājya-pāla, but they did not ascend the throne.
4	Vijayacandra Vijayapāla (*Rāso*) Malla-deva (*Rambhāmañ-jarī*).	Son of 3.	,,	Candra-lekhā (*Ram-bhāmañjarī*).	,,	1167, 1168.	*c.* 1156	During his time the struggle with the Cau-hans began.
5	Jayacandra, Jayaccandra, Jayantacandra,	Son of 4.	,,	Śubhādevī (*Puruṣa-parīkṣā*).	,, He was also ini-tiated as a de-	1170, 1171, 1173, 1174, 1175, 1176, 1177, 1178, 1179,	1170	He suffered a defeat at the hands of Sihā-

Serial No.	Name of king	Relation to predecessor	Titles	Name of queen	Religion	Known dates A. D.	Approximate date of accession	Remarks
	Jaitracandra, (also sometimes known as Pangu or Dal Pangula).				votee of Krisṇa and he extended his patronage to Buddhistsas well. The Gāhaḍavāla rulers were generally tolerant to the different systems of beliefs.	1186, 1189.		buddin Ghori.
6	Hariścandra.	Son of 5.	”		Paramamāheśvara.	1196, 1197.	1194	He is the last known ruler of the dynasty. The kingdom was afterwards annexed by the Moslems.

BIBLIOGRAPHY

Original works

Brāhmaṇas

Aitareya Brāhmaṇa, *ed. by* Th. Aufrecht. Bonn, 1879.

Pañcaviṁśa Brāhmaṇa, *ed. by* Vedāntavāgīśa. Calcutta, 1869-74.

Epics

Vālmīki Rāmāyaṇa, *ed. by* Hemacandra Bhaṭṭācārya. Calcutta, 1869-84.

Vālmīki Rāmāyaṇa, *ed. by* P. C. Roy. Calcutta, 1881-82.

Vālmīki Rāmāyaṇa, (North-Western Recension), *ed. by* Bhagvad Datta. Lahore, 1931.

Mahābhārata, *ed. by* P. C. Roy. Calcutta, 1882.

Śrīmanmahābhāratam (based on South Indian texts), *ed. by* Kriṣṇācārya. Bombay, 1906.

Mahābhārata, English Translation *by* P. C. Roy. Calcutta, 1883-96.

Works based on the Epics.

Rājaśekhara's Bāla-Rāmāyaṇa, *ed. by* Govindadeva Śāstrī. Benares, 1869.

Pracaṇḍapāṇḍava or Bālabhārata, *ed. by* Carl Cappeller. Strassburg, 1885.

Pracaṇḍapāṇḍava or Bālabhārata, *ed. by* Durgā Prasāda and Parab. Bombay, 1887.

Purāṇas.

Brahma Purāṇa, *ed. by* H. N. Āpte. Poona, 1895.

Agni Purāṇa, *ed. by* Rājendra Lal Mitra. Calcutta, 1873-79.

Matsya Purāṇa, *ed. by* Āpte (Ānandaśrama Sanskrit Series). Poona, 1907.

Vāyu Purāṇa, *ed. by* H. N. Āpte (Ānandāśrama Sanskrit Series). Poona, 1905.

Viṣṇu Purāṇa, *ed. by* Jīvānanda Vidyāsāgara. Calcutta, 1882.

Viṣṇu Purāṇa, *ed.* and translated into English *by* H. H. Wilson.

Śiva Purāṇa Calcutta, 1890.

Bhāgavata Purāṇa

Brahmāṇḍa Purāṇa

Padma Purāṇa

Harivaṁśa.

Lexicons.

Keśava's Kalpadrukoṣa, Gaekwaḍ's Oriental Series, XLII, 1928.

Śabdārtharatnasamanvayakoṣa, Gaekwaḍ's Oriental Series, 1932.

Yādavaprakāśa's Vaijayanti, *ed. by* Gustav Oppert, 1893.

Hemacandra's Abhidhāna-cintāmaṇi, *ed. by* Boehtlingk.

Śabdakalpadruma Calcutta, 1889.

Abhidhāna-saṁgraha

Abhidhānaratnamālā of Halāyudha

Amarakoṣa.

Modern Dictionaries.

Dowson's Hindu Classical Dictionary (1914).

Monier-Williams' Sanskrit-English Dictionary.

Woollaston's English-Persian Dictionary.

Works on Polity.

Kauṭilya's Arthaśāstra, *ed. by* Shamasastry. Mysore, 1909.

Kauṭilya's Arthaśāstra, English Translation *by* Shamasastry, 3rd edition. Mysore, 1929.

Kāmandakīya Nītisāra, *ed. by* Gaṇapati Śāstrī. Trivandrum, 1912.

Manusmriti, (Hindi Pustaka Agency). Calcutta, 1928.

Grammatical Works.

Pāṇini's Aṣṭādhyāyī.

Patañjali's Mahābhāṣya, *ed.* by Kielhorn.

Other Works.

Bāṇa's Harṣacarita, *ed. by* Jīvānanda Vidyāsāgara. Calcutta, 1892.

Bāṇa's Harṣacarita, *ed. by* Führer. Bombay, 1909.

Bāṇa's Harṣacarita, English Translation *by* Cowell and Thomas. London, 1897.

Bāṇa's Kādambarī, *ed. by* Peter Peterson. Bombay, 1900.

Bāṇa's Kādambarī, *ed. by* Parab. Bombay, 1896.

Bāṇa's Kādambarī, English Translation *by* Ridding. London, 1896.

Sanskrit Poems of Mayūra, *ed. by* Quackenbos, Columbia University Series, Vol. IX.

Kalhaṇa's Rājataraṅgiṇī, *ed. by* Durgā Prasāda. Bombay, 1892.

Kalhaṇa's Rājataraṅgiṇī, English Translation *by* Sir Aurel Stein. London, 1900.

Rājaśekhara's Karpūra-mañjarī, *ed. by* Konow and Lanman. Harvard Oriental Series, 1901.

Viddhasālabhañjikā, *ed. by* Jīvānanda Vidyasāgara, Calcutta, 1883.

Viddhasālabhañjikā, *ed. by* B. R. Ārte. Poona. 1886.

Kāvyamīmānsā, *ed. by* C. D. Dalal and R. A. K. Śāstrī. Gaekwaḍ's Oriental Series, No. 1, 1916.

Padmagupta's Navasāhasāṅkacarita, *ed. by* V. S. Islampurkar. Bombay Sanskrit Series, Bombay, 1895.

Mankha's Śrīkaṇṭhacarita, *ed. by* Durgā Prasāda and K. P. Parab. Bombay, 1900.

Bhartrihari's Vairāgyaśataka.

Vikramārjuna-Vijaya or Pampa-Bhārata, *ed. by* Lewis Rice. Bangalore, 1898.

Kānyakubja Mahākāvya.

Vāsavadattā, *ed. by* F. E. Hall, Calcutta, 1859.

Kālidāsa's Malavikāgnimitra, *ed. by* S. P. Pandit. 1889.

Kālidāsa's Meghadūta, *ed. by* Hultzsch. London, 1911.

Vallabhadeva's Subhāṣitāvali, *ed. by* Peterson. Bombay, 1886.

Sārngadhara's Paddhati, *ed. by* Peterson. Bombay Sanskrit Series, No. 37.

Subhāṣitaratna-Bhāṇḍāgāra, *ed. by* Parab. Bombay, 1911.

Harṣa's Priyadarśikā, *ed. by* Nariman, Jackson, and Ogden. Columbia University Series, 1923.

Soḍḍhala's Udayasundarīkathā, *ed. by* C. D. Dalal and Kriṣṇamācārya. Gaekwāḍ's Oriental Series, No. 11. Baroda, 1920.

Prasannarāghava, *ed. by* Paranjpye and Panse. Poona, 1894.

Mammaṭa's Kāvyaprakāśa, *ed. by* Jhalkīkara. Bombay, 1921.

" " English Translation by Gangānātha Jhā. 1925.

Nāgoji's Kāvyapradīpodyota, *ed. by* D. Chandorkar. Poona, 1898.

Maheśvara's Prakāśādarśa.

Maheśvara's Viśvaprakāśa, Caukhamba Sanskrit Series. Bombay, 1911.

Śrīharṣa's Naiṣadhacarita, *ed. by* Śivadatta. Bombay 1919.

Vidyāpati's Puruṣaparīkṣā, edited and translated *by* Nerurkar. Bombay, 1914.

Nayacandra's Rambhāmañjarī.

Madanavinodanighaṇṭu, *ed. by* Jīvānanda Vidyāsāgara.

Prithvīrāja-vijaya, *ed. by* S. K. Belvalkar (Bibliotheca Indica).

Prithvīrāja-Rāso, *ed. by* S. S. Das. Benares, 1904.

Rāso-Sāra " " " " " "

Hemacandra's Kāvyamīmāṅsā, Gaekwāḍ's Oriental Series, 1924.

Mañjusrīmūlakalpa, *ed. by* Gaṇapati Śāstrī. Trivandrum, 1925.

Dīvyāvadāna, *ed. by* Cowell and Neil. Cambridge,

1886.

Vākpati's Gauḍavaho, *ed. by* S. P. Pandit, Bombay, 1887.

Rājaśekhara's Prabandhakoṣa.

Merutunga's Prabandhacintāmaṇi, *ed. by* Jinavijaya Muni. Śāntiniketan (Bengal), 1933.

Merutunga's Prabandhacintāmaṇi, *ed. by* Rāmacandra Dīnānātha. Bombay, 1888.

Merutunga's Prabandhacintāmaṇi, English Translation *by* C. H. Tawney. Calcutta, 1899.

Hemacandra's Kumārapālacarita, *ed. by* S. P. Pandit. Bombay, 1900.

Prabhāvakacarita, *ed. by* H. M. Śarmā. Bombay, 1909.

Dhanapāla's Paiyalacchi, *ed. by* Bühler, Gottingen, 1879.

Chinese Works.

Samuel Beal, The Travels of Fa-hian.

" " Buddhist Records of the Western World. London, 1884.

Samuel Beal, Hwui-li's Life of Yuan Chwang. London, 1911.

Thomas Watters, On Yuan Chwang (*Si-yu-ki*). 1904.

J. Takakusu, I-tsing's Record of the Buddhist Religion in India and the Malay Archipelago. Oxford, 1896.

Works on Geography.

S. N. Majumdar Śāstrī, Ancient India as described by Ptolemy. Calcutta, 1927.

S. N. Majumdar, Cunningham's Ancient Geography

of India. Calcutta, 1924.

N. L. Dey, Geographical Dictionary of Ancient India. Calcutta, 1927.

Works on Numismatics.

C. J. Brown, Catalogue of Coins in the Provincial Museum, Lucknow. Vol. I. Oxford, 1920.

C. J. Brown, Coins of India. (Heritage of India series, 1922).

Sir Alexander Cunningham, Coins of Mediæval India. London, 1893.

J. Allan, Catalogue of Indian Coins (Gupta Dynasties). London, 1914.

Vincent A. Smith, Catalogue of Coins in the Indian Museum, Calcutta. Vol. I. Oxford, 1906.

Pt. B. B. Bidyāvinod, Supplementary Catalogue of the Coins in the Indian Museum, Calcutta. Vol. I. Calcutta, 1923.

E. J. Rapson, Catalogue of Coins of the Andhra Dynasty. London, 1908.

E. J. Rapson, Indian Coins.

Gazetteers.

Gazetteer of Farrukhabad

Imperial Gazetteer of India. Vols. VI & XIV

Mirzapur Gazetteer.

Bombay Gazetteer. Vols. I, II, and IX.

Moslem Works.

Alberuni's India, English Translation by E. C. Sachau. London, 1914.

John Briggs, Rise of the Mahomedan Power in India. (*Ta'rīkh-i-Firishta*. N. K. Press. Lucknow, 1905).

Sir H.M. Elliot and John Dowson, History of India as told by its own Historians. Volumes I & II Specially see extracts from—Kāmil-ut-Tawārīkh of Ibn Asīr.

Tabaqāt-i-Akbarī of Nizāmuddīn.

Tāj-ul-Maāsir of Hasan Nizāmī.

Ta'rīkh-i-Yamīnī of Al Utbī.

Rauzat-us-Safā of Mīr Khonḍ.

Habīb-us-Siyar of Khond Mīr.

Murūj-ul-Zahab of Al Maśūdi.

Chach-Nāmā.

H. G. Raverty's English Translation of the Tabaqāt-i-Nāsirī. London, 1881.

Miscellaneous Modern Works.

A. A. Macdonell and A. B. Keith, Vedic Index of Names and Subjects, Volumes I & II, London. 1912.

F. E. Pargiter, Ancient Indian Historical Tradition. London, 1922.

A. B. Keith, A History of Sanskrit Literature (1928).

A. B. Keith, The Sanskrit Drama. Oxford, 1924.

A. B. Keith, Classical Sanskrit Literature (Heritage of India Series), 2nd ed. 1927.

R. W. Frazer, A Literary History of India. London, 1907.

D. C. Sen, History of Bengali Language and Literature, Calcutta, 1911.

E. J. Rapson, Cambridge History of India. Vol. I. Cambridge, 1922.

Sir Woolsley Haig, Cambridge History of India. Vol. III. Cambridge, 1928.

Vincent A. Smith, Early History of India, 4th ed. Oxford, 1924.

Vincent A. Smith, Oxford History of India, Oxford, 1920.

Vincent A. Smith, Aśoka, 3rd. ed. Oxford, 1919.

T. G. Aravamuthan, The Kāverī, the Maukharis and the Sangam Age. Madras, 1925.

Edward A. Pires, The Maukharis, Madras, 1934.

R. K. Mookerji, Harṣa. Oxford, 1926.

K. M. Panikkar, Śrī Harṣa of Kanauj. Bombay, 1922.

Ettinghausen, Harṣavardhana: Empereur et Poet. Paris, 1906.

L. D. Barnett, Antiquities of India. London, 1913.

C. V. Vaidya, History of Mediæval Hindu India. Vol. I. Poona, 1921.

C. V. Vaidya, History of Mediæval Hindu India. Vol. II. Poona, 1924.

C. V. Vaidya, History of Mediæval Hindu India. Vol. III. Poona, 1926.

R. G. Basak, History of North-Eastern India, Calcutta, 1934.

B. C. Mazumdar, Orissa in the Making.

Jouveau Dubreuil, Ancient History of the Deccan, English Translation. Pondicherry, 1920.

Hemacandra Raychaudhuri, Political History of Ancient India, 3rd. ed. Calcutta, 1932.

R. G. Bhandarkar, Early History of the Deccan. 3rd. ed. Calcutta, 1928.

R. G. Bhandarkar, Report for 1882 on Sanskrit Manuscripts, No. 208.

H. D. Sankalia, The University of Nalanda. Madras, 1934.

F. Max-Müller, India, what can it teach us? London, 1892.

Vogel, Antiquities of the Chamba State. Calcutta, 1911.

Robert Sewell, A Forgotten Empire. London, 1900.

J. F. Fleet, Dynasties of the Kanarese Districts. Bombay, 1899.

E. B. Havell, Aryan Rule in India. London, 1918.

Beni Prasad, The State in Ancient India. Allahabad, 1928.

Mark Collins, Geographical Data of the Raghuvaṁśa and the Daśakumāracarita. Leipzig, 1907.

A. S. Altekar, Rāṣṭrakūṭas and their Times. Poona, 1934.

D. C. Ganguly, History of the Paramāra Dynasty Dacca, 1933.

H. C. Ray, Dynastic History of Northern India Vol. I. Calcutta, 1931.

H. C. Ray, Dynastic History of Northern India Vol. II. Calcutta, 1936.

Tod's Annals and Antiquities of Rājasthan, *ed. by* Crooke. Oxford University Press, 1920.

H. H. Wilson's Theatre of the Hindus. London, 1871.

Raverty, Notes on Afghanistan.

Crooke's Tribes and Castes of N. W. P. and Oudh.

Elliot's Races of N. W. P. and Oudh.

Cawnpore Settlement Report.

Sir Āshutosh Mookerji Silver Jubilee Volume. Orientalia.

Führer, Sharqi Architecture of Jaunpur. Calcutta, 1889.

R. C. Majumdar, Corporate Life in Ancient India. Calcutta, 1922.

U. N. Ghoshal, Hindu Revenue System. Calcutta, 1929.

B. K. Ghosh, English Translation of Jolly's Hindu Law and Custom. (1928).

B. N. Reu. History of India (Hindi).

Journals.

See the List of Abbreviations.

Add also :

Indian Thought.

Vienna Oriental Journal.

Bulletin of the School of Oriental Studies.

Asia Major.

Journal of the Royal Anthropological Institute.

Gottingische Gelehrte Anzeigen.

Asiatic Journal and Monthly Register for British and Foreign India, China, and Australia, 1836.

INDEX OF NAMES[1]

[1] I had proposed to give the references to works used or cited in the text along with the Bibliography, but unfortunately owing to certain unforeseen circumstances this could not be done. I hope to do so in the second edition, if ever it comes out.

B

E

F

G

L

M

V

CORRIGENDA

Reference	*For*	*Read*
P. 8. n. 1c, l. 3	Gādhirindrakaḥ	Gādhir-Indrakaḥ
P. 9. n. 5, l. 1	Caivājamīḍho	caiva-Ajamīḍho
P. 13, n. 3, l. 1	more than one Viśvāmitras	more Viśvāmitras than one
P. 40, n. 1, l. 1	Āndhrapatiṁ	Āndhrādhipatiṁ
P. 67, n. 3, l. 2	vānārāti	vānarāti
P. 69, n. 1, l. 2	sarva lakṣanaiḥ	sarva-lakṣanaiḥ
P. 79, l. 15	apears	appears
PP. 81, n. 3, l. 2; 113, n. 7, l. 2.	Lakṣmīḥātmī kritā	Lakṣmīḥ ātmīkritā
P. 89, l. 7; See also *Index* for other references.	Āhicchatra	Ahicchatra
P. 96, n. 3, l. 1	Rudradaman	Rudradāman
P. 113, n. 7, l. 1	Atra-puruṣottamena	Atra Puruṣottamena
P. 119, l. 15	Gujrat	Gujarat
P. 121, l. 17	Nāsāditaḥ	Nāsāditāḥ
P. 138, l. 25	ormed	formed
P. 147, l. 4	describesthem	describes them
P. 148, l. 32	onthe	on the
P. 166, l. 7	Sāgaramatī	Sāgaramati
P. 202, n. 3, l. 2.	Abhūdā Kālikātiraṁ	Abhūd ā-Kālikātīraṁ
P. 204, l. 21	de thronement	dethronement
P. 223, l. 23	prattihāra vaṁśo yaṁ	Prattihāravaṁśo-'yaṁ
P. 2:7, n. 1, l. 2	Yen āsau	Yen-āsau
P. 239, l. 18. See also *Index*.	Kālacuri	Kalacuri
P. 253, l. 7	lef	left
P. 256, n. 2, l. 1	asīt	āsīt
P. 264, n. 2, l. 2	sena	senā
P. 280, l. 22	Bhatripaṭṭa II	Bhartripaṭṭa II

Reference	*For*	*Read*
P. 294, l. 5	kīrtti śeṣaṁ	kīrtti-śeṣaṁ
P. 300, n. 2, l. 2	..vaṁṣa jāta kṣmāpāla..	..vaṁśajāta-kṣmāpāla..
P. 301, n. 3, l. 2	nripā-ṇāṁ	nripāṇāṁ
" "	..Śita..	śiti..
" " l. 3	Yāmunāṁ	Yāmunaṁ
P. 302, n. 2, l. 2	KuśikottaraKośalendra-sthānīyakani.	Kuśik-ōttara-Kośal-Endrasthānīyakāni
P. 321, n. 3, l. 4		*Put* ; after *Rāso*
P. 334, n. 3, l. 4		close the brackets.

Capital *initial* letters in Kṣitīśāḥ (p. 28, n. 4, l. 4), Kṣatārayaḥ (*Ib.*, l. 5), Śateṣu (p. 55, n. 2, l. 1), Yudhi (p. 65, n. 3, l. 2), Kaśāprahāra (*Ib.*, l. 3), Kūṭapākalaḥ (p. 79, n. 1, l. 2), Śaśi...(p. 121, l. 16), Krityavedināṁ (p. 202n, l. 1), Kuryācca (p. 216n, l. 2), Pratiharaṇavidher (p. 223, l. 9), Prātīhāryaṁ (*Ib.*, l. 21), Udāraḥ (p. 300, n. 3, l. 3), Khalu (p. 304, l. 1), should be taken as *small letters.*

For small *initial* letters in later (pp. 53, l. 11 ; 66, n. 1, l. 3), yamunā (p. 202, n. 3, l. 2), prattihāra (p. 223, l. 23), ādivarāhena (p. 243, n. 1, l. 1), substitute capital letters.

Read the following names, wherever they occur, with diacritical marks thus :

Mālava, Valabhī, Nālandā, Cauhān, Sabuk-tigīn, Maḥmūd, Sihāb-ud-dīn, Qutb-ud-dīn, Nizām-ud-dīn, Alā-ud-dīn, Sulaimān. Bakhtyār Khiljī, Mas'ūd, Jahāngīr.

Note :—The identification of Yuan Chwang's *Chi-chi-to* (pp. 113, 118) with Jejākabhukti (Jajhoti) has been doubted in view of the following verse occurring in a fragmentary Mahoba inscription :

"Jejākhyayā-atha nripatiḥ sa babhūva Jejābhuktiḥ prithor-iva yataḥ prithivī-iyaṁ-āsīt" (*Ep. Ind.*, I, p. 221, v. 10). According to Thomas Watters, it was perhaps identical with Chitor (II, p. 251). Can it not, however, be identified with Citrakūṭa, as has sometimes been suggested.

It may further be noted that Dr. Vincent Smith identified *Pi-lo-shan-na* with Bilsaṛ in the Etah district ; *A-yu-te* with the region of which Aphui in the Fatehpur district was the capital; *Mo-ti-pu-lo* with the eastern part of the Bijnor district; and *A-ye-mu-k'a* with the Partabgarh and Rae-Bareli districts in Oudh (Watters, II, Appendix, p. 338).